urch, is the site of Doctor Arthur Conan

MEDICAL CASEBOOK OF DOCTOR ARTHUR CONAN DOYLE:

From Practitioner to Sherlock Holmes and Beyond

"The Old Horse." Drawn by Arthur Conan Doyle, fall or winter, 1929. Courtesy of Dr. & Mrs. C. Paul Martin.

MEDICAL CASEBOOK OF DOCTOR ARTHUR CONAN DOYLE:

From Practitioner to Sherlock Holmes and Beyond

by

Alvin E. Rodin, M.D., M.Sc., F.R.C.P. (C)
Professor and Chairman of
Department of Postgraduate
Medicine and Continuing
Education, Wright State
University School of Medicine,
Dayton,Ohio

& Jack D. Key, M.A., M.S.
Associate Professor of
Biomedical Communications,
Mayo Medical School, and
Librarian, Mayo Foundation,
Rochester, Minnesota

ROBERT E. KRIEGER PUBLISHING COMPANY, INC.
MALABAR, FLORIDA 32950
1984

Original Edition 1984

Printed and Published by
ROBERT E. KRIEGER PUBLISHING COMPANY, INC.
KRIEGER DRIVE
MALABAR, FL 32950

Printed in the United States of America

Library of Congress Cataloging in Publication Data

Rodin, Alvin E.
Medical casebook of Doctor Arthur Conan Doyle.

1. Doyle, Arthur Conan, Sir, 1859–1930—Knowledge—Medicine. 2. Doyle, Arthur Conan, Sir, 1859–1930—Characters—Sherlock Holmes. 3. Medicine in literature. 4. Physicians in literature. I. Key, Jack D. II. Title.
PR4624.R63 1984 823'.8 83-16232
ISBN 0-89874-592-6

DEDICATION

——The Women

Dame Jean Conan Doyle
Virgie Key
Jean Rodin

SPECIAL RECOGNITION

——Major Contributions

John Michael Gibson
Richard Lancelyn Green
Andrew Malec

We are indebted to John W. Desley, Rochester artist, for the orginial drawings used for:

Section One.
Secton Two.
Section Three.
Tailpiece.
Dust Jacket.

Contents

LIST OF ILLUSTRATIONS

LIST OF ILLUSTRATIONS

Figure 1.

Figure 2.

Figure 1. The Old Quad of the University of Edinburgh, with the buildings and the golden boy the same as 100 years previously when Doctor Conan Doyle graduated in 1881. (Photograph used with permission.)

Figure 2. Conan Doyle's home from 1875–1877, No. 2 Argyle Terrace, Edinburgh. O.D. Edwards points to the second level location. (Photograph used with permission.)

Figure 3. Conan Doyle's home from 1877–1880, No. 22 George Square. It now houses the Catholic Student Union. (Photograph used with permission.)

Figure 4. Conan Doyle's home from 1880–1881, No. 15 Lonsdale Terrace (facing The Meadows). (Photograph used with permission.)

FOREWORD

It would be hard to find a more widely recognized fictional character than Sherlock Holmes. But it would not be difficult to find a number of writers more widely acclaimed than Holmes' creator, Sir Arthur Conan Doyle. There may never again be another "sodality" as widely spread and as active as is the Cult of Sherlock Holmes, led by the Baker Street Irregulars, but even the Irregulars pay only lip service to Doctor Conan Doyle. He is regarded by them as the "Literary Agent" of Doctor Watson, and they maintain that Watson, not Conan Doyle is the actual author of the Holmes adventures. Why Watson and Holmes permitted A. Conan Doyle's name to appear on the title page of the books and stories has never been fully determined, though there has been some speculation about this matter. Certainly this curious situation should have some explanation if the B.S.I. hypothesis re the "Literary Agent" can be accepted. So far no satisfactory explanation has been received. The "Conanical" toasts of the Irregulars, a part of the ritual of the cult, except for the label, include no reference to Doctor Conan Doyle, or even to the "Literary Agent." For all their activities, he might never have existed.

Were Conan Doyle alive and well I wonder how he would have regarded this omission. What would be think of societies dedicated to the study of "The Sacred Writings," i.e., his tales about Sherlock Holmes, but rarely mentioning the actual creator of their idol. Some members of the Conan Doyle family have not approved of this attitude of the Baker Street Irregulars. They have not been entirely pleased with the attention given to Holmes and the ban on attention given to Holmes' creator.

It is quite possible that Doctor Conan Doyle would not have been at all exorcised at these developments. He did not begrudge the attention given to the Sherlock Holmes stories, but he did have some reservations about them. Remember, he once in all seriousness brought Holmes to his death. In the adventure of "The Final Problem," Holmes and Moriarty, locked in a final struggle were presumed to have fallen to their deaths at the Falls of Reichenbach. In his autobiography, *Memories and Adventures,*[375] Conan Doyle said:

> *It was still the Sherlock Holmes stories for which the public clamoured, and these from time to time I endeavored to supply. At last, after I had done two series of them I saw that I was in danger of having my hand forced, and of being entirely identified with what I regarded as a lower stratum of literary achievement. Therefore as a sign of my resolution I determined to end the life of my hero. (p. 93)*

Again Conan Doyle, after having "revived" Holmes in *The Return of Sherlock Holmes,* published *The Valley of Fear,* and "His Last Bow," and wrote in the Preface to *The Case-Book of Sherlock Holmes,*

> *I had fully determined at the conclusion of* The Memoirs *to bring Holmes to an end, as I felt that my literary energies should not be directed too much into one channel. . . Had Holmes never existed I could not have done more, though he may perhaps have stood a little in the way of the recognition of my more serious literary works.*
>
> *(Doyle, Sir Arthur, Conan,*
> The Case-Book of Sherlock Holmes,
> *London, John Murray, 1927, p. 6–7)*

From this evidence it is clear that Conan Doyle did not regard the Holmes adventures as his major contribution to society, though he acknowledged in the above preface, the devotion of Holmes' followers, and thanks them for their "past constancy."

Might he not also have been willing to thank the Baker Street Irregulars for their "constancy?" And while members of the Doyle family have been disturbed at efforts of the Irregulars to dramatize and "canonize" the Holmes cult, Sir Arthur may have reacted a bit differently. In the famous filmed interview, he spoke quite warmly of the Sherlock Holmes stories even though he turned rather quickly to his later dedication to Spiritualism, and that part of the interview was much longer than the Holmes sequence. From this, one would assume that he regarded Holmes seriously but less than with the highest priority. Remember his response to a cable from William Gillette: "May I marry Holmes?" Conan Doyle responded that "Gillette could marry Holmes or murder him or do anything he liked with him."[125] (p. 117)

Conan Doyle was a man of great compassion, and a man with a fine sense of humor, witness the Knoxian "Sherlockismusses" appearing in the tales,—"the dog did nothing in the nighttime," and "That is what you may expect to see when I follow you." And note the report of Conan Doyle's first meeting with William Gillette. At the rail station there emerged from the carriage the perfect image of Sherlock Holmes. Gillette, tall, angular, attired in Inverness cloth cape and wearing a deerstalker, whipped out a magnifying glass, looked Conan Doyle up and down and remarked "obviously an English author." Conan Doyle roared with laughter. I think he would have been entertained by some of the antics of the B.S.I., for example Julian Wolff's refutation of Rex Stout's infamous article "Watson was a woman." He may very well have been amused but also sympathetic to the canonization of his hero "Sherlock Holmes" and the labeling of his adventures as "The Sacred Writings."

But it is very clear that Conan Doyle was most concerned with his contributions in other fields. In the list of subjects (Preface to *The Case-Book)* in which he had explored his literary limitations ("history, poetry, historical novels, psychic research, and the drama"), though he did not mention medicine, he most certainly would have welcomed Messrs Rodin and Key's *Medical Casebook of Doctor Arthur Conan Doyle.* As they so effectively demonstrate, Conan Doyle's medical interests and competence pervaded his entire career. They have made abundantly clear that Conan Doyle was truly *Doctor* Conan Doyle.

Certainly the literature of Sherlock Holmes, as well as psychic research, historical novels, and short stories, will benefit from this penetrating and exhaustive analysis of Conan Doyle's medical involvements. Not only are Conan Doyle's writings analyzed for medical concerns, one finds other examples of his nature and character, examples which contribute substantially to Sherlock Holmes devotee's appreciation of the Master. Quite naturally the Holmes saga contributes numerous items to their imposing list of Conan Doyle's medical involvements. And certainly Sherlock Holmes fans will welcome the extensive listing of the cases and their medical references. Truly, the detailed results of the Rodin/Key research are a significant contribution to the literature of Sherlock Holmes as well as to the career and accomplishments of Sir Arthur Conan Doyle.

The *Medical Casebook of Doctor Conan Doyle* also contributes significantly to the explanation of the almost unique popularity of the Sherlock Holmes adventures. They are so popular because they reflect the character and nature of Doctor Arthur Conan Doyle. A man dedicated to the protection of the innocent and the achievement of true justice, Conan Doyle devoted much of his energies and efforts to such cases as the Slater case, and the Edalji case. An active sportsman he loved "the game" and this book underlines that interest effectively. He was always a champion of evidence and the dependence upon facts rather than theories, as exhibited in his numerous letters regarding medical matters. Indeed he traveled at his own expense to Berlin to study and analyze the Koch treatment for tuberculosis, disdaining the easy acceptance of a new remedy. His interest in education is reflected by Holmes: "Education never ends, Watson. It is a series of lessons with the greatest for the last," and "Education, Gregson, education. Still seeking knowledge at the old university." (RedC) As the *Medical Casebook. . .* abundantly shows, Doctor Conan Doyle was continually studying and learning.

Rodin and Key in their study of Conan Doyle's medical career paint with a talented brush, the picture of a great Doctor, honest, lover of justice, supporter of the underdog, patron of learning and education and a true sportsman—all qualities with which Conan Doyle endowed Sherlock Holmes. These are indeed the qualities which they clearly demonstrate, permeated Doctor Conan Doyle's medical career.

St. Paul, Minnesota

E. W. McDiarmid, Ph.D.
Professor Emeritus
University of Minnesota

PREFACE

What began as a lukewarm interest has become a labor of love—love for the very human characteristics of a literary figure and for the worlds of the mind he has created and peopled. A benign interest in Arthur Conan Doyle on the part of both authors mushroomed into an almost enslaving passion following their first acquaintance at the 1979 meeting of the American Osler Society in San Francisco. This interest in common led to a collaboration on several Conan Doyle related presentations and publications; and to an increasing awareness of an injustice being perpetuated concerning this creative writer.

It became evident while seeking out primary source material that Conan Doyle was very much more than "Doctor Watson's literary agent"—and, indeed, much more than the great Sherlock Holmes himself. These views are contrary to the "happy pretenses" sanctioned by enthusiastic Holmesians. He lived in times of major changes in human affairs—for science, medicine, literature, culture, nationalism, technology, religion, and philosophy to note only a few of the areas. Conan Doyle's interests and activities touched on all of these, most significantly in medicine, politics and literature.

Yet the real merit of Conan Doyle is unappreciated except by a few. He does not even bask in the glory of his own creation, the master detective. Indeed, this unusual author is subjugated by the fact that he drew his fictional characters so well that they have escaped from the printed page to become living human beings for a sizable following. Compounding the offense is the laudatory credit for medical knowledge afforded the imaginary Sherlock Holmes—while Conan Doyle's own medical knowledge and contributions are obscured.

The medical Conan Doyle is the most umbrageous and unappreciated chapter in an otherwise well-publicized life. There have been numerous papers published on the medical content in the Holmesian tales, but very largely as a "telling" rather than as a comprehensive assessment in relationship to Conan Doyle's period and our own. Little attention has been paid to medicine and medical orientations in his other fictional works, or to the influences of medical training, teachers, and events on the totality of his life. In particular, Conan Doyle's scientific medical writings have not been assembled and evaluated as an entirety.

As our files of material related to the medical Conan Doyle grew so did the realization that we were caught up in a crusade, both academic and emotional, to have the full story established. Some of our fervor came from a closer contact with the subject who shouldered numerous causes and needs of others. Exposure for us to other characteristics and interests of this man also wove an inexorable magnetic appeal. Some of these alluring facets were his strength of character, humor, romanticism, humaneness, sincerity, naivety, catholic interests, sense of present and future, his work as a physician, and his medical concepts as expressed in various publications.

We found it impossible to ignore our captivation with Conan Doyle. In fact, so much so that all other avocations were displaced. Visits and/or contacts were made to various places in the United States and Canada which have significant Conan Doyle collections: the public libraries in Toronto and New York City, the Huntington Library, the university libraries of Minnesota, Texas, and Iowa. The culmination was a five-week tour of Britain and Scotland "in quest of the elusive Doctor Arthur Conan Doyle."[773] This work has been greatly enriched by the additional, and significant material, collected and collated from the extensive research of a few British Doyleans.

One result of our efforts is the first book devoted to Sir Arthur Conan Doyle as a physician and medical author. Biographical details and influences of his life as a medical student and practitioner are covered at length. Featured are his medical concepts and writings which represent a valuable contribution to both the scientific and nonscientific aspects of medicine of the late 19th century. Conan Doyle was a diversified genius who deserves to have a full accounting. That is the purpose of this book. In addition, some activities and events encountered by serendipity were too fascinating to leave buried in the dim and dusty vaults of neglected knowledge. Some of this is presented as chapter notes so as not to detract from the continuity of the overall narrative. (An "N" cited in the text refers to a relevant item in the chapter notes.)

The book has been written with general readers, scholars, Holmesians, physicians, and historians all in mind. Medical terms used by Conan Doyle are explained. More detailed scientific and medical assessments are provided in some chapter notes. Specific medical details in Conan Doyle's writings are gathered together and tabulated as appendices. These should provide an overview for the casual reader, and a source for further research for the serious scholar.

Our search for material relevant to the medical Conan Doyle was greatly hampered by the lack of specific citations of sources for definitive statements, descriptions, and quotations in the commentaries of most secondary works. Consequently, this book is amply provided with references. We anticipate that this effort will encourage and facilitate the research of other investigators. In particular the reader should be able to differentiate between someone's opinion of someone else's opinion and that of Conan Doyle himself. References have been numbered in alphabetical sequence and placed before the index. One Caveat is what we mean when the word *Canon* is used. Throughout the book this word is used strictly for designating the collective Sherlock Holmes stories.

Where possible the information has been obtained from primary sources in order to ensure an accurate portrayal—and thereby lay to rest the myths that "Conan Doyle was an inadequate physician." A flavor of Conan Doyle's style can be obtained from the quotations drawn fron his writings, including excerpts of letters to family and friends. In a similar vein we have tried to avoid the grossly exaggerated psychologic and other suppositions that characterize so much of the expository literature on Conan Doyle. Some of our own biases may have crept in, but, we hope, unobtrusively.

Implicit in the orientation of this offering is a certain predilection for the role of history as a discipline. The consideration of a historical event or personage becomes significant when put into the context of its past, present and future. This work is laced with descriptions of the age in which Conan Doyle lived and with the state of medical knowledge before, during and after his lifetime.

There are several things that this book was not intended to do. It is not a literary evaluation, although some personal biases may surface. There is a comprehensive, but not an exhaustive accounting of *all* medical writings by Conan Doyle. There are undoubtedly a few that were missed or considered too inconsequential to include. Conan Doyle's acceptance of spiritualism is taken for what it was, the religion of choice in his mature years. Nor is there the glorification of Sherlock Holmes that represents much of all related commentaries.

In Britain there are four Doylean scholars whose hard earned knowledge has enriched this book. We are greatly indebted to them for their generosity and comments. They were visited during a five-week sojourn in May and June of 1982.

Geoffery Stavert, a Commander in the Royal Navy, had the good sense to settle in Southsea where Conan Doyle practiced. He has used his opportunities to ferret out many details not heretofore known about Conan Doyle's practice days.

John Gibson, a government surveyor living in Runcton, has used his spare time for years to track down articles by and about Conan Doyle in English newspapers of the period. Many such items are incorporated into this book as a result of his tenacity and his generosity in freely sharing the fruits of his labor with us.

Richard Lancelyn Green, of London and Poulton, has what must be the most varied collection of Holmesiana and Doylean memorabilia, if not the largest. All this was unstintingly shared over a seven-hour period, including a fine lunch with his gracious parents. Green and Gibson have recently published a detailed bibliography of Conan Doyle.[488]

The fourth Doylean of note, is Owen Dudley Edwards, a historian on the faculty of the University of Edinburgh. His specialty is Conan Doyle's early days in Edinburgh. Much of this was communicated as an erudite dialogue during a three-hour walking tour of Conan Doyle's Edinburgh. His book on this subject has recently been published.[424]

We would be sadly remiss if no special mention were made of a fifth individual indispensable in the quest for Doctor Arthur Conan Doyle. It is not only because of her father that Dame Jean Conan Doyle is sought out, but also because of her warmth and graciousness as well as that of her husband, Sir Geoffrey Rhodes Bromet. Her encouragement and her insights have proved invaluable.

Many other individuals and institutions in Britain were both supportive and informative to our research efforts. Some of Conan Doyle's books were obtained through the expertise of Gaby Goldscheider of Windsor. Doctor J.T.O. Hall led a naive but inquisitive American through the complexities of the indices of the Special Collections of the University of Edinburgh Library. Other libraries consulted onsite with gratifying results were the Erskine Medical Library and the National Library of Scotland in Edinburgh; in Portsmouth, the Hampshire Public Library and the City Records Office; and in London, the British Library and its Newspaper Division, the Library of the Royal Society of Medicine and that of the Wellcome Institute. The five-week quest in Britain was as successful in developing warm friendships as it was in obtaining invaluable data.

The United States also has its own scholars important to the subjects of our research. Peter Blau, now editor of the *Baker Street Journal,* spent an afternoon in Washington, D.C. reviewing his extensive Holmes/Doyle collections with one of us, and has subsequently shared a great deal of additional information. An enthusiastic correspondence has been carried on with some of the other leaders and major collectors in the field—John Bennett

Shaw, Jon Lellenberg (an editor of *Sherlock Holmes Miscellania*), Saul Cohen, C. Frederick Kittle, Ely Liebow, D.A. Redmond, Jack Tracy (the Holmesian Encyclopedist) and Ronald De Waal (noted for his extremely useful Holmesian bibliographies).

Four individuals have made other significant contributions to this book. They served as critical readers of the manuscript. We are greatly indebted to them for their efforts, comments, and suggestions—Florence L. Schmidt, Emeritus Staff and former editor, Mayo Foundation; C. Paul Martin, M.D., Internal Medicine and Family Practice; Andrew Malec, Special Collections, University of Minnesota; and E.W. McDiarmid, Ph.D., Professor Emeritus, University of Minnesota and Sigerson of The Norwegian Explorers. Any errors or misinterpretations in the book are the responsibility of the authors.

Librarians in the United States and Canada played a significant role in our efforts. Cameron Hollyer, Curator of the Conan Doyle Collection at the Toronto Central Library, provided a detailed tour and also several important medical items. Collections of letters written by Conan Doyle were made available (with acknowledgement for publication of excerpts) by the Henry W. and Albert A. Berg Collection, The New York Public Library—Astor, Lenox and Tilden Foundations; and by the University of Minnesota Special Collections Library. These along with letters owned by John Hench, Worcester, Mass., provided significant primary source information for the understanding of the medical Conan Doyle. Our debt to these collections is immeasurable.

Most remarkable have been the ''search out and acquire'' activities of two medical libraries—the Health Science Library of Wright State University School of Medicine (Dayton, Ohio) and the Mayo Clinic Medical Library (Rochester, Minnesota). The abilities of their staffs to trace obscure articles by unknown authors in limited journals of the past is almost beyond belief—and especially noteworthy is their dogged persistence.

Often less recognized are the contributions of publishers to books. Permissions to use articles were readily given for Chapter Two by the *Journal of the History of Medicine and Allied Sciences,* the

Journal of the American Medical Association, the *Southern Medical Journal,* and *Minnesota Medicine.* Most unusual is the Krieger Publishing Company, the President of which has a keen interest in the medical Conan Doyle. To him, we appreciate the finished product.

Finally, to Jean McDowall (Key's secretary) and Pat Spitler (Rodin's secretary) we extend special thanks for their unbelievable patience. While at this point they might be thought by some to be "A.C.D. casualties," we consider them unique—they have earned their "spurs" with consistent dedication, hard work, and contribution.

Alvin E. Rodin
Jack D. Key

INTRODUCTION

A somewhat portly, self-assured, gentleman and his dog entered our view. From the firmness of his tread and the erectness of his body the man might be a general reviewing troops. He is athletic in bearing, has a friendly face, and a heavy mustache. He is fashionably dressed in a dark suit. As he moves from the door of the house down the short walk to a seat located in what appears to be well-kept grounds of a large estate, he looks more like a general than ever. He removes his hat, revealing a full head of gray hair, and with deliberation seats himself comfortably on the bench. Then, looking directly at us Arthur Conan Doyle, in a warm Scottish burr, speaks, "Let's see now. I've got to say one or two words just to try my voice, I understand." He goes on for about five minutes to relate how he came to write the Sherlock Holmes stories. This famous author then turns his conversation to a brief discussion of the psychic faith to which he was so deeply committed during the last decade and a half of his life.

Conan Doyle's manner somehow implies that time is very precious to him, and he talks with an economy of words but covers the subjects in a way which is both interesting and appropriate to the occasion. Time *is* precious with him; his plethora of interests and activities, and wide reputation combine to bespeak such a prodigious degree of vigor, endurance, and industry, that one wonders at his finding time to share the few moments with us.

At the end of eleven minutes, in total, the short film ends and the house lights come on. This, the only sound film ever made of Sir Arthur Conan Doyle, was arranged in 1927 by Jack Connolly of Fox-Case.[380] Connolly, a persuasive newsreel man, captured on sound and film many of the important personalities of his day. Believed lost for many years this Conan Doyle film, now commercially available, is a valuable introduction to a man who has brought so much pleasure to countless readers of several generations throughout the world.

It would be grossly redundant to recount in very much detail the general biographical data pertaining to the life of Arthur Conan Doyle or linger at length on his popular literary characters. So much has been published concerning them all that the combined output could fill a sizable library. Consequently, a synopsis of these much-written-about facts will be sufficient.

Arthur Conan Doyle was born in Edinburgh on May 22, 1859. His mother, concerned that he have a means of livelihood, advised Arthur to go to medical school. This he did after a preliminary education at the Jesuit College at Stoneyhurst, Lancashire, England. Conan Doyle graduated from the University of Edinburgh in 1881 with degrees of Bachelor of Medicine and Master of Surgery. Two brief sea voyages as a ship's surgeon, first to the Arctic on a whaler and later to the west coast of Africa, and several short tours of duty as an assistant to physicians in England, contributed to his reservoir of experience, much of which was subsequently incorporated into novels.

After a disappointing interval as assistant to George Budd, a flamboyant medical school colleague, Conan Doyle put up his own brass plate at Southsea, a residential district in the southern part of Portsmouth, England. In 1885 he wrote a thesis, passed the examination, and qualified for the MD degree awarded by Edinburgh University. His moderate practice left him ample time, and Conan Doyle devoted much of it to writing. Early efforts met with minimal success among the publishers, but the adventures of Sherlock Holmes became popular reading within a few years. The publishers begged for more and were obliged. To provide more time for writing, Conan Doyle decided to become an eye specialist, and left for study in Vienna. Returning from the Continent after a short stay, he set up practice (briefly) in London among the fashionable practitioners at Devonshire Place (Upper Wimpole)—but saw no patients.

While surviving a severe bout of influenza, Conan Doyle made up his mind to give full time to writing. Royalties from his books and checks for his short stories and other writings were increasing. What had started very modestly with the sale of his first story in 1879 had subsequently, with many other publications, grown to an enjoyable and comfortable business. He turned to medicine again only while treating British soldiers in the Boer War in South Africa.

In total, Doctor Conan Doyle's medical activities covered little more than 15 years. A career in medicine, originally undertaken for practical purposes, seemingly did not provide the challenges and satisfactions he sought. His gift for writing served as the vehicle to fame and fortune. Nevertheless, Conan Doyle was proud that he was a physician. In a letter to his mother, (as quoted by Bendiner)[58] he once said, "The title I value most is that of 'Doctor,' which was conferred by your self-sacrifice and determination."

Arthur Conan Doyle—the man—died on July 7, 1930, in Crowborough, Sussex; Arthur Conan Doyle the author lives on, especially through Sherlock Holmes, in the minds and hearts of multitudes.

"A Study in Scarlet" in *Beeton's Christmas Annual,* London, 1887, introduced Sherlock Holmes to the public and marks the launching of a spectacularly popular series of crime solving adventures for the scientific detective and his Boswellian partner and foil, Doctor John H. Watson. Spanning a period of some 40 years, four novels and 56 Sherlock Holmes related short stories were published. These have sold in the millions of copies, including various editions and translations.

Over the years the central figures of this fiction have been metamorphosed for many from characters in stories into real persons. They were so well drawn by Conan Doyle that they transcended the printed page and became living, breathing human beings to thousands of enthusiastic Holmesians. More than this, he established himself as a versatile author with historical novels, short stories, volumes of poems, plays, histories, science fiction, and publications on spiritualism.

For many, if not most persons, the significance of Arthur Conan Doyle is in his literary creations. To these people, in comparison with the captivating exploits of Sherlock Holmes and Doctor Watson, the fact that Conan Doyle was a physician who saw patients or wrote medical articles would be considered almost unworthy of notice. Of less importance to them, even if known, would be considerations of the quality of medicine practiced by the Doctor Conan Doyle or his thoughts on such matters as vivisection, smallpox vaccination, typhoid, and tuberculosis. It is, in fact, generally held that Conan Doyle took up literary writing because he was a failure as a doctor.[27]

Even though his literary nemesis of crime, various causes, and other interests eclipsed the medical side of Conan Doyle, medicine was nevertheless inextricably entwined with his total being. He received academic recognition in literature in the form of an honorary LL.D. Conan Doyle should also be recognized for his work as a physician and for his medical concepts expressed in various publications. He was a man of all seasons—a diversified genius—and deserves to have the full story established.

Myths which haunt Conan Doyle's medical reputation are endlessly perpetuated, especially by those enthralled with the Sherlock Holmes aspects of his life. Mainly, these involve claims that he was a failure as a physician; that he saw very few patients; that he lived in near poverty all during the years of his practice; that he possessed minimal skills as a physician; that he was responsible for few medically related publications and these few being so insignificant as to be meaningless; and that he had no real interest in medicine—in essence, the sum of his life was, so to speak, "literary agent" for Doctor Watson. In subsequent chapters of the *Medical Casebook of Doctor Arthur Conan Doyle* we will examine the facts and fictions of these myths. Perhaps, this book can detail rehabilitative substance for an otherwise rather vaporous, confusing, and neglected facet of Conan Doyle's life story. For example, as we shall see, his medical writings represent a valuable contribution to both the scientific and nonscientific aspects of medicine of the late 19th century. Up to the present, accounts of these writings have been few, and none of them have been evaluative of their scientific merit. Analysis of Conan Doyle's writings on infectious diseases in particular reveals a remarkable insight, for the 1880s, into the bacterial causation of disease and prevention through immunization. Also, scattered through Conan Doyle's considerable fiction, some of which is primarily medical, are examples reflecting his orientation to humanistic medicine which must be considered. All of this, and more, coupled with medical matters found in the Corpus Holmesiana, provides the reader an opportunity to pass through "The Magic Door" with Doctor Arthur Conan Doyle to share an important part of his life.[338]

> *I care not how humble your bookshelf may be, nor how lowly the room which it adorns. Close the door of that room behind you, shut off with it all the cares of the outer world, plunge back into the soothing company of the great dead, and then you are through the magic portal into that fair land whither worry and vexation can follow you no more. . . . There stand your noble, silent comrades, waiting in their ranks. Pass your eye down their files. Choose your man. And then you have but to hold up your hand to him and away you go together . . .* [338a] *. . . [when] we stride out together, do we not face our fate with a braver heart for all the rest and quiet and comradeship that we found behind the Magic Door?*[338b]

SECTION ONE

ARTHUR CONAN DOYLE, M.B., C.M., M.D.

1

STUDENT AND PRACTITIONER

EDINBURGH BEGINNINGS

Arthur Conan Doyle was born May 22, 1859, at No. 11 Picardy Place, only a mile from the University where he was to begin his medical career 17 years later.[N1] There were no known childhood experiences or family heritage that one associates with a bias toward medicine.[920] His maternal grandfather, William Foley, was a doctor, but only for a brief time in Ireland before dying at a young age.[424] Conan Doyle's paternal origins extended from Dublin to London, where his father, three uncles, and grandfather exhibited considerable artistic talent. The latter, John, under the initials "HB," became the leading British political cartoonist of his day. His uncle Richard drew the cover for *Punch* and illustrated works of Dickens and Thackeray. Conan Doyle's maternal roots were also in Ireland, from whence his widowed grandmother and mother (Mary Foley) came to Edinburgh. There was a French connection through a maternal uncle,

Michael Conan, who was his godfather and provided part of his name.

Conan Doyle's father, Charles, moved from London to Edinburgh to work in the Government Office of Works and there met and married Mary in 1855. Arthur was their first son. They had ten children, of which seven survived (including Arthur) when Conan Doyle was in practice at Southsea. Among them was his elder sister Annette, who died in 1888 in Lisbon. Arthur was the second child, then came Connie, Lottie [Caroline], Innes his brother, then Ida, then Julia [Dodo]. Innes lived with Arthur during the first four years of medical practice in Southsea. Arthur was the favorite of his mother. She undoubtedly influenced his literary career by reading him romantic stories of knighthood and the Napoleonic wars.

The family somehow retained its integrity on a meager salary of £240 per year, supplemented by the intermittent sales of drawings by Charles. Their early home, today obliterated by a traffic interchange, was rather spartan. Then followed a succession of rented living quarters each in the general area of the University of Edinburgh.

Conan Doyle's secondary education was not directed to any particular profession.[125] There was, however, an influence towards the priesthood since he attended the Jesuit College of Stonyhurst in Preston, England, and its branch school in Feldkirch, Austria.[125] There appears to have been some effort made by the faculty to have Conan Doyle enter the Jesuits, but his mother resisted.

The question arises as to why he entered the medical profession, which he was to abandon after 10 years as a practitioner. It has been stated that "He surprised his artistic family by choosing medicine as his career."[191] This is contrary to Conan Doyle's own statement "It had been determined that I should be a doctor, chiefly, I think, because Edinburgh was so famous a center for medical learning."[375] This certainly indicates that it was not his decision alone. Byran Charles Waller, a medical consultant who lived with the family, was undoubtedly an influence on the Doyle family and on Arthur himself.[N2]

Medicine, like religion and politics, was, and still is, attractive to genteel families of limited means as a profession for their sons. A factor in Conan Doyle's case was surely the lessened expense of attending a medical school within a short walking distance of the family residence. Both No. 22 George Square, where they lived from 1877 to 1880, and No. 15 Lonsdale Terrace, where they made their home from 1880 until after Arthur's graduation, were within hailing distance of the University. It just seemed common sense to prepare for a career in medicine at the University and to live at home. For whatever reason, Conan Doyle did enter medicine.

Edinburgh in the 18th and 19th centuries was a major center for both literature and medicine. Here, for example, Sir Walter Scott (1771–1832) invented the historical novel, a form of literature which Conan Doyle favored. Edinburgh also influenced Robert Louis Stevenson (1850–1894) with whom Conan Doyle corresponded in later years.[150] There is no evidence that they knew each other while they were students at the University of Edinburgh. Literary giants such as Carlyle, Longfellow, and Dickens visited Edinburgh, helping to create a cultural milieu which could not but rub off on an intelligent and alert lad such as Conan Doyle.[476] One of his earliest childhood recollections was of sitting on the knee of Thackeray [one of his grandfather's friends], who visited the family.[920a] With such an environment it is not surprising that Conan Doyle's literary efforts were published as early as the age of 20, while he was still a third year medical student.

Disease and medicine also had major visibility in Edinburgh after Conan Doyle's birth. The death rate in various districts of Old Town ranged from 28.8 to 37.1 per thousand in 1865, when Conan Doyle was six years old.[476] In 1866 there were at least three epidemics of cholera. One of Conan Doyle's medical teachers in later years, Doctor Littlejohn, was elected Officer of Health in 1862.

By the time Conan Doyle entered medical school, Edinburgh had a long tradition of strong medical organizations and outstanding medical practitioners. Even before the establishment of the medical school in 1726 it had two Royal Colleges—Surgery incorporated in the 16th century and Medicine in the 17th.[21] Edinburgh abounded in world-renowned medical figures, many of whom were knighted. Sir James Syme (1799–1870) developed the field of amputations and surgical excisions. Lord Lister (1827–1912) became one of humanity's greatest benefactors by applying preventive measures in the operating room derived from Pasteur's discovery of bacteria as the cause of infections.[500]

BRITISH MEDICAL EDUCATION

Until 13 years before Conan Doyle entered medical school there were separate educational systems in Britain for physicians, surgeons, and apothecaries.[143] This changed with the Act of 1858, which created a General Council of Medical Education and Registration of the United Kingdom, subsequently called the General Medical Council (GMC).[435] Every body which granted medical qualifications in Great Britain and Ireland was included.

The GMC was given the authority to blend conflicting interests into one coordinated whole. Between 1859 and 1866 the GMC urged education in general knowledge as a prerequisite for medical school. Of interest is the stipulation that these "premed" subjects should not be oriented to the special requirements of medicine, a viewpoint that has surfaced again today. Conan Doyle passed examinations in Greek, Latin, French, mathematics, practical philosophy, chemistry, and English.

By the time he entered medical school in 1876, anatomy, physiology, medical chemistry, materia medica (drugs), morbid anatomy (pathology), surgery, midwifery, therapeutics, gynecology, diseases of children, vaccination, teeth, mental diseases, and hygiene were all specified courses.[146] Such a curriculum is quite similar to that of a hundred years later, although there is no longer the same amount of stress placed on teeth and hygiene. Also required in Conan Doyle's time was that "Every student should perform the duty of clerk and dresser." This is equivalent to the modern-day clerkship in hospital wards and outpatient departments. It was in such a situation that Conan Doyle came under the influence of Doctor Joseph Bell, an occurrence that greatly influenced his subsequent literary and medical careers.

Some other important rulings of the GMC were that medical education should not be less than four years, and that medical qualification should not be conferred until the student reached the age of 21. Conan Doyle graduated at the age of 22. His medical education was extended over a five-year period because of time taken out to earn money. His need for earned income to complete medical school is further evidence of the low economic status of the Doyle family. At that time the usual cost was about £100 per school year, but this expense would be cut in half for a student living at home.[168] Much of this money was paid directly to lecturers in the form of fees.

UNIVERSITY OF EDINBURGH MEDICAL SHCOOL

The medical school of the University of Edinburgh, although one of the most prominent in Britain, was not the first. Aberdeen University established a Chair of Medicine in 1494. Cambridge followed in 1540, Oxford in 1545, Glasgow in 1637, and Edinburgh in 1726.[143] Edinburgh did for many years, however, have three Chairs in the basic medical sciences (botany, anatomy, and chemistry) before granting its first medical degree in 1705.[651]

It was not until 1726 that a medical school was officially opened in Edinburgh, being organized by a group of physicians who had trained at the famous school in Leyden, Holland.[543] This was 170 years after the origin of the University itself (1556) when it was called Town's College and consisted of two eminent scholars who were appointed to lecture publicly.

The medical school was housed in the university building on South Bridge Street now affectionately known as the Old Quad (quadrangle). This is where Conan Doyle received his medical education from 1876 to 1881. Three years after his graduation the school moved to a new building on Teviot Place.

The Edinburgh medical school was unique in that a hospital for clinical teaching was built in 1729, three years after its inception.[543a] This was the beginning of the Edinburgh Infirmary for the Poor which provided patient exposure for medical students including Conan Doyle. Bedside clinical teaching was begun in 1746 by Alexander Monro primus.[166] This combination of university education and clinical hospital instruction, so prominent today, was unique in Britain at that time and contributed considerably to the rapid rise of the medical school's reputation.[557]

Another contributing factor was the presence of several faculty members of considerable stature, whose lingering reputations at the school undoubtedly impressed Conan Doyle. For instance he may well have been influenced by the example of John Hughes Bennett (1812–1875) to write a letter in 1882 to the editor of the *Lancet*.[223] In 1845, Doctor Bennett, Professor of Physiology, was the first to describe a marked excess of white blood cells in the blood. He labeled the condition as leucocythaemia, now known as leukemia.[153] Conan Doyle was struck by the occurrence of this malignant disease in a patient who had experienced a bout of malaria. Conan Doyle's use of chloroform as a plot device in many short stories may have been influenced by Sir James Y. Simpson (1811–1870),[405] who was the first to apply this anesthetic agent in obstetrics. These medical giants and others were part of the heritage which Conan Doyle assumed on entering his medical training.

Through the reputation of its faculty and the practical nature of its educational system the University of Edinburgh Medical School extended its influence overseas during the 18th and 19th centuries.[930] For example, William Shippen (1736–1808) and John Morgan (1735–1789) returned to Philadelphia after obtaining medical degrees there and established the first American medical school in 1768.[562] The medical school at McGill in Montreal also owes its development, a half century later, to Edinburgh graduates.[1]

Arthur Conan Doyle, by fortune of place of birth, became exposed to the best in medical education. His medical student days deserve closer study because they strongly influenced his subsequent medical and literary careers, and also provides an orientation to medical education in 19th century Britain.

CURRICULUM

In 1876, when Conan Doyle began his studies, the University of Edinburgh Medical School had a curriculum resembling that of a century later—at least in emphasis on both basic knowledge and practical experience. This was a break with many centuries of academic medical education based upon reading and discussion of the written works of the great Greek and Roman physicians—Hippocrates and Galen.[733] In Edinburgh the break with the past had begun in the 18th century, some 100 years before Conan Doyle entered medical school.

Conan Doyle was exposed to practical experience in both basic sciences and clinical medicine.[407] Laboratory work, for example, was available in chemistry, not only for analytical practice but also for students wishing to do chemical investigations. In physiology, students performed analyses of urine and blood, and practiced using the ophthalmoscope and laryngoscope. Each student was provided with a microscope for the study of both normal and diseased tissue and fluids.

In anatomy the tradition of learning by dissection of human corpses began in the middle ages and has continued to the modern era. It was no different at Edinburgh where Conan Doyle dissected the human body, although dissection was more detailed than is the rule today. The Edinburgh tradition in anatomy, however, was somewhat tainted by the highly publicized episode in the 1820s of Burke and Hare, who committed murder to supply bodies for dissection to the anatomist Robert Knox.[420] According to Edwards,[423] Conan Doyle used Hare as the pattern for the main character in his short story "My Friend the Murderer."[247]

Exposure to patients was extensive during the clinical part of the medical curriculum.[407] Clinical instruction in medicine was given at the Royal Infirmary and at the Royal Edinburgh Asylum. Students had the option of studying gynecological cases at the Royal Infirmary and obstetrical patients at the Royal Maternity.

The fact that the University provided a course in Surgery is symbolic of the marked change in medicine during the 18th and 19th centuries. Prior to this time University medical graduates were disdainful of anyone who did surgical procedures. In fact, the Hippocratic oath of the early Christian era stated "I will not use the knife, not even on sufferers from stone, but will withdraw in favor of such men as are engaged in this work.''[406] Surgery was left to the ''barber surgeon'' who gained experience through apprenticeship[205] rather than in a university curriculum as did Conan Doyle. The Edinburgh school provided classes in surgery and amphitheatre observation of patients and procedures.

A bright, interested student always had an opportunity to obtain further practical experience. In 1878 Conan Doyle was selected by the surgeon, Doctor Joseph Bell, to be his outpatient clerk. This gave Conan Doyle the responsibility ''to array his outpatients, make simple notes of their cases, and then show them in, one by one, to the large room in which Bell sat in state surrounded by his dressers and students.''[375a]

This episode as outpatient clerk provided Conan Doyle valuable clinical training and an opportunity to become imbued with the powers of observation. He based the character of Sherlock Holmes in part on Doctor Bell's deductive skills and in doing so laid the foundation for the world-wide recognition of what was to become his ''master'' detective.[611] For both physicians this literary creation greatly overshadowed any repute of their own medical accomplishments.

MEDICAL STUDENT

That Doctor Joseph Bell selected Conan Doyle as his outpatient clerk would appear to indicate that the young man was an outstanding medical student. But by Conan Doyle's own account in his autobiography of 1924 ''I was always one of the ruck, neither lingering nor gaining—a 60 percent man at examinations.''[375b] The details of his medical school days are sparse, but some orientation can be achieved by reference to the impressions of his teachers and fellow students, to his medical writings, and to his actual grades.

Doctor Joseph Bell told a reporter from the *Pall Mall Gazette* ''I always regarded him [Doyle] as one of the best students I ever had. He was exceedingly interested always upon anything connected with diagnosis, and was never tired of trying to discover those little details which one looks for.''[611a] This is certainly high praise from one who was the epitome of minute observation. It also suggests that Conan Doyle derived such attributes for

Sherlock Holmes from his own characteristics, as well as from those of Joseph Bell.

Conan Doyle's graduating class of August 1, 1881, numbered 128 students.[413] None of them has become a household name in medicine or in literature as he himself has, nor to our knowledge none have written about him. One student in the subsequent class did so. In his autobiography, D. Marinus stated, that "Conan Doyle impressed me chiefly by his very kind and considerate manner towards the poor people who came to the out-patient department, whom I'm afraid some of us were in the habit of treating somewhat cavalierly."[638] This is indeed high praise for a medical student of any era.

That Conan Doyle was not a "run of the mill" medical student is also evident from his various literary activities at that time. According to Marinus he translated a German technical paper. He also had two short stories published in 1879.[217,218] More to the point, in that same year he had a noteworthy letter to the editor published in the *British Medical Journal.*[216] It describes his taking increasing doses of the drug gelsemium in order to study its side effects. The careful attention to details makes this account, especially by a medical student, a significant contribution.

In a lighter vein is the doggerel Conan Doyle wrote in the margins of his textbook on therapeutics.[75] This probably represents some release from the deadening effects of the mass of information on an active, imaginative mind, and possibly was also used as a mnemonic aid. One example relates to opium, a drug which also appears in the Holmesian *Canon.*[41]

I'll tell you a most serious fact,
That opium dries a mucous tract,
And constipates and causes thirst,
And stimulates the heart at first,
And then allows its strength to fall,
Relaxing the capillary wall.
The cerebrum is first affected,
On tetanus you mustn't bet,
Secretions gone except the sweat.
Lungs and sexuals don't forget.[75]

This is not the stuff of which poetry is made; but it is indicative of a sense of the humorous and ludicrous that Conan Doyle exhibited later in some of his medical short stories[281] and those on Brigadier Gerard.[324]

Further orientation to Conan Doyle's student days can be obtained from his novels. In *The Firm of Girdlestone* (1890) the hero, Thomas Dimsdale, attended medical courses at the University of Edinburgh.[258] Comments on the institution reveal Conan Doyle's somewhat pragmatic view of his alma mater. "The University is a great unsympathetic machine, taking in a stream of raw-boned cartilagenous youths at one end, and turning them out at the other end as learned divines, astute lawyers, and skillful medical men."[258a] This novel also contains an excellent description of a football match between Scotland and England.[258b] There is no evidence that Conan Doyle participated as extensively in sports while a medical student as he did while a practitioner.

Conan Doyle's description in this novel also provides an orientation to the atmosphere of the University which he attended for five years. Unlike the regimentation at Oxford and Cambridge, students at Edinburgh had the freedom to live where and how they wished, were given no religious expectations, and could choose whether or not to attend classes or even examinations. Such license can destroy the poorly motivated student. For Conan Doyle it meant that he could earn money by taking time off to act as a medical assistant and a ship's surgeon.

In 1880 he spent seven months as a ship's surgeon on the arctic whaler *Hope*.[554] This was just before his final year in medical school. Although there was no call for medical services from this third year student, the experience had a deep and undoubtedly maturing effect upon Conan Doyle.

Seventeen years later he was to express relief at the absence of disease in the crew of 50 men.[298]

> *I went in the capacity of surgeon, but as I was only twenty years of age when I started, and as my knowledge was that of a third year's student, I have often thought that it was as well that there was no call upon my services.*

Fortunately, scurvy was no longer a problem on whalers since the value of fresh fruit and vegetables had been recognized earlier in the century.[90] His pay was two pounds, 10 shillings a month plus three shillings for each ton of oil brought back. The steward [Jack Lamb with whom Conan Doyle had boxed] paid tribute to Conan Doyle when he said, "[he is] the best surgeon we've had. He blacked my eye." Conan Doyle also achieved some prestige in that the ship's doctor as well as the mate shared the captain's cabin on whalers.[554] In 1883, while a practitioner, he made a lengthy presentation on these adventures to the Portsmouth Literary and Scientific Society.[727] In his 1924 autobiography he devoted a full chapter to the exaltation and joys of the physical rigors of the arctic.[375c] Such endeavor was not the behavior of the typical medical student.

A further description of medical school days in Conan Doyle's novel of 1895, *The Stark Munro Letters,* is relatively brief.[293p] The hero, whose last name is that of one of Conan Doyle's classmates[413] and similar to that of three famous Edinburgh anatomists—the Monros,[945] gives an account of experiences with a fellow student named Cullingworth. Conan Doyle used the same pseudonym in his autobiography for the flamboyant George T. Budd who was a student in the class preceding his.[375d] In the novel they stole a specimen of liver containing amyloid in order to prove that the substance was composed of glycogen. This event may be fictional, although Conan Doyle attested that the novel was semi-autobiographical. The real Doctor Budd did publish papers on amyloid disease.[106]

Grades on medical school examinations are usually used as the measure of a medical student although they fail to indicate humanistic attributes such as those described by Marinus for his fellow student.[638] Conan Doyle's grades were generally average, with several exceptions.[876] He received an S (satisfactory, average) in Anatomy, Institutes of Medicine, Chemistry, Midwifery, Medical Jurisprudence, Surgery, and Clinical Medicine. Above average grades (S+) were achieved in Pathology, Botany, and Natural History; and he had two excellent grades of B—one in Chemical Testing and the other in Practice of Physic. These are not the grades of a "60 percent man at examinations," but of a good solid student. He received only one grade that was slightly below average, an S- in Clinical Surgery. This is surprising considering his experience with Joseph Bell. The explanation may be found in one of the letters which he wrote to Doctor Reginald Hoare,[385a] his preceptor in Birmingham, concerning his final examinations of June 1881. With the usual clarity, he wrote, "The writtens were good fair papers, no choice of questions . . . Midwifery was decidedly easy . . . Medicine I took honors in, the paper was hard, but suited my reading . . . The Medical Ju[risprudence] was beneath contempt."

His experience in the oral examinations in June, 1881, was more varied. "In Midwifery I took honors in my oral . . . I got a fearful raking over in Medicine, a regular honors Exam." Even worse "The Surgery oral was a beastly exam. Spence[185] [Professor of Surgery] behaved like a prig. He told me to lay out the instruments for lithotomy from a tray—I did it—He came prancing towards me with his hat bashed over his left eye, and a face like three kicks in a mud wall. 'Wouldn't I need an Artery Forceps!' . . . I remarked 'I didn't lay it out, sir, because you forgot to put one in the tray'—I had him there." And Conan Doyle also had his S- in Clinical Surgery.

A more humorous account of examinations is given by Conan Doyle in his novel *The Firm of Girdlestone.*[258] The hero, Thomas Dimsdale, narrowly passed Zoology and Botany due to lucky guesses, but succumbed to Chemistry because of an atrocious answer that greatly amused the examiner. Conan Doyle was a good enough student to survive his prig of an examiner and graduated with 127 classmates, each one a Bachelor of Medicine (M.B.) and a Master of Surgery (C.M.). His achievement is even more noteworthy in that only about one half of students, entering medical schools then, actually graduated.[424b] It is not surprising, however, that upon graduation he drew a satirical sketch of himself waving a diploma, and captioned it "Licensed to Kill."[355] Years later Conan Doyle commented on his medical training at the University.

> *[It was] . . . one long weary grind of botany, chemistry, anatomy, physiology, and a whole list of compulsory subjects, many of which have a very indirect bearing upon the art of curing. The whole system of teaching, as I look back upon it, seems far too oblique and not nearly practical enough for the purpose in view. And yet, Edinburgh is, I believe, more practical than most other colleges.*[349]

Much the same can be heard today from harassed medical students.

TEACHERS

Any school is as great as its faculty; and the University of Edinburgh Medical School was blessed with many outstanding teachers. In fact, Conan Doyle's teachers undoubtedly had a considerable effect on his future career. Of the many faculty members, listed in Appendix C, several had a specific influence even though Conan Doyle's impression was that "There was no attempt at friendship, or even acquaintance, between professor and students at Edinburgh."[375e]

Surprisingly, the teacher who is widely regarded as Conan Doyle's model for Sherlock Holmes, Joseph Bell, was not a member of the faculty. He was, instead, an "extra-academic" teacher and senior surgeon at the Royal Infirmary. Students could elect to take an extramural course with him.[611] The results of such a decision by Conan Doyle were far-reaching, as described above.

Conan Doyle undoubtedly studied Joseph Bell's *A Manual of the Operations of Surgery* which was in its third edition in 1878.[56] The book includes a description of an operation for ankylosis (fusion) of the elbow joint by Doctor P. Heron Watson, an Edinburgh surgeon, who had been an army surgeon in the Crimean War. The similarity of name and experience to Holmes' Doctor Watson may be coincidental, as may be that of James Watson, a member of his graduating class.[413] However, it supports the contention of one authority, Owen Dudley Edwards, that details of the Sherlock Holmes stories came from Conan Doyle's Edinburgh experiences.[422] More important for our study of the medical

Conan Doyle is the wealth of medical references in these tales derived from his medical education.[N3]

A specific example of the influence of Conan Doyle's medical education on his writings is related to an outstanding Edinburgh faculty member, Sir Robert Christison (1797–1882), who held an Edinburgh chair for 55 years—first in medical jurisprudence and then in materia medica.[495] A student of Christison described him as "a striking figure; tall, erect, with a commanding presence, a somewhat cold and imperious manner, we used to call him 'Dignity Bob'."[95]

Christison's paper on medical jurisprudence in the *Edinburgh Medical and Surgical Journal* of April 1, 1829,[137] described the appearance of dead human bodies which he had beaten with a heavy stick in an effort to study bruises produced after death.[N4] Can one doubt the source of Stamford's description of Sherlock Holmes' behavior in the anatomy laboratory of St. Bartholomew's Hospital? "He appears to have a passion for definite and exact knowledge. When it comes to beating the subjects in the dissecting rooms with a stick, it is certainly taking rather a bizarre shape."[244]

William Rutherford, who held the Chair in Physiology, was a professor who impressed Conan Doyle considerably. Rutherford was the first to demonstrate the determination of blood pressure to students in Edinburgh.[895] He was also an extremely popular lecturer attracting hundreds of students. Rutherford's impact is evidenced by Conan Doyle's recollection. "Most vividly of all, however, there stands out in my memory the squat figure of Professor Rutherford with . . . his singular manner. He fascinated and awed us . . . He would sometimes start his lecture before reaching the classroom, so that we would hear his booming voice . . . when the desk was still empty."[4f]

Conan Doyle acknowledged, "I have endeavored to reproduce some of his peculiarities in the fictitious character of Professor Challenger." This is a bombastic and rambunctious scientist who is the main character in two of Conan Doyle's science fiction stories, *The Lost World*[357] and *The Poison Belt,*[360] and a much later spiritualistic novel *The Land of the Mist.*[376] He is also featured in two short stories—"The Disintegration Machine" and "When the World Screamed." Challenger is drawn with considerable humor and some relish. Of related interest is that another of Conan Doyle's teachers, Sir Charles Wyville Thomas,[883] was the scientific supervisor of an actual *Challenger* expedition which spent three and a half years charting the ocean beds of the world. It seems unlikely that the similarity of names is mere coincidence and is further evidence of the influence on Conan Doyle's literary works of his medical school experience.

In his autobiography, Conan Doyle lists several other faculty members of note.[357e] Alexander Crum Brown, Professor of Chemistry, studied the salts of alkaloids, presumably much as did Sherlock Holmes. Sir William Turner,[883] who held the Chair in Anatomy from 1867 to 1903, had studied anthropology, a subject which was prominent in Conan Doyle's *The Lost World*[357] and *The Hound of the Baskervilles.*[321]

It would be misleading to leave the impression that the only, or even the greatest, influence on Conan Doyle's writings were his Edinburgh teachers. Also playing major roles were the extensive medical knowledge which he gained at the medical school, experiences with preceptors, and his own subsequent practice.

STUDENT MEDICAL ASSISTANT

While still a medical student Conan Doyle worked during summers as a medical assistant. His motivation is best given in his own words:

> *It was clearly very needful that I should help financially as quickly as possible, even if my help only took the humble form of providing my own keep. Therefore I endeavoured almost from the first to compress the classes for a year into half a year, and so to have some months in which to earn a little money as a medical assistant, who would dispense and do odd jobs for a doctor.*[375b]

Such added stress makes his medical school grades all the more remarkable.

Little information is available about Conan Doyle's experiences as an assistant aside from that mentioned in his autobiography. "My first venture, in the early summer of '78, was with a Dr. Richardson, running a low-class practice in the poorer quarters of Sheffield."[375b] After three weeks they parted company by mutual consent for reasons not given by Conan Doyle.

His second position was for four months of the same year and was with a Doctor Elliot in Ruyton-of-the-eleven-towns, Shropshire. This was a country practice which he found to be less stressful than the one in Sheffield. It is noteworthy because his account provides the first reference to a patient of his own in the sense of having full and sole responsibility. His description, of being called to an emergency when Doctor Elliot was away, is as follows:

> *. . . I found a man in bed with a lump of iron sticking out of the side of his head. I tried not to show the alarm which I felt, and I did the obvious thing by pulling out the iron . . . I then pulled the gash together, staunched the bleeding and finally bound it up, so that when the doctor did at last arrive he had little to add.*[375g]

This was certainly a trying experience for a student who had only been in medicine for two years. But it did give Conan Doyle some badly needed confidence.

His experience with a third physician for whom he was an assistant followed in the next summer. He was still a student, but now much more knowledgeable and experienced. It proved to be most gratifying for both of them. Doctor Reginald Ratcliff Hoare was a very busy physician in Aston, Birmingham and, according to Conan Doyle, was "a fine fellow, stout, square, red-faced, bushy whiskered and dark-eyed. His wife was also a kindly and gifted woman . . ."[375h] Conan Doyle's position in the house was soon more that of a son than an assistant. His main duty was to fill and dispense prescriptions. He also added to his clinical experience by visiting the poorest or the most convalescent patients. For all of this he received the much needed income of £2 a month.

It was during his second stint with Doctor Hoare, in 1879, that Conan Doyle began showing his true mettle both as a writer and as a medical scientist. He published his first two short stories[217,218] and studied the side effects of the drug gelsemium on himself.[219] Twelve years later Conan Doyle chose writing over medicine as his major career.

Without doubt Conan Doyle badly needed money during his years as a medical student, especially since his father was confined in a Convalescent Home because of chronic alcoholism.[36] But he did reap several unexpected benefits from his so necessary assistantships. He received University credit for dispensing activites in Birmingham. This also led to a very meaningful relationship with the Hoare family. Conan Doyle returned for the third time as Doctor Hoare's student assistant for several months in 1880—after his experience as ship's surgeon on the whaler. In the succeeding years he corresponded frequently with the Hoares, and addressed Mrs. Hoare as "Dear Mam," as he did his mother.[385]

Conan Doyle sent the family tokens of his respect when Doctor Hoare died. Dickson Carr states that Doctor and Mrs. Hoare attended Conan Doyle's wedding to his second wife in 1907.[125d] This may be an error since Reginald Hoare's obituary is printed in the *British Medical Journal* of April 9, 1898,[397] some nine years earlier. It is possible that the doctor referred to was his son who took over the practice after his death. Conan Doyle wrote a personal letter to the senior Doctor Hoare's daughter as late as 1921.[385c] Hoare is depicted warmly as Doctor Horton in Conan Doyle's autobiographic novel, *The Stark Munro Letters.*[293cc]

> *His heart is broad and kind and generous. There is nothing petty in the man. He loves to see those around him happy; and the sight of his sturdy figure and jolly red face goes far to make them so. Nature meant him to be a healer. . . .*

Conan Doyle's enduring relationship with the Hoares is an indication of a warmth in interpersonal relationships that he carried with him into the practice of medicine.[N5]

CONAN DOYLE ON MEDICAL EDUCATION

Three years after graduation Conan Doyle was concerned about the standards of medical education represented by medical degrees. In 1884 he wrote a letter to the editor of the *Evening News* strongly criticizing "American Medical Diplomas."[237] He referred explicitly to the "so-called University of Philadelphia" which "consisted of a small body of parchmentmongers who did a roaring business trade in worthless diplomas." Particularly vexing was their operating in Britain after having been declared illegal in the United States. That a person could buy a medical degree without training would be upsetting to anyone who had gone through a long and demanding five-year period of medical education as had Conan Doyle.[N6]

An assessment of the medical education Conan Doyle experienced is provided in his address to the medical graduating class of St. Mary's Hospital, London, in 1910. This was 29 years after he graduated and 19 after he left the practice of medicine.[349]

> *I think that our educational tendency—as is natural in all clinical courses—was to expend undue attention upon rare diseases, and to take the common ones for granted. Many men who were quite at home with strange pathological lesions found themselves in practice without ever having seen a case of scarlatina or measles. I have no doubt at all that it was our own fault, and not that of my old University, which has always had the highest reputation for practical teaching. I found it much the same in men from other schools. They all came forth with much to learn. It is not possible in five years to cover every branch of medicine, especially if allied subjects such as botany, chemistry, and zoology are added to the curriculum. A young medical man who had just entered practice said to me once, speaking of his unfortunate patients, 'When they are alive I don't know what is the matter with them, and when they are dead, I am not sure they are dead!*

Much the same can be said for the crowded curriculum of today's four-year medical schools. Conan Doyle undoubtedly benefited by seeing many common conditions as a student assistant. We shall see if he performed any better in his own practice in Victorian England than the "young medical man" to whom he referred.

THE VICTORIAN MEDICAL MILIEU

Doctor Arthur Conan Doyle graduated from medical school at a time when the practice of medicine was undergoing two major changes: one in its scientific basis and the other in its organizational pattern. The history of medical licensure in Britain is characterized by centuries of ineffective medical acts which were unsuccessful in limiting untrained practitioners until the mid-19th century.[734] For example, the Medical Act of 1512, although granting licenses to graduates of Oxford or Cambridge, also permitted licensing by Bishops of Dioceses.

Even though unlicensed healers were restricted, they were not generally prosecuted before the 19th century.[481] The real beginning of effective protection of the public from untrained practitioners was the Apothecaries Act of 1815.[734] Apothecaries functioned more or less as general practitioners and the Act restricted practice to those who were duly trained.

There still remained several different routes to medical licensure—License of the Society of Apothecaries, Fellow of the Royal College of Physicians, Member of the Royal College of Surgeons, or as a University graduate.[81] These categories were united by the Medical Act of 1858 into one designation for legally qualified practioners.[435] As a graduate of the prestigious University of Edinburgh, Conan Doyle would have had no problem becoming licensed in 1881.

A medical license in the last half of the 19th century was not a passport into guaranteed prestige and wealth.[720] In fact, medicine was then considered a marginal profession because of its technical education and because many of its members came from the lower middle class.[720a] Only the few who were well born, well placed, and prosperous achieved social prestige. And Conan Doyle, our new medical graduate in 1881, did not fit into these categories.

Conan Doyle was, however, well versed in the scientific revolution that was occurring during this period. After centuries of unfounded theories of disease and untested methods of treatment, new orientations to observation and research in the sciences were changing medicine. By the year of Conan Doyle's graduation the existence of bacteria was generally recognized and their causation of several human diseases accepted.[114] Many physiological functions of the body were being delineated such as, the actions of gastric juice[50] and the functions of the liver.[692] Also disease changes in cells and tissue were being described.[902]

Physicians in 1881 were becoming equipped with diagnostic instruments other than their own hands. Laennec's invention of the stethescope in 1819[567] had finally found its way into the physician's bag,[39] although as a hollow cylinder rather than the modern tubing. The compact clinical thermometer was available. This had been initially developed by Sir Clifford Albutt in 1868.[468] Although William Rutherford had demonstrated blood pressure measurement to Conan Doyle and his classmates, the practical air sphygmomanometer (blood pressure cuff) was not developed until much later. Nonetheless, young physicians of the 1880s, such as Conan Doyle, were the forerunners of practitioners who could base diagnosis and treatment on fact rather than fancy. Reliance on observed facts rather than on supposition was also a characteristic of the master detective created by Conan Doyle.

Such was Conan Doyle's excellent preparation for the practice of medicine. Always optimistic about his prospects, Conan Doyle once wrote his mother:

> *Let me once get my footing in a good hospital and my game is clear. Observe cases minutely, improve in my profession, write to the* Lancet, *supplement my income by literature . . . and then when my chance comes be prompt and decisive in stepping into an honorary surgeonship.*[568]

He was soon to discover, however, that lack of money was as serious a handicap in obtaining a foothold in the medical community as it was in obtaining a medical education.

EARLY PRACTICE

On receiving his medical degrees of M.B. and C.M., Conan Doyle did not immediately enter into his own private practice. He lacked the financial resources necessary to buy into an existing practice as was common at the time. In fact, Peterson, in her book on the mid-Victorian medical profession,[720b] uses Conan Doyle's semiautobiographical novel, *The Stark Munro Letters,*[293] as an example of the difficulty in getting established.

After graduation in August, 1881, Conan Doyle returned to his Birmingham mentor Doctor Hoare, now as a physician rather than as a student assistant.[375i] While there he received a telegram from a medical school friend, Doctor George T. Budd, Jr., who was in the class preceeding his. Budd had failed in his attempt to reestablish the Bristol practice of his father, which had fallen apart after his death. Budd now implored his schoolmate to give advice to him. Conan Doyle went to Bristol, advised Budd to "make a composition with his creditors," and returned to Doctor Hoare after two days.[375k]

His Birmingham stay was only a few months because of a desire to go to sea again and to get sufficient capital to start up his own practice. Conan Doyle's enquiries led to his appointment as doctor on the African Steam Navigation Company's *Mayumba.* This was a 4,000 ton cargo steamer which also carried up to 30 passengers. At a pay rate of £12 a month for the four-month journey Conan Doyle could most certainly not have raised enough capital to buy a practice of his own.

Conan Doyle devoted a chapter in his autobiography to this African voyage.[375j] The steamer left Liverpool on October 22, 1881, for the West Coast of Africa. Unlike his voyage to the Arctic, there was some need for the services of the young medical graduate. He described, in an article on photography during the trip,[222] being caught "in the middle of a terrible hurricane . . . My own cabin had been flooded by a wave, but I was too busy attending the prostrate ladies to have time to think of my own woes." More serious was exposure to "that fever haunted coast [of West Africa]. Many of our men were struck down by the miasma, and for some weeks the quinine bottle was more familiar to me than the [photographic] developing tray."

The nature of the fever is not stated specifically. The term "miasma" was used before the 20th century for an unknown cause of infectious diseases produced by "emenations" from marshes and swamps. It had a connotation of not only "ordinary" fevers but also of "intermittents"—in other words malaria which has recurring episodes of fever.[655] His treatment of the crew with quinine, a specific for this infection, supports such a diagnosis.

The ship's surgeon himself was attacked by the miasma, according to his autobiography.

> *We had reached Lagos and there . . . the germ of the mosquito or whatever it was reached me and I was down with a very sharp fever. . . . As I was myself doctor there was no one to look after me and I lay for several days fighting it out with Death in a very small ring and without a second.*[375j]

The imagery taken from boxing is indicative of his active involvement in this sport. The reference to a mosquito suggests malaria or yellow fever, both of which are spread by this vector. Such knowledge was in the early developmental stage in 1891. At any rate Conan Doyle survived, writing to a friend that "I am just recovering from a smart attack of fever, and am so weak that the pen feels like an oar. . ."[386] There is no record of subsequent recurrences as occurs in some patients with intermittent fever.[N7]

Several deaths from the fever occurred. One of the crew died during another outbreak, and was buried at sea.[222] Conan Doyle also treated "a young Frenchman dying of fever upon the West Coast of Africa . . . a sallow face with large black eyes looking out at me."[275] Fortunately for his readers he escaped such a fate. He did experience another narrow escape, not from the minute mosquito, but from a large shark while swimming off the ship.

Reference to a second patient during this voyage is made in another letter[46k] written from the steamer.[N8] "Then there is a frightful horror (Mrs. McSomething) going to Madeira for her lungs. Straight in the hair and long in the face. She won't let me examine her chest. 'Young doctors take such liberties, you know my dear'—so I have washed my hands of her." Such an experience was not unusual for a young physician. Doctor Oliver Wendell Holmes, who was highly thought of by Conan Doyle, had a similar experience. Soon after his graduation Holmes was taken by Doctor Channing to see an invalid lady. Her reaction was "Dr. Channing, why do you bring that little boy in here? Take him away! This is no place for boys."[549]

More exciting was a fire on board ship during which Conan Doyle had to calm the passengers.[375j] The *Mayumba* and its surgeon survived these rigors to return to England from the West Coast of Africa on January 14, 1882. What he did then is not clear. One of his biographers, Pierre Nordon, indicated a return to Edinburgh.[683a] However, it is likely that before going to Plymouth in May he also spent some time in Birmingham, possibly again assisting Doctor Hoare. The best evidence is found in a letter he wrote to *Blackwell Magazine* regarding a manuscript.[224] It is dated March 24, 1882, and his address given as The Elms, Gravelly Hall, Birmingham. That he was in Birmingham at this time is also evident in the footnote to a letter from Plymouth to Doctor Hoare's wife.[385b]

> *By the way I left a good clothes brush at G.H.[Gravelly Hall] and my new gloves. Would you mind sending a little parcel with those and other things I may have left. I will pay at this end. I have a couple of Sam's shirts which must go back.*

According to Carr,[125] who had access to Conan Doyle's papers, the young doctor visited his uncles in London during this period. The visit was at the request of concerned relatives to discuss his future prospects. The family members were strong Catholics and offered to use their influence with others of the same faith to help him start a practice. Conan Doyle refused on the grounds that he had become an agnostic. He would not ignore his principles by taking advantage of a faith in which he no longer believed. Such altruism, although noble, left the young doctor with no immediate prospects.

EXPERIENCE WITH GEORGE T. BUDD

Conan Doyle was saved from unemployment, or so it seemed at first, by another telegram in May 1882 from his medical school friend. Budd wired from Plymouth—"Started here last June. Colossal success. Come down by next train if possible. Plenty of room for you. Splendid opening."[375k] Conan Doyle left immediately for Plymouth. From a letter to Mrs. Hoare[385b] it is evident that Conan Doyle lived at the Budd residence, 6 Elliott Terrace, The Hoe, Plymouth. The practice was conducted in a building at No. 1 Durnford Street, Stonehouse, Plymouth.

The six-week experience with this flamboyant individual impressed Conan Doyle to the extent that he described it in a lengthy letter to Mrs. Hoare at the time[385b] and devoted 140 out of 246 pages to it in *The Stark Munro Letters* 13 years later.[293] He also included it in his autobiography 42 years later.[375k] Only in the letter does Conan Doyle refer to Budd by his real name. In the other two accounts the name is Cullingworth and in the novel the city is Bradfield. Conan Doyle also used episodes from Plymouth for some of his medically related short stories.[281]

The descriptions of Doctor Budd all present the picture of an unusual practitioner, but with varying emphasis on eccentricity. Above all, Budd was innovative in marketing his product with resultant crowded waiting rooms. As Conan Doyle described in his letter to Mrs. Hoare "Each [patient] had a ticket with the number of his turn to see Budd upon it. If any man wanted to go out of his turn he had to pay 10/6, when he had the privilege of passing over the heads of all the people before him."[385b] Conan Doyle also wrote: "Behind all [his] tomfoolery, I, watching his prescriptions, could see a quickness of diagnosis, a scientific insight, and a daring and unconventional use of drugs."[293ee]

In *The Stark Munro Letters*[293] Budd was depicted as a mercenary professional whose success was based on the attraction of large numbers of patients by various questionable practices. Newspaper stories of successful or seemingly successful cures were sought. Some consultations were free, but with charges for drugs which were prescribed in "heroic doses."

In Conan Doyle's autobiography he called Budd "half genius and half quack, [who] had founded a practice worth several thousand pounds of ready money in the year."[375k] Budd accomplished this in spite of, or because of, browbeating his patients.

> *People flocked into the town from 20 and 30 miles round, and not only his waiting-rooms, but his stairs and his passages, were crammed. His behaviour to them was extraordinary. He roared and shouted, scolded them, joked them, pushed them about, and pursued them sometimes into the street, or addressed them collectively from the balcony.*[375k]

Under these somewhat trying conditions Conan Doyle managed to develop "a steady dribble of patients." In his autobiography he provided an engaging description of one of his patients.

> *I went up country once, and operated upon an old fellow's nose which had contracted cancer through his holding the bowl of a short clay pipe immediately beneath it. I left him with an aristocratic, not to say supercilious, organ, which was the wonder of the village and might have been the foundation of my fame.*[375l]

This account indicates a good knowledge of cancer causation and surprising surgical skills for a recent graduate. Several years later he was to make a pipe a major prop for his detective—Sherlock Holmes.

Conan Doyle's surgical expertise was not to be the basis for medical fame in Plymouth. His mother had never approved of his association with Budd and so wrote in letters to her son.[375l] These letters, left lying around, were read by Budd, "a man of strange suspicions and secret plottings," who then terminated their working agreement on a cordial but cool basis. Conan Doyle, although educated at one of the most prestigious medical schools, was again unemployed and after only six weeks of practice. At least Budd promised to send him £1 a week to help establish a practice elsewhere.

George Turnarene Budd, Jr., is worthy of a few comments because of his deep and lasting effect on Conan Doyle. Was he really as eccentric and megalomaniac as depicted? His obituary in the *British Medical Journal*[686] indicates death in 1889, at the young age of 34. The statement that "He had a large private practice in Plymouth, where he had settled for seven or eight years" does not indicate gross eccentricity. Neither does the obituary in the *Plymouth Western Morning News.*[190] "The medical profession will hear with regret of the death of Dr. George Budd of Stonehouse. [He] continued to see his patients as late as Saturday last. Overwork brought on congestion of the brain."

These obituaries may have been overly kind as are most. A letter to the editor of the *Plymouth Western Morning News* in 1972[669] states that Budd "died in tragic circumstances." A feature article in the same newspaper in 1971[925] indicates that he "died in poor circumstances haunted by a suspicion that someone was poisoning him." But these two statements are not referenced to any sources and perhaps Conan Doyle exaggerated Budd's actions because of their disagreements and separation. However, Conan Doyle's letter to Mrs. Hoare[385b] describing some of Budd's peculiarities was written very shortly after his arrival in Plymouth.[N9]

Doctor George Budd, of Plymouth, may well have come to a disastrous end in his practice, as well as deteriorated mentally, as implied by two recent letters to the editor.[669,925] Similarly, Doctor Cullingworth of Bradfield had a considerable decline in practice.[293r] "People had no doubt accustomed themselves to his eccentricities, and these had ceased to impress them." In addition he "had shown renewed signs of that vein of suspicion which had always seemed to me to be the most insane of his characteristics." Doctor Cullingworth, full of grandiose schemes, moved to Brazil; whereas Doctor George Budd died in 1889, his only remembrance was his striking impression on Conan Doyle.

Conan Doyle probably came closer to a solution for the enigma of George Budd than the obituaries or the commentators. In his autobiography he provided a vital piece of information that might well explain the more grandiose and irrational aspects of Budd's character.[375d]

> *. . . I understand that an autopsy revealed some cerebral abnormality, so that there was no doubt a pathological element [brain lesion] in his strange explosive character.*

Be that as it may, the short six-week experience had a remarkable influence on Conan Doyle's subsequent careers. The descriptions in his autobiography, a novel, and several short stories seem reasonably clear. In addition, it has been suggested that some of the inspiration for the mentally energetic character of Sherlock Holmes[925] and for the bombastic one of Professor Challenger[473] were derived from Doctor Budd's character.

Influences also are evident in Conan Doyle's medical career. Both wrote letters and short items on a variety of medical subjects. Particularly noteworthy are those in common. Budd wrote on "Position of the White Corpuscles in the Blood Stream,"[112,N10] these blood cells being also described by Conan Doyle in his paper of 1884 on "Life and Death in the Blood."[231] Both published short items on gout, Budd in 1880[110] and Conan Doyle in 1884.[238] Also Conan Doyle utilized some of the same techniques to attract patients that he ascribed to George Budd.[N11]

Conan Doyle would need such techniques and all the wiles he could muster to start up his own practice in Victorian England. According to Peterson, medical graduates with limited means were likely to have lean years.[720b]

> *The proper house, the carriage, the clothing that would all have testified to his gentility and, by extension, his respectability and trustworthiness, were out of reach of the man without resources.*

Conan Doyle had no resources except for his excellent medical education, his intelligence, his elan, and the promise of £1 per week from Doctor Budd.

SOUTHSEA

After parting from Budd, Conan Doyle made a quick visit to Tavistock, a small country town eight miles north of Plymouth.[845] Conditions for practice there did not appeal to him and he returned to Plymouth to set sail for Portsmouth.[N12] The reason for choosing this site to establish himself was "that I knew the conditions at Plymouth, and Portsmouth seemed analogous,"[3751] both being seaports and naval bases.

The history of Southsea as a prominent area began in the 16th century with the completion of South Sea Castle in 1544.[180] In the following year Henry VIII observed his flagship, the *Mary Rose,* sink with all hands aboard as it left the harbor to engage an approaching French fleet. The ship sank intact having been foundered by sudden heavy winds.[N13] Southsea continued as a prominent naval base during the 17th century. It was from there that Nelson sailed on September 4, 1805, on his last voyage. His ship, the *HMS Victory,* remains today in Southsea as a tourist attraction.

Before 1800 much of Southsea was a large area of open country in Portsmouth. Land development began early in the 19th century. The first hotel, Bush Hotel, was built in 1810 on Wish Lane, now called Elm Grove, next to which Conan Doyle was to set up a medical practice 72 years later. By 1847, 66% of the population of this area of Southsea consisted of nobility and gentry. Gradually, with the influx of dockyard workers, the population became more middle class.

Between 1860 and 1885 Southsea developed as a prominent seaside resort, with pleasure piers, many hotels, ornamental gardens, bath houses, and railway lines.[759] Its population in 1881, a year before Conan Doyle's arrival, was 34,226. In August 1882, a month after his arrival, a spacious pavilion was opened by the Prince of Wales. By 1885 there were 368 lodging houses. Compatible with Conan Doyle's attitudes toward modesty of the female sex was the regulation against mixed bathing. There were separate beaches for each sex.

Southsea became a community with multifaceted characteristics. As summarized by Riley[759] "Southsea is something of an oddity, for it developed as the middle-class suburb of a great naval establishment and, since it was close to the sea, became a waterplace out of which sprang a seaside resort." Conan Doyle, writing in his autobiography 34 years after leaving Southsea, expressed a similar fascination with this city. "With its imperial associations it is a glorious place and even now if I had to live in a town outside London it is surely to Southsea, the residential quarter of Portsmouth that I would turn. The history of the past carries on into the history of today, the new torpedo-boat flies past the old *Victory* with the same white ensign flying from each . . . there is a great glamour there to anyone with the historic sense. . ."[375m]

Further descriptions of Portsmouth and its suburb are contained in his *Essays on Photography*[475] written while he practiced in Southsea.

> *Portsmouth is never at any time a dull place. The coming and going of men-of-war and transports, the large garrison, the crowds of "blue jackets," and the fashionable influx into Southsea—all prevent its ever becoming so.*[235]
>
> *There is something piquant and interesting in this union between a grim old fortified town [Portsmouth], grey with age and full of historical reminiscences, and a brand new watering place [Southsea], resplendent with piers, parades and hotels.*[236]

Another noteworthy aspect of the history of Portsmouth and its Southsea district is its association with major literary figures.[711] Charles Dickens (1812–1870) was born and spent his first two years there. It was also the birthplace of George Meredith (1828–1909) and Sir Walter Besant (1836–1901). Rudyard Kipling (1865–1936) spent the ages of 9 to 12 in Portsmouth. In Southsea itself the prolific writer, H.G. Wells (1866–1946), spent two years, from 1881 to 1883, as an apprentice in a drapery establishment in King Street. Another prolific writer, Arthur Conan Doyle, arrived in Southsea in 1882 about a year before H.G. Wells ran away from his drapery apprenticeship. Conan Doyle's location was within a mile of the site of H.G. Wells' apprenticeship. It is unlikely that they met because of the difference in their ages, 23 and 16, and in their positions in society. Conan Doyle, unlike some of the others, established his literary career while in Southsea.

It was in Southsea that Conan Doyle practiced medicine from July 1882 to December 1890. In 1882 the overall death rate in Portsmouth was 21.39 per 1,000 population and in Southsea 14.73.[756,N14] Southsea also had a lower incidence of the various infectious diseases than other districts of Portsmouth. Its birth rate of 10.39 per 1,000 was considerably lower than that of greater Portsmouth, which was 35.14. From these statistics Southsea does not appear to have been the district in most need of another physician. Its reputation as a healthy environment was noted in Conan Doyle's *The Stark Munro Letters.*[293] "I live in the queer health-giving old city of the past."

According to *Chamerlin's Portsmouth Directory of 1881–1882*[133] there were 53 Surgeons and Physicians in Portsmouth at the time of Conan Doyle's arrival. For a population of 129,872 this figure represents one physician for 2,450 people.[N15] This is a respectable ratio when compared to a rate of one general practitioner per 2,000 for Southern Western England in 1978.[428] Somewhat reducing the number of patient visits was the ratio of about nine quacks to every physician in 19th century England.[81]

At the time several hospitals were located in Portsmouth. One, the Royal Portsmouth Hospital opened on January 2, 1849.[786] In 1882 it had approximately 55 to 60 beds. Of 937 patients admitted in 1890,[787] 153 were from Southsea. The hospital was closed in 1979 and incorporated into the Queen Alexandra Hospital in nearby Cosham. Whether or not Conan Doyle admitted patients to this hospital is uncertain as the records are no longer available.[616] *Annual Reports* include only names of subscribers, donors, and committee members.

It is also possible that Conan Doyle used St. Mary's Hospital which was opened in 1883, a year after his arrival. Unfortunately, for our study, patients' records before 1976 have been destroyed because of an acute shortage of storage space. Also present in Portsmouth was the Lunatic Asylum, opened in 1879 and now called St. James Hospital. Doctor Conan Doyle's name is not included among the physicians noted in the admission records for the 1880s.[8]

Some of the diagnoses for patients in these institutions provide a flavor of the social, cultural, and medical biases during Conan Doyle's years of general practice. For example, religious excitement, childbirth, and dissipation were reasons for admission to the Lunatic Asylum.[87] Causes of death in the Royal Portsmouth Hospital were similar to those of today, although with a greater preponderance of infectious diseases.[706] The lack of knowledge in some areas is indicated by the indefinite term ''morbus cordis'' for heart disease.

The incidence of the major categories of disease have changed in a hundred years. In 1882, infectious diseases were responsible for 38% of deaths in Portsmouth and in 1979 for only .4% in England and Wales as a whole.[938] Similarly, in 1882 cancer was responsible for 1.6% of deaths and in 1979 for 21.6%. There are, of course, differences in data collection methods and unclear specificity of diagnosis over the past 100 years. The magnitude of the differences in figures suggests significant changes in the problems faced by Doctor Conan Doyle as compared to his modern counterparts.

Portsmouth also had a Municipal Throat and Ear Infirmary. The senior physician was Doctor Gordon Holmes, another individual with the name that Conan Doyle was to raise to worldwide renown.[871] The Portsmouth Eye and Ear Hospital, which he was to attend, did not open until 1884.[679] Such, then, was the historical, cultural, and medical environment which Conan Doyle chose at the age of 23 as the site to build his own practice.

PRACTICE—THE FIRST SIX MONTHS

Many statements have been published regarding Conan Doyle as a medical practitioner. Some are negative—''the patients gradually trickled in, but they trickled out as quickly, and often he was on the edge of starvation;''[525] some are lukewarn—''I find it hard to understand why Doyle was not a great success in practice;''[122] and some are erroneous—''Arthur Conan Doyle was a struggling ophthalmologist in 1887.''[775]

What then was the true nature, the degree of success and the caliber of Doctor Conan Doyle's medical practice in Southsea? Four primary sources of information are available—his autobiography, *Memories and Adventures;*[375l] his autobiographical novel, *The Stark Munro Letters;*[293b] newspapers of the time, and his personal letters. The relationship between Conan Doyle's medical practice and his novel *The Stark Munro Letters*[293] is commented on in a book review. ''We do not for a moment imply that [it] is an autobiography; but we are greatly mistaken if some pages of the book have not been written in the heart's blood of the author.''[85] Further, direct relationship to actual events is suggested by the use of Cullingworth as a name for Budd, as in his autobiography, and by almost identical accounts of some patients. In fact, the details in this novel written 12 years after he started practice are probably more accurate than those in his less detailed autobiography written 34 years later. In Conan Doyle's words:

> *In a book written some years afterwards, called* The Stark Munro Letters, *I drew in very close detail the events of the next few years, and there the curious reader will find them more clearly and fully set out than would be to scale in these pages . . . My mental attitude is correctly portrayed in* The Stark Munro Letters.[375p]

Another invaluable source of information is the ''on-site'' research carried out in the past few decades by Commander Geoffrey Stavert of Southsea.[843] Review and collation of these sources provide a fairly accurate depiction of Conan Doyle—the practicing physician.

Conan Doyle most likely arrived in Southsea from Plymouth on June 24, 1882, aboard an Irish steamer.[843] His cash balance was under £10 and his baggage consisted of ''one small trunk containing all my earthly possessions."[3751] On the very first day he was involved in a street fight with a rough who was beating his wife. Conan Doyle was ever the champion of ill-used females.

The first week in Southsea was spent obtaining temporary lodging and then a permanent site for both living quarters and practice. Conan Doyle's method for selecting the location is indicative of a very logical and methodical mind such as he created for Sherlock Holmes.

> *. . . I bought a large shilling map of the town. Then back I came and pinned this upon the lodging-house table. This done, I set to work to study it, and to arrange a series of walks by which I should pass through every street of the place . . . On my map I put a cross for every doctor. So at the end of that time I had a complete chart of the whole place, and could see at a glance where there was a possible opening, and what opposition there was at each point.*[293a]

Conan Doyle's choice was an eight-room house on the south side of Elm Grove with the St. Paul's Baptist Church to the east and another house and the Bush Hotel to the west. These structures were on the southeast corner of Elm Grove and King's Road. A photograph of the intersection taken about 1900 reveals adjoining structures. The two houses, each three stories high, were overshadowed by a four-story hotel and a church spire.[458] The address of the house was 1 Bush Villas. It served Conan Doyle's needs for eight and a half years.[N16]

According to Stavert[843] "Dr. Doyle did not know it at the time, but he could hardly have chosen a better place in which to begin his medical and literary career. Many of Southsea's leading citizens who were to play a prominent part in the next few years of his life lived within a few hundred yards of Bush Villas." But Southsea already had a sufficient number of physicians for its needs. "There were already well over a dozen doctors in the square mile of Southsea. As a young unknown he could only look to the poorer or artisan class of patients from the long terraced streets to the north of Elm Grove."[845]

Conan Doyle's impoverished financial status was not helped by a vindictive letter from Doctor Budd in which he reneged on his promise of £1 per week. Although Conan Doyle's mother sent some funds, there was not enough for a down payment on the rent of £40 per year. He managed to avoid this expense by using an uncle as a reference.[375l] He had just enough money to outfit the house with £4 worth of furniture and a red lamp, the latter being the Victorian symbol for a physician's house. Left with only "a couple of pounds in hand" he could do no more. At least Conan Doyle was able "to make one room possible for patients with three chairs, a table and a central patch of carpet."

Conan Doyle's medical paraphernalia, brought in the trunk from Plymouth, consisted of a stethoscope, several medical books, and a name plate which he affixed to the rented house.[293b] To these he added "a fair consignment of drugs on tick from a wholesale house . . ."[375l] This paucity of professional tools is totally inadequate by today's standards, but was sufficient in 1882.

Within a week after his arrival in Southsea Doctor Conan Doyle was ready to start the general practice of medicine.[N17] His first step was to place a two-line ad in the *Portsmouth Evening News* of July 1, 1882, under the category of Miscellaneous Wants.

> *Dr. Doyle begs to notify that he has Removed to 1 Bush Villas, Elm-grove, next the Bush Hotel.*[660]

The wording of the ad is noteworthy for it can be interpreted as a notice of a change in location of an established physician, although it does not say as much.

Conan Doyle's ad did not result in large numbers of patients, but he was not completely bereft of callers.

> *From the very beginning a few stray patients of the poorest class, some of them desirous of novelty, some disgruntled with their own doctors, the greater part owing bills and ashamed to face their creditor, came to consult me and consume a bottle of my medicine. I could pay for my food by the drugs I sold.*[375l]

Even today such an experience is common to most medical graduates who start their own solo practice.

According to a letter, written by Conan Doyle to Mrs. Charlotte Thwaites Drummond, an Edinburgh friend,[387] he saw his first patient about a week after opening his office. "I then sat in the bed and ate the corned beef for a period of six days at the end of which time a vaccination turned up. I had to pay 2/6 for the vaccine in London, and could only screw 1/6 out of the woman, so that I came to the conclusion that if I got many more patients I would have to sell the furniture."[378a] The humor is evident, as it is in some of his fictional writings. His classmate C.B. Gunn, who set up a practice in Peebles, Scotland, had to wait six weeks for the first patient.[497]

The first few months of practice were slow. "Patients are still rather coy. They swarm in at the rate of about two a week."[386] Conan Doyle could have taken advantage of a letter of introduction to the local Bishop which he had received from his Catholic relatives. But, still maintaining his ideals, he burnt it.[375l] To relieve the loneliness Conan Doyle had his ten-year-old brother Innes join him. This was approximately a month after opening his practice.

Innes Doyle was undoubtedly impressed by his older brother. He wrote to his mother on August 16, 1882, "The patients are crowding in. We have made three bob this week."[375m] Innes can be excused for this obvious exaggeration. In the same letter he tells of a "gipsy's child [who] had measles . . . we got sixpence out of them and that is always something." With characteristic humor Conan Doyle commented "it was the Gipsy who got sixpence out of us."

Medical practices are not made out of such incidents as these. Fortunately several events helped build Conan Doyle's clientele. According to Stavert, [843] Doctor Pike, who practiced nearby, sent Conan Doyle a few patients. Other examples are provided in a letter from Conan Doyle to his Birmingham mentor, Doctor Hoare. The letter was probably written in December 1882 some time after Hoare visited him in Southsea.[385c]

> *A dentist over the road named Kirton . . . has proved himself a great trump and sends me on anything he can. I have inherited a club too from a drunken doctor who has left.*

Also mentioned in the letter to Hoare[385c] is the type of practice-building event that Doctor Budd of Plymouth relished. ''A man had the good taste to fall off his horse the other day just in front of the window, and the intelligent animal rolled on him. I stuck him together again, and it got into all the papers and got my name known a little.''

This incident was reported in the *Portsmouth Evening News* of November 2, 1882, under the title ''Accident in Elm Grove.''[598]

> *An accident, which might have led to serious consequences, occurred this afternoon in Elm-grove as Mr. Robinson, of Victoria-road, was riding in front of the Bush Hotel, his stirrup leather snapped, and he was thrown to the ground, the animal rearing at the same time and falling partially upon him. He was conveyed into the house of Dr. Conan Doyle, of Bush Villas, and that gentleman was able to pronounce that, though considerably shaken and bruised, there was no injury of any consequence.*

Conan Doyle describes several similar incidents for Doctor Munro who ''ran down to the newspaper office on each occasion. . .''[293c] It is more likely a recollection of Doctor Budd's behavior than his own.

Conan Doyle's account of still another patient typifies how he survived while his practice was slowly developing during the first six months.

> *Some of my tradespeople gave me their custom in return for mine. . . . There was a grocer who developed epileptic fits, which meant butter and tea for us.*[375m]

By December he was reasonably established as he relates in a letter to Dearest Mam. ''The practice is still looking up. . . . There is no sign at all of any falling off. It's increase is never brilliant but always steady.''[387b]

The evidence points to Conan Doyle's having, in his own words, ''the nucleus of a little practice'' within six months of arriving in a strange city where he had no contacts.[N18] His financial position had improved by December 1882 to the point where he could take in a housekeeper. Such initial success speaks well for his perseverance, his medical skills, and his relationships with patients. There is no doubt that his outgoing personality was of assistance.[375m]

> *I mixed with people so far as I could, for I learned that a brass plate alone will never attract, and poeple must see the human being who lies in wait behind it.*

His position can best be summarized from another letter from Southsea at the end of December 1882.[386]

> *It is just six months today since I walked into this house with a small portmanteau and an ulster. . .*
>
> *I have a fine brass plate, and a big red lamp. I have paid £26 rent and taxes—and all without borrowing a penny, and I don't owe as much as I am owed now. So I think that is a very satisfactory result.*

PRACTICE—THE NEXT EIGHT YEARS

Conan Doyle wrote and spoke very little about his medical practice after the first six months. In his autobiography[375] the first six months are given six pages and the last eight years two and one half pages. A significiant section of *The Stark Munro Letters* [293] is devoted to the privations and humor of trying to establish a practice. His attitude toward his practice in March 1883 was expressed in a letter. "The practice is getting along wonderfully. Medicine brought in more than 11 pounds in February, and I hope March will be better still—in fact I have made as much already".[386] By the end of 1883 he could write that "I am up to my eyes in work. These are my own people to be looked after. Then a neighboring medico has gone away for a month and I take the Parish for him."[386]

The financial aspects of these years are well known because of Conan Doyle's statement "I made £154 the first year, and £250 the second, rising slowly to £300, which in eight years I never passed, so far as the medical practice went."[375m] These figures have been used by some as an indication of his failure as a practitioner.

This income, although low by current standards, must be evaluated in respect to the economics of the time. Pearsall[713] has pointed out "To give this figure [£300] some kind of reality, this was four times the wage of a skilled craftsman—a mason, a printer, a tailor or a carpenter." Conan Doyle himself considered even £200 adequate. "I hope this next year to make well over £200 from medicine, which with a little help from publishers will be quite a swagger income."[387b] Such a positive reaction may have been related to the fact that his father supported a large family on no more than £250 per year.[862]

To put Conan Doyle's income into further perspective, figures on incomes of physicians in the mid-Victorian era are available.[720c] A practice income of £200 was common in the first two years and £300 acceptable. In London some practices yielded as low as £150, with £370 the median. Such comparisons make it evident that Conan Doyle's practice was not a financial failure.

Stavert[845] has provided some orientation to the significance of Conan Doyle's income in respect to the number of patients seen. At a typical charge of 3/6 per visit for the period, plus medicine sales, £300 per year would signify 20 to 25 calls per week. This was not the practice of a failure. "The fact that Doyle's income did not rise much above £300 was due, in my opinion, not to any incompetence on his part but simply to the amount of competition."[845]

Conan Doyle's income from medicine was not limited to this private practice. He was enrolled in a unit of the British Army as a local civilian doctor "for temporary duty of some hours a day. The terms were a guinea a day."[375n] He also had a commission to perform medical examinations for the Gresham Life Insurance Company, the superintendent of which was a friend, Mr. Barnden.[125b] To these were added £20 to £30 a year from his writings [820] and £100 from his wife after his marriage in 1885.[N19]

In 1885 a major addition to Conan Doyle's medical status occurred. He received information about the requirements for the M.D. degree from a friend in November 1883 and went to Edinburgh for the preliminaries in March 1884.[386] By April 1885, he completed a thesis on Tabes Dorsalis[240] and defended it successfully in July for an M.D. degree from his alma mater, the University of Edinburgh.[414] This occurred one month before his marriage. Unlike medical schools in the United States, those in Britain gave the M.D. degree in midcareer as an advanced qualification rather than on graduation.[720d] This degree, attractive to patients, may have further increased his practice. Quite surprising is that Conan Doyle made no mention of this achievement in his autobiography.[375]

Some flavor of Conan Doyle's practice may be obtained from descriptions in his autobiography of specific patients seen after he became established.

> *Then there was a very tall, horse-faced old lady with an extraordinary dignity of bearing. . . . But every now and again she went on a wild burst, . . . I was the only one who had influence over her at such times, . . . I quelled her by assuming a gloomy dignity as portentous as her own.*[375m]

Conan Doyle apparently had some skills in patient/doctor relationships.

> *I was called in by a poor woman to see her daughter. Long thin limbs were twisted and coiled in the tiny couch. The face was sane but malignant. . . . "Its's a girl," sobbed the mother. "She's nineteen. Oh! if God would only take her'!" What a life for both! And how hard to face such facts and accept any of the commonplace explanations of existence!*[375m]

This episode certainly presents Conan Doyle as the compassionate physician.

> *. . . I was called in to a lady who was suffering from what appeared to be dyspepsia of a rather severe type. There was absolutely nothing to indicate anything more serious. I therefore reassured the family, spoke lightly of the illness, and walked home to make up a bismuth mixture for her, calling on one or two other cases on the way. When I got home I found a*

> *messenger waiting to say that the lady was dead. . . . The woman really had a gastric ulcer, for which there is no diagnosis; it was eating its way into the lining of her stomach, it pierced an artery after I saw her, and she bled to death.*[375m]

Such experiences happen to all physicians. Did Conan Doyle deduce that there was a gastric ulcer, or was an autopsy performed?

In 1885 Conan Doyle was advertising for a private patient to be looked after in his spare room[386] The patient came as a referral.

> *I had come into contact with them [Mrs. Hawkins, son and daughter] through the illness of the son, which was of a sudden and violent nature, arising from cerebral meningitis. His case was a mortal one, and in spite of all I could do he passed away a few days later.*[375m]

Conan Doyle kept the son in his house for several days and called in a consultant (Doctor Pike). This is an example of his compassion, which may have been influenced by his reaction to the daughter ''a very gentle and amiable girl'' who became the first Mrs. Conan Doyle on August 6, 1885.

There is a report in the *Portsmouth Evening News* (1888)[726] of another patient:

> *Yesterday afternoon the Portsmouth Coroner held an inquest at the Barley Mow, Castleroad, Southsea touching the death of James Killick, aged 47 years, a green grocer, carrying out business in Castleroad. Dr. Conan Doyle said that death arose from failure of the heart's action arising from natural causes, probably brought about by the intemperate habits of the deceased man. The jury returned a verdict in accordance with the medical testimony.*

This is indicative of the acceptance of Doctor Conan Doyle by the community.

Another patient was a rather prestigious community member. This was General Alfred W. Drayson, who was Professor of Surveying and Astronomy at the Royal Military Academy, Woolwich.[471] The General involved Conan Doyle in spiritualistic activities, which were later to dominate his life. [N20] A result was the record of yet another patient described in 1923.[372]

> *A patient of Southsea days came back [at a seance conducted by Mr. John Ticknor]. He gave the date as 1888. I had a favorite patient named Woodman at this time. I said 'I hope I was not the cause of your passing over.' He laughed loudly at this.*

It is remarkable that Conan Doyle would remember the name of a patient a third of a century later.

One description by Conan Doyle of an encounter with a patient revealed a rather disinterested and sardonic orientation. This was in an article in 1893 in which he explains his development as a writer.[271]

> *How often have I rejoiced to find a clear morning before me. Then to me enter my housekeeper with tidings of dismay. 'Mrs. Thurston's little boy wants to see you, doctor.' 'Show him in,' say I, striving to fix my scene in my mind that I may splice it when the troubles over. 'Well, my boy?' 'Please doctor, mother wants to know if she is to add water to that medicine.' 'Certainly, certainly.' Not that it matters in the least but it is well to answer with decision.*

Many a physician has felt such a reaction when his avocation has been disturbed. Conan Doyle's description, years later, undoubtedly portrays this feeling to make a point rather than depicting an actual dialogue.

In 1904 Conan Doyle was asked why he gave up the practice of medicine.[717] The reason he gave was that the work was too hard. As an example he related "My first case came to me in the middle of the night. It was January, and a cold rain was falling." He was called out to see a young girl who had taken laudanum by mistake for paregoric. When he reached the house after considerable difficulty, he was told that all was well and he was not needed. "Ye won't charge nothin' for this visit, will ye?" asked the father. Any practitioner in any era or country has one or more anecdotes of the demanding but pecunious patient. In this instance Conan

Doyle's anecdote was obviously apocryphal, since he began his practice in July, not in January.

Other recollections are by Conan Doyle's youngest child, Dame Jean. "I once met a woman whose mother 'had been brought into the world' by my father. He was the family doctor, and it seems they liked him and felt confidence in him—a doctor who would understand."[389] Conan Doyle's relationship to his family as a physician also reveals his bedside manner. Dame Jean Conan Doyle relates:

> *I suffered a lot from various pains when I was a child—earache, neuralgia, toothache, and other pains. Although my father always called in our family doctor, when a doctor was needed, he always used to comfort me by gently massaging the painful area. Although he had strong, broad hands they had an amazingly light gentle touch—very soothing and helpful when one was ill. This may be no indication of his ability as a doctor, but I felt at the time that he must have had a genuine sense of vocation for his profession.*[389]

These examples reveal a physician who was knowledgeable, compassionate and well-respected. Why, then is Conan Doyle considered by so many as a medical failure? "I saw . . . a reproduction of Dr. Doyle's shingle as it was hung out before the house where he waited in vain for patients to come."[37] There are several likely reasons for such misstatements.

The fact that Conan Doyle emphasized the first six months of struggle so much more than the next eight years has provided an overall negative bias. Related is the greater drama and fascination that is presented by striving against difficulty and by the macabre.

A second factor is the modesty with which Conan Doyle related his experiences as a physician. For example, he once said that he had "a limited, strictly limited practice."[394]

Then there was his sense of humor, often at his own expense, and the satirization of his medical activities. In 1913 at a tea for Representatives of the Medical Profession, Conan Doyle wryly recalled that once in America the chairman at a dinner at which he was present remarked "that it was a sinister fact that although

Sir Arthur Conan Doyle was supposed to be a doctor no living patient of his had ever been seen.''[349] Perhaps, his humor was a defensive reaction as indicated by the assertion ''It is well that medical practice has its humorous side, for it has much to depress one.''[375m]

Another factor relates to erroneous interpretations of his income. Even with this, Conan Doyle's adroit humor has exaggerated his lack of success. An often repeated anecdote is the following:

> *In the first year the Income Tax paper arrived and I filled it up to show that I was not liable. They returned the paper with ''Most unsatisfactory'' scrawled across it. I wrote ''I entirely agree'' under the words, and returned it once more.*[375m]

One might surmise that Conan Doyle was ''his own worst enemy.'' But, in fact, he was a human and humane practitioner who combined an excellent medical education with both humbleness and humor. These factors assisted him in establishing an adequate practice in the relatively healthy district of Southsea in spite of a surfeit of physicians.

NONPRACTICE MEDICAL ACTIVITIES

Conan Doyle's practice was not large enough to prevent him from engaging in other profession-related activities. The extent and variety of these involvements would be noteworthy even on a full-time basis. For example, he was a member of the British Medical Association.[646] There is no evidence that he held an office in its Southern Branch, as he did in many nonmedical organizations. The Southern Branch of the British Medical Association held its 13th annual meeting in Portsmouth on June 18, 1886.[98] Southsea was represented by two vice-presidents, one member of the Council and the Hon. Secretary for the District. If Doctor Conan Doyle attended it was as an ordinary member.

His special medical interest was the eye. ''Of late years I had been interested in eye work and had amused myself by correcting refractions and ordering glasses in the Portsmouth Eye Hospital under Mr. Vernon Ford.''[375q] The Eye and Ear Hospital had been established in 1884 in a small house in Clarence View, Portsmouth.[679] This location was quite convenient for Conan Doyle, being within a mile of 1 Bush Villas.[N21]

Doctor Conan Doyle was sufficiently involved with the hospital and oriented to the importance of eye problems to offer strong support to its work at the annual meetings. In 1889 he ''stressed that to the working man and the mechanic his eyes were practically his life, and the loss of his eyes a living death.''[429] In 1890 ''Dr. Conan Doyle, in an eloquent speech pointed out that one of the results of modern civilization was that it became unnecessary to use their long sights. This tended to weaken the power of the eyes.''[430] This may be a rather unfounded theory, but does illustrate interest in problems of the eye.

He learned refractions sufficiently well at the hospital to refract eyes of his own patients. One receipt for payment from W. Chapman has been preserved ''To testing child's eyes, etc. 5/. Nov. 26th/90.''[388] His teacher was undoubtedly the hospital physician and eye specialist, Doctor Arthur Vernon Ford, who was five years his senior. Ford graduated in 1876 from St. Thomas Hospital, London.[845] As were many of Conan Doyle's relationships, that with Vernon Ford was long lasting. In 1898, Doctor and Mrs. Ford were guests at a fancy ball given by the Conan Doyles in Hindhead. This was eight years after the Conan Doyles left Southsea.[833] Conan Doyle appeared as a Viking and Vernon Ford as Queen's Counsel.[N22]

Conan Doyle attended various public meetings on subjects related to medicine. On April 15, 1886, he objected to an antivivisection presentation by a minister. He spoke up at the meeting, supporting the killing of rabbits if it would alleviate human suffering.[203] He was supported by Doctor Claremont, to whom he was to leave his practice three and a half years later.[904]

On Febraury 9, 1889, Conan Doyle was one of about 20 to 30 medical and scientific men and journalists invited to see a demonstration by Professor Milo de Meyer.[555] Several individuals were successfully hypnotized and the usual hypnotic suggestions carried out. An unsuccessful attempt was made to hypnotize Conan Doyle. His views on hypnotism were not recorded, but in 1894 he did make this subject (in a greatly exaggerated form) the theme of a novel *The Parasite.*[280]

CITIZEN

Conan Doyle's Southsea tenure was characterized by numerous nonmedical activities. Although not directly related, these do round out the picture of a professional greatly involved with his community. He was very active in the Portsmouth Literary and Scientific Society.[842] Its meetings were held at various sites every other Tuesday in the winter months. This made for quite a few meetings a season, many of which were attended by Conan Doyle. Years later, in his autobiography, Conan Doyle reminisced "We kept the sacred flame burning in the old city with our weekly paper and discussions during the long winters."[375q]

Conan Doyle derived a benefit from his association with the Portsmouth Literary and Scientific Society.

> *It was there I learned to face an audience, which proved to be of the first importance in my life's work. I was naturally of a very nervous, backward, self-distrustful disposition in such things and I have been told that the signal that I was about to join in the discussion was that the whole long bench on I which I sat, with everyone on it, used to shake with my emotion.*[375q]

This is one of Conan Doyle's characteristic semideprecatory and humorous accounts.

He not only attended meetings, but also participated in discussions and presented papers. An interesting presentation on "Our Knowledge of the Brain" was delivered by Doctor C.C. Claremont, a fellow physician, on December 21, 1887.[729] It stressed the limited knowledge of its function and the contributions of phrenology (the study of shapes of the head as the basis for certain mental characteristics.) Conan Doyle stated that mistakes arose through mistaking phrenology for physiognomy (the facial look or expression as an indication of character). It is not clear whether Conan Doyle accepted the now outmoded "science" of phrenology.[N23]

After a paper given by a Doctor Nicolson in 1890 on "Witches and Witchcraft,"[934] Conan Doyle suggested that there might be some truth in Witchcraft, since it was a belief held in many countries for a long period of time. He considered witchcraft to be related to mesmerism (hypnotism) and clairvoyance, and stated that witchcraft "was a case of preternatural power, used for malevolent purposes."[N24] Such views presaged Conan Doyle's full acceptance of spiritualism about 15 years later, a belief which had been considerably enhanced by General Drayson.[367]

Conan Doyle presented three papers to the Portsmouth Society. The first one, based on his whaling trip as a student.[375c] given on December 3, 1883, was widely reported.[24,25,727] He described the history of Arctic exploration, the whaling industry and schemes for reaching the North Pole. With characteristic enthusiasm "I borrowed from a local taxidermist every bird and beast that he possessed which could conceivably find its way into the Arctic Circle. These I piled upon the lecture table, and the audience, concluding that I shot them all, looked upon me with great respect."[375q,N25]

In a letter written shortly before this presentation he expressed some concern, but with his typical touch of humor.[386]

> *I do hope it will pass off well. It will do me a lot of good in the way of getting my name known among nice people. I have a sturdy phalanx of bachelor friends—strong armed and heavy sticked who may be relied upon for applause.*

His other two talks were on literary figures. In a presentation on January 19, 1886,[728] concerning Carlyle he regretted "the strange and obscure style" in which Carlyle wrote, an accusation that cannot be made of Conan Doyle. On November 20, 1888, the presentation was on George Meredith, a native son of Southsea.[472,730] Conan Doyle praised Meredith, but was less salutary in his comments ten years later in *Through the Magic*

Door.[338a] He was also mentioned by Sherlock Holmes,[260] as was Carlyle.[244,257]

Conan Doyle's contributions to the Portsmouth Literary and Scientific Society were also organizational. He served as the Society's secretary for at least six years. His friend and patient, General Drayson, was president for several terms. Much has been made of Doctor James Watson, another secretary of the Society, in respect to serving as model for Doctor John Watson of Holmesian fame.[452] Doctor James Watson of Southsea appears to have the edge in being considered as the model for Holmes' Boswell. However, Doctor P. H. Watson, one of Conan Doyle's Edinburgh teachers, previously mentioned, cannot be ignored.[56] Although James had been overseas in China, P. H. had served in a colonial war as did John Watson of Sherlockian fame.

Not the least of Doctor Conan Doyle's activities were sports. He considered active involvement as the only true sport. "Sport is what a man does, not what a horse does."[342] According to the reminiscences of a Southsea friend he took part in rowing, amateur boxing, championship football, and cricket.[721] "He kept training religiously." Other sports in which he engaged were bowls and billiards.[561] Occasionally he paid a penalty for this extensive physical activity, as indicated in a letter written to Doctor Hoare in 1890. "At present I have strained both muscles of my back at cricket and can hardly rise from a chair."[385d]

These sports also afforded some rewards for excellence. At the end of 1883 he wrote "I have a crutch stick of ebony and silver which I won as a prize."[386] In September 1885 he received a special presentation "by the members of the Southsea Bowling Club to their popular president, Dr. Conan Doyle."[735] He was given a dinner service which "was a slight token of the esteem in which Dr. Doyle was held by members of the club, not only as President, but for his private character." This is indeed fair praise and undoubtedly also enhanced his status as a physician.

The catalog of Doctor Conan Doyle's activities does not end with sports. As secretary of a political group, the Liberal-Unionists,[375q] he met such prominent figures as Sir William

Crossman and Lord Balfour.[N26] On January 26, 1887, he was initiated into the Phoenix Masonic Lodge of Portsmouth.[42] Although he did not play an active role in Freemasonery, he continued his membership until 1911. He was in famous company, some other well-known Masons being Mesmer, Marat, Hahnemann, Jenner, and Mayo.[6] The Sherlockian stories contain four such Freemasons.[873] Another activity, which was to become a dominating life's work, relates to his being secretary of the Hampshire Psychical Society in 1887.[845] At the same time he was a member of the General Council of his alma mater.[646]

One might well ask what motivated such a massive amount of activity in a moderately successful medical practitioner. One commonly held view is that he exerted himself in order to become known and thus to attract more patients.[449] Perhaps! But this hardly does justice to an exceptional individual who showed considerable elan and catholic interests all of his life. More likely reasons are his loneliness during the first year at Southsea and his zest for human life and action in all of its infinite variety.

WRITER AND PRACTITIONER

As with Conan Doyle's community activities, his motivation for writing has been attributed to "the tedious waiting for nonexistent patients."[531] One wonders, however, after considering the foregoing review of Conan Doyle's activities, how he found time to write at all, especially after the first few years of practice. Conan Doyle did show an inclination for writing before he began practice. While still a medical student, one medical letter to the editor on gelsemium[216] and two of his short stories had been published.[217,218] Between the time of graduation and the start of practice in Southsea he wrote only three short stories: "The Gully of Bluemansdyke,"[219] "Bones,"[220] and "My Friend the Murderer."[247] In fact, as his practice grew his writing increased. Between July 1882 and December 1884 Conan Doyle wrote four medical letters to the editor, one article on infections, and one medically related short story. In 1884 he began writing his novel *The Firm of Girdlestone*[258] which was published in 1890.

It was during these busy Southsea years, 1885 to 1890, that he wrote the most—three medical letters to the editor in support of vaccination for smallpox and one on Doctor Koch and his contentious cure for tuberculosis. The latter was also the subject of a detailed paper. In addition, he had written two medically related short stories. His major achievement during this time was an extensive thesis on Tabes Dorsalis for an M.D. degree.[240] These were significant contributions to medicine!

It was in the field of nonmedical writing that Conan Doyle really blossomed out during the years of his medical practice. This output consisted of 40 short stories and five novels, including the first two of the Holmesian series—*A Study in Scarlet*[244] and *The Sign of the Four.*[257] *The White Company,*[265] which was first publishd in January 1891 (but written in 1889), should also be included in this listing.[N27]

These considerations discredit statements about the motivation for Conan Doyle's literary endeavors. For example, "It was in 1886, when fortunes were at a low-ebb, that Arthur Conan Doyle hit on the idea of an amateur detective."[819] This myth has been perpetuated from article to article, but is not supported by a study of primary source material.

Conan Doyle had his own explanation for his increased literary output which began in 1885. "After my marriage . . . my brain seems to have quickened and both my imagination and my range of expression were greatly improved."[375p] In a similar vein he explained in 1893 "It [a novel] was written in the intervals of a busy though ill-paying practice."[271] On the basis of the evidence we can surely accept Conan Doyle's statement as true.

LEAVING SOUTHSEA

By 1890 Conan Doyle seemed well entrenched in Southsea, dividing "my time between oculism, occultism and my writing, with a little cricket as a corrective."[385e] It was not to last much longer. The first indication of an imminent change began with his precipitous trip to Berlin to study Koch's newly reported cure for tuberculosis.

> *. . . I should have remained in Southsea permanently but for this new episode in my life . . . A great urge came upon me suddenly that I should go to Berlin to see him [Koch] do so [demonstrate]. I could give no clear reason for this but it was an irresistible impulse and I at once determined to go.*[375q]

And go he did, on November 16, 1890. One result was a very erudite analysis of Koch's cure. Another result was his encounter with Malcolm Morris, a London skin specialist. According to Malcolm Morris' son, the two had been friends since Conan Doyle brought him a patient for consultation.[666] Morris insisted that Doyle leave general practice, specialize in the eye, spend six months training in Vienna, and establish himself in London.[375q]

Conan Doyle, ever a man of action, lost no time in making a decision. He returned to Portsmouth on November 22 and in an interview on November 24 stated "I am leaving Southsea shortly and am busily engaged in winding up my practice."[738]

The community was quick to react. "The departure of Dr. A. Conan Doyle was made the occasion on Friday week (Dec. 12), by his friends of their sense of the advantage to this borough of his seven [sic] years residence therein."[195] The farewell dinner was held at the Grosvenor Hotel with 34 in attendance.[393] It was presided over by Doctor James Watson and included a toast by General Dryson.

Not only Conan Doyle's friends honored him. In an interview in 1892 by How,[175] he provided an example of the esteem in which his patients held him.

> *It was one of the late Khedive's dinner plates. When I was leaving Portsmouth, an old patient came to bid me good-bye. . . . Her son was a young able-bodied seaman on the* Inflexible *at the bombardment of Alexandria. . . . He found himself in the Khedive's kitchen! With an eye to loot, he took this plate, and crawled out again. It was the most treasured thing the lady possessed, she said, and she begged me to take it.*

How's article contains a picture of the Khedive's plate.

According to Conan Doyle's autobiography "There were no difficulties about disposing of the practice, for it was so small and so purely personal that it could not be sold to another and simply had to dissolve."[375q] In spite of this he did not abandon his patients. In a letter to one of them Conan Doyle stated his intention.

> *I am leaving Southsea to practice in London. My practice I am handing over to Dr. Claremont of Petersleigh, Elm Grove, who has promised to give the utmost attention to my patients. I feel that I am leaving them in the safest of hands.*[388]

Claremont and Conan Doyle had substituted for each other during absences.[385d] "I am doing Claremont's work as well as my own, he being away."[N28]

The Conan Doyles left Southsea about December 18, 1890, as indicated in a letter to Mrs. Hoare.[385f] They then visited his mother in Edinburgh beginning about December 26.[385g] In another letter to Mrs. Hoare he indicated leaving for Vienna on a Thursday morning (January 3, 1891) and arriving Saturday evening (January 5, 1891).[385h] Conan Doyle had now completely broken the bonds of his medical practice and did so within little more than a month after making the definitive decision.[N29]

NEW VENTURES

Conan Doyle's arrival in Vienna is as good a time as any to consider his abdication from general medicine. There is little basis for Ivor Brown's statement that "The experiment [practice] was courageous but unsuccessful. He was driven by poverty to alter his profession."[101] Conan Doyle provides a different perspective of his Southsea days. "My life had been a pleasant one with my steadily-increasing literary success, my practice, which was enough to keep me pleasantly occupied, and my sport. . ."[375q]

This positive view of his status in Southsea is borne out by an article, complete with portrait, devoted to him in the *Portsmouth Crescent* of September 20, 1888.[392] "He is most popular amongst all those who know him, and his tall athletic, broad-shouldered figure is extremely familiar to a large number of Portsmouth people."

It is most likely that Conan Doyle felt some limitations imposed by the growing practice in respect to his freedom to write and travel. After returning from Berlin he stated, "I had spread my wings and had felt something of the powers within me."[375q] He was not, however, absolutely certain about literary success and so chose a medical specialty that could provide a living and yet permit enough time to write. To this might be added the prestige factor of being a London Consultant. Thus, one could attribute Conan Doyle's leaving general practice for ophthalmology to the fact that it was not a failure, but sufficiently successful to inhibit his writing.

It is interesting to note at this point an excerpt from Conan Doyle's *The Stark Munro Letters*.[293] In a conversation between Stark Munro (Conan Doyle) and Cullingworth (Budd), the following comment appears:

> *I've taken to the eye, my boy. There's a fortune in the eye. A man grudges a half-crown to cure his chest or his throat, but he'd spend his last dollar over his eye. There's money in ears, but the eye is a gold mine.*

This was published three years after his abortive attempt to establish himself as an ophthalmologist in London. Surely he is satirizing his own experience.

Another example of Conan Doyle's thoughts on ophthalmology as a career appears in a letter he wrote to his sister, Lottie.[832] One also sees the hint of ambivalence concerning the financial role literature was to play in his destiny.

> *If it* [Micah Clarke] *comes off, we may then, I think, take it as proved that I can live by my pen. We should then have a few hundreds in hand to start us. I should go to London and study the eye. I should then go to Berlin and study the eye. I should then go to Paris and study the eye. Having learned all there is to know about the eye, I should come back to London and start as an eye-surgeon, still, of course, keeping literature as my milk-cow.*

This letter was written in 1888, about two years before his departure from Southsea. It is evidence that his decision to leave general practice for ophthalmology was not an abrupt one. It was not due to his chance meeting with Malcolm Morris in November 1890, although his final break was precipitated by it. One of his goals was to settle in London which was the mecca for writers, both American and British, during the last quarter of the 19th and first quarter of the 20th centuries.[921] A gossip item in a Portsmouth paper of March 29, 1889 indicated more publicly his desire to specialize in eye work.[613]

> *Dr. Conan Doyle soon forsakes Portsmouth for good. The best men in London have come from the country. Dr. Doyle has a desire to become an eye specialist. He goes to Berlin, Vienna, and Paris, for study, and ultimately settles down in London as an eye specialist and novelist. He is not a little chagrined at the Hants Post's Nonconformist bitter criticism of his characters in Micah Clarke.*

OPHTHALMOLOGIST

Conan Doyle finally chose Vienna to study ophthalmology because of its reputation and because of the influence of Malcolm Morris. Vienna had a long and excellent reputation for this specialty with the first medical school chair being established in 1812.[607] Much of the basic studies on diseases of the eye were carried out in Vienna. It was here that the ophthalmoscope, invented by Helmholtz of Berlin in 1851, was developed into a clinical instrument. Cocaine, promoted by Sigmund Freud, was first used in Vienna as a local anesthetic for the eye in 1884. It was, however, a feature of Conan Doyle's Holmesian stories before his Vienna experience.[244] Albrech von Graefe, an outstanding eye surgeon, revolutionized cataract surgery by development of a knife permitting removal through the smallest wound possible. Conan Doyle used Graefe's cataract knife as a device in *The Adventure of Silver Blaze.*[267] published in 1892. It was used to cut the leg tendon of a race horse, leaving a very small, imperceptible wound—imperceptible that is to anyone but Sherlock Holmes.

Many other notables were in the Vienna eye school.[607] Students flocked there from many countries during the last quarter of the 19th century. There were also other reasons besides educational ones. One ophthalmology student who chose Berlin suggested that "there was another reason for the popularity of Vienna. It was a gay and merry city, and there was not that undercurrent of jealousy of Britain and America which was already in process of development in Berlin."[855]

It was to this environment that Doctor and Mrs. Conan Doyle arrived during a blizzard on the evening of January 5, 1891. Their stay was apparently pleasant, but somewhat unsatisfactory in respect to learning about the eye.

> . . . *I attended eye lectures at the Krankenhaus but could certainly have learned far more in London, for even if one has a fair knowledge of conversational German it is very different from following accurately a rapid lecture filled with technical terms.*[375r]

Lectures in English had been provided in Vienna since 1879 by Ernest Fuchs, who obtained the Chair in Ophthalmology at the Vienna Medical School in 1885.[607a] Perhaps these were not available during Conan Doyle's sojourn. At any rate he managed to keep occupied. "I say a little of gay Viennese Society."[375r] He also continued his literary work by writing *The Doings of Raffle Haw,*[262] possibly one of Conan Doyle's weakest novels. It was written between the day after his arrival in Vienna (January 6) and January 23.[715] At least he received £150 for the novel—sufficient to pay for his travel expenses. The name Raffles was used by his sister Constance's husband, E. W. Hornung (1866–1921), for his fictional gentleman thief[808] eight years later.

Little additional information has been found on Conan Doyle's Vienna interlude. There are, however, conflicting versions of the length of his stay in that city. The most accurate account is that of Pearson[715] who had access to Conan Doyle's diary, begun in

January of 1891. His stay was not four months as indicated in his autobiography written 23 years later.[375r] It extended from his arrival on January 5 to departure on March 9. This was a period of two months rather than the six suggested by Malcolm Morris. It is doubtful, given the short period of time, language difficulties, and busy social and literary activities, that Conan Doyle increased his knowledge of ophthalmology. His departure from Vienna on March 9 was undoubtedly influenced by the unsatisfactory nature of the educational experience—due in part to a lack of preparedness.

> *. . . it is usually taken for granted that he [the student] has exhausted his own country before going abroad, which was by no means the case with me. Therefore as far as eye work goes, my winter was wasted. . .*[375r]

Conan Doyle's departure may also have been accelerated by financial concerns, being down to "the very few hundred pounds which were absolutely all that I had in the world." In spite of this comment he had sufficient funds to spend about ten days touring Italy. On March 19 they reached Paris where a few days were spent with Edmund Landolt, a leading French ophthalmologist. Edmund Landolt (1846–1926) wrote one of the first large modern treatises on diseases of the eye.[73b] It was published between 1880 and 1889.

Conan Doyle arrived in London on March 24, 1891. Living quarters were obtained at No. 23 Montague Place, Russel Square, opposite the rear of the British Museum. No. 23 Montague Place has now been replaced by a building of the University of London. It is one and a fourth miles walking distance to Conan Doyle's office site. He chose for his office No. 2 Devonshire Place, which is only two blocks from Harley Street, the prestigious address of London consultants. Devonshire Place is only one block long being the continuation of Wimpole and Upper Wimpole Streets. In 1891 this block may have been part of Upper Wimpole Street as it is so designated on his letterhead paper.[385i] It lies between Marylebourne and Devonshire Street. No. 2 is only one fourth mile from Baker Street of Sherlock Holmes fame. Although Conan

Doyle is credited with saying that he never set foot in Baker Street, he meant, of course, before writing his first Sherlock Holmes story.

According to Conan Doyle's diary the consulting room was ready on April 6. He also had partial use of a waiting room. With characteristic humor he recalled "I was soon to find that they were both waiting rooms. . ."[375r] Rent was £120 per year. He walked from home to his office daily. Office hours were from 10 a.m. to 3 or 4 p.m. By his own account he saw no patients and spent most of the time writing. He did, however, undertake associations with ophthalmologic groups. He became a member of the Ophthalmologic Society of the United Kingdom and was so registered from 1891 to 1893.[875]

Conan Doyle also affiliated with an eye hospital. In a letter to Doctor Hoare he indicated "I have now hooked on at the Westminster Ophthalmic."[375r] The Royal Westminster Eye Infirmary is now the Moorfields Eye Hospital located in High Street only a third of a mile from Montague Place. A history of this institution, written in 1929, includes list of honorary consultants since 1810.[149] Conan Doyle is not listed. Perhaps his career as an ophthalmologist was too short for an official hospital appointment.[N30]

It is not known if he made other efforts to become known as a specialist. One interesting comment noted "I was aware that many of the big men do not find time to work out refractions . . . I was capable in this work and like it, so I hoped that some of it might drift my way,"[375r] The proximity to the "big men" in Harley Street did not result in any patients. In his own words "I started a waiting room—which is a room where a doctor waits for something to come along. The only thing which came along to me was the tax collector, so I left my profession."[349]

Some disagreement prevails as to how long Conan Doyle maintained his specialty practice. In his autobiography he gave the month of termination as August 1891.[375r] But again his diary, written at the time, disagrees.[715] On May 4 he was "prostrated" by a severe attack of influenza. During this illness he decided to leave medicine and become a full-time writer.[714] Upon recovering he searched for another home. By June 25 the Conan Doyle's had moved to No. 12 Tennyson Road in the London Suburb of South Norwood. The break with medicine appeared to be complete.[N31]

It is apparent that Conan Doyle had an office open for the practice of ophtahlmology for only a month—from April 6 when his consultation room was ready to May 4 when he was suffering from influenza.[530] This was far too short a period to become established as a consultant and accounts for the dearth of patients. His so-called failure as a specialist in ophthalmology was really due to lack of motivation.

Conan Doyle's decision to leave medicine was related, at least in part, to the fact that during April he received £177 for his literary efforts,[832] more than half his yearly income from practice in Southsea. His illness provided the opportune excuse.

> *It was then, as I surveyed my own life, that I saw how foolish I was to waste my literary earnings in keeping up an oculist's room in Wimpole Street, and I determined with a wild rush of joy to cut the painter and to trust forever to my power of writing.*[375r]

Thus, Conan Doyle at last committed himself to his true vocation, but one which was to be inextricably influenced by previous experiences.

THE BOER WAR

No. 2 Devonshire Place was not the last place where Conan Doyle was to be identified as a practicing physician. Ten years after closing his London office he served as a voluntary physician with the British Forces in Bloemfontein, South Africa, during the Boer War. The main sources of information on this episode are four Conan Doyle publications—a book *The Great Boer War,*[316] a large pamplet *The War in South Africa,*[320] an article on typhoid,[314] and four chapters of his autobiography.[375s] Such extensive coverage is indicative of the intensity for him of the experience, including its medical aspects.

The war between the British and the Boers began in October 1899. Its causes need not concern us here except for Conan Doyle's own perceptions. "There was never a war in history in which the right was absolutely on one side. . . . Britian had it [Cape Colony] by two rights, the right of conquest and the right of purchase."[320] Regardless of this, England had a "black week" from December 10 to 17 when it lost three major battles. This stimulated a large increase in volunteer enlistments—including Conan Doyle. He had a spirtit of genuine patriotism and any cause involving his country attracted him.[N32]

In the following week he attempted to enlist in ranks of the Middlesex Yeomanry. Because of age (40) he was put on a waiting list for a commission. Soon after this, Conan Doyle received an offer from philanthropist John Langman who was outfitting, at his own expense, a hospital to be sent to South Africa. Conan Doyle was to be a "supplementary medico" and an unofficial general supervisor. He accepted this offer shortly before he received an inquiry from the Yeomanry—which he in turn rejected—"much to the relief of his numerous friends and innumerable admirers."[813]

Conan Doyle, patriot and author, thus entered the war as a physician rather than as a combatant. Other physicians in the hospital unit were Robert O' Callaghan, F.R.C.S., gynecologist, and senior surgeon, and Charles Gibbs and H.J. Scharlieb, both F.R.C.S. and younger surgeons.[911] Also present were Major M. Drury, Army medical officer in charge, and Langman's son, Archie, general manager. With supporting personnel the entire party totalled 50. The hospital had 100 beds with marquees and 35 tents.[N33]

The entire hospital company underwent a ritualistic review by the Duke of Cambridge in London on February 21, 1900.[911] On the 28th the field hospital sailed for Capetown from Tilbury on the *S.S. Oriental.* Three weeks later, on March 21, Conan Doyle arrived in Capetown for what he considered to be one of the major episodes in his life—both politically and medically. In the meantime he had sent his wife, Louise, to Naples in the hope that the warmer climate would cure her tuberculosis.

At Capetown Conan Doyle stayed at the Mount Nelson Hotel. He exhibited considerable humanistic concerns by visiting the internment camp for Boer prisoners. "They were certainly a shaggy, dirty, unkempt crowd but with the bearing of free men." Two years later, in describing the camps for their wives and children, Conan Doyle showed a basic understanding of the relationship between sanitation and disease.[320] "Camp life without cleanliness is unhygienic."

Conan Doyle was quite modern in his concept of epidemiology.

> *Had the deaths [of children in camps] come from filth-disease, such as typhus fever, or even from enteric [typhoid] or diphtheria, the sanitation of the camps might be held responsible. But it is a severe form of measles that the high mortality is due. Boer mothers, with a natural instinct, preferred to cling to the children and make it difficult for the medical men to remove them in the first stages of the disease. The result was a rapid spread of the epidemic, which was the more fatal as many of the sufferers were in low health owing to the privations unavoidably endured in the journey from their own homes to the camp.*[316a]

He was ever the champion of the underdog, even when on the opposing side, although in this instance he was also defending Britain against criticism.

On March 26 the field hospital left Capetown by boat and arrived in East London on the 28th. Here the unit was divided between two trains. Only one reached Bloemfontein and "the other half had wandered off and was engulfed in the general chaos."[375s] Conan Doyle was to find the missing half on a railway siding within a few days.

On April 2 at 5 a.m. Conan Doyle arrived at Bloemfontein, capital of the Orange Free State.[N34] "[We] were dumped down outside the town in a great green expanse covered with all sorts of encampments and animals."[375s] The hospital was given the cricket field as its camp and the pavillion as the main ward. "Before evening our beds were up and our hospital ready for duty. Two days later wagons of sick and wounded began to disgorge at our doors and the real work had begun." Bloemfontein had an existing general hospital of 500 beds,[316a] but it was the field hospital at its outskirts that was to be Conan Doyle's headquarters for three months.

Bloemfontein had been under British control since 1848 when a garrison was located there.[316b] After Lord Roberts' defeat by Conje on February 27, 1900, he retreated to Bloemfontein, which was reached on March 13. Lord Roberts had failed to take the waterworks 20 miles away and the Boers cut the water supply. By the time Conan Doyle arrived (April 2) typhoid fever, which was usually only endemic in the area, had reached epidemic proportions. According to the newly arrived physician the epidemic was due to the use of the old town wells, necessitated by the loss of the waterworks.

In his history of the Boer War, Conan Doyle vigorously supported preventative medicine.[316c]

> *If bad water can cost us more than all the bullets of the enemy, then surely it is worth our while to make the drinking of unboiled water a military offence.*
>
> *It is heart rendering for the medical man who has emerged from a hospital full of water-born pestilence to see a regimental water-cart being filled, without protest, at some polluted pool.*

The effect of such neglect of basic hygiene was disasterous. "One general hospital with five hundred beds held seventeen hundred sick, nearly all enterics [typhoid]. A half field hospital with fifty beds held three hundred and seventy cases."[316b] Conan Doyle's estimates of the total number of typhoid cases at Bloemfontein varied from 5,000 in his autobiography to 7,000 in his history of the war. With many deaths a day "coffins were out of the question, and the men were lowered . . . into shallow graves at the . . . rate of sixty a day."[375s]

Menpes[649] has provided a description of Doctor Conan Doyle working in the field hospital at the height of the epidemic.

> *It was difficult to associate him [Conan Doyle] with the author of* Sherlock Holmes: *he was a doctor pure and simple, an enthusiastic doctor too. I never saw a man throw himself into duty so thoroughly heart-and-soul. . . . He threw open the door of one of the . . . wards, and what I saw baffles description. The only thing I can liken it to is a slaughter house.*
>
> *It fascinated me to watch their cheery doctor carrying the sunshine with him wherever he went, worshipped by all.*

The severity of the situation in Bloemfontein was also described by Sellers.[198] "Tales of horror crowd upon one; stories of men in delirum, wandering about the camp at night; stories of living men in the agonies of disease, with dead men lying on either side." It was in such a hell that Conan Doyle managed to maintain his equilibrium and his human sensitivity. This was not true of some others. At one point he settled a serious dispute, close to mutiny, between Major Drury and many of the supporting staff.

Conan Doyle not only did general administrative duties at the field hospital but also practiced medicine. He has provided us with an account of one of his patients.[375s]

> *One of my enteric patients was obviously dying and kept murmuring that he would like some solid food. Of course the first law in treating enteric is, or was, that diet must be fluid, as the intestine is ulcerated and puncture of it means death by peritonitis. I said to Gibbs: "Do you consider that this man is sure to die?" "He is certainly as bad as he can be," said Gibbs. "Well then," said I, "I propose to give him a solid meal." Gibbs shook his head and was shocked. "It is a great responsibility you take." "What's the odds," I asked, "if he has to die anyhow?" "Well, it's just the difference whether you kill him or the disease does." "Well, I'll take the chance, said I—and I did so."*
>
> *M. Hanlon was my enteric patient and he had never looked back from the day he had that square meal. But I don't say it was an example for the family practitioner to copy.*

It appears that he could be both compassionate and unorthodox in practice.

Another patient encounter occurred on the battlefield. Conan Doyle left Bloemfontein May 1 with Lord Roberts' troops on the first stage of their march to Pretoria. During enemy action Conan Doyle exmined a soldier who had been shot in the stomach.[315]

> *I pull up his shirt, and there is the Mauser bullet lying obvious under the skin. It has gone round instead of penetrating. A slit with a pen-knife would extract it, but that had better be left for chloroform and the field hospital.*[375s]

In this instance he appeared to be acting as an unofficial triage officer.[N35]

The waterworks were captured by the British during this stage of the march. After Conan Doyle returned to Bloemfontein (May 7), the combination of restoration of safe water and onset of colder weather produced an abatement of the typhoid epidemic. Shortly thereafter Conan Doyle himself had a mild illness—possibly typhoid. He attributed its mildness to having been inoculated, a preventative measure which he stressed in a paper on typhoid in the *British Medical Journal* of July 7, 1900.[314] Then, as in Southsea, he received a sports injury—this time "a severe bruising of the ribs caused by a foul in one of the inter-hospital football matches which we had organized in order to take the minds of the men from their incessant work."

Amidst all this activity Conan Doyle also found the time and energy to write a history of the war. With the epidemic almost over, he left by train for the recently taken Pretoria on June 22, to obtain more information for his book. He interviewed Lord Roberts, visited Johanesburg, and was back at Bloemfontein on July 4. He then encountered another disease. This was erysipelas, an acute febrile infectious disease of the skin from which several orderlies died. Only at the time of World War II, when penicillin became available, was it no longer a frequently fatal disease.[639]

Conan Doyle soon left for Capetown and on July 11 sailed home to England on the *S.S. Briton*.[683b] He had spent three and one half months in South Africa of which about two and a half were spent close to the front lines in Bloemfontein. Conan Doyle was not finished with the Boer War following his departure. He had yet to make it a personal crusade which led to a recognition he never sought.

He finished *The Great Boer War*[316] within two months of his return. This was a remarkable achievement encompassing a 552 page detailed account of innumerable battles and related politics. Interspersed with battlefield descriptions were his medically related concerns of sanitation and the organization and needs of military medicine.

> *A medical reserve could be formed at very small cost which would ensure to the soldier the very best skill which the country can produce. At the same time there is room for improvement in the personnel of the [medical] department and in the spirit in which they approach their work . . . . there is too much that is military and too little that is medical in the relations between the department and those whom they serve.*[316c]

Even in war the patient was Conan Doyle's primary concern.

His most influential writing was *The War in South Africa. Its Cause and Conduct,*[320] published early in 1902. Its purpose was to "distribute abroad, in the different languages of Europe, a simple and direct statement of the British case in the Boer War, and an answer to those charges of inhumanity against our soldiers which were rife upon the continent."[328] This work was so successful that Conan Doyle has been credited with turning world opinion in favor of Britain. He was knighted for this service on August 6, 1902, by Edward VII. Conan Doyle was *not,* as some suggest, knighted because he created Sherlock Holmes. "I have no doubt that it was to the latter (Boer War pamphlet) that my knighthood, and my appointment as Deputy-Lieutenant of Surrey . . . were due."[375t] According to Nordon he at first considered refusing the title as he was no lover of decorations.[683c] His mother convinced him otherwise. Conan Doyle used this episode in his story of the "Three Garridebs."[374] Watson relates "Holmes refused a knighthood for services which may perhaps some day be described." Although the story was written in 1924 Conan Doyle set the date as June 1902, two months before he, himself, was knighted. Even before the Boer War he included a justification of empirialistic activities in a novel, *The Tragedy of the Korosko.*[305]

Even in such a propagandist work the physician emerged. There was concern with epidemics of smallpox, diphtheria, and measles among Boer children in camps. Conan Doyle's emphasis on the needs of sick soldiers is shown by his description of efforts to protect them from the rain.

> *When we applied for leave to use the deserted villas to put our sick soldiers into—the hospitals being full—we were told that it could only be done by private treaty with the owners, who at that time were on commando against us. I remember suggesting that the corrugated-iron fencing round the cricket field be used for making huts, and being told that it was impossible as it was private property.*[320a]

In showing the concern of the British for private property of the Boers he has also shown his own for the patient in need.

Other but lesser activities were related to the Boer War. In August, 1900 Conan Doyle gave evidence to the South African Hospitals Commission.[836] He denied that there was any deliberate neglect of patients in hospitals, but deplored the shortage of beds and utensils. A further presentation was made on November 13, 1900, to the Author's Club of which he was chairman.[395] Again he reiterated the negative effect of military protocol on medical services. "The moment they began to give military titles to doctors they took a step backwards and not forwards."

Conan Doyle played several roles in the Boer War. He was a war historian whose work has been neglected. He was a patriot and a very successful propagandist for which he was knighted. He was a medical writer whose farsighted support of typhoid vaccination is almost unknown. Above all he was the humane military physician who placed the patient above politics and protocol.

The Boer War was over in May 1902, and so was Conan Doyle's involvement with it—and again he gave up the "practice" of medicine. It was not the end, by any means, of his "involvement" with medicine.

GELSEMINUM AS A POISON.

SIR,—Some years ago, a persistent neuralgia led me to use the tincture of gelseminum to a considerable extent. I several times overstepped the maximum doses of the text-books without suffering any ill effects. Having recently had an opportunity of experimenting with a quantity of the fresh tincture, I determined to ascertain how far one might go in taking the drug, and what the primary symptoms of an overdose might be. I took each dose about the same hour on successive days, and avoided tobacco or any other agent which might influence the physiological action of the drug. Here are the results as jotted down at the time of the experiment. On Monday and Tuesday, forty and sixty minims produced no effect whatever. On Wednesday, ninety minims were taken at 10.30. At 10.50, on rising from my chair, I became seized with an extreme giddiness and weakness of the limbs, which, however, quickly passed off. There was no nausea or other effect. The pulse was weak but normal. On Thursday, I took 120 minims. The giddiness of yesterday came on in a much milder form. On going out about one o'clock, however, I noticed for the first time that I had a difficulty in accommodating the eye for distant objects. It needed a distinct voluntary effort, and indeed a facial contortion to do it.

On Friday, 150 minims were taken. As I increased the dose, I found that the more marked physiological symptoms disappeared. To-day, the giddiness was almost gone, but I suffered from a severe frontal headache, with diarrhœa and general lassitude.

On Saturday and Sunday, I took three drachms and 200 minims. The diarrhœa was so persistent and prostrating, that I must stop at 200 minims. I felt great depression and a severe frontal headache. The pulse was still normal, but weak.

From these experiments I would draw the following conclusions.

1. In spite of a case described some time ago in which 75 minims proved fatal, a healthy adult may take as much as 90 minims with perfect immunity.

2. In doses of from 90 to 120 minims, the drug acts apparently as a motor paralyser to a certain extent, causing languor, giddiness, and a partial paralysis of the ciliary muscle.

3. After that point, it causes headache, with diarrhœa and extreme lassitude.

4. The system may learn to tolerate gelseminum, as it may opium, if it be gradually inured to it. I feel convinced that I could have taken as much as half an ounce of the tincture, had it not been for the extreme diarrhœa it brought on. —Believe me, yours sincerely, A. C. D.

Clifton House, Aston Road, Birmingham.

Figure 5. Conan Doyle's first published medical item. It appeared in the *British Medical Journal* (1879).

OTHER MEDICAL INVOLVEMENTS

Arthur Conan Doyle was a medical student and practitioner for 15 years, from 1876 to 1891. For the remaining 40 years of his life, except for the several months in Bloemfontein, he had no vocational or official relationship to his primary profession. Yet his medical experience surfaced in many activities as author, politician, citizen, and spiritualist.

Evidence is found that Conan Doyle continued to relate to some individuals as a physician. His empathic approach to illness in members of his own family has previously been mentioned.[389] A receipt for £10 was given by Conan Doyle to a Mr. Blackburn Adams in 1902, probably for medical services.[487] More interesting is a prescription written by Conan Doyle, M.D., for his younger brother, Captain Hay (Innes) Doyle, in 1904.[214] It was for alum in water to be used as a gargle three times a day. It has been reproduced by Symons.[862] The prescription was filled by Thomas Read, a dispensing chemist in Camberley, where Captain Doyle was undoubtedly stationed at either the British Army's Staff College or the nearby Royal Military Academy.

Conan Doyle also related to at least one well-known individual as a physician. Sir James Barrie, the author, was not only his friend but also his collaborator on the libretto for an unsuccessful comic opera titled "Jane Annie."[44,N36] Conan Doyle had been asked to help complete the libretto "because Barrie's health failed on account of some family bereavement."[375u] According to Higham[525a] "When Barrie grew weak from bronchial attacks and had to take to his bed, Conan Doyle proved an excellent physician." This occured in Kirriemuir, Scotland, in 1892 about a year after Conan Doyle left practice. Once a doctor always a doctor!

Aside from patients, Conan Doyle also maintained contact with organized medicine. In July 1913, the British Medical Association held its annual meeting in Brighton. On a Sunday the Assembly of over 100 traveled by motor coaches to Windlesham, Conan Doyle's home in Crowborough, for a reception.[22] Acknowledgment of the hospitality indicates his continuing sympathy and support of the medical profession.

Most medical men have on innumerable occasions received refreshments and entertainment at Sir Arthur Conan Doyle's hands. . . . There are a good many men who have left the profession of medicine to attain eminence in other walks of life, but not all of them acknowledge the claims that it still has upon them in a corresponding altruistic fashion. . . .

Conan Doyle was also quite sensitive to contentious issues in society. He strongly supported the Daylight Saving Bill of 1908 at a hearing of a Select Committee of the House of Commons.[189] Typically, the orientation related to health. He stated that the Bill would promote health and happiness of the majority of the community, especially the children. Also characteristic was concern for the future. He stated that the Daylight Saving Bill would increase the general standard of health and the stature of the next generation.

Venereal disease spread by prostitution did not escape Conan Doyle's attention. In 1883, while in Southsea, he wrote his first letter to a newspaper on the subject.[227] He severly chastised opponents of the Contagious Disease Act because "dreadful evils are to result, men to suffer, children to die, and pure women to inherit unspeakable evils." His indignation was aroused again during the first World War. "Is it not possible in any way to hold in check the vile women who at present prey upon and poison our soldiers in London?"[363] "These women are the enemies of the country. They should be treated as such."[364] Conan Doyle could bring a scathing command of the language to bear on any cause he felt to be justified.[N37]

Prostitution, the military, and venereal disease are no different today than in Conan Doyle's Southsea and London days.[907] In a 1971 account "The soldiers VD problem is like the merchant sailor's, exaggerated by the even greater need for release when opportunity offers, . . . from his situation, which make his life forfeit anyway."[718] But, antibiotics are now available unlike Victorian London where, in 1859, there were 2,828 brothels and 8,600 prostitutes known to the police.[812] An estimate by an author of the time was between 50,000 and 80,000 prostitutes.[644]

Conan Doyle also took part, in 1909, in the humanitarian campaign to ameliorate conditions for natives of the Congo.[345] One can empathize with Conan Doyle's reactions of moral indignation and intense concern for the innocent victims. In his usual forthright manner he took to task the Christian and civilized nations who observed

> *. . . a helpless race, whose safety they have guaranteed, robbed, debouched, mutilated and murdered, without raising a hand or in most cases even a voice to protect them. . .*[346]

In such intense concern for "the horrible beatings, the mutilation of limbs, the starving," Conan Doyle exhibited the same humanism that he did for his patients—the emotional and physical sanctity of the human being.

Another of Conan Doyle's medical causes was support for vivisection (research upon living animals) needed for the advancement of medical knowledge to benefit humanity. Strong antivivisection forces in Victorian society were supported by such prominent figures as Tennyson, Browning, Carlyle, Ruskin, and Queen Victoria.[51] As a practitioner in Southsea (1886) he had objected strongly to a minister who denounced Pasteur's torturing of thousands of "poor dumb creatures to save us from hydro-phobia."[203] Twenty-four years later, in 1910, Conan Doyle was still in support of vivisection. The *Daily Express* of October 29 contained a letter by A. Wall, Honorary Treasurer of the London Anti-vivisection Society, stating that there is not "an atom of evidence" that any lives had been saved by the torture of animals.[908] In quick response the paper of November 1 carried a letter from Arthur Conan Doyle.[348] He referred to the population of a District of India in which many lives had been saved from the plague by inoculations developed in animals. In characteristic rhetoric he also referred to "the anti-human campaign with which Mr. Wall is associated." Conan Doyle, thus, was in the public eye as a vivisection supporter as were such scientific figures as Darwin, Huxley, and Lister.[436]

Conan Doyle also made references to vivisection, in the sense of any experimentation on animals, in several of his writings. His master detective, Sherlock Holmes, investigated the death of Drebber, in *A Study in Scarlet,*[244] published in 1887, a year after the confrontation with the clergyman. Holmes gave a pill found in the suspect's room to a dog. ". . . it gave a convulsive shiver in every limb, and lay as rigid and lifeless as if it had been struck by lightening." The conclusion by Holmes was that Drebber had been poisoned by an alkaloid arrow poison.

In this episode Conan Doyle felt the need to justify the implicit cruelty of such an act by describing the dog as a poor little terrier in chronic pain. He also referred to a concern for cruelty to animals by Pheneas, the spirit guide for his family's seances.[381] "Animals will be saved from all future suffering and when the spirit first touches the earth that particular suffering will at once be eliminated." Conan Doyle objected to injudicious hunting.[342] He also had a marked aversion to cruelty to animals.[315]

> *A fat white pig all smothered in blood runs past. A soldier meets it, his bayonet at the charge. He lunges and lunges again, and the pig screams horribly. I had rather see a man killed.*

More directly related to experimentation was Conan Doyle's reaction to the research activities of one of his medical school teachers at the University of Edinburgh. His autobiography, published 43 years after his graduation, contains a criticism of William Rutherford, Professor of the Institutes of Medicine.

> *He was, I fear, a rather ruthless vivisector, and though I have always recognized that a minimum of painless vivisection is necessary, and far more justifiable than the eating of meat as a food, I am glad that the law was made more stringent so as to restrain such men as he.*[375a]

Such an orientation is characteristic of the more conservative approach to vivisection—a compromise between the desire to help humanity through science and the psychological revulsion against inflicting pain on living creatures.

Conan Doyle's medical orientation also surfaced during his spiritualistic activities, which dominated the last 15 years of his life.

He proposed that in "pulse variations or in spirographic records we have an excellent check against fraud (of mediums)."[371]

> *The normal pulse [of the medium] before the sitting was steady and full at 78. He then sank into a trance and spoke for some time in the character of Colonel Lee. During this time his pulse rose swiftly and ended at 127, a rate which was sustained for 20 minutes. When Colonel Lee disappeared I was dismayed to find his pulse vanish altogether, and for some minutes there was an unperceptible thrill rather than a throb of the radial artery . . . the Black Hawk control began to manifest. The pulse was then steady at 100, and remained full and bounding up to the end of the sitting when it dropped once more to 78.*

One may disagree with his interpretation, but cannot deny the orientation to objective evidence which is the mainstay of medicine.

Different sorts of evidence exist and Conan Doyle also accepted some of those of spiritualism. In a letter to the editor in 1927[378] he objected to criticism of attributing cure of a terminal case of cancer by spirit healing. Doctor Worth had suggested that the disease was not cancer but hysteria. The letter from Arthur Conan Doyle, M.D., cited the patient's physician as stating that she was "in extremis" and that the healing medium "is said to have been cured of cancer which had been certified by three medical men, before she was chosen as a special instrument." There have and continue to be rare cases of substantiated "miracle"cures that are beyond the comprehension of medical science of the times in which they occur.

Two further examples of the relationship of Conan Doyle's spiritualism to medicine are provided by Walsh in his book on spurious cures.[910] On his speaking tour of the United States in 1922 he extolled Andrew Jackson Davis whose contact with great medical authorities of the past had given him the knowledge to heal diseases.[910a] Conan Doyle also gave a more personal example of spirit medicine.[910b] A communication, through a medium, from

Conan Doyle's dead brother told of his sister-in-law's illness and that she must see a healer who cured by magnetic powers—and so she was. Conan Doyle, however, did not support another spiritualistic approach to healing. "While in Boston I spent an hour or so in the magnificent temple of the Christian Scientists. I confess that I have little sympathy with these people. . . . Faith healing and healing by what we now call suggestion are as old as history."[372]

Conan Doyle was not and is not the only physician to accept spiritualism. He wrote a preface in 1928 for the autobiography of Doctor D. Marinus in which he fully supported his psychic experiences. He went even further.[382] "You have to bear in mind that spiritualism does not consist mainly of phenomena or of messages from those whom we have loved and lost. The most essential thing of all is the teaching from the higher entities beyond. . . ."

In respect to more traditional biologic science Conan Doyle believed in Darwin's theory of the "survival of the fittest." In 1892, after a presentation on marine animals, he noted "that in the lives of humans, as in animal life, the weakest went to the bottom . . . working towards some glorious goal."[886] The latter phrase was a characteristic belief of Victorian society. Years later, in 1927, Conan Doyle in supporting spiritualism over traditional Christianity stated:

> *Unless matters have changed since I was a student of biology, the foetus of man and of animal are undistinguishable from each other in the early months of gestation. This has always seemed to me a strong argument for Darwin.*[379]

Total immersion in spiritualism did not exclude his knowledge of and acceptance for biologic theory and fact.

Conan Doyle was involved in still other areas related to health and the afflicted. He strongly supported, at the annual meeting of the related association, trained educators for the oral teaching of the deaf and dumb.[694] He was attracted to physical culture and in 1907 provided a foreword for Sandow's manual of exercise *The Construction and Reconstruction of the Human Body.*[337] "That which is physically beautiful stands in the main for that which is mentally sane and spiritually sound.'' He recommended a national system of compulsory gymnasia. (Conan Doyle had taken a course in physical development from Sandow.)[38] Later he rejected Sandow's methods as evidenced by a toast given at a luncheon for J.P. Muller who had invented a different system.[618]

> *Some time ago he [Conan Doyle] had tried a system which developed muscles. . . . He found that he put on muscle, but became 'stupider and stupider' in the process so he gave it up and the muscle melted like butter in the sun.*

In a more direct manner Conan Doyle used his knowledge of medicine, in particular ophthalmology, to campaign for the release of an individual whom he considered wrongly convicted. This was in part due to the foreign (Parsee) origin of his father. With typical dedication Conan Doyle entered the lists for George Edalji, a solicitor, who lived near Birmingham. In 1903, Edalji was accused of ripping open at night the stomachs of horses and cattle.[375v] On the basis of some anonymous letters he was convicted and sentenced to seven years imprisonment. In late 1906 Conan Doyle chanced to read a statement written by Edalji and rose to the defense.

One of Conan Doyle's main items of evidence was Edalji's severe myopia which is detailed in letters to the *Lancet*[336] and the *British Medical Journal*[335] of January 19, 1907. Eye specialists were asked to answer the following question.

> *Do you consider it physically possible for Mr. George Edalji, whose degree of myopic astigmatism as determined by retinoscopy under homatropine is*
>
> *Right Eye—8.75 diop. spher.*
> *—1.75 diop cylind. axis 90°*
> *Left Eye —8.25 diop. spher.*
>
> *to have set forth without glasses on a pitch dark night with neither moon nor stars, to have crossed country for half a mile, climbing fences, finding gaps in hedges, and passing over a broad railway line; to have found and mutilated a pony which*

was loose in a large field, to have returned half a mile, and to have accomplished it all under thirty-five minutes, the limit of time at his disposal?

Conan Doyle's first writings on the Edalji case were not in medical journals but in a newspaper, the *Daily Telegraph* of January 11[330] and 12,[331] 1907. The reaction was extensive. The issues of January 14[151] and 15[732] carried eleven news items on the subject and seven letters sympathetic with and two against the cause. Both of the latter disagreed with Conan Doyle's interpretation of Edalji's eyesight.

To an objection from an eye specialist, Mr. Aitchison, that the degree of myopia could be corrected by eyeglasses,[9] he replied that Edalji had none.[332] The other objection was that Edalji's eyesight may have deteriorated after three years in prison—at which time they had been examined.[732] Conan Doyle replied that "astigmatic myopia depends upon a congenital shape of the eye, and could not have been brought about by prison."[333]

A further correspondence from Aitchison pointed out that eyes do change from infancy to adulthood.[10] Conan Doyle replied in a somewhat sarcastic vein.[334]

When I spoke of there being no change in Mr. Edalji's eyes, I meant his adult eyes. There are some things one takes for granted, unless one is talking to a very youthful audience.

As usual in his crusades for various causes he had the last word.

George Edalji was released from prison, having served three of his seven years sentence, in time to attend the wedding of his benefactor to Jean Leckie on Sept. 18, 1907. Conan Doyle had demonstrated that the methods of logical deduction could be applied in the real world as well as that of Sherlock Holmes.[N38]

This account of the Edalji episode does not complete the story of Conan Doyle's involvement with medical matters after leaving practice. Subsequent chapters include discussions of his writings in the medical literature, medically related short stories, a novel with hypnotism as the theme,[280] an address to medical students,[349] and medical references in his extensive nonmedical fiction, not the least of which are the Holmesian stories.

One other medical item, a small but personally significant one, was written by Conan Doyle. The *Guy's Hospital Gazette* of 1915[362] contains his obituary for Captain Malcolm Leckie, the brother of his second wife and an officer in the Royal Army Medical Corps. He was killed by shrapnel during the Battle of Mons on August 28, 1914, aged 34. Emphasized was his devotion to patients, for which he received a posthumous D.S.O.[N39] Conan Doyle was also to lose during the war (in 1918), but due to influenza and pneumonia, his first son, Captain Kingsley Conan Doyle (in London), and his younger brother, Colonel (Adjutant-General) Innes Doyle (in Belgium), who had shared the first few years in Southsea with him.[375gg]

ASSESSMENT

We have now traveled with Doctor Conan Doyle from the start of his medical education in 1876 through medical assistantships, general practice, ophthalmology, military medicine, and medicine beyond practice. What then was his caliber as a physician? His own assessment is biased by modesty laced with deprecatory humor. He did recognize, however, the extent and variety of his medical experience. In an address to medical students in 1910 he emphasized "that I am not an amateur, and that there are few phases of medical life, from the sixpenny dispensary to the two-guinea prescriptions, that I have not had personal experience."[349]

In this retrospect of 30 years, Conan Doyle had a clear perspective of the practical medical climate in which he had practiced.

> *Wondrous was the science which combined so many powerful drugs, and yet so accurately balanced them that they never modified the action of each other. I suppose it was really based on the same principle as that of a country practitioner, whom I knew, who dispensed his own medicines. He used to empty all the bottles which had not been claimed into one huge jar, from which he occasionally dispensed draughts for his more obscure cases. 'It's*

> *like grape-shot,' he explained. 'If one misses, another may hit.' The patient's constitution could be trusted to pick out what was best for it in the splendid selection which the old physicians used to lay before it.*[349]

How did others rate Doctor Conan Doyle? Some of his patients were complimentary, but his contemporary confreres wrote no comments. Perhaps obituaries written within two weeks after his death on July 7, 1930, will help. A review of eleven of these reveal no mention of the medical Conan Doyle in eight instances. The doctor is not acknowledged in two that stress the "wealth of interesting features" in his history and personality.[156,522] One obituary highlights his business acumen as director of the Raphael Tuck and Sons, Limited,[881] another his historical novels,[794] one his spiritualistic activities,[602] and two his creation Sherlock Holmes.[157,745] Conan Doyle would have been disturbed by the latter category, because "he bore such a deep hatred toward Sherlock Holmes."[866]

Such an attitude to the master detective is far harsher than his creator actually had. His daughter, Dame Jean, recalls that:

> *Although my father sometimes got weary of Holmes, he always had an affection for him and we were brought up with the same feeling. [personal communication]*

Of the three obituaries that acknowledged Conan Doyle, the doctor, one merely mentions that "His interests first turned to medicine"[688] and that he practiced in Plymouth (sic). Another provides a negative assessment. "It was in 1886, when his fortunes were at a low ebb, that Arthur Conan Doyle hit on the idea of an amateur detective"[819] and this in a medical journal! Only one of the eleven obituaries provides an unbiased statement of his medical life and its positive influence on his writings.[818]

Has the half-century or so after his death treated the doctor any better? Some commentators are puzzled by the fact that he was not more successful in medical practice. "He was certainly an acute observor, and it is difficult to see why he was not an outstanding success in practice"[121] and "It is unclear why this man of magnificent mental equipment did not indeed reach the heights in medicine.''[635] This seems damning with faint praise.

An analysis of Conan Doyle now as a medical practitioner is difficult. Perhaps the best measure is against guidelines provided during his own time. In August 1879, Thomas Grainger Stewart provided such criteria in an address to medical graduates at the University of Edinburgh.[853] Conan Doyle may have been in the audience as a third year student.

The first criterion was to ''avoid entering at once upon the responsibility of private practice.'' This precept Conan Doyle followed, but probably because of insufficient funds to set up on his own. Fulfilling a second charge to ''take care that no thought about yourselves intrudes as you discharge your duties'' was certainly met in Bloemfontein. He also met a third criterion ''keep up the kindly feelings which animate you towards [your professional brethren]'' as evidenced by his reception for the British Medical Association in 1910.

Doctor Stewart's two remaining charges to the medical graduates dealt with keeping abreast of medical knowledge and seeking to advance it. We have seen that Conan Doyle's professional knowledge was adequate for his times, but did he advance it? Was Pearsall correct in stating that ''there was never any indication that Doyle had any revolutionary ideas about medicine, or that he thought that he was especially privileged to carry the banner of Hippocrates?''[713]

Answers to this question will be dealt with in subsequent chapters which assess Conan Doyle's medical writings and medicine in his nonmedical writings.

Figure 6. The Arctic steam-whaler *Hope* on which medical student Conan Doyle served as ship's surgeon for seven months in 1880. (Photograph used with permission from Hodder & Stoughton Ltd., London.)

Figure 7. Conan Doyle, third from left, aboard the *Hope* in 1880.

Figure 8. Conan Doyle's sketch of his elation at achieving his medical school diploma in 1881.

2

MEDICAL WRITINGS

Arthur Conan Doyle's *reputation* as a medical author leaves much to be desired in both quantity and quality. Negative comments are found even in medical journals. "His only strictly medical writings appeared as brief notes in the *Lancet* and the *British Medical Journal*."[580] "His strictly medical writings were scanty, mostly letters-to-the editor."[775] "In all Dr. Doyle's writings only one volume is of a medical nature and that in no wise technical—*Round the Red Lamp*."[416]

Yet, as we have seen in the review of Conan Doyle's professional activities many strictly medical items were encountered. Key[569] listed 13 of his writings as medical, with one being fictional. In a more recent exposition 22 are cited.[772] In Appendix B, 57 Conan Doyle writings are listed as medical. These are an admixture of nonfiction and fiction and include six chapters from his autobiography and three from his novel *The Firm of Girdlestone*.[258] His most significant nonfictional items were written as a medical student and as a practitioner—between 1879 and 1890 and one in 1910.

What follows is an analysis of the content of the more significant items in Conan Doyle's medical bibliography. Others have been described in the previous chapter. Relationships of his knowledge and concepts to those of the time reveal the measure of this medical man.

SELF-EXPERIMENTATION WITH A DRUG

As stated previously, the first of Conan Doyle's medical writings was published in 1879, while he was still a third year medical student. It is not only his earliest but also his only writing related strictly to medical research. He conducted research on himself and by doing so joined a long list of individuals who have contributed to medical knowledge by using themselves, rather than others, as subjects. Conan Doyle lived at a time when self-experimentation was common.[443]

Such a personalized approach to research has certain advantages. The investigator is considered more ethical in being willing to subject himself as well as others to human experimentation.[859] With oneself as the subject the effects of a drug can be directly perceived. There are also disadvantages.[52] Preexisting biases of the researcher are likely to be magnified when he uses his own body. Also, any conclusions derived are based on reactions to a drug in only one individual.

In spite of limitations, significant advances in pharmacological knowledge have been made by means of self-experimentation with drugs. Some recorded episodes have been quite dramatic. In 1822, Doctor E. Hale of Boston injected his own antecubital (elbow) vein with a drachm of castor oil.[504] Effects were a taste of oiliness, stiffness of the jaw, nausea, diarrhea, and fatigue. He concluded that emetics and cathartics have a greater and more rapid action when given intravenously. In 1825, Johann Purkinje described the effects on himself of orally administered digitalis.[511] These included flickering of vision, nausea, diarrhea, slow pulse, calf pains, and lassitude. He concluded that many of the manifestations were caused by stimulation of the vagus nerve.

Tonery, in 1830, convinced the French Academy that charcoal can absorb toxic alkaloids by taking charcoal with an otherwise lethal dose of strychnine.[52] In 1855 Christison chewed one-fourth of a Calabar bean (eserine), with resultant severe giddiness, torpidity, and irregular pulse.[138] He did not, however, notice its best known effects, on the eye.[774] Christison did recommend the use of the Calabar bean for the humane execution of criminals. Only recently has execution by drugs been legalized in a few places.[574]

Self-experimentation with drugs has also occurred in more recent times. In 1943, Hofmann of Switzerland began the study of the effects of lysergic acid diethylamide (LSD) by administration of the substance to himself.[532] In 1947, Scott Smith of Salt Lake City had a colleague administer intravenously to him two and one-half times the dose of curare (d-tubercurarine chloride) necessary for complete respiratory paralysis.[829] Artificial respiration with oxygen was used for maintenance of air exchange. Because there were no changes in his electroencephalogram, his consciousness, or his sensorium, Doctor Smith concluded that curare does not have a cerebral effect.

In 1948, Jans Hald and Erik Jacobsen of Denmark delineated by self-experimentation the effects of taking alcohol after Antabuse.[503] In 1967, Cutler of Seattle induced hyperthyroidism in himself with a drug (L-triiodothyronine) in order to determine its effects on the concentrating function of the kidney.[181] He concluded that it produces a mild concentrating defect due to decrease in renal sodium concentration.

There have been numerous other instances of self-experimentation with drugs. Many of these have not been recorded or at least widely acknowledged. One such example relates to Arthur Conan Doyle who undertook such a study in 1879 as a medical student assistant to Doctor Hoare of Birmingham.[375h] An account of this episode is provided by Conan Doyle in a letter to the editor published in the *British Medical Journal* of September 20, 1879.[216] Because of persistent neuralgia he had been taking tincture of gelsemium. Such therapy was highly recommended for neuralgia in William Osler's textbook of 1892.[696]

Gelsemium is the dried rhizome (root) of yellow jasmine.[905] Its actions are similar to those of nicotine, but with a stronger central depressant action.[N40] There is no pharmacological explanation for the use of gelsemium in neuralgic conditions. According to Proctor,[737] gelsemium was discovered accidentally by a Mississippi Planter whose servant used, in error, the root of jasmine to make a tea for his master who was suffering from a bilious fever. There was a resultant complete loss of muscular power and a disappearance of the fever. In the middle of the 19th century it was used chiefly by eclectic (not following any one system) practitioners of the Midwest.[526] By the seventh decade gelsemium was included in both United States and British Pharmacopoeias.[491] Recommended uses were for pneumonia, pleurisy, neuralgia, and intermittent and yellow fevers. Although described in the 1973 edition of the *United States Dispensatory*,[702] it is no longer included in the United States and British Pharmacopoeias.[N41]

Conan Doyle took increasing doses of the tincture of gelsemium in order to "ascertain how far one might go with the drug."[216] He began at 40 minims (two ccs.) on the first day, with six daily increments. Giddiness developed with 90 minims (6 ccs.) on the fourth, and severe headaches and diarrhea at 150 minims (7.5 ccs.) on the fifth day. Conan Doyle persisted until the seventh day when 200 minims (10 ccs.) resulted in severe depression in addition to the other symptoms.

This episode is of interest for several reasons. First, it is an apparent example of the selfless contribution of a medical student to the delineation of the side effects of a drug. Second, it suggests a curiosity and a dedication to medical knowledge that Conan Doyle did not often exhibit. In his autobiography[375q] he stated, "I had . . . no great interest in the more recent developments of my own profession, and a very strong belief that much of the so-called progress was illusory." In 1890, he did rush to Germany to see firsthand Koch's tuberculin cure for tuberculosis. But, this may have been related to some restlessness in being tied down to a medical practice.

Quite surprising is the fact that Conan Doyle undertook self-experimentation with gelsemium even though he was aware that fatalities had been reported in patients taking the drug. His letter of 1879[216] refers to "a case described some time ago in which 75 minims proved fatal." Prior to 1879 there were many reports of deaths ascribed to gelsemium in German, American, and English medical journals. Death was due to respiratory arrest. A report that may have been seen by Conan Doyle was a letter to the editor of the *Lancet* of September 27, 1873,[460] six years before his own self-experimentation. One death is described after 50 minims of tincture of gelsemium and another after 120 minims. In 1882, Doctor Wormley collected a series of 25 deaths related to gelsemium.[939] The smallest doses involved were 12 minims in a three-year-old child and 60 minims in a healthy male adult. Sollmann's *Manual of Pharmacology* of 1948[834] states that "A drachm of fluid extract [60 minims, four ccs.] is said sometimes to cause death, and 30 minims are dangerous." Conan Doyle took 3.3 drachms (200 minims).

Why Conan Doyle disregarded the possibility of death while taking gelsemium in not known. We can make some inferences on the basis of his other activities and his writings. Altman,[17] in discussing reasons for the selection by investigators of themselves as experimental subjects, included reliability, dependability, convenience, suicide, ethical code, and a spirit of adventure. Conan Doyle is unlikely to have taken gelsemium in any sort of suicide attempt, because of the complete lack of any such indications in his autobiography[375] or his exploits, and because of his keen zest for life. His disregard for the possibility of a fatal outcome was also not likely due to a belief in life after death, because his complete acceptance of spiritualism did not occur until 1916. As an individual not overly interested in research or new medical knowledge, Conan Doyle is unlikely to have been motivated by concerns for experimental reliability, dependability or convenience.

Conan Doyle's apparent defiance of an awkward result was most likely a reflection of the bravado, the sense of the dramatic, and the spirit of adventure already noted in many of his endeavors—experiences as a ship's surgeon and involvements in war and sports. In addition to the Boer War, Conan Doyle was a war correspondent in Egypt in 1896, observing Kitchener's desert campaigns; a trainer of volunteer defense militia in England in 1901;[878] and an observor of the French and Italian battle fronts in 1916.[375w] He engaged in high-risk sports such as auto racing and skiing in the Alps.[158] Such bravado is also evident in his fiction. The Sherlock Holmes stories contain many episodes of daring, such as the confrontation with the Hound of the Baskervilles.[321] His novels of knighthood, of which *The White Company*[265] is the best known, are all accounts of valor and heroics.

We cannot be certain of Conan Doyle's motivation for overdosing himself with gelsemium. In part, he may have been stimulated by the example of his teachers at the University of Edinburgh. But, he was even more a man of his period—the late Victorian and early Edwardian ages. These were times in which considerable value was placed on the dramatic gesture, the romance of insurmountable odds, and the heroic sacrifice to a cause. Today, people hold different values. Perhaps this is why self-experimentation, such as that of Conan Doyle, has decreased in incidence and prominence.[767]

MEDICAL LETTERS ON TWO DISEASES

Doctor Conan Doyle's further medical writings did not deal with any personal research activities. Two letters to medical journals were concerned with specific diseases—leukemia and gout. His first medical item after graduation was a letter to the editor of the *Lancet*, dated March 25, 1882.[223] (Haunting any author is the uncharitableness of fate—here his name was misspelled as A. Cowan Doyle.) This was during the period between his return from West Africa and his involvement with Doctor Budd. That he was in Birmingham at the time is evidenced by the Aston address. In fact, he described the patient as a 29-year-old man who "came to my friend Mr. Hoare," his Birmingham mentor.

Conan Doyle's succinct clinical history describes a sharp attack of ague (malaria) a few years prior, and, on examination, "an enormously hypertrophied spleen.'' Interestingly, his medical education had been sufficiently up-to-date to lead him to examine the patient's blood with a microscope, an instrument not as yet in general use in medical offices. Conan Doyle's interpretation was ''that the leucocytes were enormously increased in number . . . The proportion of white to red [cells] was calculated at one to seven.'' This indicates a total of perhaps 400,000 to 500,000 white cells per cubic millimeter, an enormous increase in number that is indicative of leukemia—a cancer of the blood.[N42]

The patient was much wasted, having lost 42 pounds in a few weeks. The major treatment was large doses of arsenic, a regime that was used for many years before and after 1882.[905a] A more effective treatment of leukemia did not become available until after the mid-20th century with the use of chemotherapeutical agents. Nonetheless, the greatly enlarged spleen of Conan Doyle's patient did decrease considerably in size. One wonder's if this was a result of the arsenical treatment or only a ''natural'' remission that can occur in leukemia—usually temporary.

Conan Doyle's main point in reporting this case was the fact that malaria preceded leukemia, which he interpreted as a possible cause-and-effect relationship. It appears that he may have fallen into the trap of mistaking a relationship in time to one of causation. Most amazing, however, is some recent experimental evidence that malaria may indeed predispose to a group of tumors (lymphomas) that arise from tissues related to white blood cells.

Malarial infection in mice depresses their immune response sufficiently to result in lymphomas.[919] In humans, a connection is suggested by the fact that the geographic distribution of a type of lymphoma frequent in African children is the same as that for chronic malaria.[116] This is not to say that Conan Doyle (or any of his contemporaries) had any knowledge of viruses or the immune system. His simplistic logic, which could well have been erroneous, was a harbinger of the future.

More was known about the basic nature of another specific disease that was the topic of his letter to the *Lancet* of 1884.[238] Gout has a long history, having been described in ancient Egyptian mummies,[100] in the writings of Hippocrates,[722] and in Byzantine writings of the 12th century.[120,N43] It was not until 1848 that uric acid was discovered by Garrod to be the abnormal substance in the blood of gouty patients.[165]

Conan Doyle must have been aware of the relationship of uric acid to this joint disease because the 1880 note by his former compatriot, George Budd, stated, "Now and again the attempt [to eliminate uric acid] may be successful; but more commonly it is only partly so, and uric acid accumulates."[110] Conan Doyle's former mentor (Doctor Hoare) objected, in a memorandum, to Doctor Budd's statement that uric acid was drained from tissues by lymphatics.[528] Doctor Budd had the last word by a rebuttal a week later with yet another memorandum.[111]

Unlike those of Budd and Hoare, Conan Doyle's letter was clinically oriented. He described various manifestations of gout in three generations of one family, including a grandfather with joint disease, his son with psoriasis, and his granddaughter with eye disease. He was evidently well abreast of current literature, there being an extensive dissertation by Hutchinson on "The Relation of Certain Diseases of the Eye to Gout" in issues of the *Lancet* published one and two weeks before his own letter appeared.[442A, 553] It is now a well-established association.[800] His knowledge of pathology was detailed enough to associate the contracted granular kidneys of the grandfather to his gout, which results in deposits of urate crystals in the kidneys as in the joints.

Conan Doyle's designation of psoriasis as a gout-related event is interesting in that such an association is today recognized in modern textbooks as possible, although uncommon.[668,N44] The inheritance of gout in some instances has been known for some time, but is often overlooked, because of the increase in severity of the joint disease with excessive intake of port and meats.[696b,N45]

Clinical acumen on Conan Doyle's part is evident by the fact that he suspected the granddaughter's eye disease to be related to gout because the congestion and blindness occurred "whenever her digestion was deranged."[238]

> *Recognizing this to be a gouty symptom, and bethinking me of the obscure skin disease which afflicted the father, I made somewhat minute inquires into the previous family history. I found that the grandfather . . . had been a martyr to gout for many years.*

This is a display of the art of clinical diagnosis at its best—in part intuitive and in part based on a broad knowledge of disease.

Conan Doyle's letter on gout did not merely describe findings in patients, as did so many published medical notes of his day. As in his other two early medical letters, it presented careful observations which were then used as the basis for conclusions. Gelsemium for example, is not necessarily fatal in large doses, malaria may predispose to leukemia, and gout can have different manifestations in different generations of the same family.

In Conan Doyle's major scientific medical work, a thesis on tabes dorsalis, he also proposed several theories, this time based on a review of published observations of others.

THE M.D. THESIS ON TABES DORSALIS

Four years after graduation from medical school, Conan Doyle wrote and successfully defended a thesis for an M.D. degree from his alma mater, the University of Edinburgh.[240] As previously mentioned, in Britain, unlike America, this was and still is a graduate degree awarded only after several years of practice and the writing of an acceptable thesis.[720] He completed his thesis in April 1885, about a year after he began it,[386] and received the degree in July 1885, one month before his first marriage.

Several recent publications[568,579] have alluded to an M.D. thesis by Conan Doyle on "The Gouty Diathesis," submitted to the University of Edinburgh. There is, however, no extant record of such a thesis. Communications with his Alma Mater make it certain that Conan Doyle wrote only one thesis, "An Essay Upon the Vasomotor Changes in Tabes Dorsalis."[240] The misinformation may have originated from a statement in a paper on Conan Doyle written in 1935.[629] In 1884 he did publish a letter in the *Lancet* entitled "The Remote Effects of Gout,"[238] which may have become, with the passage of time, transmogrified into an elusive pseudothesis.[771]

Conan Doyle's thesis on tabes dorsalis is not well known, because, aside from a few excerpts,[421] it has never been published. Also, he made no mention of it in his autobiography written 30 years later.[375] It still rests at the University of Edinburgh Library in its original handwritten form.

The thesis is his most impressive medical work. Its literary style is as graphic in parts as is his fiction. An excellent example is found in the introduction (p.3):

> *The protean nature of it's [sic] symptoms, it's [sic] strange and varying course extending over lengthy periods, baffling all treatment and dragging on from one variety of torture to another until the emaciated sufferer hails the death which relieves him of his pain, have excited the interest both of pathologists and of clinical observers.*

This is indeed as gripping an account of tabes as are Doctor Watson's descriptions of the activities of Sherlock Holmes.

Although scientific contemporaries of Conan Doyle wrote with more literary embellishments than is true today, Conan Doyle managed his with uncommon maturity and elegance. Note his caveat (pp 3–4):

> *It is with diffidence that a young medical man must approach a subject upon which so many master minds have pondered—more particularly when the views which he entertains differ in many respects from any which he has encountered in his reading.*

On visible symptoms in an ideal case of tabes (pp 31–32):

> *In many cases he is of that swarthy neurotic type which furnishes the world with an undue proportion of poets, musicians, and madmen . . . His wife calls his attention to the fact that he has*

> *developed a squint, or he finds a dimness come over his sight and the lines of his morning paper become blurred & blotted. Very commonly one of his eyelids drop [sic] and he finds he cannot raise it.*

and then (p 32):

> *The patient returns home after this examination and may notice little or no change in his condition for years. Various little symptoms show him however that the demon which has seized him has not relaxed its grip*

Even a literary citation is written in an engaging manner (p 36):

> *Here are the words of Heine the great German Jewish poet when after seven years of this torture he saw the shades of death gather round his couch. They are interesting as showing the thoughts evolved by a great brain when linked to what was practically a dead body.*

Conan Doyle provided a table of contents for his thesis. Contents include anatomic, physiological, pathological, clinical, prognostic, and therapeutic aspects of tabes dorsalis. Also provided are some 50 references, although with incomplete citations. The bulk of the thesis is an excellent summation and an assessment of the then-current knowledge of the disease. The term "tabes" originates from the Latin and its Greek counterpart "phthisis," meaning decay, collapse, consumption, or wasting.[863] Hippocrates wrote of phthisis notias (consumption of the back) as occurring in newlywed husbands and lechers and resulting in infertility, copious seminal discharge, and excessive urination and defecation. Some commentators consider the ancient description not to be of tabes dorsalis.[801]

The modern clinical pathological entity of tabes dorsalis was developed during the second and third decades of the 19th century, largely by Ernst Horn of Berlin and his students.[681] Most notable is the description by Loewenhardt in 1817 of what was then called "locomotor ataxy, chronic myelophthisis, sclerosis of the spinal cord, or tabes."[801] Conan Doyle mistakenly attributed the original delineation to Duchenne, the great French neurologist, who mentioned its relationship to syphilis in 1859.[801] According to Conan Doyle, "Duchenne a quarter of a century ago first picked the disease out of the chaos which then existed among all things nervous and gave it an individuality of its own." Conan Doyle recognized "the existence of an exciting influence being probably the syphilitic poison in the case of tabes." He also referred several times to the prevalence of syphilis among tabetic patients. In 1885 tabes dorsalis was still considered by many to be related to a variety of causes.[707] However, Conan Doyle in his 1885 thesis,[240] referred to one likely cause—"the syphilitic poison." Four years after his thesis, some major textbooks, such as that of Delafield and Prudden[193] did not even mention syphilis as a possible etiologic agent. Even in 1892[696c] Osler considered syphilis as only one of several possible causes including excessive fatigue, overexposure to cold and wet, and sexual excesses.

Conan Doyle, by his own account, obtained his descriptions of the normal spinal cord from textbooks on anatomy, such as those by Turner of 1877[884] and Stewart of 1884,[852] and on physiology, such as that by Foster of 1880.[453] His clinical description is extensive and similar to those provided by Bramwell in 1882[94] and by Althaus in 1885.[15] It is certainly as erudite and extensive as that found in Osler's medical textbook.[696c] Modern textbooks include little information on tabes dorsalis. For example Harrison's textbook of medicine[7] devotes only four sentences, undoubtedly due to the notable decrease in prevalence since the general introduction of penicillin in about 1945.[588]

Conan Doyle's description of the pathological changes in tabes dorsalis was not taken from his own observations, but from books by Althaus in 1877[15] and by Strümpell in 1884.[858] It is surprising that he makes only brief reference to Charcot, whose lectures included both clinical and pathological descriptions and drawings of the effects of tabes. These were published in an English translation in 1881.[135] The delineations of gross and microscopic alterations in the posterior columns of the spinal cord are the same as those found in modern textbooks,[93] but are much more detailed and engaging.

A clear and graphic description of the symptoms of tabes dorsalis can be obtained from Conan Doyle's thesis (pp 33–36):

> *Strange flushes come over him and he perspires profusely without obvious cause. Numbness and pricklings alternate in different parts of his frame. His sexual desire which has possibly for some time lags back been inordinate begins (sic) to wane. Vague pains which have been flitting about his lower limbs and which he has probably ascribed to rheumatism, become more intense and sudden in their character until he can only compare them to electric shocks. . . .*
>
> *For some time the friends of the patient have observed an uncertainty in his gait, which continues until walking becomes a matter of difficulty. He himself makes the discovery some night that without a light he is helpless, and falls to the ground. With this fresh budget of symptoms he seeks his medical man once more.*
>
> *On examination the latter finds that the knee-jerk is gone, and possibly the cremasteric and gluteal [muscle] reflexes as well. On being asked to shut his eyes the patient totters. . . .*
>
> *The victim seldom escapes vescical [bladder] troubles however, with cystitis and a constand desire to micturate, or the bladder may be sluggish, so that there is no desire to micturate, or there may be vescical crises causing intolerable agony during many hours.*
>
> *Occasionally stranger symptoms may come upon the sufferer. A small raw spot upon the plantar aspect of his foot may deepen and enlarge until a perforating ulcer is established. Or certain of his joints may become flooded by a sudden copious effusion, which rapidly bursts the ligaments, destroys the joint and causes atrophy of the articular ends of the bones. Or there may be changes in the shafts of the bones themselves by which they are rendered brittle and liable to fracture. . . .*
>
> *Slowly the unfortunate victim sinks from one gradation of misery to another and can only look forward to the death which may reach him from pure exhaustion or may come from the involvement of the vital centres in the medulla.*

Conan Doyle's major objective in writing his thesis on tabes[240] was essentially scientific: "to endeavour to show that it is secondary to a preceeding [sic] pathologic condition"—in other words, cause-and-effect relationships (pathogenesis). His conclusion was that the antecedent was some irritant, possibly syphilitic in origin, that "excites the sympathetic system and so causes constriction of the small arterioles." According to Conan Doyle, such a decrease in blood supply would have an effect "first upon the posterior column—that being the part of the cord which is most sensitive to vascular influences." His reasons were that the lower end of the cord is farthest from the origin of its blood supply in the neck and that ergot, which is a vasospastic substance, produces lesions and symptoms similar to tabes.

His vasospasm theory of tabes led him to suggest vasodilators in therapy. The prevailing therapeutic modes of the time included silver nitrate, bromides, arsenic, mercury, hydrotherapy, morphine, and galvanism.[858] Of interest in the popularity of treatment with ergot,[16] even though ergot was known to cause sclerosis of the posterior column similar to that of tabes.

The only therapy mentioned by Conan Doyle in his thesis is a vasodilator agent, nitroglycerin. In fact, he treated a tabetic patient with a 1% alcohol solution of this drug, called "Murrell's solution" after William Murrell, a London physician[827] who promoted its use in the treatment of angina pectoris.[673] Unfortunately, the patient moved to a different locality soon after onset of treatment (pp 82–83).

> *Only on one occasion have I been able to try this drug upon a tabid patient. Empiric experiments of the sort should only be tried with the knowledge and consent of the patient, and this makes it a delicate matter for a young practitioner. He is liable to fall a victim to the 'post hoc propter hoc' fallacy, and all subsequent developments of the malady be laid to the door of that unfortunate innovation in the treatment. In this one case however the sufferer being an intelligent man I proposed to him that he should try this remedy to which he readily consented. He had loss*

of reflexes, Brauch Romberg's symptom, amblyopia and every other sign of the malady. For two or three weeks he appeared to improve considerably both in his general health and in his particular symptoms. Though confined to a bath chair he pursued his avocation as a commercial traveller, and following this he passed on to another town, taking some of the drug with him. I have never heard from him since nor can I find out his address. It is such cases which tend to make medical men cynical.

Of special interest is Conan Doyle's statement that "I have myself taken as many as forty minims [2.4 ml] of Murrell's solution without inconvenience"(p 82). This suggests another episode of self-experimentation by Conan Doyle similar to that with gelsemium.[216] Both gelsemium and nitroglycerin were used to treat neuralgia, from which Conan Doyle suffered. Surprisingly, he experienced no side effects, as even two minims (0.12 ml) has resulted in dizziness, headache, flushing, and hypotension.[723] Considerable individual variability, however, is reported in respect to toxic effects.[N46]

Of considerable interest in Conan Doyle's thesis[240] is his reasoning in concluding that the lesions in tabes dorsalis were caused by decreased nutrient (i.e., blood) supply to the lower dorsal area of the spinal cord. He begins by asserting that the vascular supply of the spinal cord comes from the vertebral arteries at its upper end. Although acknowledging that small vessels enter along nerve roots, he negates any importance to their contribution.

Such views on the blood supply to the cord were not generally held in his time. For example, Turner, in his anatomy book of 1877,[884] stated that "the spinal cord is well supplied with blood by numerous arteries." Modern descriptions[846] delineate the blood supply to all levels of the spinal cord as being derived from many vessels, including vertebral, ascending cervical, costovertebral, intercostal, lumbar, and sacral arteries.

Conan Doyle's unique views on the cord blood supply were taken from the Croonian Lectures of Walter Moxon, which were published in four parts in the *British Medical Journal* of 1881.[670]

Moxon, a physician to Guys Hospital, had asked Doctor Carrington, a demonstrator in anatomy, to investigate the blood supply of the cord. This was done by injecting the femoral artery of seven cadavers, with consequent filling of the anterior spinal artery from above only but not extending to the lower end. Only the "reinforcing" arteries of the upper third of the cord were filled. Moxon did not provide details as to the substance injected or the pressure used.

Moxon's other "proofs" consisted of experiments showing that cats given prussic acid became paralyzed in their hind legs, presumably owing to "lower tension of the blood." To support his position, he used the observation that in some patients paraplegia developed after rupture of an abdominal aortic aneurysm. Moxon concluded that anemia of the tip of the cord can occur in two circumstances: (1) too much activity of the cerebral circulation pushing cerebrospinal fluid out of the skull into the spinal column where it compresses arteries to the spinal cord, and (2) tremendous reduction in atmospheric pressure, as in Caisson's (diver's) disease, resulting in loss of blood from the vessels of the central nervous system.

Conan Doyle accepted Moxon's hypothesis as one of the major basic premises in his chain of reasoning. Modern experiments, however, reveal that ligation of the aorta will result in anterior lesions of the spinal cord[882] and not in posterior lesions such as occur in tabes dorsalis. Furthermore, paraplegia is related to changes in the anterior segment of the cord and not in the posterior segment as in tabes. If Conan Doyle is to be faulted for such misconceptions, it would be because his thesis is based on a review of the literature rather than on personal investigation.

Conan Doyle's second major premise is that vascular derangement in tabes is due to constriction of small arterioles because ergot, which acts through vasospasm, produces the same lesions as tabes. He is on sounder ground here because ergot does cause vasospasm (is adrenergic),[484] and can produce sclerosis (hardening) of posterior columns and a clinical syndrome similar to tabes.[93] He did not realize, however, that a lesion located similarly could be produced by another mechanism. More remarkable is that some authors of his era, including Osler, held not only that ergot poisoning can cause lesions like tabes, but also that ergot be recommended as a treatment for tabes.[696d]

Conan Doyle concluded that the vasospasm in tabes was due to irritation of the sympathetic nervous system, because the spasmodic action of this system is compatible with the "passing away and then recurring again" of the signs and symptoms of tabes dorsalis. He supported the primacy of vascular involvement by the fact that, in tabes, small arteries of the lower part of the spinal cord show thickening, which he attributed to lack of blood supply. Such histological observations were recorded in his time[16] and have been verified in more recent times.[93] Now, however, we know that hypoxia (decreased oxygen) as such is not the cause. After such a chain of reasoning, it was only logical for Conan Doyle to recommend a vasodilator, such as nitroglycerin, as treatment for tabes.

In spite of the fact that several of his basic premises are now known to be erroneous, Conan Doyle deserves credit on several points. He was familiar with and used the latest basic science and clinical information of his day. He based therapy on considerations of the scientific knowledge of his day rather than on universal therapeutic systems then in vogue, such as hydrotherapy, galvanism, and homeopathy.[784] A final word in Conan Doyle's defense is that even today we do not know the manner in which syphilis produces the posterior column lesions of tabes.[575]

According to Edwards, Conan Doyle's "thesis deeply depended on a pamphlet of Professor Pitres."[424] The thesis provides the reference as "Pitres. Sur troubles vasomotor et secrétores dans tabes." It was published in January 1884 in the *Journal de Médicine de Bordeaux*. Conan Doyle states that he used it to extract a brief epitome of these two cases for illustrating the escape of blood in the tissues after lightening pain (p 66). He also cites Pitres along with many other authors as contributing to the description of lesions in tabes (pp 5, 22, 57, 65). Conan Doyle's references in the thesis to many foreign and British works on the anatomy, physiology, signs and symptoms, complications, and treatment make it quite unlikely that he relied on Pitres' work any more than on that of others.

Conan Doyle applied deductive reasoning not only in his M.D. thesis but also, to an even greater extent, in his Sherlock Holmes stories. Commentators have considered Holmes to be a "spectacular diagnostician,"[589] and his use of logic and deduction brilliant.[566] Of interest is the comparison of Conan Doyle's medical reasoning with his fictional reasoning. An intrinsic similarity exists between the approach of the medical diagnostician and the detective. Both reason from effect to cause.[527] In medical diagnosis it is the backward tracing from disease manifestations; in crime solving from the effects of a criminal activity. Another similarity is the close attention to minute details.[533]

An example of Sherlock Holmes' reasoning is found at the beginning of *The Hound of the Baskervilles*,[321] Conan Doyle's best known detective story (first published in 1901 and 1902). Holmes had returned to 221B Baker Street to find the walking stick of a departed visitor. From its appearance he derived, accurately of course, considerable information about the visitor. A band on the stick was imprinted with the name James Mortimer, followed by M.R.C.S., obviously denoting a physician who is a member of the Royal College of Surgeons. The stick, a gift from friends at CCH, undoubtedly Charing Cross Hospital, indicated he was well liked and amiable.

Such a gift would only be given on leaving the hospital, which indicated a lack of ambition, especially as he went into a country practice, begin obvious from the rough and worn nature of the cane, certainly unbecoming for a city physician. He had undoubtedly been a house physician because a staff member would have been too well established to leave the hospital. As the cane was inscribed only five years previously (1884), Doctor James Mortimer was obviously still under 30 years of age.

What an amazing series of inferences, especially as all were proved to be correct on the return of Doctor Mortimer. A suspicion arises, however, that Holmes may not have been quite as accurate if Conan Doyle had no control over the denouement. For example, the walking stick may have been left on purpose instead of forgotten; or CCH, may have been a hunt club as suggested by Watson; or Mortimer, a middle-aged physician, may have been tired of city and hospital stresses. Certainly the manner in which Holmes arrived at his conclusions is not consistent with his well-known adage—"Eliminate all other factors and the one which remains must be the truth." The fallacy is that one can never be certain that one is aware of all possible factors. Another basic defect is that "Holmes sometimes speaks as if it were possible to reach inferences that are certain rather than probable."[790]

One of the few critical analyses of Holmes' reasoning was written by Mackenzie[624] who provided many examples from the so-called "sacred writings" to prove that "quite as liberal a proportion of sophistry as logic is there embodied." Conan Doyle's M.D. thesis,[240] on the other hand, should not be accused of such superficially plausible reasoning, its fundamental error lying in the lack of validity of the basic premises which he selected from the literature.[N47] But we must judge Conan Doyle on the basis of his times and not on ours.

Conan Doyle committed several errors of reasoning both in his M.D. thesis and in his Holmes stories. He confused cause and effect in attributing cord lesions to sympathetic imbalance instead of the reverse. He assumed that vasospasm caused the tabetic lesion because ergot, which has a vasospastic action, causes a similar lesion. Another category of error is evident in his analysis of the forgotten cane when he assumed that he had all the relevant facts. It was Conan Doyle's control of events in his fiction which saved Holmes from failure. A more basic defect is building a chain of reasoning on false premises, such as accepting one writer's conclusions that blood supply is less to the lower than to the upper part of the spinal cord. Another error in reasoning relates to the assumption that an event or occurrence has only one interpretation, as for example that thickened vessels are due to hypoxia, or that going into country practice could only be due to a lack of ambition.

Conan Doyle, however, was circumspect with his assertions, as the following example, from among several in his thesis, illustrates (p 63):

> *The four fold corroberation [sic] of the view which makes tabes dorsalis a disease dependant [sic] upon vascular disturbance arising from a morbid state of the sympathetic system appears to me to be as conclusive as scientific circumstantial evidence can ever be.*

Such caution and the attempt to base scientific theory on observed facts are in the best tradition of medical science. He deserves considerable credit for his thesis.

Furthermore Conan Doyle's thesis serves as proof that scientific medical writing need not be monotonous. His other medical writings exhibit a similar engaging literary style.

WRITINGS ON THE CAUSE AND PREVENTION OF INFECTIOUS DISEASE

Perhaps, of even greater interest than Conan Doyle's M.D. thesis are four of his medical items which are concerned with infectious disease, particularly prevention through vaccination (inoculation). Three were written between 1883 and 1890 while he was practicing in Southsea, and one was written in 1900. This period of time was one in which knowledge of the microbial cause of disease was being established, but not as yet fully accepted by or even known to many medical people. Yet Doctor Conan Doyle, an unknown general practitioner trying to build up a practice, wrote on basic concepts of this newly developing and revolutionary field, actively supported unpopular preventative measures, and made some far-sighted predictions.

The first article, "Life and Death in the Blood," was published in a magazine called *Good Words*, in 1883,[231] only one year after he entered practice. Conan Doyle's introduction is a forerunner of his later science fiction stories[357,360] and, most amazingly, of a 1966 movie, *Fantastic Voyage*.[432] He asked the reader to imagine a man reduced in size to less than one thousandth of an inch, so that he could travel through the bloodstream.

> *Had a man the power of reducing himself to the size of less than the one-thousandth part of an inch, and should he, while of this microscopic structure, convey himself through the coats of a living artery, how strange the sight that would meet his eye!*

Once there he would see the red blood cells that carry oxygen and the white blood cells (leukocytes) that envelop and ingest material. Conan Doyle cautioned that there would be "small hope for our poor little mite of humanity should one of these floating stomachs succeed in seizing him in its embrace." His knowledge of recent concepts of medicine is indicated by the fact that Metchnikoff's first presentation on phagocytosis was in 1883,[652] the same year that Conan Doyle's paper was published. Observations on the engulfing abilites of leukocytes, however, had been made by Langhans in 1870 and by Birch-Hirschfield in 1876.[114]

Very striking are the vivid analogies used in describing blood cells.

> *[The red blood cells] jostle through their brief existence without any claims to a higher function than that of the baker's cart, which carries around the necessities of life, and so valuable not for itself but for its burden.*
>
> *Gelatinous in consistency [white blood cells] and irregular in shape, capable of pushing out long prehensile tentacles with which to envelope its food and draw it into its interior, this creature would appear from his point of view as a polyp of gigantic proportions and formidable aspect.*

This is not only gripping imagery but also surprisingly detailed description of the functions of red and white blood cells. They would be a credit for any modern day lecturer!

The major part of this engaging paper delineates other elements found in the blood in diseased conditions as "little organisms, which lie upon the debatable ground between the animal and vegetable kingdoms." By 1883, the existence of bacteria was known, having been described by Leeuwenhoek in a letter to the Royal Society in 1676[204] and recognized as pathogenic (disease causing) organisms by Bassi of Lodi in 1836, in relation to silk worms.[114] But popularization did not occur until the studies of Louis Pasteur on fermentation in 1857 and on spontaneous generation in 1862 and 1863.[888] However, even in the 1870s and 1880s there were some prominent skeptics on the extent of bacterial causation of disease, among them Virchow and Bernard.[4]

In Conan Doyle's article of 1883,[231] he referred to several diseases in which microorganisms had been found. He referred to the only two diseases of humans which had been well established before 1880 to have a bacterial cause: relapsing fever by Obermeier in 1873 and anthrax by Koch in 1876.[114] He mentioned the isolation of the tubercle bacillis by Koch in 1882,[441] but did not include that of glanders discovered by Loeffler in the same year.[114] He was aware, however, that some diseases of animals, such as pig-typhoid and fowl-cholera were caused by bacteria.

Conan Doyle's major orientation in this article was on the prevention of bacterial disease by inoculation of material from an infected patient. He referred to Jenner's work on smallpox vaccination in 1796[48] and to Pasteur's work on attenuated anthrax organisms in 1881. His grasp of this immunological concept is demonstrated by his prediction that an attenuated inoculum would be developed for rabies; a year later, in 1884, this was accomplished by Pasteur.[399] Conan Doyle also suggested the possibility that "inoculating with the weakened infusion" of the tubercle bacillis could prevent such an infection. Interestingly, when Koch did make such a claim in 1890,[586] Conan Doyle was the first to be skeptical.[252]

The stature of Conan Doyle in respect to medical concepts is evident from two more general predictions in his 1883 paper.[231]

> *Given that a single disease, proved to depend upon a parasitic organism, can be effectually and certainly stamped out, why should not all diseases depending upon similar causes be also done away with?*

> *It is probable that in the days of our children's children, consumption, typhus, typhoid, cholera, malaria, scarlatina, diphtheria, measles, and a host of other diseases will have ceased to exist.*

Some of the diseases listed had not as yet been linked definitely to a microorganism. More remarkable is that "in the days of our children's children" constitutes two generations, or 60 years, a future date that corresponds with 1943, which was the beginning of the era of practical antibiotic therapy for infectious diseases.[744] It has taken 96 years for his prediction of the total eradication of an infectious disease to come true—that is, smallpox in 1979.[55]

Conan Doyle's "Life and Death in the Blood"[231] fits into the category of a tour de force, being not only superbly written but also at the very vanguard of medical knowledge, and even beyond in the uncanny accuracy of his predictions. Highlighting this are the contents of a graduation address given by his former teacher William Rutherford in 1891, 10 years after Conan Doyle's graduation.[391] The same infectious diseases are described in the same manner, but without any further scientific knowledge than Conan Doyle espoused eight years earlier. "Life and Death in the Blood" deserved (and deserves today) some recognition as an outstanding work. That it has not, may be a reflection of the fact that it was written by a young practitioner and published in a literary magazine rather than in a medical journal.

Also relatively unknown is Conan Doyle's letter on "Compulsory Vaccination"[242] published in the *Portsmouth Evening Mail* on July 15, 1887. This letter was written 91 years after Jenner's first vaccination for smallpox, 47 years after the first English vaccination act,[785] and seven years before the viral inclusion bodies were identified by Guarnieri.[468d] Smallpox as a disease has a long history, having been described in ancient Chinese writings, and found as skin lesions in the mummy of Ramses V who died in 1100 B.C.[55]

Prevention of smallpox by injection of material from a pustule of an afflicted individual was recognized in the Middle East long before Jenner's work.[401] Its use in England was pioneered by Lady

Mary Montagu on her return from Turkey in 1718.[857] By 1740 such inoculation was being practiced by some physicians in a few towns including Portsmouth.[748,N48] After Jenner's cowpox-related discovery in 1796, considerable opposition developed to the inoculation of humans with either smallpox or bovine cowpox material.[402] Such opposition continued until the complete eradication of smallpox in 1979.

Opposition to such preventive measures occured in the face of the extensive endemic and epidemic presence of smallpox in England. For example, in 1723, a smallpox epidemic resulted in the death of about one in five in Portsmouth.[748] In 1887, when Conan Doyle wrote his letter, there were only 23 cases of smallpox with three deaths reported in Portsmouth.[671] Severe epidemics were occurring elsewhere at the time. An epidemic in Sheffield resulted in 6,088 cases, 590 deaths, and untold numbers of facial disfigurement by scars.[48] The value of vaccination was established by the fact that for children less than 10 years of age, incidence in the vaccinated was five per 1,000 and in the unvaccinated 101 per 1,000; death cases were 11 and 372, respectively. Five years later, in 1892, William Osler wrote "Smallpox is one of the most virulent of contagious diseases, and persons exposed, if unprotected by vaccination, are almost invariably attacked."[696e] Nevertheless, antivaccinationists persisted in their vigorous denouncements.[N49]

An example of such opposition occurred in York in 1876, and is commemorated by a display in Castle Museum.[773] The heading of the display is "Keighly Guardians confined in York Castle for not obeying a mandamus to enforce the Vaccination Law. August to September, 1876." Pictures are included of seven distinguished appearing citizens. This incident occurred 80 years after Jenner's development of his vaccine, 60 years after the first British vaccination acts, and 11 years before Conan Doyle's letters.

Despite opposition, the English Parliament established a series of acts, beginning in 1840, after an epidemic of smallpox resulted in 42,000 deaths. The Vaccination Act of 1840 provided free vaccination.[785] The first compulsory Vaccination Act was passed in 1853.[152] It mandated that every child be vaccinated within three months after birth. Offenders "shall forfeit a sum not exceeding twenty shillings." The fee for vaccination was set at threepence, and powers for enforcement of compulsory vaccination were provided in the Public Health Act of 1858, but they were rather vague.[785] By 1887, 83% of newborns were vaccinated. The effectiveness of the act was reduced in 1898 when another Act of Parliament exempted conscientious objectors. Finally, in 1946, compulsory vaccination was abolished.[630]

Arguments against vaccination varied from irrational fears to well-founded observations. Concern was expressed that the skin injections might result in skin infections such as erysipelas and sepsis.[402] With respect to inoculation with infected material from a patient, it was stated that tuberculosis and syphilis also could be transmitted. It was recognized that a vaccinated individual became resistant to smallpox by being given the disease itself, albeit relatively slight.[117] Thus he could infect others, and a few such minor epidemics were reported.[48] Some opponents to vaccination were also opposed to other medical procedures such as vivisection for research purposes.[927]

Opposition to inoculation of cowpox from infected cows included reasons that varied from the bizarre to the religious to the scientific. One type of reaction is illustrated in Gillray's etching, "The Cow Pock" (1808),[478] depicting various inoculated individuals in whom bovine-like features and excrescences developed. Other types of opposition, however, were more thoughtful and rational. It was such reactions that Conan Doyle countered in 1887.

Conan Doyle's letter[242] dated July 14 was a strong reaction against such opposition. It was in response to one dated July 13 by Colonel S.B. Wintle of Southsea who raised several objections to vaccination.[931] The first objection was a moral one, contending that it was immoral to prevent smallpox as it had been sent by Providence. Conan Doyle countered by asking the question, "Is it immoral to preserve a child from a deadly disease by methods that have been proven by science and experience?'' He compared the opposition to vaccination with that to the use of chloroform to relieve pain during surgery or labor.

To the objection that smallpox vaccination was unsuccessful, Conan Doyle cited decreased rates of incidence, severity of the disease, and death from it since the inception of vaccination. He described the experience at the London Smallpox Hospital where no cases had occurred in vaccinated nurses, doctors, and dressers who had been exposed to the disease. Conan Doyle concluded his letter with a positive statement: ''As long as that case is so weak as to need the argument of morality to enforce it I think the Vaccination Acts are in no great danger of being repealed.''

Four day's after Conan Doyle's rebuttal, Colonel Wintle responded,[932] countering that in spite of vaccination there were still epidemics of smallpox, especially in London and Liverpool. Conan Doyle soon followed with another rebuttal,[243] pointing out that ''the death-rate varies from less than one in a hundred among the well-vaccinated to the enormous mortality of 37 per cent among Colonel Wintle's followers.'' He gave as the reason for the greater prevalence of disease in Liverpool and London the fact that they have a larger floating population than any other English city making it more difficult to enforce vaccination acts. Having thus answered Colonel Wintle's arguments with reason and clarity, Conan Doyle concluded with a severe accusation.

> *But he [Wintle] undertakes a vast responsibility when, in the face of the overwhelming testimony of those who are brought most closely into contact with disease, he incites others through the public press, to follow the same courses and take their chance of infection in defiance of hospital statistics.*

Conan Doyle's motivation for publishing these rebuttals is provided by a quotation from his first letter.[242]

> *The interests at stake are so vital that an enormous responsibility rests with the men whose notion of progress is to revert to the condition of things which existed in the dark ages before the dawn of medical science.*

Such a statement indicates a very strong interest in and support of medical progress. It is contrary to the equally strong statement in Conan Doyle's autobiography in 1924 in which he refers to his attitude at this time as "a very strong belief that much of the so-called progress was illusory."[375q] This statement, however, may reflect a strong orientation toward other interests and causes during the succeeding 26 years. Conan Doyle was always a fighter for causes that he believed in, whether they were medical, political, legal, or spiritualistic.

Conan Doyle's response to a vaccine for another infectious disease, tuberculosis, was skeptical rather than supportive. His views are found in a lengthy letter to the *London Daily Telegraph* of November 20, 1890,[252] relating to a fascinating yet frustrating episode in the history of medicine, which occurred during 1890 and 1891.

The episode began with the Tenth International Medical Congress held in Berlin from August 3 to 9 with the great pathologist, Rudolph Virchow, presiding.[61] Attendance was between 5,000 and 6,000, including prominent English physicians such as James Paget and Joseph Lister.[62] On August 6, the *Daily Telegraph* reported Robert Koch's presentation of his finding of several substances that had destroyed the tubercle bacillus in vitro [outside the living body] and one that could do so in affected tissues of guinea pigs.[63] The story related the anticipation, by several eminent physicians, that the substance would be effective in man. The reason given was that "what takes effect on vertebrate animals of a lower species can be applied with success to the human frame."

It was not until November 13, 1890, that Koch published in the *Deutsche Medizinishe Wochenschrift* an account of investigations on human beings.[585] He described beneficial results of treatment with lymph, stating that "phthisis [tuberculosis] in the beginning can be cured with certainty." It is likely that the reprint of Koch's article in the *British Medical Journal* (November 15)[586] caught Conan Doyle's eye. In his autobiography he stated:

> . . . *in 1890 Koch announced that he had discovered a sure cure for consumption and that he would demonstrate it upon a certain*

> *date in Berlin. A great urge came upon me suddenly that I should go to Berlin and see him do so. I could give no clear reason for this . . . at a few hours' notice I packed up a bag and started off alone upon this curious adventure.*[375q]

Until November 19, the day before Conan Doyle's letter, the *Daily Telegraph* contained daily stories on Koch's so-called lymph cure. Included were accounts of tubercular patients who were greatly improved,[64] financial support from Kaiser Wilhelm,[65] Koch's self-injection with his own lymph,[758] his refusal to reveal the composition of the lymph,[66] and various laudatory comments[67] and lectures.[68] It is possible that Koch had been pushed into premature release of information on his cure by Kaiser Wilhelm.

Conan Doyle arrived in Berlin on Sunday, November 16, being one of the first of many who invaded Berlin to learn about Koch's remarkable cure for tuberculosis. He was unsuccessful in gaining entrance to an overcrowded lecture by Professor von Bergmann on the treatment of patients with the lymph.[253] Accounts of Conan Doyle's encounter with Professor von Bergmann are found in his article[253] and in a newspaper interview.[738] On his arrival Sunday morning, he learned of a lecture to be given that evening by the Professor. He approached von Bergmann to ask if there was any way whereby he could attend the oversubscribed session. The reaction, according to Conan Doyle, was violent. He shouted that "There's no place. Perhaps you would like to take my place, it's the only one vacant." Conan Doyle, as in many of his activities, was not to be thwarted. "I was enabled [through Doctor Hartz of Michigan] next morning to turn the Professor's flank by seeing in his wards the same cases which he had lectured upon the night before." Conan Doyle characterized von Bergmann as "a man of some character, gruff in manner, and showing a hatred for all English doctors, while all the other German doctors were courageous and obliging." He attributed the cause of such a hatred to a quarrel with Sir Morell Mackenzie.

The following day, however, he saw treated patients on the wards of several clinics. It was on that day, November 17, presumably in the evening, that Conan Doyle wrote his letter from Berlin, to be published on November 20.[252] On the 20th he wrote a postcard to his former mentor, Doctor Hoare, referring to this letter, and indicating that he was the first Englishman to arrive in Berlin to study Koch's cure, and "the first to leave with full knowledge of the process."[385j] The second English physician to arrive was most likely Malcolm Morris, who had brought a patient for treatment.[738] Doctor Morris considered the patient improved after injection of Koch's fluid.

His letter on "Consumption Cure" emphasized certain difficulties, such as very incomplete knowledge and an insufficient supply of the lymph. Conan Doyle stressed that the lymph did not kill the bacillus but the tissue in which it lies, that the system established tolerance for lymph, and that lymph could activate dormant tubercular processes. He gave credit to Koch for recognizing these attributes. Conan Doyle, however, went further when he doubted that the bacilli, which are so numerous, minute, and widely spread in organs, would be cleared out of the body. Thus they could "cause by their irritation fresh tubercular tissue to form." His view that the lymph "forms an admirable aid to diagnosis" was originally suggested by Koch.

Within a month of his letter, an article by Conan Doyle was published in the *Review of Reviews*[253] in which he recounted very favorably the facts of Koch's life and work, and ended with the same material included in his letter. Added were three drawings of the tubercle bacilli as seen under the microscope. Also added were literary flourishes, some of which were in the form of analogies. "It [Koch's lymph] continually removes the traces of the enemy but it still leaves him deep in the invaded country." Conan Doyle was very careful that his doubts about Koch's lymph would not be construed as a criticism of the man himself. His motivation for writing the letter was to provide a more balanced view of the efficacy of Koch's lymph.

Great as is Koch's discovery our knowledge is still very incomplete. The sooner that this is recognized the less chance will there be of serious disappointment.

Subsequent to publication of Conan Doyle's letter in November and until January 15, 1891, the *Daily Telegraph* contained 13 stories on Koch's cure, all of which were generally positive, and two letters. One letter suggested that tubercular persons consult their medical advisers before going to Berlin because the lymph was in short supply.[708] Articles in the medical press, such as the *British Medical Journal*, were not as uniformly accepting of the validity of Koch's cure. For example, on November 22, two days after publication of Conan Doyle's letter, an editorial suggested that Koch had overinterpreted the results of his studies.[396] Three weeks later, however, on December 13, Joseph Lister published a favorable account of Koch's remedy.[612] It was based on a lecture at King's College Hospital in which he characterized the results as "simply astounding."[436] Unlike Conan Doyle, he was not concerned about live bacilli being released by tissue necrosis because "the bacilli may be quite unable to maintain their growing" in the adjacent healthy tissues.

A review of issues of the *Daily Telegraph* from January 16 to March 31, 1891, failed to reveal any further reports or letters on Koch's lymph. This sudden cessation of interest may have been due to Virchow's presentation to the Berlin Medical Society on January 7, 1891, of 21 autopsies of patients treated with Koch's lymph, as reported in the *British Medical Journal*, January 17.[903] In all cases the lymph had spread the infection by producing necrotic tissue, which carried the bacilli into bronchi of lower lobes where further foci of infection were created—a possibility that had been suggested by Conan Doyle two months earlier.[252] Only at this time did Koch reveal that his lymph was a glycerine extract of a pure cultivation of bacilli, which he now called "tuberculin."[587]

The hope that tuberculin was therapeutic for tuberculosis, however, did not disappear for several years.[403] William Osler, for example, in his *Principles and Practice of Medicine* (1892),[696q] stated, "It will probably be several years before we can speak with decision upon the true position of this remedy." Osler referred to 23 patients treated with tuberculin at Johns Hopkins Hospital, only three of whom were benefited; the condition of the others was aggravated. In summary he stated that "our knowledge warrants us in urging extreme caution in its use"—a conclusion that Conan Doyle had arrived at in 1890. As late as 1913, George Bernard Shaw found it appropriate to satirize Koch's tuberculin cure in his play "The Doctor's Dilemma."[810]

Rene Dubos, in his history of tuberculosis,[400] evaluated Conan Doyle's article on Koch and his cure as:

> *. . .a statement of the mode of action, potential usefulness, limitations and dangers of tuberculin of such intelligent understanding that little of importance has since been added to his analysis of the subject.*

Also striking is the fact that Conan Doyle had arrived at such an assessment within only a few days after arriving in Berlin.

Conan Doyle's grasp of the then current frontiers of medical science was even broader, as evidenced by his summation that "herein lies that vast difference between Koch's treatment of consumption and the action of vaccine in the case of small-pox. The one is for a time at least conclusive, while in the other your remedy does not treat the real seat of the evil."[253]

The "Consumption Cure" episode of Conan Doyle occurred about one month before he left general practice in Southsea for ophthalmologic training in Vienna, and about six months before he gave up medical practice for full-time writing. It suggests yet another indication that had he been suitably motivated he might have become as eminent a medical personage as he became a writer of detective stories.

Unlike Conan Doyle's writings on smallpox and tuberculosis, his article on enteric fever (typhoid) was the result of direct experience of an epidemic during the Boer War. This disease was, however, also severe among civilian populations. In 1895 it caused over 5,000 deaths in England and Wales, representing a 20 to 30% death rate in infected persons.[147,N50] Conan Doyle was to find an even severer epidemic soon after he arrived at Bloemfontein, South Africa, on February 28, 1900, to serve as a physician at the Langman hospital.[314] He remained for four months, leaving for

England on July 1, 1900. Meanwhile, on June 5, he had written an account for the *British Medical Journal* on the epidemic of typhoid at Bloemfontein. It was published July 7.[314]

Conan Doyle's article refers to vaccination against typhoid fever. Sixteen years after Klebs' discovery of the organism, a typhoid vaccine consisting of heat-killed bacilli was developed in 1896 by Almroth Wright (1861–1947), a professor of pathology at the Army Medical School in Netley.[944] His vaccine was used extensively by the army on a voluntary basis in England, India, Egypt, Cyprus, and South Africa between 1899 and 1902.[605] In South Africa only 20,000 of 200,000 soldiers were vaccinated.[470] This was due to opposition based on side effects and supposed ineffectiveness. Statistics on use at various locations, gathered by Wright in 1902, indicate a sixfold to twelvefold reduction in incidence among the inoculated, with a fourfold decrease in death rate.[941]

The typhoid epidemic in Bloemfontein reached its height in April, about a month after Conan Doyle's arrival, and lasted until August, about a month after his departure. In his autobiography Conan Doyle stated, "We lost more from enteric than from the bullet in South Africa."[375s] His article is more specific in listing 10,000 to 20,000 cases of typhoid in one month among troops in South Africa, and 600 deaths at Bloemfontein alone.[314] Conan Doyle provided proof of the diagnosis by starting that "Our senior surgeon, Mr. Gibbs, performed post-mortems on several cases, but never without finding the characteristic ulcers [in the intestine]." Although he had no statistics, he indicated a strong impression from his own experience that the vaccine could prevent the disease, and when it did not prevent it, the course of the disease was modified. As support he cited the fact that, as of June 5, there had been no deaths among the inoculated patients. Wright's statistics on the typhoid epidemic at Bloemfontein indicated a 14.8% incidence in those inoculated as compared to 33.5% in those who were not.[941] This supported Conan Doyle's impression. One inoculated patient did die, however, undoubtedly after Conan Doyle left South Africa on July 1.

Conan Doyle's scientific orientation to typhoid was related to prevention through vaccination, as it had been for Jenner's cowpox. In this instance, unlike that of tubeculin, he came out strongly for its use on a compulsory basis, as he had for smallpox vaccine. "There is one mistake which we have made, and it is one which will not be made in any subsequent campaign. Inoculation for enteric was not made compulsory. If it had been so I believe that we should have escaped from most of its troubles."[314] This recommendation by Conan Doyle was even more remarkable in that typhoid vaccine was not widely known at the time.[493] For example, the Goulstonian Lectures of 1900 on Typhoid Fever by Horton-Smith did not even mention the vaccine.[546] In fact is was 15 years after Conan Doyle's letter that compulsory vaccination for typhoid fever was instituted in the British Army.[147] Even after the outbreak of World War I Almroth Wright found it necessary to publish a long letter in the *Times* on the subject.[942]

Conan Doyle was also quite aware that typhoid bacilli were water-borne, being spread by uncontrolled water supplies. This concern was expressed in both his autobiography[375s] and his history of the Boer War.[316] His frustration at the lack of corrective actions by the military lasted even after his return from South Africa. This is seen in his evidence given to the South African Hospital Commission in August 1900[836] and his presentation to the Author's Club in November 1900.[395] A year later he was still critical of the military. In a comment after a presentation on "Typhoid and the Army" by Doctor Leigh Cannery,[885] Conan Doyle characterized himself as "one who had witnessed the horrifying results of the neglect of the most ordinary precautions among the soldiers in South Africa, without the slightest remonstrance from anybody."

Conan Doyle's orientation to typhoid was that of prevention by two means—by immunizing the possible hosts and by controlling spread of the bacilli. But, unlike some, the scientific aspects of disease did not blind him to the more human aspects. In his article of July 7, 1900, he extolled the selfless activity of orderlies and nurses. Eight of 18 orderlies became infected and one died. One of eight nurses also died. Although Conan Doyle was critical of the army command, he found it impossible not to speak highly of the courage and patience of soldiers in the hospital and of their concern for each other.

Although containing considerable scientific information, Conan Doyle's four items on infectious disease all have another common theme—a concern for the more human qualities of suffering humanity.

CONTINUING ROMANCE WITH MEDICINE

The Bloemfontein adventure with typhoid is not the only evidence that Conan Doyle was oriented to the broader aspects of disease. This is exemplified in his introductory address to the medical students of St. Mary's Hospital in London in 1910.[777] He was honored by being chosen to present the prizes and awards for the past session. He also had a later connection with this School; his son Kingsley entered the medical school in 1911, but left for the war in 1914 before qualifying.[211,N51]

Conan Doyle's address was printed in full in the *St. Mary's Hospital Gazette* of October 1910[349] and was condensed in the *Lancet* of the same month.[350] It contained several categories in its content—his own experiences as a practitioner, various exhortations about medical practice, general beneficial results of medical knowledge, the effects of disease of leaders on history, the past and present status of medical science, historical aspects of infectious disease discoveries, and a final idealistic statement. This presentation, given 20 years after Conan Doyle left medical practice, provides a much greater breadth of orientation to medical matters than is evident in his other talks or writings.

Conan Doyle's description of his activities as a physician was unpretentious as usual. He does, however, indicate some pride in the many different places and types of medical practice in which he had engaged. It was from this broad experience that he based his advice to the medical students—being concerned about the undue materialism which was part of the period during which he had received his own education.

> *I would ask you then, gentlemen, in your studies of matter, not to be precipitate in your conclusions as to spirit. . . . And besides an undue materialism, there is another danger upon which I would warn you. It is intellectual priggishness.*

He was also concerned that undue emphasis on the disease to the exclusion of the person would produce an incomplete and unsatifactory physician.

> *There is another facet which life will teach you, . . . the value of kindliness and humanity as well as of knowledge. . . . A strong and kindly personality is as valuable an asset as actual learning in a medical man.*
>
> *I have known men in the profession who were stuffed with accurate knowledge, and yet were so cold in their bearing, and so unsympathetic in their attitude, assuming the* rôle *rather of a judge than a friend, that they left their half-frozen patients all the worse for their contact.*

This contrast between the disease-oriented, nonempathic physician and the humanistic one was written in the same year that Abraham Flexner published his review of medical schools.[440] Flexner recommended a close connection with universities and emphasis on basic biological sciences. Although greatly improving medical education, one result was decreasing emphasis on the human being harboring the disease. A reaction against such depersonalized medical care became quite evident in the 1960s[766] and led to increasing concern for the sentiments expressed by Conan Doyle a half-century before[427]

A significant segment of Conan Doyle's introductory address is a fascinating account of the effect on history of diseases of famous figures. As one might expect from his detailed studies for his novels on the Napoleonic wars,[265] the incidents all relate to French History. For example, a molar abscess weakened Louis XIV's resistance to advisors who wanted him to revoke the Edict of Nantes of 1598, which had protected the Huguenots. The revocation, in 1685, led to the loss of 250,000 of France's Protestant citizens who fled to other countries, all because of the lack of dental hygiene. Conan Doyle's novel, *The Refugees*, is a tale of a Huguenot family who escaped to the New World.[273]

Not widely known is that Francis I of France invented the wig to cover areas of alopecia, bald patches on the scalp, caused by a skin disease. Some of the inhumanity of the French Revolution was attributed by Conan Doyle to disease in two of its more radical leaders. Marat had a severe, generalized skin disease that may have increased his paranoia.[N52] With respect to Robespierre, whose liver was diseased. Conan Doyle stated, "A man whose veins are green in color is likely to take a harsh view of life." And finally, Napoleon's defeat at Waterloo may have been due to lethargy caused by his gastric carcinoma.[N53]

Conan Doyle concluded his address by extolling several dedicated physicians whose research had greatly benefited mankind. Again his choices were in an area he had previously written upon—infectious diseases. ". . . in language calculated to arrest the attention and excite the emulation of the student he told of the untiring patience of Sir Patrick Manson in his pursuit of the methods by which filaria (filariasis) was transferred from one human body to another."[637] Major Ronald Ross had discovered how malaria is spread by mosquitoes and thus improved life around the Mediterranean and in the West Indies.[788] Sir David Bruce discovered the germ that caused Maltese (Malta) fever and its spread by milk of goats.[102] Resistance to infection was better understood because of Sir Almroth Wright's study of opsonins (which make bacteria more susceptible to engulfment).[943] He did not neglect the subject of a previous letter and article—Koch. Of these five advances in knowledge, three took place some time after Conan Doyle had left practice (Ross 1897, Wright 1903, Bruce 1907). His accounts in this presentation indicate a continuing interest in and understanding of new medical advances.

Conan Doyle's 1910 address presents an orientation toward medicine that is similar to that of Sir William Osler, including humanism, medical history, renowned physicians, and the frontiers of medical science.[698] Osler lived in England from 1905 until his death in 1919, but there is no evidence that he ever met or communicated with Conan Doyle. That Osler knew of him is evident by several items in his *Bibliotheca*, including a copy of Conan Doyle's 1918 article on spiritualism and 11 of his books.[701] Unlike Osler, however, he did not achieve a reputation as an outstanding scientific and humanitarian physician. In fact, although deserving, the opposite occurred.

William Osler would have wholeheartedly embraced the concluding sentiments of Conan Doyle's address of 1910 to medical students.

> *Unselfishness, fearlessness, humanity, self-effacement, professional honour—these are the proud qualities which medicine has ever demanded from her sons. They have lived up to them. It is for you youngsters to see that they shall not decline during the generation to come.*

SUMMARY

Conan Doyle was an exceptional medical personage. It would be as unusual today as it was in the 1880s for a medical student to engage in self-experimentation and to publish the results; for a general practitioner to write a thesis for a higher degree; to strongly react against public opposition to an issue such as vaccination; and to be the first to criticize, on the basis of analysis, a supposed cure developed by a world-renowned physician.

The question arises as to why Conan Doyle's medical writings are not more widely known or acknowledged as valuable contributions. There are several reasons. Four of his contributions in medical journals were letters to the editor, a form frowned upon by medical elitists. Even worse, his astute article on microbiology and his analysis of Koch's life and work were published in lay magazines. And, most unfortunately, his M.D. Thesis has not been published.

Conan Doyle's medical education, experience and writings were not wasted efforts. In his address on "The Romance of Medicine"[349] he indicated that "a medical training was a most valuable possession for a man, even if he did not afterwards engage in practice." This was certainly true for himself in respect to his fiction. Some of the attraction of the Holmesian stories is due to numerous references to signs and symptoms of diseases and their treatment. Not the least of his fiction are the 19 short stories and two novels that have a predominantly medical theme.

Figure 9. Doctor Conan Doyle in academic regalia for his graduation in August 1881.

Figure 10. Doctor George T. Budd for whom Conan Doyle worked as a physician assistant at Plymouth during May and June 1882. (From *Conan Doyle: His Life and Art* by Hesketh Pearson (Taplinger Publishing Co., Inc., 1977). Copyright 1977 by Michael Holroyd. Reproduced by permission.)

Figure 11. Conan Doyle, a general practitioner, in Southsea from July 1882 to December 1890.

SECTION TWO

ARTHUR CONAN DOYLE, LL.D. (HON)

3

MEDICAL FICTION

The quantity of Conan Doyle's nonfictional writings is greatly exceeded by the number of his fictional works, of which the Holmesian stories are actually the lesser amount. As one might anticipate from his background, the medical orientation of some and medical references in others are quite extensive. Such nonscientific content is now referred to as "Literature and Medicine," which, beginning in the 1970s has become a prominent area of study.[N54] In 1978, for example, an anthology of such writings was published under the title *Medicine in Literature*[132] and in 1982 as *The Physician in Literature.*[177] A bibliography of hundreds of items relating to *Literature and Medicine* was published in 1975[877] and in 1982, the first volume of a journal devoted to the subject was issued.[742]

Several reasons have been given for the increasing interest in "Literature and Medicine." Most can be related to the wider human and humane outlook that resulted with the merging of C. P. Snow's two cultures—literature and science.[831] Both cultures become enriched, that of the nonscientist by an appreciation of the natural wonder of the world, and that of the scientist through a wider world view. Conan Doyle was well suited to combine these two cultures. His medical background was extensive, including both education and practice, and he wrote his first two stories at the ages of six and ten.

In order to determine how Conan Doyle's fiction fits into the category of "Literature and Medicine" we must determine the meaning of this phrase, which is not specifically defined in most related books. Literature containing medical content is an obvious meaning, but the word literature in itself is open to several interpretations and dictionary definitions. Included are all writings of a people, era, or activity (i.e., medical literature); elegant and refined artistic writings (Bellé Lettres); and writings of universal interest, excluding scientific and technical works.[847] It is the latter definition that most closely defines the meaning of "literature" in this context. Included are works that are nonfictional (history, biography, autobiography, philosophy) and fictional (novels, short stories, plays, poetry).

The 1982 bibliography on *Literature and Medicine*[877] does not distinguish between writings that have a primary medical orientation, such as Shaw's *The Doctor's Dilemma*,[810] and those that contain an occasional reference, such as Shakespeare's works. For discussion and assessment of medicine in Conan Doyle's fiction it is useful to separate these two categories. Those with a major medical orientation can be labeled "Medical Fiction" and the others, "Medical References in Fiction."

Conan Doyle's medical fiction has received some recognition by inclusion of several items in the two anthologies already mentioned. His medical fiction, however, was much more extensive. Included in the appendices is a list of 18 short stories, two novels, three chapters of another novel, and two poems. To place this in perspective, he published close to 150 short stories and approximately 20 novels, excluding writings on Sherlock Holmes and Brigadier Gerard. Many of these include references to medical matters, but do not constitute medical fiction by our definition. The term "medical fiction" as used herein is applied to a writing that has a physician or patient as one of the major characters, with the plot line being dependent upon that fact, or to a writing that has a medically-related condition as a major theme.

CONAN DOYLE AS LITTÉRATEUR

There appears to be a fascination with medical graduates who become successful literary figures.[485] Most frequently cited are Somerset Maugham, John Keats, Anton Chekhov[82] and, more recently, William Carlos Williams.[148] Both Somerset Maugham and John Keats graduated from medical school in London, the latter in 1816 and the former in 1897. Neither of these two developed medical careers. Both Chekhov,[160] who graduated from the Moscow Medical School in 1884, and Williams,[924] who graduated from the University of Pennsylvania Medical School in 1907, combined medical practice and literature throughout most of their lives. Not to be overlooked is Oliver Wendell Holmes who was one of Conan Doyle's idols.[872]

Conan Doyle differed from all of these literary physicians, in that, although he practiced medicine, he ended this career ten years after graduation for a primarily literary career. Like Keats[564] he published poetry, although of a much lesser quality. Like Williams he also wrote novels,[210] and like Maugham, plays. But unlike all of these men, Conan Doyle has not been considered as a literary figure in the sense of being characterized by "beauty of expression and form and by universality of intellectual and emotional appeal."[847] Instead, he is generally regarded as a good teller of tales. Thus, "Conan Doyle is eminently readable. He has no tricks of style and writes in lucid straight-forward English. He wrote quickly, and his work sometimes suffered from the speed."[629]

For several reasons Conan Doyle is not included in the ranks of the literary giants. His literary novels, such as *The White*

Company,[265] *Sir Nigel*,[329] and *Micah Clarke*,[248] are vitually unknown, being neglected in the veneration of his Sherlockian detective stories. Some of his other novels are essentially adventure stories with emphasis on action rather than introspection, as for example, *The Lost World*[357] and *The Tragedy of the Korosko*.[305] Finally, some of his novels are rather weak in respect to both plot and concept, such as *The Doings of Raffles Haw*,[262] *The Land of Mist*,[376] and *A Duet*.[310] But, so were some works of those acknowledged as literary greats, such as the later writings of Joseph Conrad.[496]

Another difference between physician writers is the amount of medical material in their literary works.[657] With Keats it is minimal, and with Maugham, Chekhov,[747] and Williams somewhat more. Conan Doyle, however, not only had more individual works that were of basic medical orientation but also had more references included in his other works. Even more so, his writings are among the best examples of permeation of fiction by medical experience, as expressed by Pellegrino.[716]

> *More usually, physicians who become serious writers abandon the clinic wholly or visit it only intermittently. But they retain the clinician's way of looking. Their writing carries that special imprint peculiar to those who have felt, smelled and dwelled among fevers, madness, blood and abscesses. We think of Rabelais, Crabbe, Smollett, Chekhov, Maugham, Keats, Celine and Walker Percy who completed their medical training. . . .*

Whether or not Conan Doyle belongs in such an august group of medical writers is a moot point. We could well ask, as has Rousseau "What kind of literature results when a practicing physician such as Andre Soubiran writes a prolific number of medical novels? How would (they) have been different if Soubiran had not been a physician?"[789] A review and analysis of Conan Doyle's medical fiction can assist in determining the extent to which his medical experience influenced his fiction.

THE MEDICAL SHORT STORIES

Conan Doyle wrote 18 short stories which fall under our definition of medical fiction, that is, having a plot or theme that is primarily medical. Five were written while he was a practicing physician and 13 within the next three years. In 1894, he published a collection of 15 of these medical stories under the title *Round the Red Lamp*,[281] the red lamp being a Victorian symbol of a physician's house.

Before discussing these stories, it is useful to consider Conan Doyle's orientation to medical fiction. He has provided us with such comments in the preface to this collection.

> *[Being an extract from a long and animated correspondence with a friend in America]*
>
> *I quite recognize the force of your objection that an invalid or a woman in weak health would get no good from stories which attempt to treat some features of medical life with a certain amount of realism. If you deal with this life at all, however, and if you are anxious to make your doctors something more than marionettes, it is quite essential that you should paint the darker side, since it is that which is principally presented to the surgeon or physician. He sees many beautiful things, it is true, fortitude and heroism, love and self-sacrifice; but they are all called forth (as our nobler qualities are always called forth) by bitter sorrow and trial. One cannot write of medical life and be merry over it.*
>
> *Then why write of it, you may ask? If a subject is painful, why treat it at all? I answer that it is the province of fiction to treat painful things as well as cheerful ones. The story which whiles away a weary hour fulfils an obviously good purpose, but not more so, I hold, than that which helps to emphasise the graver side of life. A tale which may startle the reader out of his usual grooves of thought, and shock him into seriousness, plays the part of the alterative and tonic in medicine, bitter to the taste, but bracing in its result. There are a few stories in this little collec-*

> *tion which might have such an effect, and I have so far shared in your feeling that I have reserved them from serial publication. In book form the reader can see that they are medical stories, and can, if she or he be so minded, avoid them.*
> *—Yours very truly,*
>
> *'A. CONAN DOYLE'*[281]

These sentiments cover a variety of rationales: the desire to present doctors as humane, to have the bitter side of life represented in fiction, and to write about the nobler qualities that are evoked by suffering. One suspects that the preface was written after the collection was ready for publication, primarily because Conan Doyle's fiction is often not related to philosophic motivation, introspection, and abstract ideation. We shall see if his medical fiction has features similar to the rest of his works—heroic action, ideals of behavior, pixyish humor, and the romance of life. His medical short stories can be discussed on the basis of major themes and also lesser references to medical items. Three are based upon the practice of medicine as such. Two describe the difficulties of starting a practice. "Crabbe's Practice"[278] is another version of the George Budd and Conan Doyle relationship. Crabbe (Budd) and Barton (Conan Doyle) both graduated from Edinburgh, the latter a year earlier. As related in *Memories and Adventures*[375] and *The Stark Munro Letters*,[293] Barton was called to visit Crabbe who was quite anxious because he failed in "making a bid for a high-class practice at once." Conan Doyle's solution was to have Barton fall into the water, drown, and be resuscitated from death by Crabbe with an electric battery, much to the amazement of selected influential citizens. Crabbe then became a great success with a busy practice.

The outrageous humor implicit in such a situation was fully exploited by Conan Doyle.

> *Whether it was an accident or whether Tom's innate reckless devilry got the better of him I cannot say. He himself always swore it was an accident, but at any rate he sent the strongest current of a most powerful battery rattling and crashing through my system. I gave one ear-splitting yell and landed with a single*

bound into the middle of the room. I was charged with electricity like a Leyden jar. My hair bristled with it. . . . Never was there such a stampede! The inspector of police and the correspondent of the Chronicle sprang down the staircase, followed by the twelve respectable citizens. The landlady crawled under the bed.[278]

"Crabbe's Practice" does have a rather cavalier approach to the serious business of establishing a practice; but surely Conan Doyle's own experience entitles him to some levity.

In "A False Start"[285] Conan Doyle included humorous episodes more reminiscent of his own early days of practice in Southsea. Doctor Horace Wilkinson had recently set up practice in Sutton, but had no patients as yet and his scanty resources were running somewhat low. Wilkinson was depicted as "a very reliable plodder as a physician, and nothing more"—compatible with Conan Doyle's modest view of his own medical capabilities.

Some of Conan Doyle's humor was based upon the time-honored ploy of mistaken identity. The doctor attempted to diagnose the medical problem of a burly man who appeared at the door in the manner of some of his old professors who "would have electrified the patient by describing his own symptoms before he had said a word about them." The ruddy face suggested alcoholism, and the doctor advised no beer, but the stranger said he was already an abstainer. He coughed and Wilkinson considered it to be bronchial, but he said it came from chewing tobacco. Finally, the stranger said he was not a patient but an inspector from the Gas Company, collecting money owed on the meter. This episode is also included in *The Stark Munro Letters*,[293d] published one year later. It is surely a satire of the methods of both his own teacher, Doctor Joseph Bell, and his creation, Sherlock Holmes.

Another instance of mistaken identity is that of the gypsy, whom Wilkinson began to treat for a bruised eye until she told him that she had come to show her baby with measles. This is likely a true episode as it was related in both Conan Doyle's autobiography[375m] and his semifictional work—*The Stark Munro Letters*.[293] Conan Doyle was not adverse to poking fun at himself or his experiences. "Dr. Horace Wilkinson was beginning to be a little doubtful as to the advantages of quick diagnosis. It is an excellent thing to be able to surprise a patient, but hitherto it was always the patient who had surprised him."[285]

A third story with medical practice as its theme is "Behind The Times."[282] In this case, the narrator, a relatively new medical graduate, has returned to his home town where still in practice is Doctor James Winter who had delivered him and treated him for serious illnesses. Conan Doyle used this situation to compare the new with the old in medical education and science.

Doctor Winter had been educated by being apprenticed to a surgeon, learned anatomy on bodies stolen from graves, learned vaccination, and would have practiced bleeding freely "but for public opinion." Similarly Conan Doyle had been an apprentice, but as a student, to Doctor Joseph Bell,[611] was educated in a school with the most famous of criminal anatomical episodes,[743] and supported vaccination as a practitioner.[243] There is no evidence that he practiced bleeding. Blood letting finally went out of vogue as a panacea for most ailments about the middle of the 19th century, over 2,000 years after its introduction on the basis of the humoral theory of Hippocrates.[576]

Furthermore, Doctor Winter regarded advances in medical science "as a huge and ludricous experiment," much as Conan Doyle claimed he himself did while in practice.[375q] Winter saved the narrator's reputation by finding the stone at bladder surgery when he himself could not. Nevertheless, he and another young practitioner, Doctor Patterson, were concerned about Winter's neglect of modern instruments and treatment.[282]

> *It is all very well for the poorer people. . .but after all the educated classes have a right to expect that their medical man will know the difference between a mitral murmur and a bronchitic rale. It's the judicial frame of mind, not the sympathetic, which is the essential one.*

When the narrator became sick with "a splitting headache and pains in every joint" during an influenza epidemic, he of course, considered calling Doctor Patterson.

> *. . .but somehow the idea of him had suddenly become repugnant to me. I thought of his cold, critical attitude, of his endless questions, of his texts and his tappings. I wanted something more soothing—something more genial.*

Such a viewpoint is now heard frequently in respect to the overly scientific physician and his technology. According to an analysis of the doctor and patient relationship in 1972:

> *In modern medical practice, which is now focused predominantly on technical knowledge, the physician may be engrossed in technical concerns and arcane terminology that mystify the patient. Moreover, many physicians no longer attach high importance to personal rapport with the patient; to some the 'bedside manner' seems a concession to salesmanship not befitting a medical scientist.*[590]

A doctor as a patient is, however, more a patient than a doctor. Thus, the narrator sent his housekeeper, Mrs. Hudson, to get not Doctor Patterson but Doctor Winter! She returned quickly. "Dr. Winter will come round in an hour or so, sir; but he has just been called in to attend Dr. Patterson." Conan Doyle was to reiterate his concern for the sympathetic and caring orientation of physicians 16 years later in his talk "The Romance of Medicine."[349] Today, he would be considered as an enlightened medical man.

Two of Conan Doyle's stories are centered on activities of medical students. The weakest one is "Lot 249,"[226] concerning three students living in rooms at an old College at Oxford. They were taking anatomy at the time. One of them, Edward Bellingham, was experimenting with an unwrapped mummy in his room. A series of attacks occurred on individuals against whom Bellingham had a grudge. The implication is that the culprit is his mummy; and another student forced him to cut up and burn it. The story does not succeed as literature nor as science fiction nor even as horror fiction.

More successful is"His First Operation,"[283] much of which was directly related to Conan Doyle's days as a medical student. A first year man was being taken by a third year man to view his first operation. On the way they stopped at Rutherford's Bar, which is still in existence in Edinburgh. It is located at No. 3 Drummond Street, around the corner from the Old University. According to Edwards it was a favorite of Conan Doyle and Stevenson.[773]

The students then entered the infirmary and passed through a corridor in which patients were waiting. Only a medical author would list their conditions, which included a carbuncle, pemphigus, popliteal aneurysm, Colle's fracture, spina bifida, tropical abscess, and elephantiasis. Such a catalogue of diseases does not further the story line, but does contribute to realism.

On reaching the operating room the tiers of benches were crowded with both students and physicians. Several of the latter characters were based upon physicians in Edinburgh during Conan Doyle's tenure there. "Anthony Browne, who took a larynx out successfully last winter" was undoubtedly P.H. Watson, to whom Doctor Bell attributed the first such operation.[56] The operating surgeon was Archer "one of the carbolic acid men," who may well have been Joseph Lister, the Edinburgh surgeon who prevented infection in the operating room by use of a carbolic acid spray to kill germs.

Archer's opponent in the story is Hayes, "the leader of the cleanliness-and-cold-water school, and they all hate each other like poison." He probably represents the Edinburgh obstetrician, James Simpson[405] who favored a more hygienic approach. He may well have made a satirical remark similar to that of Doctor Winter in "Behind The Times":[282] "Shut the door or the germs will be getting in." The difference in opinion was not related to acceptance of the germ theory of disease, but to the methodology of control of germs in the operating room.[N55]

Conan Doyle's description of the patient for surgery indicates a familiarity with the details of pathology. It was a woman with a "Cancer of the parotid [gland]. It's the devil of a case; extends right away back behind the carotids [artery]." It was "originally cartilaginous but now [was] assuming malignant characteristics." It is evident that he was well taught and had an excellent memory.

"His First Operation"[283] ends with the first year man fainting while chloroform was being given to the patient. On awakening he found that the operation had not been performed because the patient could not tolerate the chloroform. Such an unexpected and final turn of events is reminiscent of O'Henry's short stories, as is also the ending of "Behind the Times."[282]

The fainting of a medical student while watching an operation is not an unheard of event. It is similar to Charles Darwin's experience during his two years at the University of Edinburgh Medical School (1825-1827).[184] He became deeply disturbed by "two very bad operations, one on a child, but I rushed away before they were completed. Nor did I ever attend again." Such a universal theme and the realism make "His First Operation" one of Conan Doyle's most successful medical stories.

More universal themes are found in two short stories in which physicians describe various patients they have seen and their relationships with them. "A Medical Document"[288] begins with the reason why some physicians become emotionally unresponsive or disinterested in the dramatic events they encounter. "A life spent in watching over death beds. . .takes something from a man's sense of proportion, as constant strong waters might corrupt his palate. The over stimulated nerves cease to respond."

Conan Doyle provided another reason for an apparently unsympathetic doctor.

> *'I shall never go to that doctor again,' says she afterwards. 'His manner is so stiff and unsympathetic.' Unsympathetic! Why, the poor lad was struck dumb and paralyzed. I have known general practitioners who were so shy that they could not bring themselves to ask the way in the street. Fancy what sensitive men like that must endure before they get broken in to medical practice.*

Here he is more oriented to the problems of physicians, unlike in his address "The Romance of Medicine,"[349] 16 years later, in which his interest lay with the patient. But, even in 1894 Conan Doyle did have such an awareness of the importance of the doctor and patient relationship. For example, Doctor Winter who was "Behind the Times"[282] had "the healing touch—that magnetic thing which defies explanations or analysis. . . His mere presence leaves the patient with more hopefulness and vitality."

The patients described in ''A Medical Document''[288] by three physicians are those whose plight engenders emotional reactions. There was the 16-year-old girl, hideously contorted and wicked appearing, whose mother prayed that God would take her. This pathetic creature was an actual 19-year-old patient of Conan Doyle's, being described also in his autobiography.[375m] The cause of the deformities may have been decreased oxygen to the brain during birth.

Another medical episode related in this story was taken directly from Conan Doyle's sea voyage in 1892 to West Africa.[385k]

> *It's no joke when the doctor of one of these isolated gunboats himself falls ill. . . . You might think it easy for him to prescribe for himself, but this fever knocks you down like a club, and you haven't strength left to brush a mosquito off your face.*[288]

Fortunately, Conan Doyle survived to write engrossing medical tales. Also significant for Conan Doyle's practice days is the income of £2,500 per year of one of the general practitioners—eight times that of his own.

Other patients described in ''A Medical Document''[288] are pitiful. A famous beauty wore ever higher collars because of a malignant skin ulcer which was spreading up her neck. And then there was the couple in love, who could never meet, because the man had tuberculosis and could not come down to low levels, and the woman had rheumatic heart disease and could not go up to high levels. This is a rather grossly exaggerated statement as to the effect of oxygen concentration on these diseases, but it does serve Conan Doyle's romantic inclination.

The relationship between the sexes is further described in ''The Surgeon Talks.''[290] For example, the wife of a ''sporting baronet'' was told he had a peculiarly malignant case of cancer. She did not want him to be told until the next day as it would spoil his evening dinner with two old friends. The fortitude of patients is exemplified by the case of the wife who needed an amputation of the arm and shoulder for a sarcoma of the bone ''but the woman took it as bravely and brightly as could be, and she has done very well since.''

As in "A Medical Document"[288] Conan Doyle intermixed homilies of medical activities with accounts of patients.

> *Men die of diseases which they studied most. . . . It's as if the morbid condition was an evil creature which, when it found itself closely hunted, flew at the throat of its pursuer. If you worry the microbes too much they may worry you.*

Evident in this quote is the very effective use of similies which contribute to the vividness of his fiction.

A medical aphorism can be found in the description of a surgeon's first patient, a hysterical elderly woman who wanted her dog put to death. He decried that the love and affection she should have given her family was squandered on an uncouth little animal, and that her payment for his services was only four and sixpence.[288]

> *The whole incident struck me as so whimsical that I laughed until I was tired. You'll find that there's so much tragedy in a doctor's life, my boy, that he would not be able to stand it if it were not for the strain of comedy which comes every now and then to leaven it.*

Worth quoting at length is what appears to be Conan Doyle's concept of a physician.[288]

> *And a doctor has very much to be thankful for also. . . . It is such a pleasure to do a little good that a man should pay for the privilege instead of being paid for it. Still, of course, he has his home to keep up and his wife and children to support. But his patients are his friends—or they should be so. He goes from house to house, and the step and his voice are loved and welcomed in each. . . . It is a noble, generous, kindly profession.*

This is indeed an ideal, if not overly romanticized, view of the physician. One is reminded of romantic tales of the ideals of knighthood.

Several of the items of medical fiction are essentially love stories in which physicians are involved. In "The Doctors of Hoyland,"[274] both are doctors. Doçtor James Ripley is a young, studious, and successful practitioner in Hoyland who had inherited his father's practice, thus avoiding the tribulations of Conan Doyle who started on his own. When a new medical office opened nearby, Ripley called to pay his respects on the doctor, whom he discovered, much to his amazement, was a female named Verrinder Smith.

> *He had never seen a woman doctor before, and his whole conservative soul rose up in revolt at the idea. He could not recall any Biblical injunction that the man should remain ever the doctor and the woman the nurse, and yet he felt as if a blasphemy had been committed.*

To make matters worse Smith had studied with distinction at Edinburgh, Paris, Berlin, and Vienna, and had received a gold medal and the Lee Hopkins scholarship for original research. Furthermore, she pointed out that the very basis of his paper in the *Lancet* on locomotor ataxia had been repudiated. Doctor Smith proved to be as successful in practice, attracting many of Ripley's patients because of successful cures of such diseases as skin ulcers, birthmarks, clubfoot, and even of Ripley's own fractured leg.

Ripley fell in love with Smith, but to no avail because she was devoting her life entirely to science. "I came down here while waiting for an opening in the Paris Physiological Laboratory. I have just heard that there is a vacancy for me there." And so Hoyland again had only one doctor, but one who "had aged many years in a few months," and "a weary sadness lurked always in the depths of his blue eyes."

This is indeed a positive picture of the female physician, even for the late Victorian era. Interestingly, Conan Doyle had a reputation for being very traditional in respect to the woman's role in society. This was partly deserved because of his strong opposition to the vote for women, accentuated by the suffrage movement in the first two decades of the 20th century.[740] His chivalrous orientation to women was greatly offended by their militant, unwomanly conduct.[862c] In "His Last Bow"[365] Conan Doyle referred to "window-breaking furies," undoubtedly the more violent of the suffragettes. As a public figure and as an ardent advocate for his beliefs, Conan Doyle's statements drew considerable attention. The headline of an interview with him in the *New York American* of May 28, 1914, proclaimed "Conan Doyle Says: 'Let the Militants Die of Starvation'. He Predicts Lynching if Depredations Continue. . . ."[155] He also suggested that, to increase the public's opposition to the suffragettes, their "window smashing, house burning and picture mutilating" should be supported.

Conan Doyle did support women's rights in another contentious arena—divorce laws. A husband could get a divorce solely on the grounds of unfaithfulness of his wife, but a woman needed additional grounds, such as desertion and brutality. In his autobiography Conan Doyle stated that there was no decrease in morality in countries with more liberal divorce laws.[375x] He deplored that "unions which are obviously disgusting and degrading are maintained in this country." Conan Doyle's feelings on the subject were so strong that he served for ten years as president of the Divorce Law Reform Union. As usual in one of his campaigns, he wrote a pamphlet on "Divorce Law Reform."[344] He considered the opposition of the organized church responsible for lack of reform. Evidently Conan Doyle found no conflict of interests in the fact that reform of divorce laws was a substantial plank in the British suffrage movement.[515] His sense of righteous indignation was aroused more by the image of an ill-used woman than by a mass of militant women.[N56]

No extant evidence indicates that Conan Doyle took a position on female doctors. The year of publication of "The Doctors of Hoyland"[274] (1894) was in the latter part of an era in which women were struggling to be accepted in medical schools. At the University of Edinburgh a group of five women were admitted to study medicine in 1869 after considerable opposition by faculty and subsequent riots by male students.[515] Male students at the University College Medical School in London petitioned for discontinuance of admission of women as late as 1920.[619] This was 36 years after Conan Doyle's benevolent depiction of the skillful but feminine Doctor Smith.[N57]

In spite of Conan Doyle's frequently used ability at humorous but incisive satire, he did not level it at female students. To others of his era, however, they became the butt of many a deprecatory remark.[650] The following quotation is an especially sexist example written in 1888. "A man if he has nothing the matter with him, might call in a female doctor; but if he was sick as a horse, the last thing he would want around him would be a female doctor. And why? Because when a man has a female fumbling around him he wants to feel well."[596] It is to Conan Doyle's credit that he did not descend to such levels in any of his campaigns.

A more humorous approach to relationships between the sexes is the theme of "A Physiologist's Wife."[256] Doctor Ainslie Grey was the epitomy of the dedicated professor, devoted to his physiologic research and teaching. He and his sister Ada "lived in a serene and rarefied atmosphere of scientific calm, high above the petty emotions which affect humbler minds." His explanation for even his own emotions was in terms of physiologic aberrations. "I slept badly. Some little cerebral congestion, no doubt due to overstimulation of the centres of thought."

The story is replete with biting satire of the purely scientific mind. "'You believe in nothing.' 'On the contrary, my dear Ada, I believe in the differentiation of protoplasm.'" Or further "Protoplasm may prove to be the physical basis of love as well as life." Grey explained sentiment as "vague hereditary tendencies stirred into life by the stimulation of the nasal and auditory nerves." Thus we see Conan Doyle satirizing pure science by writing sans human emotion.

As happens to most good men, even scientists, they fall in love and propose marriage, as did Doctor Grey to Mrs. O'James. In feeling emotion on her acceptance, he explained it as "some little congestion of the pons and medulla due to the chlorophyll in rich greens." His explanation of love to his betrothed is purely scientific and yet cosmic.[256]

When the atom of hydrogen draws the atom of chlorine towards it to form the perfected molecule of hydrochloric acid, the force which it exerts may be intrinsically similar to that which draws me to you.

Even the rational scientist may be misled by his emotions. Doctor Grey married Mrs. O'James who turned out to be the wife of Doctor O'Brien whom she had deserted years before. She then departed with her first husband—with Grey's blessing. Grey reacted with no evident emotion—"I have my work on Vallisneria"—but he soon died of a broken heart.

"A Physiologist's Wife"[256] was published in 1890, when Conan Doyle was still practicing in Southsea. It contains more references to his own activities than any other of his short stories. The location is Birchespool, a name which he also used for Portsmouth in *The Stark Munro Letters*.[293] Grey had studied in Edinburgh and Vienna, as had Conan Doyle. He won a fellowship for his pamphlet on nerve roots; Conan Doyle was awarded an M.D. for his thesis on tabes dorsalis which also affects nerve roots.[240] Frequent allusions were made to bacteria, which Conan Doyle stressed in his article on "Life and Death in the Blood"[231] of 1883.

Grey draws several conclusions about the mental status of women. "The great advance of the human race, . . . was when, by the development of their left frontal convolutions, they attained the power of speech. The second advance was when they learned to control that power. Woman has not yet attained the second stage." Even more negative is the statement that women are less intelligent than men as their cerebrum is of less weight. The direct relationship between brain size and intellect was a common belief in the 19th century and beyond.[207] Conan Doyle's only nonfiction publication in this area related to the geographic distribution of intellect.[246,N58]

The deprecatory remarks about women in "A Physiologist's Wife"[256] may be more a satire on the male scientist than on females, especially in light of the author's glowing characterization of Doctor Smith, of "The Doctors of Hoyland."[274] It is reasonable to assume, however, that so complex an individual as Conan Doyle had mixed opinions on women, as evidenced by his views on chivalry, divorce, and suffragettes.

Another short story, "Sweethearts,"[279] has a considerably greater sentimental orientation to romance. This time the physician plays the role of a concerned observer, one who could escape from the pressures of practice only in the early hours of the morning.

> *It is hard for the general practitioner who sits among his patients both morning and evening, and sees them in their homes between, to steal time for one little daily breath of cleanly air. . . .*
>
> *But it was by the sea that I lived . . . And who cares for the town when one can sit on the beach at the headland, and look out over the huge, blue bay, and the yellow scimitar that curves before it.*

Conan Doyle was undoubtedly expressing some nostalgia for the days of his practice in Southsea on the channel. The imagery is particularly striking; for example, the big ships that "went past, far out, a little hillock of white and no hull, with topsails curved like a bodice. . . ."

One morning the doctor, enjoying the sea, noticed an old man. "As he approached, my eyes caught Nature's danger signal, that faint bluish tinge in nose and lip which tells of a labouring heart." This is a rather striking description of cyanosis due to early heart failure. It, in contrast to the serenity of the sea, does much to set the mood of incongruity and anticipation.

The old man appeared to be very depressed, but when seen four days later, was quite bright and merry. On being asked by the narrator why the change, he explained that his wife was returning from Scotland after being away for four days. He described her as still young and very beautiful. "She's one of those women, you know, who have youth in their hearts, so it can never be very far from their faces." But when she arrived "she was thick and shapeless, with a ruddy, full-blown face." But, how she looked to his eyes!

"Sweethearts"[279] might well have been only another slight tale of the close attachment of an elderly couple. But, it is the elements drawn from the actual experience and knowledge of a practitioner, along with skills in imagery, that raises this story above the ordinary. It is also an example of the influence of loss and pain on physical well being. One can well imagine Conan Doyle, after such an episode, returning to his practice "braced afresh to the reek of a sick-room, and the dead, drab weariness of practice."

Of less intrinsic quality is another story of romance, "A Question of Diplomacy."[287] It concerns the daughter of a foreign minister who could not attend to affairs because of gout—"a little piece of inflamed gristle. . . a huge undeniable, intrusive, red-hot toe."—resulting in a brain clouded by gout or colchicum.[N59] Colchicum is a plant, the active principle of which is colchicine, used in the treatment of gout. Conan Doyle had shown an interest in gout in a letter to the editor of the *Lancet*[238] ten years before this story. In short, the daughter, in this story, Ida, was in love with Arthur, a poor Lord with no prospects. He was given a post in Tangier which would separate the two. When "our medical autocrat," Sir William, physician and medical baronet, visited the prime minister, he examined Ida for pain in her side. He found some dullness and crepitations in the lung (possibly tuberculosis) and recommended a dry climate such as Tangier. And so the lovers were reunited.

"A Question of Diplomacy"[287] lacks the imagery found in "Sweethearts," and has a more sardonic outlook on love. Again it was impossible to separate the doctor from the author. For example, the medical baronet was asked if he had read Hahnemann, the founder of homeopathy.[N60]

Another story related to a romantic escapade, "The Case of Lady Sannox," is in a macabre vein.[272] The physician is an integral part of the plot—Douglas Stone "the celebrated operating surgeon, the man of steel nerves," had "the third largest [income] of all professional men in London." "Again and again his knife cut away death," but "deep in his complex nature lay a rich vein of sensualism, at the sport of which he placed all the prizes of his life." Stone's downfall was due to an affair with the notorious Lady Sannox, a former actress, whose husband plotted revenge. Disguised as his own Turkish servant he came to Stone one night because his master had fallen and cut his lip on a poisoned dagger. The wound needed excision to save him. When the surgeon arrived, the patient had already been sedated with a heavy dose of opium, and had been veiled except for the mouth. Stone quickly cut out a broad V-shaped segment of the lower lip. There was a scream, the veil was lifted, and Lady Sannox revealed. Douglas Stone went insane and Lady Sannox entered a convent.

This short story is noteworthy as an example of Conan Doyle's penchant for inappropriate surgery, either by error or by deception. Several other examples are included in his short stories. In "The Retirement of Signor Lambert,"[304] the husband whose wife was having an affair with an opera singer, visited a famous throat surgeon of Cavendish Square to learn the anatomy of the vocal cords. He then called on his wife's lover, overpowered him with his strength and with chloroform. Using a lamp and instruments, the husband cut the vocal cords of the opera singer, who then could no longer sing.

In the medical story, "The Surgeon Talks,"[290] a patient with Bell's palsy was being prepared for an ear removal when he became violent while being given chloroform and kicked over the candle. In the dark, he was picked up, restrained, and given chloroform, and his face was draped. After removal of the ear, it was found to be an assistant surgeon on the table "and it led to a good deal of ill-feeling." Bell's palsy is a paralysis of one side of the face caused by a lesion of the seventh cranial nerve, first demonstrated in 1829, by Charles Bell (1774–1842), a London anatomist who was educated in Edinburgh.[468e] Conan Doyle's explanation for the rather unusual method of treatment was that the surgeon "got it into his head that removal of the ear would increase the blood supply to the part." Rather fanciful, but necessary to justify this major plot element.

Another "ear" episode occurs in Conan Doyle's humorous account of "How the Brigadier Lost His Ear."[323] During the French occupation of Venice, Brigadier Etienne Gerard lost the tip of his right ear when he took the place of a senora in a dark cell where she was imprisoned for collaborating with the enemy. The gallant Gerard, thus, had part of his ear excised, a punishment that was meant for the senora. The story is a mixture of humor, chivalry, and pathos, as are many of the Gerard stories.

Less humorous, but with more sensitiveness, was Conan Doyle's handling of aging in "A Straggler of '15."[263] Old Daddy Brewster about 90 years old, had been a corporal, was a veteran of Waterloo, and had a medal, a pension, and a housekeeper, Mrs. Simpson. Well depicted are the psychologic aspects of aging, such as the distrust of the new, and the heightened reality of the past. "And that battle, it might have been yesterday. I've got the smell of the burned powder in my nose yet." The battle of Waterloo took place on June 18, 1815, three miles south of Waterloo which is a village near Brussels.[915] Brewster would have been one of Wellington's 68,000 troops which decisively defeated Napoleon's 72,000 soldiers. Conan Doyle also featured the Napoleonic wars and Napoleon himself in his novel *Uncle Bernac*.[299]

Also high-lighted are the more physical ailments of the elderly.[263]

> *Come in doctor! Yes, I'm better. But there's a deal o'bubbling in my chest. It's all them toobes. If I could but cut the phlegm I'd be right.*

This suggests early heart failure with edema of the lungs, and possibly chronic bronchitis.

Of particular interest in our environment-conscious society of today is Conan Doyle's description of the location in which old Daddy Brewster lived. It was close to an arsenal, described as a manufacturing plant.[263]

> . . . *the huge smoke-spouting monster, which sucked in the manhood of the town, to belch it forth, weary and work-strained, every night.*

This is not to say that he necessarily recognized the connection between air pollution and respiratory disease, but the terse description is worthy of Dickens.

The doctor provided a diagnosis for Brewster's niece. "Ninety years ails him. His arteries are pipes of lime. His heart is shrunken and flabby. The man is worn out." In our modern era we cannot provide any better summation of these effects of old age—arteriosclerotic arteries and the senile heart.

When Brewster's condition became terminal both his body and mind were affected. "All day the man lay with only his puffing blue lips and the twitching of his scraggy neck to show that he still held the breath of life"—an effective description of cyanosis of the lips and distended, pulsating veins of the neck caused by congestive heart failure. At the same time his mind reverted in time. "The guards need powder," he cried, then collapsed. Conan Doyle's concluding comment is "that the third guards have a full muster now." "A Straggler of '15" is a sentimental appreciation of the elderly, as was his story of the aged couple in "Sweethearts."[279]

Conan Doyle's medical short stories also include one with insanity as its theme. In "The Surgeon of Gaster Fell"[255] James Upperton went to Gaster Fell in the moors to isolate himself for his studies of mystic Egyptian papyrus. The drama is set by his encounters with Eva Cameron "she with dark, dreamy eyes looking sadly out over the somber fells." And then the mystery is engaged by Eva's declaration that "I will never marry . . . I dare not . . . The risk would be with the man who married me. . . ."

The plot thickens when Upperton observes that a large man is keeping an elderly man prisoner in a hut. He becomes even more perplexed when the "jailer" introduces himself as a surgeon and Eva's brother. The last scene is one of the elderly man opening the door of Upperton's hut, but then being chased across the fells by the surgeon.

The explanation is given in a letter to Upperton. The elderly man is the father of the surgeon and Eva. He had been "a hard-working general practitioner in Birmingham, where his name is still remembered and respected"—as was the Doctor Reginald Hoare, Conan Doyle's student perceptor. In this instance, however, Doctor Cameron had begun at the age of 50 to deteriorate mentally, attributed to overwork and a sunstroke. Fraser Brown, an alienist (psychiatrist) indicated that his insanity came in paroxysms with long periods of sanity. His children kept him in seclusion in an isolated area to keep him out of an asylum.

Such paroxysmal episodes of insanity may be caused by porphyria, a defect of metabolism of the hemoglobin in red blood cells.[654] The result is an excess of porphyria compounds in the blood and urine with untoward effects on various organs, and in some types on mental status.

Supporting such a diagnosis is the reference to exacerbations by sunlight, a characteristic of porphyria. It also suggests the reason why Eva Cameron could not marry, porphyria being inherited. Conan Doyle could not have had porphyria as such in mind as this metabolic defect was not delineated in the 19th century. He could, however, have observed some individuals with the characteristic episodic pattern of insanity.[N61]

Conan Doyle's understanding of psychiatry was excellent for his time, the early Freudian era.[12] He appreciated the relationship between a disease of the body and "a disease of the soul."[288]

> *Is it not a shocking thing—a thing to drive a reasoning man into absolute Materialism—to think that you may have a fine, noble fellow with every divine instinct and that some little vascular change, the dropping, we will say, of a minute spicule of bone from the inner table of his skull on to the surface of his brain may have the effect of changing him to a filthy and pitable creature with every low and debasing tendency? What satire an asylum is upon the majesty of man, and no less upon the ethereal nature of the soul.*

Here, Conan Doyle exhibits his ability to range from medicine to philosophy within the same context.

Conan Doyle also had an appreciation of the more personal aspects of the psychiatric specialist.[288]

> *'Don't you find it a very wearing branch of the profession?' asks Foster after a pause. 'My dear fellow, it was the fear of it that drove me into lunacy work.'*

Apparently the maxim that psychiatrists are the ones most in need of their own services originated in the early days of the development of this specialty.

Another medical specialty featured in Conan Doyle's medical stories was that of obstetrics. In "The Curse of Eve"[286] Robert Johnson, a commonplace man, a gentleman's outfitter, was characterized as one for whom "it seemed impossible that any of the mighty, primitive passions of mankind could ever reach him." Yet, Conan Doyle elevated both Johnson and this tale to a universal theme.

> *Yet birth, and lust, and illness, and death are changeless things, and when one of these harsh facts springs out upon a man at some sudden turn of the path of life, it dashes off for the moment his mask of civilisation and gives a glimpse of the stranger and stronger face below.*

Johnson's one positive trait was his affection for his wife Lucy, pregnant for the first time. With the onset of labor he calmly went to fetch Doctor Miles of Bridford Place. The doctor was out making house calls. As Johnson tried to reach him, just missing him at every place, his prim and staid nature turned to one of panic. It became one of frantic horror when he finally caught up with the doctor. "My dear sir, there can be no very pressing hurry in a first case . . . . You can't get an engine to go without coals, Mr. Johnson, and I have had nothing but a light lunch." Conan Doyle's comment shows little empathy with the patient's spouse.

> *He [Johnson] had not imagination enough to realize that the experience which seemed so appallingly important to him, was the merest everyday matter of business to the medical man who could not have lived for a year had he not, amid the rush of work, remembered what was due to his own health.*

This is readily recognizable as the sentiments of one who had been exposed to the harassments of medical practice, as had Conan Doyle.

Doctor Miles finally arrived. To his credit he tried to soothe Johnson by chatting about other matters, such as the watchmaker down the street whom he saw "through the typhoid when they took up the drains in Prince Street."[N62] Then complications developed. In Johnson's "dim brain he was asking himself questions which had never intruded themselves before. Where was the justice of it? . . . Why was nature so cruel? He was frightened at his own thoughts. . . ."

Miles finally indicated that it was "a nasty case" and sent Johnson to obtain a bottle of A.C.E. (one part alcohol, 2 parts chloroform, 3 parts ether) as straight chloroform was too strong for her heart. Also needed was a consultant, Doctor Pritchard, to whose house the distraught husband sped frantically. Here the response was rather abrupt. "My consultation fee is three guineas, payable at the time." Again Conan Doyle shows his understanding of the strains of medical life.[286]

> *The consultant was a man who had been hardened by a life of ceaseless labor, and who had been driven, as so many others have been, by the needs of his own increasing family to set the commercial before the philanthropic side of his profession. Yet beneath his rough crust he was a man with a kindly heart.*

Johnson spent agonizing hours until the doctors came downstairs and reported that his newborn son and the mother were both well. Conan Doyle used this opportunity for some more philosophy. "He felt that he was a stronger and a deeper man. Perhaps all this suffering had an object then. . . . If there had been a harrowing, there had been a planting too." The theme of maturing through tribulations is a common one. In Conan Doyle's own life stressful events may have played a similar role.[N63]

In summary, "The Curse of Eve" has two universal themes—the enobling nature of suffering, and the hardening effect of a demanding profession. A third such seminal topic related to obstetrics is found in "A Medical Document."[288] A woman insisted that her husband, a policeman, be handcuffed to her during her entire labor, which lasted eight hours. With the twisting during pain the "iron had fairly eaten into the bone of the man's arm." She showed no remorse. "He's got to take his share as well as me. Turn and turn." There was no acceptance here of the eternal consequences of Eve's biblical downfall; but a hostility to the fact that men are spared the pain resulting from their own pleasurable actions.

A fourth theme is found in "The Third Generation"[284]—the retribution for the sins of one generation falling upon another one. Doctor Horace Selby lived in Scudamore Lane, London, a secluded street. His patients did not consider seclusion a disadvantage because of his specialty, presumably syphilology. Although Conan Doyle does not use the word syphilis, as befits Victorian fiction, the allusions are clear.

Sir Francis Norton called on Doctor Selby because of the sudden development of a serpiginous ulcer of the skin. The specialist also indicated an abnormality of his teeth and interstitial keratitis (clouding of the cornea).[N64] The diagnosis given was a strumous diathesis (a widespread condition of many tissues). A diagnosis of syphilis is certainly indicated by the signs and symptoms described. Such findings are characteristic of congenital syphilis, that is, infection of the fetus in the uterus with spirochetes which cross the placenta from the infected mother. Although diseased at birth, the newborn infant may appear healthy and the lesions may not become manifest until later in life,[780a] as in the cases of Sir Francis and his father.

Conan Doyle again exhibits an intimate knowledge of the reactions of a medical practitioner. As Selby examined Sir Francis' eyes:

> *. . . a glow of pleasure came over his large, expressive face, a flush of such enthusiasm as the botanist feels when he packs a rare plant in his tin knapsack, or the astronomer when the long-sought comet first swims into the field of his telescope. . . . He had so forgotten the patient in his symptom that he had assumed an almost congratulatory air towards its possessor.*

Only the physician can appreciate the thrill of seeing an unusual but characteristic disease manifestation; but only the patient can feel the implicit callousness of such a reaction.

Sir Francis indicated that his father also had similar problems, but strongly denied any culpable behavior on the part of either.

The doctor agreed that his disease was based on "a constitutional and hereditary trait," initiated by his grandfather.[N65]

> *. . . a notorious buck of the thirties, who had gambled and duelled and steeped himself in drink and debauchery until even the vile set with whom he had consorted had shrunk away from him in horror. . . .*

This strong moralistic statement is reminiscent of the three letters to the editor written by Conan Doyle protesting the lack of control of prostitutes who spread this vile disease.[227,363,364]

Like Johnson in "The Curse of Eve," Sir Francis' reaction was one of anguished protest.

> *Haven't I a right to ask why? Did I do it? Was it my fault? Could I help being born? And look at me now, blighted and blasted, just as life was at its sweetest! Talk about the sins of the father! How about the sins of the Creator!*[N66]

His suffering was not to ennoble him as it did Johnson. His plight was made worse by the obvious need to cancel his wedding which was to take place within a week. Doctor Selby recommended immediate immigration to Australia. Instead Sir Francis committed suicide by purposely slipping and falling under the wheels of a heavy two-horse dray.[N67]

The two remaining medical short stories of Conan Doyle are not related to medical specialties, but to two modes of therapy in vogue during the 18th and 19th centuries. Both are noteworthy for their "tongue-in-cheek" humor. The narrator of "The Los Amigos Fiasco"[289] used to be a leading practitioner of Los Amigos, a city in the west of the United States.[N68] This city had a great generating gear, and the suggestion was made that it be used for electrocutions. Its massive amount of electricity, 12,000 volts, would guarantee instantaneous death, unlike the slower deaths with the 2,000 volts used in New York. "The charge should be six times greater, and therefore, of course, it would be six times more effective. Nothing could possibly be more logical."

The first electrocution was planned for Duncan Warner—"Desperado, murderer, train robber, and road agent, he was a man beyond the pale of human pity." A committee of four was organized to oversee his execution. Included were the narrator and the old German, Peter Stulpnagel, an eccentric who worked with wires, insulators, and Leyden jars. He warned that the increased dose would not necessarily increase the effect of a small dose, but could have a different effect.

The chairman of the committee objected that "all drugs increase their effect when they increase their dose." Conan Doyle, the experienced medical man, provided Stulpnagel with a contrary example.[289]

> *Your argument is not very good, . . . When I used to take whiskey, I used to find that one glass would excite me, but that six would send me to sleep, which is just the opposite. Now, suppose that electricity were to act in the opposite way also, what then?*

They were soon to find out. Duncan's electrocution resulted in his hair turning white and falling out, and in his feeling healthier than ever. Attempts to kill him by shooting or hanging were unsuccessful. The old German's explanation was that the massive dose of electricity had so increased Duncan's vitality that he could defy death for centuries. "Electricity is life, and you have charged him with it to the utmost."

This story was first published in December, 1892. The electric chair was first used at Auburn State Prison in New York on August 6, 1890.[425] The event may have stimulated Conan Doyle's imagination. In any case the story serves as a vehicle to satirize electrotherapy. This was one of the many popular "cure-all" systems of therapy promulgated during the 18th and 19th centuries.[910]

Electrotherapy was used in the last century for many ailments and in many forms, such as "electric belts." It gained considerable acceptance among both the public and physicians, although instruments stated to be "electrical" were likely not to be such. According to a book on the subject,[577] published in 1889, "at present the medical profession as a whole believe more or less in its [electricity] therapeutic value."[N69]

Conan Doyle probably was not one of the believers in the efficacy of electrotherapy as evidenced by the orientation of "The Los Amigos Fiasco." Similarly in "Crabbe's Practice,"[278] published eight years earlier, the friend of a struggling physician pretended to drown and then be brought back to life by galvanic current from a battery, in order to gain notoriety and patients. In both stories electricity is depicted in a comic manner as enhancing life rather than death.

In another story, "The Great Keinplatz Experiment,"[239] mention is made of an experiment upon a student. "Did I not stand two hours upon a glass insulator while your poured electricity into my body? Have you not stimulated my phrenic nerves, besides ruining my digestion with a galvanic current round my stomach?" The use of medical students as subjects for human research has a long history, but usually not for anything as drastic as herein described.[52] Biological experimentation with electricity (but not human) had begun over 100 years before this story and its application for treatment of disease about the same time.[468i,N70]

"The Great Keinplatz Experiment"[239] was based on another mode of therapy that was in vogue before the 20th century—mesmerism (hypnotism). Professor Alexis von Baumgarten, Regius Professor at the University of Keinplatz, was a celebrated anatomist, profound chemist, and one of the first physiologists in Europe. He was attracted to psychology, especially relationships between mind and matter. He would often call for student volunteers to be put into a mesmeric trance for his experiments. One of these students, Fritz von Hartmann, was in love with his daughter, Elise. Her mother did not approve of Fritz because of his licentious ways. The Professor was interested in whether the human spirit could exist apart from the body. He asked Fritz to volunteer for an experiment in this area. Fritz at first refused but finally agreed if the Professor would give him his daughter's hand.

Professor von Baumgarten published an account of his theory that "the soul or mind does separate itself from the body" when the individual is mesmerized. He also described an experiment which he planned to conduct soon.[239]

> *It is my intention, therefore, shortly to mesmerise one of my pupils. I shall then mesmerise myself in a manner which has become easy to me. After that, if my theory holds good, my spirit will have no difficulty in meeting and communicating with the spirit of my pupil, both being separated from the body.*

The experiment was attended by the chief men of science of all South Germany, Professor Lurcher of London who had written a treatise on cerebral centers, a Swedenborgian minister, and several great lights of the spiritualistic body. The Professor mesmerized Fritz and then himself. They remained in a trance for an hour before awakening. Their spirits had entered each other's bodies. They did not, however, realize the interchange, which resulted in considerable consternation in their families and friends, who could not understand their unusual behavior. The Professor finally noticed his appearance was that of Fritz when he saw his face reflected in a pool. The spirits were then returned to their rightful bodies by repeating the experiment. Fritz, of course, married Elise, and they lived happily ever after.

"The Great Keinplatz Experiment"[239] could be considered as a science fiction story, or as an outrageous comic ridicule of a therapeutic fad that had been in vogue for over a century at the time the story was written in 1885. Conan Doyle himself had attended a demonstration of hypnotism in 1889, but could not be hypnotized.[555] He did link mesmerism with spiritualism in this story. "It was his [von Baumgarten's] ambition to build a new exact science which should embrace mesmerism, spiritualism, and all cognate subjects."

Conan Doyle at this time (1885) had come under the influence of General Drayson and was attending some seances in Southsea. Although it was about 30 years before he completely accepted spiritualism, von Baumgarten's views indicate that the seed was already well planted.[239]

> *In the case of a mesmerised person, the body lies in a cataleptic condition, but the spirit has left it. Perhaps you reply that the soul is there, but in a dormant condition. I answer that this is not so, otherwise how can one account for the condition of clairvoyance, which has fallen into disrepute through the knavery of certain scoundrels, but which can easily be shown to be an undoubted fact.*

The term mesmerism takes its origin from Friederich Anton Mesmer (1734–1815) of Mersburg in Southwest Germany who studied at the University of Vienna.[623] His treatment originated from a system of cures by magnetic plates, which he soon replaced with a theory of animal magnetism.[506a] This was practiced in groups of patients through touching and a seductive atmosphere, while each patient held a rod that connected to the lid of a tub filled with bottles of powdered brass and iron filings to give the impression of a gigantic galvanic cell. Mesmer combined both the effectiveness of suggestibility and the belief in electrotherapy.

Mesmer moved to Paris in 1778 and soon achieved considerable renown by winning the favor of Marie Antoinette. This was enhanced by the conversion of Charles d'Eslon, physician to the King's brother. Eventually, the flamboyant claims and the suggestive sexuality in applying hands to sensitive parts of the female anatomy led to the formation of a Commission in 1874. Its report refuted all claims of Mesmer. The effects could be produced without any of his manipulations or equipment. There were no effects if used without the patient's knowledge and therefore imagination was important. Mesmer's reputation was ruined, but his methods continued to spread throughout Europe and America.[N71]

By the time of Conan Doyle's tale, "The Great Keinplatz Experiment,"[239] mesmerism had been shorn of its trappings and reduced to hypnotism as we know it today. There is some evidence that in later years he believed in mesmerism (hypnotism) as a method of treatment[374A]. As a writer he took advantage of its elemental appeal. Conan Doyle also used the same theme, but to an even more grotesque extent, in his novel *The Parasite*.[280]

Conan Doyle's medical short stories are of interest, not only because of their individual contents but also because of certain recurring subjects. The most frequent is the anesthetic, chloroform, mentioned in no less than seven of the stories. In "Behind the Times"[282] it was used to develop the character of Doctor Winter who regarded it as a dangerous innovation. In the "Curse of Eve"[286] it heightened the tension of the situation by being too strong for a weak heart. In "His First Operation"[283] the fact that the patient did not tolerate it well provided an unexpected ending.

In two instances the use of chloroform was associated with nefarious schemes, both as punishment for infidelity. The vocal cords of Signor Lambert,[304] an opera singer, were cut, as was the lower lip of the beautiful Lady Sannox.[272] In "The Surgeon Talks"[290] the ear of the wrong individual is removed. Only in the case of Doctor Verrinder Smith's operation on a clubfoot is chloroform used in a standard manner.[274]

Without doubt Conan Doyle utilized chloroform fully and effectively in his stories for comic and shock effects. His introduction to the anesthetic was during his medical education in Edinburgh, where Doctor James Simpson was the first to use it for obstetrical anesthesia in 1847.[405] It gained notoriety in 1853 when it was used for Queen Victoria's confinement and delivery of her ninth child, Leopold.[199] Conan Doyle's high regard for chloroform is evidenced by his response in 1897 to a request by a magazine for his opinion on the most striking and beneficial achievement during Queen Victoria's reign.[296]

> *I am often sent conundrums of this sort by various magazines, and I never remember answering one before. Since you make a point of it, however, I send you my opinion for what it is worth—which is, that chloroform is the most beneficient invention of Her Majesty's reign.*

Of ten replies, Conan Doyle's is the only one which elects chloroform. Another two mention anesthetics in general along with other items.

Still another common element was reference to diseases of the nervous system. Two stories mention locomotor ataxia (tabes dorsalis), which was the subject of Conan Doyle's thesis in 1885.[240] In one,[274] Doctor Smith criticized Doctor Ripley's paper on the subject, and in the other[278] old Doctor Hobson "doesn't know the difference between locomotor ataxia and a hypodermic syringe."

Another reference relates to Doctor Walker, one of the most noted authorities in Europe on nervous diseases.[290] He not only wrote a book on the lesion in tabes dorsalis (sclerosis of the posterior columns) but also was given symptoms characteristic of this lesion by Conan Doyle

> *Walker had few reflexes, could not put his heels together with eyes shut without staggering, and suffered from lightening pains and ptosis [drooping eyelid].*

This terse description of the symptoms of tabes dorsalis was written nine years after his M.D. thesis. Again Conan Doyle recognized the cause to be syphilis. "Walker was a single man, which means that he was not restricted to a single woman."

A patient with another disease of the nervous system caused by syphilis (general paresis) is described in "A Medical Document."[288]

> *Something about the man's way of talking struck me and I watched him narrowly. His lip had a trick of quivering, his words slurred themselves together, and so did his hand-writing . . . one of his pupils was ever so larger than the other.*

These are indeed two clear and succinct clinical descriptions that are made all the more interesting because of their identification with specific patients, albeit fictional. The diagnoses are evident to a physician by the descriptions alone. Conan Doyle again exhibits his ability to write engagingly and accurately on clinical matters, as he did earlier in his M.D. thesis.

Several other matters are referred to in common. The income of a physician was mentioned in three of the tales,[272,274,286] all much in excess of his own while in practice. These stories were written several years after Conan Doyle left Southsea and may be meant as a satire on his own income from medicine. As one might expect from his efforts to become an ophthalmologist, there are some references to the eye. Doctor Ripley of Hoyland practiced iridectomies and extractions on sheep's eyes sent to him by a butcher.[274] In this instance, the comment effectively lets the reader know that the doctor has a scientific orientation and is conscientious and perhaps obsessive about his work. The presence of a large glass model of the human eye in Selby's waiting room helps to create a different effect, that of a prosperous and prominent specialist.[284]

One wonders about another characteristic of Conan Doyle's medical stories—the citations of scientific papers published by medical men. Ripley's paper on locomotor ataxia has been mentioned,[274] as has Walker's on posterior column disease.[290] By coincidence, Selby had written a monograph on the very disease about which he was consulted by Sir Francis. The somewhat bombastic Professor Grey had written a pamphlet "On the Mesoblastic Origin of Excitomotor Nerve Roots."[256] As will be seen, even Sherlock Holmes is credited with scientific publications. Conan Doyle's penchant for medical publications was first exhibited as a medical student and continued throughout his practice days at Southsea.[772] Perhaps, in both fact and fiction, this was his way of validating the scientific stature of both himself and his creations. It also contributed to the fullness of characterization of his fictional doctors.

His references to publications were not all in a serious vein. Crabbe[278] had published "one most deep and erudite paper in a medical journal, entitled 'Curious Development of a Discopherous Bone in the Stomach of a Duck' . . . and some remarks on the embryology of fishes." As Crabbe explained to Barton "Why, man, it was a domino which the old duck had managed to gorge itself with. It was a perfect godsend. Then I wrote about the embryology of fishes because I knew nothing about it and reasoned that ninety-nine men in a hundred would be in the same boat."

Further humorous mention of publications by Barton borders on the satiric.[278]

> *He [old Hobson] writes once a year to the British Medical [Journal] and asks if any correspondent can tell him how much it costs to keep a horse in the country. And then he signs himself in the Medical Register as 'The contributor of several unostentatious queries and remarks to scientific papers.'*

Such levity sprinkled with cynicism may have been evoked by Conan Doyle's exposure to the competitiveness of beginning his own medical practice. In Barton's words "A desperate disease needs desperate remedies."

The appreciation of *Round the Red Lamp*[281] by Conan Doyle's contemporaries was somewhat ambivalent. A review in *The Speaker* of December 1894[433] raised the same question that he answered in the preface to the book. "Ought the tragic realities and the painful common-places of the sick-room and death bed to be made the theme of fiction?" The review does not provide a definitive answer, but suggests that (in Conan Doyle's book) the painful effects of such gruesome subjects are not offensive because "he has a lightness of touch, and an instinctive delicacy of feeling. . . ." The review[433] of *Round the Red Lamp* provides a much more favorable assessment than that of a previous medical fictional work, *The Diary of a Late Physician*, by Samuel Warren,[914] of which it "is immensely in advance in power and realism" as well as beyond comparison in knowledge. Our review of Conan Doyle's medical short stories almost a century later agrees with such an assessment of its humanistic medical and literary worth.[N72]

OTHER MEDICAL FICTION

The short story is not the only literary form used by Conan Doyle as a vehicle for predominantly medical themes. There are also two novels, five chapters of a third novel, and two poems. The only major work among these is the novel *The Stark Munro Letters*,[293] previously referred to because of its semiautobiographical focus on his first five years of medical practice.

The *Stark Munro Letters* is in the form of 16 letters written by Doctor Munro to his friend Herbert Swanborough of Lowell, Massachussets.[N73] They are dated from March 30, 1881, to November 4, 1884, approximately the time between Conan Doyle's graduation and his establishment of a significant practice. The period of time Munro spent with Doctor Cullingworth is given as March and April, 1882, whereas Conan Doyle's sojourn with Budd was only a month later, May and June. It does include Munro's marriage to Miss La Force in May 1884. Conan Doyle married Miss Louise Hawkins in August 1885.

The first nine of the 16 chapters are devoted in large part to Munro's experiences with Cullingworth. Its basis in actual fact is evidenced by Conan Doyle's 1882 letter to Mrs. Hoare[385b] (this is only thinly disguised). In particular, the description of George Budd as Doctor Cullingworth, a man who might be in the first stage of lunacy, could be considered libelous. The novel, however, was first published in 1895, 13 years after Conan Doyle's Plymouth experience and six years after Budd's death. In the story, Plymouth becomes Bradfield. Southsea, where Conan Doyle established his own practice, is even further disguised as Birchespool, being 53 miles from Bradfield (Plymouth) and an hour inland. The actual distance by sea or rail is approximately three times the distance.

It is uncertain why Conan Doyle chose the fiction route to detail his practice experiences in Southsea. Possibly the year of first publication (1895) was too close to the time of his departure from practice in 1890. The fact that he repeats many of the incidents in his autobiography, *Memories and Adventures*,[375] 30 years later, provides evidence of the factual basis of much of *The Stark Munro Letters*.[293] Even patients are in common between these fictional and the nonfictional books—the epileptic grocer who kept him in food,[293f,375m] the gypsy with the sick baby,[293f,375d] the unfortunate (or fortunate for the doctor) accident victim,[293c,375m] and the patient whose cancer of the nose was removed.[293g,375l] The case of the gypsy is also repeated in a short story. One wonders whether these patients were recalled directly by Conan Doyle over 30 years later or if he reread *The Stark Munro Letters*[293] before writing his autobiography of 1924. He was noted for having an especially retentive memory.

Several individuals important to Conan Doyle can be readily identified in this novel—as already described, himself (Doctor Munro), his colleague (Doctor Cullingworth), and his wife.[293h] In addition, Munro's younger son Paul stayed with him (Innes);[293i] a neighboring doctor, Porter,[293h] sent him some patients (Pike);[843] and he corresponded with his well-read mother.[293j] Munro's father, however, was a physician[293k] unlike Conan Doyle's clerk and artist father, although both were ailing for a long time.

As might be expected, Hoare, Conan Doyle's student preceptor, was not omitted—being called Doctor Horton. Munro "had the kindest of leave takings from [Dr.] Horton. If he had been my brother he could not have been more affectionate."[293l] In both instances the mentor visits his former student assistant after he had started his own practice. Another commonality is that both Munro and Conan Doyle were 25 years of age in 1884. Many other points of similarity could be made between the fictional and the nonfictional autobiographies. One Oakley Villa was in fact One Bush Villa. In both he was involved in saving a woman from a beating.[293a,375l] The hiring of and experiences with housekeepers are featured in each. Both Munro's and Conan Doyle's uncles proved to be useful references in avoiding a rental deposit, and both worked for insurance companies.[N74]

Several prominent events in the life of Stark Munro were not experienced by Conan Doyle. Munro was engaged to look after the psychotic son of Lord Saltire, a name which the author was to use again ten years later. In a Sherlock Holmes story, Lord Saltire's only son disappeared from the Priory School.[325] The most significant difference is that Doctor Munro and his wife were killed in a railroad accident just as his practice was on the verge of success. Conan Doyle, however, continued to practice at Southsea for about six years after his practice became well established.

Like Conan Doyle's medical short stories, *The Stark Munro Letters*[293] contains references to specific disease states and treatment. In common are waxy material in the liver,[293m] the gas man mistaken for a patient,[293d] a spicule of bone on the brain,[293n] mania developing after being struck down by the sun,[293p] and Cullingworth's opinion that large doses are more curative than small ones.[293q] These similarities are not unusual, given the fact that the stories and novels were written within a few years of each other. New in the novel are complications of placenta previa (which obstructs the cervical opening),[293s] rheumatic fever (in Cullingworth),[293t] and the many diseases of Captain Whitehead, Doctor Munro's friend—"mitral regurgitation [heart], cirrhosis of the liver, Bright's disease [kidney], an enlarged spleen, and incipient dropsy."[293u]

Another major feature of *The Stark Munro Letters*[293] is the amount of theological and philosophical discussion. Fifty-four of 346 pages are devoted to these topics. To Conan Doyle's credit such discussions are not uninteresting, partly because of the narrative style of letter format, and partly because of allusions to clinical medicine and basic medical sciences as supporting evidence for his views. The views of religion expressed by Conan Doyle in this novel were probably not developed to such a degree while he was in practice. They represent a transition from the rejection of his inheritance of Roman Catholicism about 1891 to his complete acceptance of spiritualism 35 years later.

Conan Doyle does not reject religion as such, but rather, its various formalized attributes. He objects to the nonprogressive nature of the dogma;[293v,293w] to "the persecutions, the torturings, the domestic hatreds, the petty spites, with *all* creeds equally blood-guilty. . .;"[293e] to the ridiculous doctrinal points which are so useless;[293x] and to the hypocrisy of the formal church which does not live by its own doctrines.

Conan Doyle, however, did reject atheism.[293e] He saw evidence of a deity in the very heavens.

> *Wisdom and power and means directed to an end run all through the scheme of Nature. What proof do we want, then, from a book? If the man who observes the myriad stars, and considers that they and their innumerable satellites move in their serene dignity through the heavens, each swinging clear of the*

> *other's orbit—if, I say, the man who see this cannot realize the Creator's attributes without the help of the book of Job, then his view of things is beyond my understanding.*

Conan Doyle's religious views were not quite as simplistic as the above may seem. Nothing is too small for the "intelligent force."[293e]

> *We see the minute proboscis of the insect carefully adjusted to fit into the calyx of the flower, the most microscopic hair and gland each with its definite purposeful function to perform. What matter whether these came by special creation or by evolution? We know as a matter of fact that they came by evolution, but that only defines the law. It does not explain it.*

His orientation to Darwin's theory of the evolution of the species was similar to his own religion—both were still developing. "Is it not glorious to think that evolution is still living and acting—that if we have an anthropoid ape as an ancestor, we may have archangels for our posterity?"[293e]This is quite compatible with his comment after a speech in 1892 that "the weakest went to the bottom, and that we are working to some glorious goal."[886] He still supported Darwinism in 1927.

Given Conan Doyle's extensive medical background it is not surprising that it permeated his religious and philosophic thoughts. For example, he saw Nature as strengthening the race through evolution, pictured as "two great invisible hands hovering over the garden of life and plucking up the weeds."[293y] The weeds included drunkards, debauchees, and people afflicted with struma, tubercle, and nervous disease. These have at one time or other been considered as attributes of morally weak people.

His concept of evil was that it only appears to be evil. Rationale for this puzzling statement was provided by clinical references to pain.[293z] Death, "as I have seen it, has not been a painful or terrible process," there being less pain, "as would have arisen from a whitlow or an abscess of the jaw." Although there is pain associated with cancer "in the greater proportion of serious maladies, there is little suffering." A vivid example was his observation of cautery with a white hot iron applied in a case of spinal disease. In spite of "the nauseating smell of burned flesh" there was no pain as the nerves were "so completely and instantaneously destroyed." Conan Doyle saw this "dulling of the nerve and the lethargy" as nature's way of preventing man's cruelty to other men. He does not discuss mental and emotional cruelty.

Conan Doyle's philosophy included views on the human body. Not surprising, he had a high respect for the human body.[293aa] He disagreed with the phrases used by divines and theologians—"our gross frames" and "our miserable mortal clay"—which he considered as blasphemy.

> *It is no compliment to the Creator to depreciate His handiwork. Whatever theory or belief we may hold about the soul, there can, I suppose, be no doubt that the body is immortal. Matter may be transformed . . . but it can never be destroyed.*

This statement was the closest Conan Doyle came to spiritualism in *The Stark Munro Letters*.[293] Conan Doyle was also concerned about the soul. The inmost essence of the man does not lie in his physical body[293n]—not "in the bony framework which is the rack over which nature hangs her veil of flesh," nor in "An arched whitish putty-like mass, some fifty odd ounces in weight, with a number of white filaments hanging down from it, looking not unlike the medusa which float in our summer seas, . . . but there—somewhere there—lurks that impalpable seed, to which the rest of our frame is but the pod." His religious philosophy may not be considered sophisticated by some, but his anatomical imagery is superb!

The novel includes other medical references. His previous bacteriology experience is evident in one of the similes.[293z]

> *They tell me that the interplanetary spaces are full of the débris of shattered asteroids; so, perhaps, even among them there are such things as disease and death. Yet just to look at them must remind a man of what a bacillus of a thing he is—the whole human race like some sprinkling of impalpable powder upon the surface of one of the most insignificant fly-wheels of a monstrous*

> *machine. But there's order in it, Bertie, there's order! And where there is order there must be mind; and where there is mind there must be sense of Justice.*

This may seem like a rather "cold," emotionless theology to some, but Conan Doyle's enthusiasm radiates from the page.

Conan Doyle ranges from the cosmic universe to the individual cell.[293aa] ". . . every tiny organic cell of which a man is composed, contains in its microcosm a complete miniature of the individual of which it forms a part." A hundred years later this could be interpreted as genes and their genetic code present in the chromosomes of each cell nucleus.[N75] Conan Doyle, however, compares this cellular propensity to the dermoid cyst which he saw in practice. It contained "some hair and a rudimentary jaw with teeth in it." He considered this cyst to be "a clumsy attempt" to reproduce an individual, induced by "some obscure nervous or vascular excitement." Such an event, then, supports the thesis that every cell in the body has the power to reproduce the whole individual. By today's knowledge, this appears as a jumbled mess of ideas relating to imperfect understanding of genetics and embryology. For Conan Doyle's era it was an astute observation.

Similar to the cell is the ovum which has "the potentiality, not only for reproducing the features of two individuals, but even their smallest tricks of habit and of thought." The two individuals may refer to the two sexes.[N76] The influence of inheritance on minor characteristics would be too deterministic even for some geneticists of today. In the Victorian era, however, all of one's traits were considered to be based on familial inheritance and the environment not influential in even emotional characteristics.[N77]

Conan Doyle also addressed one of the central issues in the Victorian outlook. Cullingworth considered that "the human race is deteriorating mentally and morally."[293z] But, Doctor Munro forecasts a much brighter future for mankind, because the more we progress the more we tend to progress. "We advance not in arithmetical but in geometrical progression." As evidence, he compared the paultry advances in the previous 80 thousand years with those of the past ten—the railway, the telegraph, applied electricity, and chloroform (again!).

His predictions were that men will live in the air and below the water, that preventative medicine will develop much further, that crime will disappear, that war will become rare but more terrible, "that one universal creed will embrace the whole civilized earth, which will preach trust in that central power." It is unfortunate that Conan Doyle's view of the future (our present) has been proven true only for technology, but not for human interrelationships.

In summary, the novel *The Stark Munro Letters*[293] is a mixture of autobiographical events, theology, and philosophy, all permeated by the medically trained mind. Some of the issues, such as the nature of man and God, are still of major concern. The sophisticated mind may well reject the philosophy because the clarity of style and its vivid imagery carry a connotation of intellectual simplicity.

In Conan Doyle's time the reaction to his novel was somewhat mixed, but generally favorable. One review in *The Spectator* of October 1895[749] considered the novel to be a "human document" of the early struggles of a professional man, with Cullingworth a very striking creation. Considered disappointing "is the record of the young doctor's spiritual experiences . . . . The vehicle of fiction does not readily lend itself to the precision of thought and language which is essential to useful discussion of these great themes." Perhaps not, but the attempt in itself is fascinating!

Another review, in *The Speaker* of September 1895[434] considered the novel a disappointment for "those who turn to so popular an author as Mr. Doyle merely for purposes of being amused." But "allowing for altered days and changes in style, *The Stark Munro Letters* remind us not a little of Defoe and of Defoe at his best." Most lauded were the overpowering realities of the situations and the feelings of truth. These are high words of praise, but ones which have been lost on posterity. Perhaps the recent reprint of *The Stark Munro Letters*[294] will rekindle an appreciation of its literary value.

There have been other fictional biographies by physician writers who have included their own medical experience. An outstanding example is *Of Human Bondage*[642] by Somerset Maugham (1874–1965), who graduated from St. Thomas Medical School (London) in 1897. Like Conan Doyle he abandoned medicine, but within a year.[706] The hero of Maugham's novel, Philip Carey, had considerable financial difficulty, and consequent delays, during his medical education.

As one might expect in two medical works, even fictional, there are similarities. Mentioned in both are diseases such as tuberculosis, cirrhosis, and enteric fever. Conan Doyle's novel, however, includes more diseases and more detailed descriptions. Carey's statement that "Often you could guess their trades by the look of their hands" has a Holmesian ring to it.

Although both novels are similar in some of the content, they evoke a different reaction in the reader. Conan Doyle's work provides interest by shock effect, clever phrases, and clarity of writing. Maugham's work, in contrast, evokes deeper feelings. Emotions are from the heart, not the head. It contains a broader range of human interactions and problems. One feels a little different after reading *Of Human Bondage*, and not just entertained, as after reading *The Stark Munro Letters*. Perhaps this is why the former is considered as "literature" and the latter as a "good story" (aside from its use as a vehicle for Conan Doyle's philosophy).

Nonetheless, both novels provide the lay person with unique glimpses into the medical world. They are also similar in their relationship to the authors, as expressed by Somerset Maugham in the foreword to his book.

> *Of Human Bondage is not an autobiography, but an autobiographical novel; fact and fiction are inextricably mingled; the emotions are my own, but not all the incidents are related as they happened. . .*

The literary worth of another novel by Conan Doyle, *The Parasite*,[280] is much more questionable, although written at about the same time. It has been considered as "his first approach to Spiritualism in book form,"[581] but it does not deal with spirits of the dead. The villainess, Miss Penclosa, although a clairvoyant, achieves her satanic control over individuals by hypnotism and suggestion. As the tormented Professor Gilroy laments, "this dreadful thing which has sprung out at me is neither supernatural nor even preternatural." It is related, in part, to the exchange of souls through hypnotism that also occurred in Conan Doyle's short story, "The Great Keinplatz Experiment."[239]

The Parasite[280] is organized on the basis of dates, as is *The Stark Munro Letters*,[293] but as a diary rather than letters. It was between the short period of March 24 and May 5 that the narrator, Professor Gilroy, almost met his total ruination. A complete materialist, he rejected the "nebulous pseudoscience" of Professor Wilson. But, Gilroy did have a sensitive nature which he had suppressed. Perhaps, Conan Doyle was describing himself. "And yet I may claim to be a curious example of the effect of education upon temperment, for by nature I am, unless I deceive myself, a highly psychic man." Gilroy's suppressed psychic nature was to be released by Miss Penclosa, the 40-year-old clairvoyant for whom Conan Doyle provided sinister overtones by reference to her lame leg and her origin in Trinidad. Miss Penclosa converted Gilroy by demonstrating posthypnotic suggestion on his fiance, Agatha Marden. Ever the man of science, he threw himself enthusiastically into investigating the phenomenon, primarily by being repeatedly hypnotized by Miss Penclosa. Gradually he became more and more sensitized so that she achieved complete control through hypnotic suggestion, even at a distance. She, of course, had fallen in love with Gilroy, who was repulsed by her malignant nature and fortified by his love for Agatha. Because he continued to spurn her, she brought about the loss of his lectureship by hypnotic suggestions to include in his lectures "the most outrageous and unscientific heresies." And there were inexplicable antisocial behaviors such as attacking his neighbor and robbing a bank.

Even more dastardly was the posthypnotic suggestion that her intended lover throw sulphuric acid in the face of his betrothed.

All was not lost. Miss Penclosa, who had been ailing, died just at the moment that Professor Gilroy was to disfigure the innocent Agatha.

In summary, the theme of *The Parasite*[280] is more related to the cult of mesmerism, developed by Mesmer for treatment of disease, than to the belief in communication with the dead, as fully accepted by Conan Doyle about 30 years later. Since the days of Mesmer, hypnotism has developed into a mode of treatment for various psychological states. The power of posthypnotic suggestion is now, however, limited to more benevolent activities than suggested by Conan Doyle in *The Parasite*.

The Parasite[280] is related more to the literature of demonical possession, such as Robert Louis Stevenson's *Dr. Jekyl and Mr. Hyde*,[851] although the demon originates externally rather than internally. The theme is similar to that of Conan Doyle's short story "The Great Keinplatz Experiement"[239] published nine years before. In that instance hypnotism also resulted in complete control, but by interchange of two souls rather than domination by one.

The two novels *The Parasite*[280] and *The Stark Munro Letters*,[293] are symbolic of the dichotomy exhibited by Conan Doyle in various ways. On the one hand, he was the logical thinker who created the world's most famous thinking detective, and provided 55 pages of reasoned rationales for his belief in a nonsectarian diety. On the other hand, he fully accepted all aspects of spiritualism and conceived a pseudoscientific tale of demonical possession in *The Parasite*.[280] The effective combination of medical science and feeling is well illustrated in the opening pages of *The Parasite*, in describing nature in the spring.

> *We also have our spring when the little arterioles dilate, the lymph flows in a brisker stream, the glands work harder, winnowing and straining. Every year nature readjusts the whole machine. I can feel the ferment in my blood at this very moment, and as the cool sunshine pours through my window I could dance about in it like a gnat.*

In respect to Conan Doyle's many interests and enthusiasms, it might be suspected that he frequently felt "the ferment in my blood," even when it was not springtime.

Another novel published by Conan Doyle, but earlier (1890), has already been considered, in part, because of chapters on a medical student's experience at the University of Edinburgh. In *The Firm of Girdlestone*,[258] chapters V through IX are descriptions of the activities of Tom Dimsdale as a medical student.[N78] In chapter V the University of Edinburgh is described as an unsympathetic machine, but one in which confidence and self-reliance is learned—features certainly exhibited by Conan Doyle throughout his life.

Tom Dimsdale is depicted (during his period of probation) in his rooms which contained various medical textbooks "arranged with suspicious neatness, as though seldom disturbed." Of the four books mentioned, two are listed in the *Edinburgh University Calendar for 1876–1877*,[407] the year Conan Doyle entered medical school. These are Quain's *Anatomy* and Huxley's *Invertebrata*. As we shall see, student Dimsdale did not make as good use of these books as had student Conan Doyle.

In the next chapter, Tom Dimsdale is visited by his father, a physician who has retired from practice with a moderate fortune. But, he brought with him the cause of Tom's eventual failure, Kate Harston, whose father was his father's second cousin. Together they attended a rather riotous election. His study time was further eroded by playing as a halfback in the international football match between England and Scotland. (Conan Doyle was a forward.)[N79] The immediate result of the game was quite joyous. "It had been an eventful day with the student. He had saved his side, he had broken his collar-bone, and now, most serious of all, he had realized that he was hopelessly in love."

Apparently love and study for examinations were incompatible. He spent his time observing, from a hidden vantage point, the sitting room of the hotel where resided his beloved. "Thus, when Dr. Dimsdale fondly imagined his son to be a mile away grappling with the mysteries of science, that undutiful lad was in reality perched within sixty yards of him, with his thoughts engrossed by very different matters."

Tom Dimsdale received a passing satis bene minus for his first examination in Zoology, even though he did not know the number of teeth in a rabbit. He received the same barely passing grade in Botany, primarily because one of the professors recognized him as the hero of the football game (an event not unknown today). But chemistry was his "nasty cropper." On being asked the composition of the gas in bubbles at the bottom of a pond, his reply was so outrageous (an organic explosive compound named cacodyl instead of marsh gas) that his examiners laughed so heartily that Dimsdale committed the ultimate breech of decorum. He walked out of the room and thus into failure in his preliminary examinations.

Conan Doyle's skill in writing humorous accounts does not completely obscure the moral of this story, one which was very well expressed by William Osler in his address to medical students at the University of Toronto in 1903.[697] "A jealous creature (the heavenly Aphrodite) brooking no second, if she finds you trifling and conquetting with her rival, the younger, earthy Aphrodite. . . , she will whistle you off and let you down the wind to be a prey, perhaps to the examiners, certainly to the worm regret."

Tom Dimsdale did not have many regrets, having entered medical school to please his physician father rather than having any strong desire for medicine (another event not unknown today). He then entered into the world of commerce in the employment of the firm of John Girdlestone, African Merchant. The remainder of the novel is an account of the trials and tribulations of Tom and Kate and need not concern us further.

In fact, Conan Doyle would rather that *The Firm of Girdlestone*[258] had not been read at all. His own review of this novel, written 40 years after he began writing it, was less than tolerant.

> *I had for some time from 1884 onwards been engaged upon a sensational book of adventure . . . "The Firm of Girdlestone," which represented my first attempt at a connected narrative. Save*

for occasional patches it is a worthless book . . . . When I sent it to publishers and they scorned it I quite acquiesced in their decision and finally let it settle . . . a dishevelled mass of manuscript at the back of a drawer.[375p]

Fortunately, at least for our "medical" chapters, it was published in 1890.

A more recent review,[610] by Ely Liebow in 1981, has a much higher rating than Conan Doyle's. "It is episodic, melodramatic, genuinely funny, overly sentimental, and above all-romantic." "There is also comedy here to rival Dickens and Fielding . . . ." Liebow's assessment is closer to the mark than Conan Doyle's.

MEDICINE IN POETRY

Such plaudits, however, cannot be applied to another literary form in which Conan Doyle wrote. One would not be surprised to find some emphasis on medical subjects in his three volumes of poetry.[370] But of 90 poems, only two have any significant medical orientation. Both were published in *Songs of the Road* in 1911.[354]

"Religio Medici" is written as a religious creed, presumably that of a physician.[N80] Some verses extoll the attributes of God, such as goodness and wisdom. Three have specific medical content.

He strews the microbes in the lung,
The blood-clot in the brain;
With test and test He picks the best,
Then tests them once again.

The above lines have a connotation of Darwin's survival of the fittest, which Conan Doyle supported.

He chokes the infant throat with slime,
He sets the ferment free;
He builds the tiny tube of lime
That blocks the artery.

He lets the youthful dreamer store
Great projects in his brain
Until He drops the fungus spore
That smears them out again.

In *The Stark Munro Letters,*[293z] Conan Doyle implied that disease is not evil because pain is fleeting. In this poem disease is God's means of testing man. It is uncertain whether he believed this or whether it was written for poetic effect.

Interestingly, this poem was also included in *The Stark Munro Letters*, published 16 years earlier. The title, therein, is "With Either Hand,"[293bb] presumably indicating that God both gives and takes. Aside from the title, the poem is identical to the 1911 version, but with the addition of two final verses. The omission in its reprinting in *Songs of the Road* was a wise one! "So read I this—and as I try/To write it clear again, /I felt a second finger lie/ Above mine on the pen."

The other medical poem, "Darkness,"[354] is of somewhat better quality. The first verse describes a gentleman of wit, charm, kind heart, and cleanly mind who went riding one winter day.

And then—the blunder of a horse,
The crash upon the frozen clods,
And—Death? Ah! no such dignity,
But Life, all twisted and at odds!
At odds in body and in soul,
Degraded to some brutish state,
A being loathsome and malign,
Debased, obscene, degenerate.

Pathology? The case is clear,
The diagnosis is exact;
A bone depressed, a haemorrhage,
The pressure on a nervous tract.
Theology? Ah, there's the rub!
Since brain and soul together fade,
Then when the brain is dead—enough!
Lord help us for we need Thine aid!

The last three lines could serve as an excellent commentary on the current controversy over the definition of death in relation to termination of life support systems.[736]

Conan Doyle was quite taken with the fact that morphologic change in the body could result in a change in personality. Pressure of a spicule of bone on the brain was also referred to in both "A Medical Document"[288] and *The Stark Munro Letters*.[293n]

> *To think that you may have a man of noble mind, full of every lofty aspiration, and that a gross physical cause, such as the fall of a spicule of bone from the inner table of his skull on to the surface of the membrane which covers his brain, may have the ultimate effect of turning him into an obscene creature with every beastial attribute!*

A comparison with the same theme, treated in poetic format, leaves little doubt as to the literary form in which Conan Doyle was most skilled.

In spite of writing these poems (medical or otherwise), Conan Doyle, the poet, is not well known. Rolleston, in his paper of 1926[776] on poet-physicians, does include him in a section on those who practiced medicine as well as wrote verse. Also included are John McCrae (1872–1918), pathologist, who wrote "In Flanders Fields,"[621] and Oliver Wendell Holmes who was as prolific in poetry as he was in other forms of literature.[540] Rolleston does not provide an evaluation of Conan Doyle's poetry except to say that he was "ever active and endowed with the great gift of imagination."

Conan Doyle, the poet, cannot be considered in the same category as McCrae, the Canadian pathologist, or Holmes, the American anatomist. McCrae's poems literally exalt the glory of death in battle for one's country.[764] Holmes wrote poems that have become classics, such as "Old Ironsides" and "The Chambered Nautilis,"[540] He also wrote several poems that are medically oriented. A few lines from his poem "The Morning Visit" illustrates the caliber of his poetry.

Of all the ills that suffering man endures,
The largest fraction liberal Nature cures;
Of those remaining, 't is the smallest part
Yields to the efforts of judicious Art;
But simple Kindness, *kneeling by the bed*
To shift the pillow for the sick man's head,
Give the fresh draught to cool the lips that burn,
Fan the hot brow, the weary frame to turn,—
Kindness, *untutored by our grave M.D.'s*
But Nature's graduate, when she schools to please,
Wins back more sufferers with her voice and smile
Than all the trumpery of the druggist's pile.

Such sensitivity to the psychological needs of the sick were also exhibited by Conan Doyle. But the difference is that Conan Doyle's "poetic words" lack the cadence, imagery of phrase, and emotion evoking talent of those by Oliver Wendell Holmes. Lacon Watson,[916] in a paper written the year before Conan Doyle's death, did not consider him to be a great poet, but rather as a writer having the "root of the matter" in him. So, perhaps in the classic sense, Conan Doyle is best considered as a versifier rather than a poet.[183] His medical poems, like his others, were straightforward and heartfelt, but suffered from the same lucid simplicity that made his short stories and novels so effective.[N81]

Perhaps it is just as well that Conan Doyle's poetry is almost unknown. It is nowhere near the quality of his fictional works that have medical matters as their major theme. Still to be considered are his novels and short stories that are not essentially medical in nature.

Figure 12. Doctor Conan Doyle standing beside the door to his practice site, with a Baptist church to the left and another house to the right.

igure 13. Kings Road and Elm Grove—Southsea. No. 1, ush Villas, between the hotel and the church, is the site of Doctor rthur Conan Doyle's practice from 1882-1890 and is where herlock Holmes was "born," in 1887. Photograph is circa 1900. hotograph used with permission.)

Figure 14. Conan Doyle in his study at No. 1 Bush Villas.

4

NONMEDICAL FICTION

The sheer bulk of Conan Doyle's nonmedical fiction far outweighs the combined amount of his medical, medical fiction, and Canonical writings in both number and extent. The recent superb bibliography of Conan Doyle by Green and Gibson is almost 600 pages in length.[488] Each individual nonmedical work does not in itself contain a significant amount of medical references; but when all are reviewed in their totality the sum is impressive as well as informative about the medical orientation of the author.

The effectiveness of Conan Doyle's nonmedical works does not rely on the fascination that medical matters have for the layman. The exceptions are in the ''Canonical writings'' which owe their popularity, in part at least, to the numerous references to disease. The remainder of his nonmedical writings do contain scattered medical items, but these are usually secondary or incidental to the themes. These items fall into four categories—physicians, diseases, treatment, and biology.

PHYSICIANS IN CONAN DOYLE'S NONMEDICAL FICTION

In a partial list prepared by Curjel,[178] 20 physicians are included in the nonmedical, non-Sherlockian works of Conan Doyle. Of these, six are major characters in the short stories. Aloysuis Lana, "The Black Doctor"[303] of Spanish extraction, was a capable surgeon and accomplished physician. He took patients away from Doctor Edward Rowe because of his elegance of manner, the charm of his conversation, and the remarkable surgical cure of Lord Beton's second son. Doctor Lana soon became engaged to the stately Miss Frances Morton. The engagement was broken off when his behavior became reprehensible. He was soon found dead and his fiancee's brother was charged with murder. But, the dead man proved to be the twin brother of Doctor Lana, who had left to avoid his evil sibling, but returned in time for a happy ending.

"The Black Doctor"[303] is not a "medical" story because it could be told with any other professional as the main character. It is intensified by the status of the hero.

A different plot is seen in "The Brown Hand"[308] which belonged to an Afghan tribesman, before it was removed by Sir Dominick Holden, a famous Indian surgeon, because of "a soft sarcomatous [cancerous] swelling of one of the metacarpal joints." Doctor Holden was interested in comparative pathology and therefore kept the hand in preservative in spite of the religious objections of the native. Years later he was haunted by the native, returned from the dead to reclaim his hand, but it had been destroyed in a fire. The surgeon's nephew, Doctor Hardacre, was a general practitioner and a member of the Psychical Research Society. He obtained a brown hand that had been amputated at the Shadwell Seamen's Hospital and with it appeased the dead native. "The Brown Hand" could not be written without a physician as the main character, but its theme is that of the psychic rather than the medical.

In another short story, "The Fiend of the Cooperage,"[341] there is no specific reason for the hero to be a physician. Doctor Severall was employed as a medical officer by the Armitage and Wilson Trading Company in South Africa. On confrontation, the fiend that had devoured two natives and a white man was discovered to be "the great python of the Gaboon."[N82] In a similar vein it was not necessary that the discovery of "The Terror of Blue John Gap"[347] be made by a physician, Doctor James Hardcastle, who managed to survive his encounter with the huge shaggy monster.

Even the diary of the shipwrecked Doctor Jephson, "J. Habakuk Jephson's Statement,"[232] could have been written by a nonphysician. The tale was Conan Doyle's fictional solution in 1884 to an actual American ship, the *Marie Celeste,* which was found abandoned in 1874 with no clue as to the reason.[43] Doctor Jephson was a specialist in consumption, with which he himself came down and took a sea voyage for his health. Medical allusions include a description of the setting sun as a "long track like a trail of blood upon the water," a statement that "medicine doth make cynics of us all," and the diagnosis of a nightmare as "a vascular derangement of the cerebral hemispheres." Only Doctor Jephson survived the horrible shipboard murders committed by Goring, the vengeful black.

Another physician, Doctor Sinclair, advised an overworked accountant during his startling experience with "The Silver Mirror."[340] The doctor, "who is, it seems, a bit of a psychologist" made a diagnosis of "straining my nerves, risking a complete breakdown, even endangering my sanity." The accountant had witnessed a slaying in the silver mirror in his room. The doctor interpreted his description as the slaying of Rizzio in the presence of Mary, Queen of Scots, in 1566, several centuries before. From an inscription on the back of the mirror it was evident that it had belonged to her and that the accountant had "witnessed" the scene. The vivid impression became evident to him because of his mental state.

A similar event, but not related to an image in a mirror, occurred when the narrator slept beside "The Leather Funnel."[313] He had a terrifying dream in which a female prisoner was chained and had water forced into her through a leather funnel. His wealthy and educated friend, Lionel Dacre, identified the dream as "the trial of Marie Madeleine d'Aubray, Marquise de Brinvilliers, one of the most famous poisoners . . . of all time." This was an actual event.[97] The Marquise had tested poisons on hospital patients and used them on her two brothers and her husband. She was beheaded in 1676.

The experiences in both "The Silver Mirror"[340] and "The Leather Funnel"[313] are examples of psychometry—the ability to perceive the history of an object by close proximity to it. As Dacre explained:

> *. . . any object which has been intimately associated with any supreme paroxysm of human emotion, whether it be joy or pain, will retain a certain atmosphere or association which it is capable of communicating to a sensitive mind.*[313]

Conan Doyle's attraction to the more mystical nature of man and his world is evident. These stories are also indicative of his effective use of actual historical individuals in his fiction.

In the more civilized setting of London, but still unusual, is the adventure of "The Beetle Hunter."[300] Doctor Hamilton, the narrator, "had just become a medical man," and lived in Gower Street (undoubtedly around the corner from Conan Doyle's residence in 1891). His interest in beetles led him to be hired by Lord Linchmere to certify that his brother-in-law, Sir Thomas Rossiter, the world's outstanding authority on beetles, was insane. This plot necessitates that there be a physician although not as the main character. It could possibly be labeled as a "medical story" although the emphasis is upon collecting beetles. In the words of the insane Sir Thomas "People can find time for such trivialities as sport or society, and yet the beetles are overlooked."

Other physicians in the nonmedical short stories play much lesser roles. For example, Doctor Atherton was given the notebook of an aviator discovered after he had disappeared into "The Horror of the Heights."[359] Doctor Baldy Stable was surgeon to the infamous pirate, Captain Sharkey, when he was confronted by a beautiful but leprous woman in "The Blighting of Sharkey."[353] Doctor Stable had once held the first practice in Charleston until misusing a patient. In another Sharkey adventure, he escaped from hanging in St. Kitts (Carribean) by disguising himself as the governor whose throat he had cut; but he did not take along Doctor Larousse, the Governor's personal physician.[297] Even further removed from Conan Doyle's time was the Roman Senator Emiluis Flaccus who, in A.D. 92, suggested to his friend Caius Balbus a cure for headache after a night of drinking with the Emperor.[352] "My Greek physician Stephanos has a rare prescription for a morning head."

The physicians in Conan Doyle's nonmedical novels are as numerous as those in his short stories. In *The Doings of Raffles Haw,*[262] written while Conan Doyle was studying the eye in Vienna, Haw's father had been a country physician whose death caused Haw to leave medical school just before his final exam. He went into chemistry and discovered how to transmute substances into gold. This rather weak novel ends with a moral—helping others may lead to their ruination. In the relatively slight *The Mystery of the Cloomber,*[249] Doctor John Easterling, F.R.C.P., Edinburgh, plays a minor role by making an unimportant statement relative to the mystery. A baby is delivered by a Doctor Jordan in the innocuous story, *A Duet.*[310] A partial exception, Achille Letour, was one of the main characters in the novel about Huguenots—*The Refugees.*[273] He had studied medicine at Montepellier, but did not practice.[N83]

Beyond the City[264] was set in a suburb, most likely akin to Norwood, where Conan Doyle moved after closing his ophthalmology office. It presents us with two extremes of medical men. There is Doctor Balthazar Walker who wrote a paper on "Gouty Diathesis," and a treatise on "Affections of the Vasomotor System," as did Conan Doyle eight and seven years respectively, before this novel, published in 1892. He exhibited his expertise in examining Mrs. Westmacott who had been struck unconscious with a blow to the head by her evil brother, Jeremiah. "Her pulse is full and slow. There is no stertor [heavy breathing]. It is my belief that she is merely stunned, and that she is in no danger at all." On the other hand, there is Doctor Proudie, a fake, who found a nonexistent organic murmur in Denver, as part of a scheme to cheat him of his pension. This in one of the few references to quacks in Conan Doyle's works, although they were numerous in 19th century England. A somewhat more idealistic comment is made by the Prussian surgeon at the battle of Waterloo when confronted with a wounded French soldier, "I will do my best for my patients, but I will do no more."[322]

A physician in another historical novel, *The White Company*[265] is described as:

> *. . . a seller of pills and salves, very learned in humors, and rheums, and fluxes, and all manner of ailments. He wears, as you perceive, the vernicle of Sainted Luke, the first physician, upon his sleeve. . . . He is here tonight for herberage. . . .*

Another historical novel set in the time of the Napoleonic Wars is *The Great Shadow,*[268] in which there are three physicians. Two are noted in passing—Surgeon Purdie set a leg and Doctor Horscroft of Ayton was the father of Jim who "went off to Edinburgh to study his father's profession." But "He should have been a doctor years back if his brain had been as strong as his head." Like Conan Doyle, whose problem was mainly financial, he stuck to it and obtained his diploma, only to be killed by bayonets in one of the French wars.

Medical students are featured in four other works. In two instances the medical aspects are rather sparse. The narrator of "Uncle Jeremy's Household,"[241] Hugh Lawrence, "was working hard for the final examination which should make me a qualified medical man." He lived in Baker Street, as did Sherlock Holmes who was created at about the same time. Lawrence came to the aid of his friend Thurston by visiting the unusual household, which had a dangerous connection with Indian mysteries. Uncle Jeremy was depicted as being senile, "garrulous and imbecile, shuffling about in his list slippers and composing, as is his wont, innumerable bad verses.'' The fact that Lawrence was a medical student, however, is not an integral part of the plot. Neither is that of Solomon Baker, who was reading for his medical examinations, and was rejected by Eleanor Montague.[221]

The journal kept by John M'Alister Ray, medical student and acting surgeon under the insane ''Captain of the Polestar''[225] (an Arctic whaler), is of interest. This tale was published in 1883, only four years after Conan Doyle served in the same position in the Arctic. Unlike Conan Doyle's autobiographical account,[375c] Ray's Captain was the major character.

The fact that Robert Montgomery was a medical student is a much more integral part of ''The Croxley Master.''[309] He was dispensing medicine as a student assistant because of his urgent need for money. Conan Doyle appears to be writing of his own experience 20 years prior to this short story.

> *He should be back again at the University completing the last year which would give him his medical degree; but, alas! he had not the money with which to pay his class fees. . . . Sixty pounds were wanted to make his career, and it might have been as many thousands for any chance there seemed to be of his obtaining it.*

The author's own frustrations are evident. But at least Conan Doyle had a very sympathetic mentor, Doctor Hoare, and not Oldacre of ''prim manner and austere face'' who refused Montgomery a loan.

Montgomery's problems were compounded when he knocked out an insolent and brutal Barton, a miner who was to take on the boxing champion. The athletic student was finally convinced to take his place. He beat the champion and thereby won £100 to complete his medical education. He refused further fights in spite of the pleas of the miners. ''Well, we've plenty of doctors, but you're the only man in the Riding that could smack the Croxley master off his legs.'' Such a priority may reflect Conan Doyle's frustrations in establishing a practice in a location (Southsea) containing many other physicians.

Another one of Conan Doyle's medical students had financial difficulties and dropped out after two winter sessions at the University of Glasgow.[259] After his return home to the Island of Uffa his violent father died in an attempt to obtain a stolen diamond. Archie MacDonald then resumed his studies and "settled quietly down into a large middle class practice." In respect to the plot he could as well have been a law student.

The tragic story of "John Barrington Cowles"[233] is even less dependent on the fact that he was a medical student. Reminiscent of Conan Doyle is the setting in Edinburgh and the winning of a prize (in physics), as he had in a bursary examination. The short story is an account by his friend, Robert Armitage, of Cowles' hopeless and fatal love for the beautiful Kate Northcott. It was her cruelty and her "preternatural powers" of controlling minds that resulted in the deaths of her first two fiancees, and then of John Barrington Cowles, her third.

The theme is quite similar to that of *The Parasite,*[280] published ten years later (1894). Both depict essentially evil women who seek love and domination through their powers of mind control by mesmerism (hypnotism). In the instance of Kate Northcott, however, there is more implicit implication of the supernatural—"wher-wolves" and "a vampire soul behind a lovely face." Although Higham has stated that Conan Doyle's chief interest was "his obsession with the supernatural,"[525f] it does not constitute a majority of his literary output, either nonmedical or medical.

Physicians abound in *The Land of Mist*[376] which features again the scientific, daring, and bombastic Professor Challenger of two much earlier science fiction stories—*The Lost World*[357] and *The Poison Belt.*[360] In this novel the central character meets his greatest challenge—pressures to accept spiritualism—and, unlike his conquest of a prehistoric environment and a meteor, he succumbs. The telling blow was that two individuals, whom he thought he had killed with a drug overdose while a young physician, returned from the other world to assure him that they died of their diseases.

The practicing physicians in *The Land of Mist*[376] are all believers in spiritualism. At St. Mary's Hospital there were Doctor Robinson and Surgeon Atkinson, who did a resection of the cord. There was also Doctor Ross Scotton, the author of two works, one on the favorite subject of Conan Doyle, the sympathetic nervous system, and the other on "The Fallacy of the Obsonic Index."[N84] But, he was dying of disseminated (multiple) sclerosis, a widespread disease of the central nervous system. To the rescue came a most intriguing healer, Doctor Felkin, a physician who had long since passed away. He cured Scotton by entering the body of a young girl, presumably a medium, and providing a consultation.

> *Time was, my dear colleague, when a snuff-box was as much a part of my equipment as my phlebotomy case. I lived before the days of Laennec, and we carried no stethescope, but we had our little chirurgical battery, none the less.*

Conan Doyle was not necessarily striving for humor in *The Land of Mist*[376] which was written ten years after his overt conversion to spiritualism. He did refer his sister-in-law to a spirit doctor, with good results. It is evident that he was both consistent and fervent in his beliefs.[947]

DISEASES IN CONAN DOYLE'S NONMEDICAL FICTION

Diseases are, with a few notable exceptions, not a prominent feature of Conan Doyle's nonmedical, non-Sherlockian fiction. Disseminated sclerosis, for example, is not a major part of *The Land of Mist,*[376] but is a device to further the conversion of Challenger. Conan Doyle's familiarity with sea voyages is indicated by two passing references to scurvy. It occurred during the flight of *The Refugees*[273] and aboard the *H.M. Hecate* which found traces of Captain Sharkey.[353]

Only in passing is it mentioned that "Gentlemanly Joe"[226] is a loudly dressed scorbutic-looking youth. Afflicting the Duke of Bridgewater with gout acknowledges a common disease of the Victorian upper class.[384] Of lower social status was Doctor Otto van Spee who was beset by a variety of misfortunes.[230] For example "I swallowed a trichina [intestinal worm] in my ham, and was prostrated for weeks." He also acquired erysipelas, a streptococcal skin disease.

In a science fiction story, *The Poison Belt,*[360] a comet passing close to earth resulted in the apparent death of all except Challenger and his friends who were prepared with oxygen cylinders. The professor labeled the effect as catalepsy. On passing away, the population returned to life, even though his description of rigor mortis and risus sardonicus would indicate irreversible death.

Death and the lack of its finality is featured in another story. "How It Happened"[358] was revealed through a medium by a spirit who had not realized he had been killed in an auto accident until Stanley reassured him that he had been. Stanley had "died of the enteric at Bloemfontein," as had many soldiers seen by Conan Doyle in 1900. This short story also contains the concept, enunciated in the earlier *The Stark Munro Letters*[293z] that death is not painful.

> *'No pain of course?' said he. 'None,' said I. 'There never is,' said he . . . 'Stanley, you are dead.' He looked at me with the same old, gentle wistful smile. 'So are you,' he answered.*[358]

Conan Doyle was involved in a serious automobile accident in 1913, about two years before this story was published.[375hh] Fortunately, he was not even injured.[N85] This tale is also evidence that he was quite oriented to spiritualism before World War I.

Automobile accidents were only one of the detrimental results of the Industrial Revolution on health. Conan Doyle was aware and concerned about air pollution, as we have seen in the industrial town in which "A Straggler of '15'"[263] lived. In "The Croxley Master"[309] one wonders if he was describing the manufacturing city of Birmingham where he did an assistantship.

> *Outside, through the grimy surgery window over a foreground of blackened brick and slate, a line of enormous chimneys like Cyclopean pillars upheld the lowering, duncoloured cloud-bank. For six days in the week they spouted smoke. . . . Sordid and*

> *polluting gloom hung over a district blighted and blasted by the greed of man.*

This last sentence, published in 1899, could well serve as the rallying cry of today's environmental protectionists.

Several infectious diseases are included in these nonmedical writings, but only in a cursory fashion. Quartan ague (malaria) was one of the afflictions of the governor of St. Kitts.[297] Malaria is given as one of the hazards of colonization in "De Profundis."[276] This short story of marital devotion concerns John Vansittart, a coffee exporter, who sailed on the *Eastern Star.* A letter from the Captain of the ship informed Vansittart's young and beautiful wife Emily that her husband had contracted smallpox. She immediately went "to the doctor's . . . to learn how to nurse a smallpox case," and then took a boat for Madeira. On arriving in port, Vansittart's head was seen arising out of the water "His face . . . mottled here and there with dark scabs." He had died eight days before and was buried at sea!

One reference to an infectious disease is included in *The White Company,*[265] Conan Doyle's epic romance of knighthood set in the 14th century. The physician shows some intuitive knowledge of the spread of the black death (plague) which was recognized in the 14th century.[5]

> *For the rat, mark you, a foul-living creature, hath a natural drawing, or affinity for all foul things, so that the noxious humors pass from the man into the unclean beast.*[265]

Thus, he proposes that the cutting open of a rat will cure the plague by drawing the humors from the human.

Conan Doyle further exhibited his understanding of history by calling the black death "the best friend that ever the common folk had in England." With the death of half of the population, "the other half could pick and choose who they would work for, and for what wage." He was, among other things, an astute historian.

Other disease items are relatively sparse. Doctor Easterling, on examining General Heatherstone of *The Mystery of Cloomber,*[249] observed "that his reflexes were feeble, his arcus senilus (of eyes) well marked, and his arteries atheromatous." The general also had an abscess of the liver (possibly amebic). Like Conan Doyle's fictional Doctor Watson, he had been shot by a Jezail bullet, but in the region of the heart. He was saved because "what does it do but glance upon a rib, and go clean round and out at the back without so much as penetrating what you medicos call the pleura." By an amazing coincidence in 1900, a year after this tale was published, Conan Doyle examined a soldier who had had a bullet traverse the abdominal skin from front to back.

Two conditions are considered as diseases today that are of some prominence in his fiction—chronic alcoholism and insanity. Alcohol addiction is the theme of the "Japanned Box"[307] in which Sir John Bollarmore, a chronic alcoholic, kept a phonograph message from his wife, made as she was dying. It implored him never to drink again. Conan Doyle's understanding of the alcoholic is evident in his description of the victim. It is quite striking when compared with the World Health Organization's (WHO) modern definition.[578]

1899	*1951*
I began to understand that strangely human look in his eyes, those deep lines upon his careworn face. He was a man who was fighting a ceaseless battle, holding at arm's length, from morning till night, a horrible adversary, who was for ever trying to close with him—an adversary which would destroy him body and soul could it but fix its claws once more upon him.	*Alcoholism is any form of drinking which in extent goes beyond the traditional and customary 'dietary' use, or the ordinary compliance with the social drinking customs of the community concerned, irrespective of etiological factors leading to such behavior, and irrespective also of the extent to which such etiological factors are dependent upon heredity, constitution or acquired physio-pathological and metabolic influence.*

The WHO definition is couched in currently acceptable scientific terms, but Conan Doyle's description of a half century earlier is timeless in its humanity and empathy. Surely a chronic alcoholic would be better served by a physician more attuned to the latter than to the former.

It has been suggested that Conan Doyle wrote of alcohol with clinical detachment because he was a medical man.[424e] But this empathy exceeds that shown by most physicians. His father's prolonged addiction could have led him to be excessively moralistic about alcohol, but instead it provided a detailed knowledge and sympathy—at least for Sir John Bollarmore.

Conan Doyle also used alcoholism for comic effect. Wat Danbury, a huntsman, was warned by Doctor Middleton "about the possibility of delerium tremens, or even of mania." He became convinced he had these effects when the fox he was chasing resembled a huge creature ("The King of the Foxes.")[245] He swore off drink for life, but the apparition was discovered to be a Siberian wolf that had escaped from a menagerie. Again Conan Doyle's touch is gentle and amused, rather than moralistic.

Not all references to alcohol and intoxication are sympathetic. His historical novels describe drunken soldiers, undoubtedly in his attempt to recreate the totality of his segment of the past. The ghost of Hickman, "The Bully of Brocas Court,"[369] was tormented by the ghost of the dog he had murdered with a poker during a drunken rage.

Another reprehensible drunkard was old McIntyre who schemed to obtain the transmuted gold of Raffles Haw.[262] Although depicted as churlish and rapacious, Conan Doyle understood the cause of the condition, as perhaps he did of his father's debility. Old McIntyre was one of the richest gunmakers in Birmingham, but went bankrupt, and at the same time lost his wife. He was one:

> *. . . whose life now was one long wail over his misfortunes, and who alternately sought comfort in the Prayer-book and in the decanter for the ills which had befallen him.*

There is an underlying suggestion of lack of moral fiber, as Conan Doyle might have felt of his own father, and of the futility of traditional religion, which he rejected.

Conan Doyle's own experience with alcohol was more successful.

> *. . . I swore off alcohol for the rest of the voyage. I drank quite freely at this period of my life . . . but my reason told me that the unbounded cocktails of West Africa were a danger, and with an effort I cut them out. There is a certain subtle pleasure in abstinence, and it is only socially that it is difficult.*[375j]

One further alcoholic, Mr. Raby, had lost his job because of delerium tremens after "a long course of secret drunkeness."[261] Like Conan Doyle's father, he "had some leanings towards art" which he tried to sell. His wife barely supported them by sewing dresses. But he hocked a valuable one in a pawn shop for liquor money. And yet Mrs. Raby rescued him while in a drunken stupor and consoled him. Surely Conan Doyle's mother richly deserved the acalade given at the end of this tale. "Oh, blind, angelic, foolish love of woman! Why should men demand a miracle while you remain upon earth?"

Another frequent event in his fiction is insanity, his father's terminal condition. It has been mentioned as characterizing "The Captain of the Polestar"[225] and "The Beetle Hunter,"[300] in which it provides major plot themes. In the adventure of "The Great Brown-Pericord Motor,"[327] however, Pericord's insanity occurs only at the end, after he disposes of Brown's body in the weird machine that then disappeared into the heavens.

Another instance of insanity is described in *The Stark Munro Letters.*[293p] Munro, on graduating, obtained a position looking after Lord Saltire's son James who "was struck down by the sun while fishing without his hat last July. His mind has never recovered from the shock." Such a cause of insanity is not likely, but it fitted Cullingworth's advice to Stark. "Get a lunatic, my boy." Munro soon established a good relationship with the boy, but lost the position because his freethinking approach to religion angered Lady Saltire. Conan Doyle achieved two ends—an interesting event in the life of Doctor Munro and an exposition of his religious skepticism.

A more serious condition than James' insanity was the homicidal maniac of Feldkirch, a setting undoubtedly chosen by Conan Doyle because of his sojourn there for a year before entering the University of Edinburgh. Father Verhagen was "A Pastoral Horror"[254] who struck down his parishoners with a small pickaxe. He was discovered because of scratches on his arm the day after an unsuccessful murder attempt on Frau Bischoff. His insanity was attributed to "overwork and brain worry."

A rather more unlikely cause of insanity was the basis for the story of the "Silver Hatchet."[229] This ancient weapon was bequeathed to the University of Buda-Pesth. It was used to kill Doctor Otto von Hopstein, Regius Professor of Comparative Anatomy, and Professor Schiffer, whose heads were split in half. Most remarkable was the attempt by Schlegel, a student, to kill his bosom friend Straus with the same instrument. The cause of such temporary insanity was in the handle of the hatchet. It had been annointed with some diffusable poison by the Rosicrucians in the early Middle Ages. Its penetration through the skin produced a homicidal mania. The premise is fanciful, but resulted in one of Conan Doyle's interesting little stories.[N86]

TREATMENT OF DISEASES

Treatment of disease is not mentioned frequently. At an audience with the Prince in Brighton, *Rodney Stone* [295] hears the Prince complain "I am bloodied fifty ounces a month." This is equivalent to the amount of blood withdrawn for about three blood transfusions per month—a rather excessive amount. It was not, however, unusual as a general health measure in the days of Rodney Stone, the early 19th century. Conan Doyle, if anything, was meticulously accurate in his historical novels. He also included some of his personal interests. Thus, boxing was a major plot element and humor was of the essence.

A more specific use of blood-drawing occurs in *Micah Clarke*[248] when veins of the arm were opened to relieve the rush of blood to the head that occurred from being hung by the ankles. Its efficacy is doubtful.[N87]

In *The Lost World*[357] the resourceful Professor Challenger used carbolic acid to cleanse a wound made during an attack by the venemous pterodactyls. Years later in *The Land of Mist,*[376] the professor admitted to giving, while a young physician, "a new drug under discussion at the time," to two men who then died.

> *. . . it was of the datura family which supplies deadly poisons as well as powerful medicines. I had received one of the earliest specimens, and I desired my name to be associated with the first exploration of its properties.*

Professor Challenger did not have the inclination to determine the effects of the drug by trying it on himself, as Conan Doyle did with gelsemium while a medical student.[216]

Datura, a plant of the Solanaceae family, is found in Britain.[923] Species include Datura Stramonium, which is found in waste places, and Datura Tatula, which grows in abundance on hillsides. Its main pharmacologic properties are due to alkaloids, such as atropine. Datura is also known as Jimson weed in the United States. Toxic reactions include dry mouth, blurred vision, weak and rapid pulse, restlessness, weakness, and muscular incoordination.[479] Fatalities are rare, but may occur in children. The spirits of the two patients of Professor Challenger were therefore correct. Datura was not likely the cause of their death, even though the symptoms may have been alarming.[N88]

Conan Doyle's historical novels contain a variety of therapeutic agents and methods. Some orientation to treatment in the 16th century is obtained from Micah Clarke's description of his mother's attributes.[248]

> *She made salves and eyewaters, powders and confects [herbal compounds], cordials [heart stimulants] and persico [fruit kernels in alcohol] . . . herbs and simples [medicinal herbs]. The villagers and the farm laborers would rather any day have her advice upon their ailments than that of Dr. Jackson of Purbrook, who never mixed a draught under a silver crown.*

Our own society still has a concern about health costs[521] and has an increasing interest in herbs as medication.

When Micah Clarke left for the wars his mother provided him with medical advice. "A hare's foot suspended round the neck driveth away colic." Animal parts were considered to have healing powers from prehistoric times to the middle ages, and perhaps even today.[867] Even more useful was Daffy's elixir which "possesses extraordinary powers in purifying the blood and working off all phlegms, humours, vapours or rheums." This may have been Narcissus pseudo-narcissus made from the root of the daffodil.[404] It was used as an emetic and a cathartic.

Micah Clarke's mother packed the phial of elixir in the barrel of his pistol. He forgot about it and fired his gun at a hound that was attacking his companion. "Saved my life by shooting a dog with a bottle of Daffy's elixir!" Conan Doyle's refreshing sense of humor was irrepressible, even in the midst of an historical novel.

Another method of treatment of the time was amputation of severely traumatized extremities. Micah Clarke encountered a soldier who was cutting off his own arm which had been almost severed by a cannon ball. Such a drastic recourse was necessitated by the frequency of gangrene with open wounds in the days before the discovery of bacteria in infections led to antiseptic measures.[130]

A less drastic treatment was the King's cure for the white plague (tuberculosis). French and English monarchs from the 5th to the 17th centuries were considered to have the power of curing scrofula (tuberculosis of neck glands).[400a] An actual incident involving Monmouth's cure of an afflicted girl is cited in detail by Conan Doyle in the appendix (Note G) of *Micah Clarke*.[248] He also attributed the healing powers of touch to Lady Tiphaine of *The White Company*.[265] "Was it not she who was said to lay hands upon the sick and raise them from their couches when the leaches [doctors] had spent their last nostrums?" Conan Doyle's historical novels were as accurate in depicting the medical practice of the time as they were of the culture and environment.

An epidemic of the white plague is included in "The Ring of Thoth."[250] It occurred in the Egypt of 1600 B.C. Sosra, the son of the Chief Priest of Osiris, had developed a substance which "would endow the body with strength to resist the effects of time, of violence or of disease." He injected himself and was able to nurse the stricken unscathed. But his love, Atma, the daughter of the King, refused the universal preventative and died of the infection. Sosra then longed for death, but could not die. In the 19th century he finally found the ring of Thoth, in the Louvre, which contained the antidote to his substance. Atma's mummy was also there. He unwrapped it, took the antidote and died embracing her body.

This rather fanciful tale of faithful love over the centuries is characteristic of Conan Doyle's ideals of romance and enduring love. It is also related to his nonfiction article on "Life and Death in the Blood,"[231] published seven years earlier. The universal preventative of Osiris is the fictional equivalent of vaccination material which Conan Doyle predicted would eradicate infectious diseases (and has in some instances).

In stories set in Conan Doyle's own period, more conservative methods of treatment are used. For example, the private tutor in Sir John Bollarmore's ancestral home took chlorodyne, a chloroform and morphine tincture, for the pain of neuralgia. Like morphine, this can result in addiction.[905a] Conan Doyle suffered from neuralgia, but treated himself with gelseminum.[767]

A more fanciful use of a drug was used by Abrahams to convince D'Odd that he was indeed seeing an unearthly parade from which to select a ghost for his newly acquired feudal mansion, Garesthorpe Grange.[228] The ghost-procurer had given him "at least eighty grams of pure [chloral] hydrate." According to Doctor Stube it was enough to put D'Odd in a semi-comatose state, and to have bizarre visions. Abrahams' motive was robbery. Conan Doyle's purpose for writing this spoof was undoubtedly to provide entertainment and humor. He was to take the subject of spirits much more seriously 35 years later.

Of interest is the story of "Hilda Wade," written by Grant Allen, except for the last episode which was completed by Conan Doyle during his friend's final illness.[311] Brandy was administered to the nearly dead Sebastian, who suffered from plague and had been shipwrecked. He and Doctor Bannerman had conducted "an investigation into the nature and properties of the vegetable alkaloids, and especially of aconitine." Alkaloid poisons are featured in the Sherlock Holmes stories. Aconitine is possibly a derivative of the plant Aconitum (monkshood) that has both medicinal and poisonous properties.[923] Bannerman was accused of poisoning Hilda Wade's uncle, Admiral Scott Prideaux, with the drug, but he actually died of a weak heart.

Poisons are featured in several of Conan Doyle's short stories. Stanislaus Stanniford, the banker involved in a scandal, left a letter to his wife indicating he was leaving the country. Instead he took a poison in "The Sealed Room"[302] of his home. His motive for concealing his suicide was admirable—"He had been told by the first doctor in London that his wife's heart would fail at the slightest shock." This is only one of several depictions of marital devotion in Conan Doyle's fiction.

All of his married couples, however, are not exemplary. In "The Nightmare Room"[368] Archie Mason, the American banker, confronted his wife Lucille, the beautiful French dancer, with the bottle he had found in her purse. Doctor Angus had analyzed its contents as antimony,[656] a metal which has a poisonous effect similar to that of arsenic.[391] She had been poisoning him for love of his friend Campbell. Campbell arrived and they drew cards to see who would drink the poison. This rather simplistic melodrama was interrupted when the movie director stopped the scene. The unexpected ending does not quite rescue the shallow tale.

Much more complexity of character and story presents in "The Pot of Caviare."[339] Old Professor Mercer, the Californian entomologist, was hopelessly beseiged with eight other whites during the Boxer insurrection. He fed the contents of the pot of caviar, which he had poisoned with cyanide, to himself and the others. His motive was to save them from the horrible torture for which the Chinese were noted. He lived only long enough to see the unexpected arrival of English troops. Mercer's final recognition of the enormity of his action—"What have I done? Oh, good Lord, what *have* I done?"—reminds one of Kurtz's anguished

"The Horror! The Horror!" in Joseph Conrad's masterpiece *The Heart of Darkness*.[159]

Further references to medical matters are found in one of Conan Doyle's excellent historical novels. *Micah Clarke*[248] is an adventurous account of the rebellion in 1685 of the Duke of Monmouth against James, the Papist King. The hero was born at the site of Conan Doyle's practice, Portsmouth, as was Rodney Stone. Chest wounds of two soldiers, one by bullet and the other by knife, resulted in coughing up blood, as one might expect if the lung was punctured. A fanatical Doctor Ferguson is mentioned, but his activities not delineated. Much more complimentary is the description of a skilled chirurgeon (surgeon) who treated a blade wound.

> *A skilful leach is better far,*
> *Than half a hundred men of war.*

BIOLOGICAL SCIENCE

In addition to clinical medicine, several of Conan Doyle's other scientific interests are evident in his nonmedical writing as they were in his medical ones. Anthropology, for example, entered even into *The Land of Mist*.[376] Materialized during a seance was "a mis-shapen figure, crouching, ill-formed, with some resemblance to man." "It is the Pithecanthropus," said Maupuis the French metaphysician, to Challenger.

A somewhat more scientific discussion of the origin of the species occurred in *The Lost World*[357] when a younger Professor Challenger disagreed with Mr. Percival Waldron, a naturalist of some popular repute, who was giving a lecture on "The Record of the Ages."

> *Popular lecturers are in their nature parasitic. . . . Mr. Waldron is very wrong in supposing that because he has never himself seen a so-called prehistoric animal, therefore these creatures no longer exist . . . I have visited their secret haunts . . . I have seen some of them.*

In the audience at the lecture hall of the Zoological Institute were many good natured but mischievous medical students whose interest in comparative anatomy was greater than that of such students today. It is not surprising, therefore, that the fiction of a former medical student and practitioner of the era contains allusions to biological as well as medical science.

Professor Challenger had his prototypes in two individuals who had made a lasting impression upon Conan Doyle, his teacher, the bombastic William Rutherford, and his medical confrere, the egocentric George Budd. He also gave him some of his own characteristics—a zest for life, curiosity, and imagination and an interest in the nervous system. Challenger did research involving vivisection, which Conan Doyle supported in moderation. One result was the knowledge that the heart of an animal stopped only when the ganglia (nerve centers) ran down.[357]

Even when threatened by the monstrous primitive toadlike creatures "larger than the largest elephant" he exhibited his biological interests.

> *Their slow reptilian natures cared nothing for wounds, and the springs of their lives, with no special brain centre but scattered throughtout their spinal cords, could not be tapped by any modern weapons.*

Only after being shot by natives with poisoned arrows did they collapse. But, again, their hearts did not stop beating. "It was upon the third day that the ganglia ran down and the dreadful things were still." Conan Doyle can be forgiven for this exaggeration of the potency of ganglia because of the effectiveness of his imaginative melding of prehistory and zoology.[47] As was his custom, he consulted textbooks to make the fictional work as accurate as possible.[N89]

Of less ancient vintage than dinosaurs, but still old, was the spirit guide for the Conan Doyle family, beginning in December 1922. Pheneas had lived in the city of Ur in the days before Abraham.[381] He was concerned about Conan Doyle's health.

Look after your health. You are like an instrument that a great master has to play upon. The strings must not be stretched to breaking point, or the master will not be able to play the full chord.

That was excellent advice for someone as energetic as Conan Doyle!

SUMMARY

In Conan Doyle's "A Medical Document"[288] Doctor Foster comments that "There's no need for fiction . . . in medicine for the facts will always beat anything you can fancy." Perhaps! But, Conan Doyle combined the best of both worlds by introducing into fiction the medical facts he had learned and directly experienced. The significance is, as Cousins[177] has stated, "Literature helps . . . to make connections between the experiences of the race and the condition of the individual, and to fit the individual into a world that is not as congenial as it ought to be for people who are more fragile than they ought to be." Conan Doyle's medical stories may not be as erudite as this statement, but their effectiveness is increased by his clarity and often by his humor.[635] And their very effectiveness provides insight into human nobility and frailty.

Even Conan Doyle's nonmedical fiction shows the marks of an experienced physician. Not only are some of the narrators physicians, but also some of the diseases or lesions are referred to in terms not used by the nonphysician writer. The uncertainty of the reader when confronted with such words adds not only to the realism but also to the aura of mystery—as for example, atheromatous artery. This is not to say, that nonmedical writers do not include physicians in their works, but that the depth and authenticity of characterization and the use of medical terminology are less.

Charles Dickens, for example, included physicians in many of his novels and stories.[186] But, his doctors were all of one mold—good humored, somewhat portulent, bluff, and hearty. They play minor and somewhat incidental roles in his writings. Even when incidental, Conan Doyle's physicians were a more varied and interesting lot. Of more importance than the entertainment value of his tales, he has preserved for us a view of medicine and its practice as it was in his day and before,[202] albeit heightened for dramatic or comic effects.

His complexity is evident in the manifold areas of knowledge and interests encountered in his fiction. Conan Doyle was able to move freely through many periods of history—prehistory, ancient Egypt, classical Greece and Rome, the era of English knighthood, the French Huguenot upheavals, the French and British wars in America, the Napoleonic era, 19th century Britain, and the future. The subjects are as varied and intermingled—science fiction, adventure on sea and land and in the air, sport, biology, zoology, anthropology, astronomy, pollution, mysticism, and elemental human psychology and emotions. Not the least were medical topics—practice, diseases, treatment, and history. Such a cross section of human endeavors, knowledge, and interests resembles that of H. G. Wells,[60] but, in part only, because Wells had a scientific background and Conan Doyle a medical one.[N90]

Conan Doyle's fiction, however, tells us as much about himself as it does of his society. In fact, in responding to a toast at the Manchester Edinburgh University Club in 1893 "It seemed to him that it [medical practice] had tinged his whole view of life."[394] Others have agreed with him.[818]

> *Though it is not to medicine that he owed his fame, his knowledge and experience were of service to him in more than one way. He introduced them again and again into his novels, and not only into the specifically medical stories, such as "Round the Red Lamp."*

Conan Doyle's fiction reveals more than just a knowledge of medicine. A psychiatrist has written that his "humanitarian qualities thus clearly show themselves in his medical stories . . . we have ample proof of his understanding of human relationships and continue to benefit from his insights."[3] As John Fowles has indicated, in a review of Higham's biography of Conan Doyle, "One may argue over his true artistic worth; but one cannot deny that he was a quite exceptionally complex and interesting example of his species, both human and literary."[457]

Perhaps it would be best to let Conan Doyle speak for himself, as he did for all authors in *Through the Magic Door*[338a]

> *Each [book] is a mummified soul embalmed in cere-cloth and natron of leather and printer's ink. Each cover of a true book enfolds the concentrated essence of a man. The personalities of the writers have faded into the thinnest shadows, as their bodies into impalpable dust, yet here are their very spirits at your command.*

From his own works it is evident that the medical "essence" of Conan Doyle consisted of a knowledgeable and humane physician, sensitive to the needs, feelings, and frailties of both patients and their physicians. It remains to be seen if the same is true for the writings involving Sherlock Holmes.

LIFE AND DEATH IN THE BLOOD.

HAD a man the power of reducing himself to the size of less than the one-thousandth part of an inch, and should he, while of this microscopic stature, convey himself through the coats of a living artery, how strange the sight that would meet his eye! All round him he would see a rapidly flowing stream of clear transparent fluid, in which many solid and well-defined bodies were being whirled along. These are the smooth straw-coloured elastic discs which act simply as mechanical carriers of oxygen and jostle through their brief existence without any claim to a higher function than that of the baker's cart, which carries round the necessaries of life, and is valuable not for itself, but for its burden. Here and there, however, on the outskirts of the throng, our infinitesimal spectator would perceive bodies of a very different character. Gelatinous in consistence, and irregular in shape, capable of pushing out long prehensile tentacles with which to envelop its food and draw it into its interior, this creature would appear from his point of view as a polyp of gigantic proportions and formidable aspect. No differentiated organs are to be seen in it, save a dark mass of pigment in its centre, which may represent some rudimentary visua[illegible] [illegible]r [illegible]uditory appar[illegible]us. Digestion is its [illegible]

which gradually separates itself by a constriction at the base, and hurries away into the blood stream as an independent organism.

These creatures are the leucocytes, or white corpuscles, and in spite of their being very much less numerous than the carriers of oxygen, there are still several millions of them within the healthy human body. In certain diseased conditions they multiply enormously until they outnumber the straw-coloured discs. When removed and placed upon a surface kept at the same temperature as that to which they have been accustomed, they are capable of carrying on an independent existence for some time. They have indeed a prototype, wandering at large, from which they are hardly recognisable, viz.: the tiny amœba which may be washed from damp moss and detected under the microscope.

This then is the only creature possessing the attributes commonly associated with life, which is found in healthy human blood; but in diseased conditions numerous others appear, differing from each other as widely as the flounder does from the eel, and presenting an even greater contrast in the effects which they produce. The existence of these little organisms, which lie upon the debateable ground between the animal and vegetable kingdoms, ma[illegible] have been suspected by our [illegible] fathers [illegible] it is [illegible] in the last few [illegible]

Figure 15. Part of the first page of Conan Doyle's article on infectious diseases which appeared in *Good Words* (1883).

An Essay
Upon the vasomotor changes in tabes dorsalis and on the influence which is exerted by the sympathetic nervous system in that disease, being a thesis presented in the hope of obtaining the degree of the Doctorship of Medicine of the University of Edinburgh.

by.

A. Conan. Doyle. MB. CM.

1 Bush Villas
Southsea.
April. 1885.

Figure 16. Title page of Conan Doyle's thesis for the M.D. degree, which he received in August 1885. (Used with permission from the University of Edinburgh.)

Figure 17. No. 2 Devonshire Place (Upper Wimpole Street), London, where Conan Doyle had his ophthalmology office from April to June 1891—first doorway on the right. (Photograph used with permission.)

SECTION THREE

CONAN DOYLE, HOLMES, AND WATSON

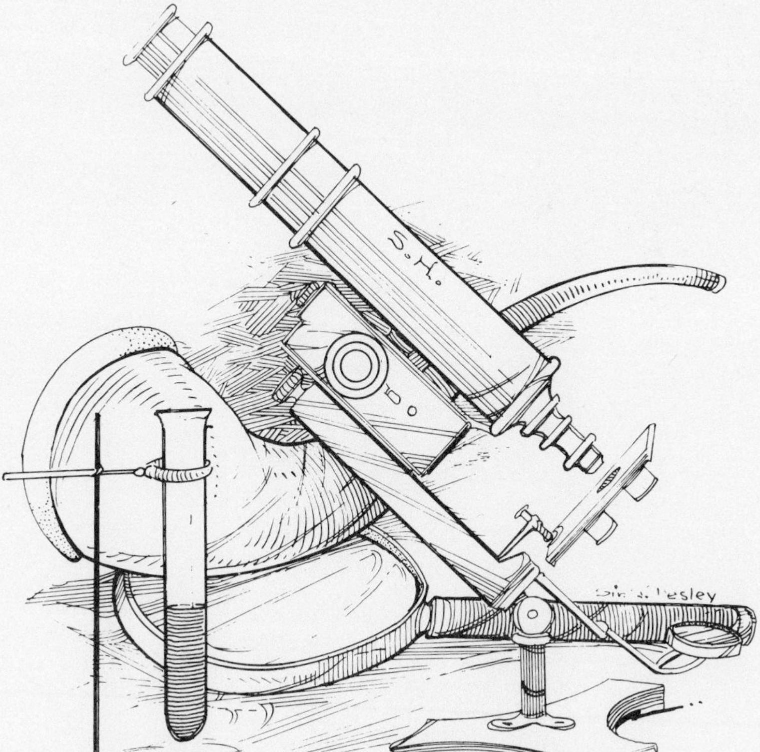

5

DETECTIVES, DOCTORS, AND DISEASES

The significance of the medical content of the Canonical writings in respect to Conan Doyle, as physician and to his times, has been obscured rather than enhanced by the enormous volume of commentaries on these stories. The majority approach the subject from a perspective of the historical coreality of Sherlock Holmes and Doctor Watson. Therefore, considerations of medicine usually consist of compilations of related items or attempts to explain various discrepancies of time, place, and events in the 60 Canonical works. An example is the extensive literature on the contradictory descriptions of the location of Watson's war wound.[92]

Another factor which dampens the critical study of Holmesian medicine is the so-called "serious study of Sherlock Holmes which begins with the premise . . . that Sir Arthur Conan Doyle was only Watson's literary agent."[83] In attempting to delineate the historic aspects of the medical Conan Doyle, one begins to appreciate the frustration of his son, Adrian, as expressed in his letter to *The Sherlock Holmes Journal* in 1963.[215]

> *. . . in regard to . . . reference to 'the literary agent,' do you not think, Mr. Editor, that the time has come when this childish and stupid joke should be dropped among members of an English Society who, presumably, have a personal regard for the creator of Holmes and Watson?*

This problem of obfuscation is not only the concern of a loyal son. Hollyer[535] has written that "Holmesian scholarship and the Holmes myth make serious criticism of the Sherlock Holmes stories quite difficult." This applies to their medical assessment as well.

Of somewhat more validity, in the historical sense, are commentaries on the source of the names "Holmes" and "Watson." It is generally stated that the latter name was suggested by the presence of Doctor James Watson, in Southsea at the time of Conan Doyle's practice.[452] Recently, Edwards[424] has suggested that the names of the two major characters in the *Canon* were derived in part from a textbook probably used by Conan Doyle. Joseph Bell's manual of surgery[56] refers to a Mr. Holmes in respect to excision of hip joints and P.H. Watson in relation to knee joints. Patrick Heron Watson (1832–1907) received his M.D. degree from Edinburgh in 1853. He was an Assistant Surgeon during the Crimean War. Joseph Bell became his assistant in 1865. This linkage in the Edinburgh faculty suggests a similar one in the derivation of the Holmes character and the name Watson in the *Canon.*[606]

Holmes and Watson are not unusual or rare names and their possible derivations need not detain us here. Sufficient, is to note the usual statement that Conan Doyle derived the name for his master detective from Oliver Wendell Holmes (1809–1894), American physician, anatomist, essayist, novelist, and poet.[872] Although often stated that Conan Doyle himself made such an assertion,[86] no such verification has been found. Actually, the possibility was first suggested in 1932 by Starrett, based on Conan Doyle's high esteem for his American colleague.[838] A statement has been made that O. W. Holmes angrily denied that the detective was named after him, but no source is provided.[531]

More pertinent to the medical orientation of this book is the individual who served as the model for Sherlock Holmes. The front-ranker for this honor is Doctor Joseph Bell, Edinburgh surgeon and teacher of the student Conan Doyle,[514] to whom Conan Doyle dedicated *The Adventures of Sherlock Holmes.*[270] The evidence is quite clear, being provided by Conan Doyle himself in his autobiography of 1924.[375p]

> *I thought of my old teacher Joe Bell, of his eagle face, of his curious ways, of his eerie trick of spotting details. If he were a detective he would surely reduce this fascinating but unorganized business to something nearer to an exact science. . . . It is all very well to say that a man is clever, but the reader wants to see examples of it—such examples as Bell gave us every day in the wards.*

He made a similar acknowledgement much earlier, during an interview in 1892.[548] "The remarkable individuality and discriminating tact of my old master (Bell) made a deep and lasting impression on me, though I had not the faintest idea that it would one day lead me to forsake medicine for story writing."

A fellow student of Conan Doyle's, Doctor H. E. Jones, wrote in 1904 a similar account of Joseph Bell's acuity, and labeled him "the king of deduction."[560] He also suggested that Conan Doyle's adaptation of Bell's skill to crime detection was influenced by another one of his professors. Sir Henry Littlejohn was Lecturer on Forensic Medicine and the City of Edinburgh Police Surgeon. Students flocked to murder trials at which he gave evidence.

In 1927, Conan Doyle provided additional insight into the genesis of his detective in a filmed interview.[380]

> *It often annoyed me how in the old fashioned detective stories, the detective always seemed to get at his results by some sort of lucky chance or fluke or else it was quite unexplained how he got there. . . . I began to think about this and . . . of turning scientific methods . . . onto the work of detection. . . . I used as a student [to] have an old professor whose name was Bell who was extraordinarily quick at deductive work.*

This is further evidence that Sherlock Holmes owes his creation to the medical training of Conan Doyle, and his overwhelming success, in part, to the author's medical knowledge.

Joseph Bell, in a letter included in a published interview,[548] made a very humble recognition of the honor. "Dr. Conan Doyle's genius and intense imagination has on this slender basis [using one's senses accurately] made his detective stories a distinctly new departure, but he owes less than he thinks to yours truly." Joseph Bell, however, may have been less than flattered, writing in a letter that "I'm sure he [Doyle] never imagined that such a heap of rubbish would fall on my devoted head in consequence of his stories."[796] In fact, he may have obtained a reputation as being a superficial teacher of surgery because of the association with Sherlock Holmes.[687]

In spite of the overwhelming evidence of the Bell-cum-Holmes relationship, a few other contenders for the honor have been proposed. It was suggested by Joseph Bell, in 1892, that the tradition established by John Syme (1799–1870) at Edinburgh of precise surgical diagnosis influenced Conan Doyle.[57] One would not be amiss to extrapolate even further that the intellectual aspects of Sherlock Holmes' character were derived in good part from the scientific orientation to medical diagnosis that was part of the educational milieu which greatly influenced Conan Doyle as a student. But, there is yet another candidate for the position of the Holmes model, and one who has excellent credentials. Conan Doyle himself exhibited the mental acuity of deduction from detailed observation, both as a physician[121] and as a public citizen applying logic to save wrongly convicted individuals, such as Edalji[336] and Slater.[356] Conan Doyle also solved several disappearances by Holmesian type reasoning, including that of a gentleman and a young foreigner.[366,N91]

Conan Doyle's narrator in a non-Sherlockian story of 1895[880] was a medical man who "used rather to pride myself on being able to spot a man's trade or profession by a good look at his exterior. I had the advantage of studying under a Professor at Edinburgh who was a master of the art. . ." The author is crediting himself with such skills, and his teacher with developing them.

The most ardent supporter of the Holmes-out-of-Doyle school of thought has been his son Adrian, supported by Starrett.[839] Adrian, however, was not fanatical to the extreme on this subject. He concluded a letter to *The Times* of London in 1943[212] with the following statement.

> *Dr. Joseph Bell did indeed help to develop my father's immense power of observation and conclusions, but it must be placed on record that these powers were indubitably innate, and for the mental prototype of Sherlock Holmes we need search no farther than his creator.*

Such a statement is quite sound in respect to the fact that what an author writes comes from his own knowledge, experience, and attributes. "Anybody knows that any creative writer . . . is bound to write to some extent from an autobiographical viewpoint."[73] How much of Sherlock Holmes was innate in Conan Doyle and how much seeded by Joseph Bell is a moot question, and need not interfere with our assessment of his detective stories and their medical content.

THE DETECTIVE STORY

In order to evaluate Conan Doyle's medical knowledge and experience as demonstrated in the Holmesian works, we must first place this type of fiction in the broader perspective of his times, his predecessor, his contemporaries, and his successors.

The Sherlockian *Canon* fits into the broad definition of crime fiction, defined by Keating as "fiction that is written primarily as entertainment and has as its subject some form of crime, crime taken at its widest possible meaning."[563] Conan Doyle was certainly not the first to write such stories, nor was he even the originator of one of its categories, the detective story.[870] He acknowledged his debt to predecessors. "Gaboriau had rather attracted me by the neat dovetailing of his plots, and Poe's masterful detective, M. Dupin, had from boyhood been one of my heroes."[375p]

Conan Doyle, however, provided Sherlock Holmes with quite a different attitude toward his two fictional predecessors.[244]

> *'Now in my opinion, Dupin was a very inferior fellow. . . . He had some analytical genius, no doubt; but he was by no means such a phenomenon as Poe appeared to imagine.' 'Have you read Gaboriau's works?' I asked. . . . Sherlock Holmes sniffed sardonically. 'Lecoq was a miserable bungler,' he said, in an angry voice.*

Such deprecatory statements were undoubtedly given to Holmes in order to characterize him as having a high opinion of his own skills.

Emile Gaboriau (1833–1873) was a French novelist who made his detective, Lecoq, a young policeman.[490] Two of his works are *The Mystery of Orcival*[465] (1884) and *The Lerouge Case*[466] (1885), both published several years before Conan Doyle's first detective story. Much better known and widely appreciated is the American author, Edgar Allen Poe (1804–1849).[861] Like Conan Doyle he wrote in several different literary genres, including science fiction, mystery, horror and detective stories, as well as poetry.[725] He far excelled Conan Doyle as a poet, but was surpassed by Conan Doyle as a writer of detective stories.

Poe's detective, Monsieur C. Auguste Dupin of Paris, used the same type of deductive reasoning from facts as did Sherlock Holmes; he succeeded where the police failed; and he had his exploits narrated by a friend. But, therein end the similarities. Dupin's best case, for example *The Murders in the Rue Morgue* (1842),[725] depicts a "thinking machine" without the fullness of characterization provided by the human foibles and eccentricities of Sherlock Holmes. The style of writing is not as engaging as that of Conan Doyle, there being pages of discussion on the value of observation and reason by the narrator and lengthy explanations by Dupin.

The fact that Conan Doyle was a better narrator of detective tales than Poe in no way detracts from his debt. He obtained the central concept of a thinking, nonpolice, detective as well as certain plot ideas. For example, Conan Doyle's "A Scandal in Bohemia"[270] contains the challenge of finding a shrewdly concealed letter as does Poe's "The Purloined Letter."[270] The deciphering of a cryptogram in his "Dancing Men" is also found in Poe's "The Gold Bug."[N92]

A closer predecessor of Conan Doyle was the Australian barrister, Fergus W. Hume,[563b] who published *The Mystery of a Hansom Cab*[551] (1886) a year before the first Sherlock Holmes story.[244] It had a wide sale in both Great Britain and America. The hero, however, is a police detective, Mr. Gorby, who eventually arrives at the correct solution to the murder in the hansom cab, to the consternation of Kilsip, the private detective. Quite similar to Sherlock Holmes, Gorby engages in considerable ratiocination. Also included are a few medical items such as the realistic description of postmortem findings, the use of chloroform to commit murder, and reference to an aneurysm of the heart. In 1884, two years before Hume's mystery, Conan Doyle wrote of a murdered man being given as a passenger to the cabman of a growler (four-wheeler).[234]

MEDICAL CONTENT IN DETECTIVE STORIES

Conan Doyle was not the first to conceive of a reasoning detective. He was the first, however, to include more than a few allusions to medical matters in this type of fiction and to such an extent that it forms one of the major literary characteristics of the Canonical writings. The introduction of such material is enhanced by creating a medical practitioner as the narrator. But Holmes himself, as we shall see, also had considerable knowledge of medical matters.

The Holmes stories did not remain for long as the sole example of major medical content in detective stories. In the 1890s Mrs. L.T. Meade collaborated with medical men to write detective short stories with medical subjects. "The Sorceress of the Strand

(Madame Sara)''[645] was coauthored by Robert Eustace, probably Doctor Robert Barton Eustace, MRCS, LRCP.[490] The plot revolves around Madame Sara, a mysterious and beautiful female who comes to London from Brazil as a beautifier of women, but actually practices medicine and dentistry. In order to gain control of a large amount of money, she placed poison (a hyoscine-like toxic alkaloid) in the heroine's dental filling. The hero is a police surgeon, Mr. Eric Vandeleur, who realizes such a possibility and removes the tooth in time. As in some of the cases of Sherlock Holmes, the culprit was not convicted of the crime. Doctor Eustace was undoubtedly the same physician who coauthored *The Documents in the Case* with Dorothy Sayers and provided details on poisons such as muscarine and arsenic.[89] Conan Doyle, the experienced physician, required no such collaborator.

Also medically oriented are the ''Dr. Thorndyke'' stories, the first one, *The Red Thumb Mark,*[461] being published in 1907. The author, R. Austin Freeman (1862–1943), was, like Conan Doyle, a physician, graduating from the Middlesex Hospital Medical College in 1887.[208] Also like Conan Doyle, he did not have the financial resources to buy a practice. Instead of attempting to start his own, he joined the colonial service and was sent to the Gold Coast as an assistant surgeon. There he contracted blackwater fever (malaria). On returning to England he was forced to eke out a living in relatively menial medical sidelines—a prison physician and examiner of immigrants and army inductees. The same erroneous statement made about Conan Doyle has been made of Austin Freeman; he was driven to writing out of financial desperation.[79]

Like Doctor Watson, the narrator, Christopher Jervis, was a physician. But the detective himself, Doctor Thorndyke, was also a medical man—a forensic physician. Thorndyke was more a scientific investigator than Sherlock Holmes, the ratiocinator. Many references are made to testing, including chemical, physical, and microscopic techniques,[870a] many of which Freeman tested himself.[798] Thus, the Thorndyke exploits tend to have more realistic investigations than those of Holmes. They have not, however, achieved any general acceptance or resulted in rampant cultism as has the creation of Conan Doyle. One reason may be the fact that the large amount of character detail and eccentricities provided for Holmes and Watson are missing for Thorndyke and Jervis. Also missing are the fascinating relationships and stimulating interplay between Conan Doyle's characters.[N93]

Freeman's stories are less suspenseful than those of Conan Doyle because he used an inverted format. They begin with a description of the crime and an identification of the criminal. Then Thorndyke picks up the trail to eventual identification of the culprit through scientific methods. Like Conan Doyle, Freeman modeled his detective after a medical school professor, Doctor Alfred Swayne Taylor of Guy's Hospital, London.[531] But he was a professor of medical jurisprudence and not of clinical surgery, as was Joseph Bell. Thorndyke is characterized by "careful adherence to the probable and a strict avoidance of physical impossibilities," and Sherlock Holmes, by untested hypotheses and irrelevant details.[912] It is these irrelevancies, however, along with interesting personal idiocyncracies that make Sherlock Holmes the better "read."

Conan Doyle's Sherlock Holmes stimulated the development of a criminal with a twist—the gentleman burglar. The name, *Raffles,*[545] was derived from Conan Doyle's *The Doings of Raffles Haw*[262] by his brother-in-law E. W. Hornung. The first book, *The Amateur Cracksman*[544] (1899) was dedicated "To A.C.D. This form of Flattery."[544] Raffles may well be the somewhat comic antihero counterpart of Sherlock Holmes. Like Holmes he kept his assistant in the dark as to his plans. Like Holmes he used chloroform to subdue a foe. Bertillon, the famous French criminologist, objected to the concept of a gentleman burglar, even though he was caught and sent to prison.[71] Holmes and Watson had a much more successful record and became more famous.

The other antihero of the period, Arsene Lupin created by Maurice Leblanc, was also placed in prison, but by his own choice.[602A] A French burglar rather than a detective, he outwitted the police using Holmesian logic. Also like Holmes he had some medical knowledge. One of Lupin's disguises was that of a Russian physician. In Saint Louis he attended the laboratory of Doctor Altier who was astonished "by the ingenuity of his hypotheses on subjects of bacteriology and the boldness of his experiments in diseases of the skin." Like Holmes, who simulated a dying detective, Lupin put a drug, atropine, in his eyes as part of a disguise. He went further by altering his skin appearance with pyrogallic acid, injections of paraffin, and applications of celandine which causes eruptions.[923] But in comparison to the crime chronicles written by Conan Doyle, Lupin's medicine is minimal in amount.

Generally not as well known as Sherlock Holmes and Doctor Watson is the specific medical content in the accounts of their adventures. Such items have been referred to and detailed by various authors. For example, Guthrie[501] has provided an overview, and Beerman[54] and Carter,[126] samplings. Maurice Campbell[121] has organized his compilation on the basis of Doctor Watson's knowledge of medicine and on his medical practice. The many papers by Van Liere on Holmesian medicine have been collected into a book.[898] Clark[139] has published an alphabetical listing of many of the diseases and signs and symptoms included in the *Canon*. Some can also be found in encyclopedic type books containing information culled from these stories.[N94]

The various content areas related to medical knowledge, skills, and practice are analyzed in the following pages. Assessment is oriented to insights provided for understanding the caliber of Conan Doyle's own medical practice, with consideration of the state of medical knowledge and the mores of the later Victorian and Edwardian eras. Perhaps we can come closer to answering questions that have been raised regarding Conan Doyle's worth as a medical man and to the contributions of a medical background to the success of a writer of fiction.

Medically related items are so numerous in the Holmes stories that it is not possible (let alone productive) to discuss each one individually. Consequently, they are detailed in Appendix E, which constitutes a comprehensive listing of such items. Citations for each story are given according to abbreviations used by De

Waal.[197] Page numbers refer to those in Baring-Gould's two-volume, annotated publication.[41] The medical content is divided into categories of doctors, specialties, diseases, drugs, forensic, Holmes, and miscellaneous. It is on this framework that the following assessment of the Canonical writings as a reflection of the medical Conan Doyle is made.

DOCTORS OF THE CANON

A unique feature of the Sherlock Holmes stories is the incorporation of a large number of doctors.[499] Not counting a professor of physiology (Cree) and one of comparative anatomy, (Cree) there are 34 physicians in all. Over 50% of these (19) are general practitioners, as was Doctor Conan Doyle. The remainder consists of a variety of specialists including four surgeons, (Danc, Glor, Houn, Illu) an endocrinologist, (Cree) a dermatologist, (Blan) and a tropical disease consultant. (Dyin) The rest are nonspecified.

Most play a minor or cameo role, being almost peripheral to the plot.[752] For example, Doctor Moore Agar of Harley Street recommended complete rest for the great detective if he was to avoid a breakdown. (Devi 508) Some are mentioned only in passing, as was Doctor Ainstree, the greatest living authority on tropical disease, whom Watson wanted to examine Holmes because of his apparent fatal disease. (Dyin 441) Another use of a doctor was to introduce a mystery, as did Doctor James Mortimer in the case of the mysterious hound. (Houn 3)[667]

Several Holmesian physicians play more pivotal roles. The best known is young Doctor Stamford who had served under Watson as a dresser and who introduced him to Holmes. (Stud 145) Maligned at first is young Doctor Ray Ernest who disappeared with old Mr. Amberley's young wife, along with his life's savings. (Reti 546) A more developed characterization is that of Doctor Grimesby Roylott, the villain who committed murder by the use of a poisonous snake. (Spec 243) Fortunately the other physicians in the *Canon* are not criminals for, as Holmes extrapolated,

"When a doctor goes wrong he is the first of criminals. He has nerve and he has knowledge." (Spec 257) This statement is substantiated by a recent study which describes 36 well-known cases of murder by physicians.[555A] The methods used were usually drugs or poisons.

The attributes of some of these physicians are reminiscent of various aspects of Conan Doyle's own medical career. Doctors Jackson (Croo 226) and Anstruther (Bosc 134) looked after Watson's practice during his escapades with Holmes—much as Doctors Claremont and Maybury must have done during Conan Doyle's involvement in various sports and travel. Doctor Becher was named after G. T. D. Beecher who received his L.R.C.P. in the same year (1885) and from the same institution, the University of Edinburgh, (Engi 223) as Conan Doyle received his M.D. degree.[752a] Doctor Trevelyan did general practice because he could not get an opening to specialize in nervous disease, (Resi 268) whereas Conan Doyle gave up a successful practice to find that he could not make a living as an eye specialist. More reminiscent of Conan Doyle is Doctor Leslie Armstrong, lecturer and consultant, who "does not care for general practice, which distracts him from his literary work."(Miss 485)

The presence of these physicians does not make the Holmes' stories medical ones. Most are fleeting with but a brief moment on Conan Doyle's stage. They do provide elements of reality and heightened drama engendered by the presence of physicians at the site of homicide or illness and references to physicians not on the scene. These details contribute to the enormous amount of background detail that fascinates readers of Sherlock Holmes. One of the physicians, Doctor Watson, unlike the other physicians, is an integral part of the *Canon* and contributes much to the flavor of the narrations.

Doctor John (James) H. Watson undoubtedly is the best known practicing physician in English literature, even though his practice was frequently interrupted by involvements with Sherlock Holmes. His prominence is remarkable because he is not the main character. But part of the success of the *Canon* is due to the interactions, the interdependency, and the contrasts between the brilliant detective and his plodding confrere.

Much commentary has been written about Watson, almost all of it oriented to a historical figure.[797] There is a eulogy to this well-known physician born in 1852, whose "father was an eye specialist in Portsmouth, England,"[437] where Conan Doyle also practiced. Watson is even purported to have written 14 medical articles and books.[643] Dissertations abound on his character,[164] his amorous affairs,[929] and inconsistencies in the stories regarding the number of his marriages and the location(s) of his war wound.[659]

Also detailed are accounts of Watson's medical career, based upon the availability "of his reminiscences, which fortunately, have been edited for posterity by Sir Arthur Conan Doyle. . . ."[2] Maurice Campbell, in particular, has provided comprehensive accounts not only of Watson's practice, but also of his medical knowledge as documented in the Holmesian works.[121] Our interest, however, lies not in Doctor Watson as a historical figure, but in his being a reflection of Conan Doyle's own medical knowledge and attitudes.

It is uncertain how much the depiction of Watson's medical career was influenced by that of Conan Doyle. One commonality is that Watson, like Conan Doyle, had stayed in Southsea, and later yearned "for the glades of New Forest or the shingle [beach] of Southsea." (Card 193) Unlike Conan Doyle's early practice experience, Watson purchased old Mr. Farquhar's practice in Paddington, London, shortly after his marriage. (Stoc 153) He then sold his practice to Verner. (Norw 414) It is not known if Conan Doyle merely turned over his own practice to Claremont or was paid for it. He exhibited no more reluctance in suddenly leaving his practice for his Berlin trip than did Watson in leaving immediately for Baskerville Hall. (Houn 32)

One suspects that Conan Doyle became sufficiently bored by the practice of medicine to leave it "In an instant" as did Watson on Holmes' request. (Stoc 154) In neither case was it due to a small practice. "My practice had steadily increased." (Engi 209) One of Holmes' observations was that Watson had a better practice than that of a neighboring doctor. In response to Watson's usual amazement at such deductions, the master detective explained. "By the steps, my boy. Yours are worn three inches deeper than his." (Stoc 154)

Certain other similarities are noted between the actual biography of Doctor Conan Doyle and the fictional one of Doctor Watson.[103] Both married more than once—their first marriage being to the sister of a patient and the heroine of a Holmes' adventure. (Sign) Such forced comparisons, although common in the so-called "higher criticism" of the *Canon,* contribute little to knowledge of Conan Doyle's own career. It must be emphasized that the depiction of Watson as a plodding and somewhat slow-witted individual is no reflection on Conan Doyle as a physician, but is his genius as a writer in creating a very effective foil for the brilliant Holmes. The mercurial nature of the master detective is cleverly highlighted by his foil. "Good old Watson! You are the one fixed point in a changing age." (Last 803)

Watson has been considered as

> . . . *a typical product of the Hospital [St. Bartholomew] at the latter half of the last century; frank, honest and industrious, a sympathetic observor, a comforter and a friend.*[835]

Such an impression of the good doctor undoubtedly comes from Conan Doyle's own opinion on the proper behavior of a physician.

The descriptions of Doctor Watson and other physicians in the *Canon* do not provide us with a detailed picture of the practice of medicine in Victorian England. We do learn, however, that then as now, practices were bought and sold; that there were both general practitioners and consultants; that some physicians were less successful than others; and that the social status of general practitioners was relatively low. At least one difference in appearance from that of today can be discerned from the basis for Holmes' deduction that Watson has entered practice after his marriage—" a bulge on the side of his top hat to show where he has secreted his stethoscope." (Scan 349) Further orientation to the medicine of the last century can be obtained from a consideration of the special areas mentioned in the *Canon.*

SPECIAL AREAS OF MEDICINE

Several basic science areas are included. There are a surprising number of anthropological descriptions, especially in *The Hound of the Baskervilles.*[321] Doctor Mortimer, physician to the Baskerville family, described Holmes' skull as being dolichocephalic with well-marked supra-orbital development, (Houn 7) and he was interested in the comparative anatomy of the Bushman and the Hottentot. (Houn 12) The moor about Baskerville Hall contained the remains of prehistoric homes of Neolithic man.

> *On all sides of you as you walk are the houses of these forgotten folk, with their graves and the huge monoliths which are supposed to have marked their temples. As you look at their grey stone huts against the scarred hillsides you leave your own age behind you, and if you were to see a skinclad, hairy man crawl out from the low door, fitting a flint-tipped arrow on the string of his bow, you would feel that his presence there was more natural than your own. (Houn 52)*

Doctor Mortimer had excavated a prehistoric skull from a barrow "which fills him with great joy." (Houn 54) But Mr. Frankland "intends to prosecute [him] for opening a grave without the consent of the next of kin." (Houn 55) This is a superb example of Doylean humor.

Traces of a vanished race in the moors were mentioned again in "The Devil's Foot." (Devi 509) The client in "The Three Garridebs" (3Gar 647) had plaster skulls of Neanderthal, Heidelberg, and CroMagnon men. Conan Doyle further demonstrated his interest in anthropology by visiting two or three times the excavation site of the Piltdown Man (1912),[922] its exposure as a hoax not occurring until 1953.[507] In 1912, he was writing *The Lost World,*[357] which also contains descriptions of primitive man.[N95]

Conan Doyle had Holmes apply the techniques of physical anthropology, mainly measurements, in solving crimes. Such an orientation is not surprising because anatomy courses in British schools contained a considerable amount of this subject during the

19th century.[592] For example, one of the clues that helped clear young McCarthy of the murder of his father was related to footprints. "His height I know that you might roughly judge from the length of his stride." (Bosc 148) Holmes determined that the murderer was more than six feet high. "Why, the height of a man, in nine cases out of ten, can be told from the length of his stride. It's a simple calculation enough, though there is no use my boring you with figures." (Stud 173) Unfortunately, Holmes does not give his formula or indicate how he compensates for variables such as speed of movement.[690] Conan Doyle attributed to the detective a monograph on the preservation of footprints using plaster of paris. (Sign 612) Thus, his study of very small footprints led to the conclusion that Jonathan Small's accomplice was an aborigine of the Andaman Islands. (Sign 655)[880] If Conan Doyle had any attribute, it was a widely ranging imagination.

The science of chemistry is as much or more an integral part of the *Canon,* being of prime importance for a scientific detective. In fact, Sherlock Holmes himself admitted to a profound knowledge of the subject. (Stud 156) To emphasize Holmes' chemical expertise Conan Doyle provided him with a "chemical corner" in his sitting room, containing an acid-stained deal (wood)-topped desk. (Empt 345) As evidence of active research his hands were stained with chemicals. (Stud 153)

But how profound was Holmes', and thereby Conan Doyle's, knowledge of chemistry? Perhaps, it was more superficial than profound. For example, a carbuncle is not composed of charcoal (Blue 457) unlike diamonds which are. It is an iron-aluminum silicate.[32] Holmes' statement that "I had succeeded in dissolving the hydrocarbon" (Sign 662) has been criticized because there is no difficulty in doing so.[142] His use of the term bisulphate of baryta (Iden 413) has been questioned because a chemist would call it barium bisulphate.[477] Holmes has even been taken to task for using the plural, acetones, for a specific chemical compound. (Copp 120)[32] But, Redmond has risen to Conan Doyle's defense, stating that "acetones" was occasionally used for "ketones" in his day. Osler's textbook of medicine of 1892 does, however, refer to the singular acetone.[696,N96]

Conan Doyle did have some accurate knowledge of chemistry. He appreciated the significance of litmus paper. (Nava 169) Mention is made of the uncertainty of the guaiacum test for blood. (Stud 150) Holmes recognized the smell of iodoform and "a black mark of nitrate of silver upon his [Watson's] right forefinger," (Scan 349) both of which are substances used by practicing physicians. Both Watson and Holmes were familiar with the characteristic "pleasant almondy odour" of prussic acid, a poison which Mrs. Ronder considered using for suicide because of the horrible mutilation of her face by a lion. (Veil 461) These chemical references provide interesting detail in the stories, but are hardly indicative of a profound knowledge of chemistry.

Isaac Asimov, a biochemist himself, has described Conan Doyle as "surprisingly poor in chemistry."[32] Even his very dramatic use of phosphorus on the jaws of the horrible hound of the Baskervilles has been questioned on a chemical basis.[750] Clark is somewhat kinder, pointing out that "the average G.P. of that period was perhaps not as chemically sophisticated as might have been desirable."[142] Conan Doyle, however, did receive a grade of S (satisfactory) in his chemistry examinations[876] but that was six years before the first Holmesian story. And even today, when medical education includes an intensive orientation to chemistry, the knowledge of general practitioners in this area is often less than desirable.

The *Canon* does contain some references to another basic science—anatomy. Watson identified the object burnt to a black cinder found in Sir Robert Norberton's furnace, as the upper condyle (protuberance) of a human femur (thigh bone). (Shos 635) This bone does have a condyle, but it is not labeled as upper. The familiarity of the author, as a physician, with anatomy corpses for dissection is evident in analysis of two ears sent to Miss Susan Cushing in a cardboard box. (Card 195) Holmes rejects the possibility that they were sent by students from dissecting rooms because the ears were preserved in salt, whereas "carbolic or rectified spirits would be the preservatives which would suggest themselves to the medical mind, certainly not rough salt." (Card 197)

The questionable science of phrenology, based on anatomical features of the head, is very effectively used by Conan Doyle for a classic confrontation between Holmes and Watson. Watson could not understand how Holmes had reached his conclusions after examining the hat of Mr. Baker who had misplaced his goose.

> *'I [Watson] have no doubt I am very stupid; but I must confess that I am unable to follow you. For example, how did you deduce this man was intellectual?' For answer Holmes clapped the hat upon his head. It came right over the forehead and settled upon the bridge of his nose. 'It is a question of cubic capacity,' said he: 'a man with so large a brain must have something in it.' (Blue 454)*

The surprise is that the hat was much too large for Sherlock Holmes, who came close to genius in his intellectual powers of ratiocination.

Conan Doyle's knowledge of yet another area basic to medicine—genetics—was consistent with that of his time. Familial similarity in physical characteristics has, of course, long been known. One example is the recognition of the villain Stapleton, as a relative of the ancestral Hugo Baskerville, from a painting. (Houn 91) More detailed was Holmes' observation that an ear in a cardboard box was identical to those of Miss Sarah Cushing. (Card 202) "There was the same shortening of the pinna, the same broad curve of the upper lobe, the same convolution of the inner cartilage." Thus, the ear could only belong to a blood relative.

Several less substantiated genetic items are alluded to. Handwriting characteristics, such as the shape of p's and g's, are hardly heredity in origin, as suggested by Holmes for the Cunningham father and son. (Reig 345) A racial trait was inherited by Mrs. Grant Munro's daughter through a previous marriage to John Hebron, who was of African descent. (Yell 588) She was a coal-black negress, an unlikely genetic event when the mother was white and the father quite light.[N97] But, the plot gave Conan Doyle an opportunity to feature his own noble and altruistic feelings. Her second husband, Munro, after a few minutes hesitation, kissed the little child and held his hand out to his wife. A story featuring and approving a mixed marriage was quite unusual and farsighted for 1893. It is another example of Conan Doyle's essential humanism.

Several references are made to inherited mental characteristics. Holmes' own skills in observation and deduction are attributed to inheritance. (Gree 590) "How do you know that it is hereditary?" asks Watson. "Because my brother Mycroft possesses it in a larger degree than I do," replies Holmes. The trait may have originated from "my grandmother, who was the sister of Vernet, the French artist. Art in the blood is liable to take the strangest forms." Conan Doyle, himself, had a great uncle, Michael Conan, who was a French artist.

The Canonical writings also contain examples of the familial transmission of cruelty and criminality. Holmes is quite concerned for the safety of Miss Hunter because her pupil is a child whose "disposition is abnormally cruel, merely for cruelty's sake, and whether he derives this from his smiling father, as I should suspect, or from his mother, it bodes evil for the poor girl who is in their power." (Copp 129) Holmes was proved right.

Even the criminal traits of Holmes' arch enemy, the evil master criminal Moriarity, were inherited. (Fina 303) "But the man had hereditary tendencies of the most diabolical kind. A criminal strain ran in his blood, which instead of being modified, was increased and rendered infinitely more dangerous by his extraordinary mental powers."

In discussing Colonel Sebastian Moran, Moriarity's Chief of Staff, Holmes develops his thesis even further.

> *I have a theory that the individual represents in his development the whole procession of his ancestors, and that such a sudden turn to good or evil stands for some strong influence which came in the line of his pedigree. The person becomes, as it were, the epitome of the history of his family. (Empt 347)*

On Watson's rejoinder that "It is surely rather fanciful," Holmes concedes that "I don't insist upon it." And rightly so! As Conan

Doyle knew, the human embryo does go through stages of physical resemblance to progenitors, such as gills and tail. This so-called recapitulation theory was acknowledged in the 19th century.[680a] Our present day knowledge of genes and chromosomes does explain inherited, familial physical features. But, the inheritance of behavioral characteristics is doubtful and cannot be proved because of the known influence of postbirth environmental influences.[N98]

We must not be too hard on Conan Doyle, author and physician. A writer should be allowed some latitude in compromising facts for the sake of effect as was done so effectively by Conan Doyle. And a physician, educated and practicing in the 1870s and 1880s can hardly be expected to have genetic knowledge not apparent until the next century. His genetic views were accepted by the medical community in his own day.[674] His readers would also accept them and be thrilled by their association with mystery and crime. Today's readers are really no different.

The Holmesian *Canon* also includes references to several medical specialties as such. Although Doctor Percy Trevelyan wrote a monograph on obscure nervous lesions, he could not limit his practice to neurology because of financial constraints. (Resi 268) Only a physician, and one experienced in ophthalmology, would use a cataract knife as the key feature in a mystery story.[170] The race horse, Silver Blaze, had his leg tendon cut by such an instrument because it left a very small and inapparent skin wound. (Silv 271, 280)[N99]

Not as many references are made to the specialty of pathology as one might expect in the tales of a detective. Mentioned is a postmortem on Sir Charles Baskerville that revealed organic disease. (Houn 12) His physician, Doctor Mortimer, was a corresponding member of the Swedish Pathological Society, (Houn 5) and Doctor Trevalyan had done some research on the pathology of catalepsy. (Resi 269) Possibly even more useful was "the latest treatise upon pathology" into which Watson plunged furiously to take his mind off Miss Morstan. (Sign 620)[N100] Conan Doyle showed an appreciation of the enthusiasm of pathologists by comparing Holmes' excitement at being told about the creeping man "with the air of a pathologist who presents a rare specimen." (Cree 755)

Surgeons are more numerous than other specialists in the *Canon.*[896] Doctor James Mortimer is labeled as a surgeon, although he appears to do general practice. (Houn) Sir Leslie Oakshott, the famous surgeon, stitched Holmes' scalp wounds which resulted from an attack by two ruffians. (Illu 683) A local surgeon, unnamed, reported that Mrs. Cubitt's wound was serious but not necessarily fatal, even though "The bullet had passed through the front of her brain." (Danc 536) And finally the surgeon of the clipper, *Gloria Scott,* was bound and gagged by mutineers and later killed. (Glor 119) Fortunately the most serious occurrence on Conan Doyle's two voyages as a ship surgeon was a severe bout of fever.

Other specialties are mentioned in passing. There is the Tropical Disease Specialist, Doctor Ainstree, whose presence would have ruined Holmes' trap for the poisoner, Culverton Smith. (Dyin 441) It was a Prague endocrinologist, Lowenstein, who sent the elderly Professor Presbury the life rejuvenating serum from a Langier monkey. (Cree 765) And it was a skin specialist, Doctor James Saunders, who saved the ex-soldier from permanent isolation by recognizing that his skin was blanched due to noninfective ichthyosis rather than leprosy. (Blan 721)

The inclusion of this relatively small number of specialists by Conan Doyle in the Holmes series is a reflection of his times. Specialization developed slower in Great Britain than in the United States.[174] It often arose as special interests of general practitioners, a good example being Conan Doyle and ophthalmology. Even more interesting than the study of such specialists are the numerous diseases included in the *Canon.*

DISEASES IN THE CANON

The most remarkable feature of the Sherlockian works, aside from their immense popularity, are the many diseases mentioned. Compiled in a listing, as in Appendix E, these diseases resemble the index of a textbook of medicine. They include involvements of many different organs and tissues of the body, as well as of the mind. However, two major deficiencies exist in the medical Holmes. As Conan Doyle points out in his short story, "A Medical Document,"[288] "The small complaints simply don't exist [in fiction]," and "The novelist never strikes below the belt." But, he can be forgiven because even modern textbooks of medicine make relatively little of the common cold[444] and because diseases of the genital organs would hardly be a fitting subject for a Victorian novelist. However, one reference is made to Watson having had "a severe chill for three days last week." (Stoc 154) Holmes deduced that he had had a summer cold because his slippers were new and the soles slightly scorched. This indicated sitting with feet outstretched to the fireplace, which would not be done ordinarily in June.

The realtively common and nonserious diseases in the *Canon* include a few of the spine and the extremities. Ferguson's son "went off with a curious, shambling gait which told my [Watson's] eyes that he was suffering from a weak spine." (Suss 470) We are told earlier that his condition was due to a fall in childhood and a twisted spine. (Suss 466) The twisted deformity of the crooked man was also traumatic, being caused by rebels in India. (Croo 236) Another back ailment, lumbago (painful back), was suggested by Watson as the reason Professor Presbury was seen creeping—much to the amusement of Holmes who pointed out that "he was able to stand erect in a moment." (Cree 755)

The slipped kneecap of Staunton, the missing three quarter rugger player, "was nothing." (Miss 480) Rheumatism was the reason for Watson to go to "A Turkish bath . . . what we call an alternative to medicine." (Lady 656) The *Canon* contains mention of four individuals who have had a lost leg replaced by a wooden one. (See Appendix E.) There are only two descriptions of the much more common limp. Such changes in appearance contribute to providing a sinister connotation for a character. Gout, on the other hand, is a joint disease of the more opulent. Lord Mount-James, "one of the richest men in England . . . could chalk [gouty material] his billiard cue with his knuckles.'' (Miss 478) This disease was the subject of a contribution to the *Lancet* by Conan Doyle in 1884.[238]

It is surprising that so little was made of abnormalities of the eye, given Conan Doyle's propensity to ophthalmology.[431] A cataract operation was needed by the mother of the Honorable Robert Adair, whose murder was the first crime solved after Holmes' return from his apparent death. (Empt 330) Shortsightedness is given more play. Holmes surprises Miss Mary Sutherland, who consulted him about her vanished bridegroom, by observing that ''with your short sight it is a little trying to do so much typewriting.'' (Iden 406) He provided no explanation. There is one reference to blindness, that of Von Herder, the German mechanic. (Empt 344) He had constructed the air gun which Moriarity's lieutenant, Colonel Moran, used in an attempt to murder Holmes.

More central to the solution of a mystery was Holmes' analysis of the golden pince-nez glasses which led to the murderess of young Willoughby Smith. (Gold 356)

> *She has a remarkably thick nose, with eyes which are set close upon either side of it. She has a puckered forehead, a peering expression, and probably rounded shoulders. . . . As her glasses are of remarkable strength, and as opticians are not very numerous, there should be no difficulty in tracing her.*

This is a graphic description of shortsightedness, which is managed through refraction of eyes, a skill which Conan Doyle learned at the Portsmouth Eye and Ear Infirmary. He also used such knowledge in the real world to free Edalji from prison—on the basis that his very weak eyes would not have allowed him to find and mutilate horses at night.[336]

Also common, but much more serious, are diseases of the heart. And here Conan Doyle exhibits considerable knowledge and understanding. Several characters are afflicted with heart failure. Sir Charles Baskerville's death while being chased by the family curse, the monsterous hound, was attributed to cardiac exhaustion and confirmed when postmortem examination revealed "long-standing organic disease." (Houn 12) This had resulted in decreased ability of the heart to withstand for long the terror and supreme exertion of outrunning the apparition. Questionable, however, is the statement that the "almost incredible facial distortion . . . is a symptom which is not unusual in cases of dyspnoea and death from cardiac exhaustion."

A long-standing case of heart failure was that of Lady Beatrice Falder whose weak heart resulted in dropsy (swelling of tissues by fluid). (Shos 633) Her condition was undoubtedly aggravated by "drinking like a fish." Even after death from dropsy there was no peace. Her brother, Sir Robert, hid her body because word of the death of his benefactor would bring down his creditors. (Shos 641) Captain Arthur Morstan, father of Watson's bride-to-be, also had a weak heart, which undoubtedly contributed to his sudden death when, during a paroxysm of anger over the division of ill-gotten treasure, "he suddenly pressed his hand to his side, his face turned a dusky hue, and he fell backwards." (Sign 628) The dusky hue was undoubtedly due to cyanosis caused by the sudden cessation of circulation of the blood. If the sudden death was due to a "heart attack" (myocardial infarction) one would expect Morstan to clutch not the side of his chest, but the front where such pain occurs. Pain in the side could be due to a lung embolus (clot carried in the blood stream), also with resultant rapid death.

Another presumed heart case is that of Major Sholto, Morstan's partner in crime. "He was propped up with pillows and breathing heavily" and was in pain. (Sign 627) This has variously been interpreted as orthopnea (difficulty in breathing when lying down),[126] and heart failure due to hypertension,[121] although shortness of breath can have other causes, such as pneumonia. Death, as in Sir Charles Baskerville, was sudden and induced by terror, in this instance seeing an unexpected, familiar, but cruel face in the window. (Sign 629)

At the time *The Sign of the Four* was published (1890), pain in the area of the heart was called angina,[696g] as it is today.[663] There was some recognition even then that it was related to blockage of coronary arteries, usually by arteriosclerosis.[769] Conan Doyle, himself, had angina for months before his death—undoubtedly caused by a myocardial infarct.

The Sign of the Four has reference to yet another type of heart disease. Thaddeus Sholto, a brother of the erstwhile Major, showed hypochondriacal tendencies in being concerned about the mitral and aortic valves of his heart. (Sign 625) The good Doctor Watson, however, assured him of their normality. More significant was the heart disease of Fitzroy McPherson, the science master, whose inexplicable death was a major challenge for the master detective. He was ''a fine upstanding young fellow whose life had been crippled by heart trouble following rheumatic fever.'' (Lion 777) A permanent disability caused by rheumatic fever is most likely due to disease of the mitral or aortic valves or both.

The most fascinating disease in the *Canon* related to the heart is found in Conan Doyle's first Holmes story, *A Study in Scarlet*,[244] published in 1887 while he was practicing medicine. It involves the first portion of the aorta, the great artery arising from the heart. Jefferson Hope (the villain-hero) was captured and desired to tell all because he ''may never be tried.'' In explanation he asked Watson to place a hand on his chest.

> *I did so; and became at once conscious of an extraordinary throbbing and commotion which was going on inside. The walls of his chest seemed to thrill and quiver as a frail building would do inside when some powerful engine was at work. In the silence of the room I could hear a dull humming and buzzing noise which proceeded from the same source. Why, . . . you have an aortic aneurysm! (Stud 223–224)*

Hope's explanation for its cause was ''over-exposure and underfeeding [while] among the Salt-Lake Mountains.'' There are, in reality, two major causes of an aneurysm (local dilatation) of the first part of the aorta, Marfan's syndrome and syphilis. The former is found in tall individuals who have an inherited degeneration of the tissue in the wall of the aorta.[456,N101] Because Hope is described as six feet tall, such a cause has been proposed.[163]

And because Conan Doyle wrote this story ten years before the syndrome was described by Marfan, he has been given credit for an earlier recognition.[751]

For several reasons, however, our hero cannot be given credit for the first description of an aneurysm due to Marfan's syndrome. The type of aneurysm in this disease is not the usual local dilatation of the lumen, but a false passageway of blood through the wall of the aorta due to a tear in its inner lining. One would not expect to find the throbbing commotion and quivering so dramatically described by Conan Doyle. In addition, a prolonged survival after the onset of the aneurysm is minimal, only 10% of patients living more than one year.

Much more common and likely, at least in Conan Doyle's era, would be an aneurysmal dilatation of the lumen of the proximal aorta caused by syphilis.[N102] This is quite consistent with the findings observed by Watson. The aneurysm may be present for many years, slowly growing until it finally ruptures with consequent rapid death due to internal hemorrhage, as occurred to the unfortunate Jefferson Hope. (Stud 230) Further evidence that he was infected with syphilis was suggested by Bates,[45] who considered that Hope's lapse of memory leading to his capture was due to involvement of his nervous system by this pernicious infection. Conan Doyle's intent here is not known.

Two remaining conditions are much more popular than aneurysm in fictional works. A "weak place in my heart" was the reason for old Trevor's fainting when Holmes reminded him of a past association. (Glor 110) Blessington used a weak heart as an excuse to sponsor Doctor Trevelyan's office in his own house. (Resi 270) Medical men now, as in Conan Doyle's day, do use the term "weak heart." Surprising, however, was his use of the condition mentioned so often in romances—a broken heart. For example, a noblewoman's husband died of a broken heart when he received some letters from a blackmailer whom she refused to pay. (Chas 568) Douglas Maberley, an Attaché at Rome, died of pneumonia a month after his heart was broken in a love affair. (3Gab 725) In Conan Doyle's defense is that such a diagnosis was not given by Watson or Holmes, and it is a colloquism, not necessarily referring to the heart as such.

The *Canon* contains considerably fewer references to diseases of the liver, lung, and skin than to those of the heart. The only indication of a liver problem was that of a prisoner on the clipper *Gloria Scott* who "was suffering from jaundice and, could not be of any use to us" in the mutiny. (Glor 119) Conan Doyle also referred to jaundice in his address to medical students at St. Mary's Hospital Medical School, attributing Robespierre's harsh nature to its presence.[349] Jaundice as such, however, would not make one any more morose than would any other chronic condition. There is no indication as to the extent of his knowledge of causes of jaundice.

Only one mention of a definitive disease of the respiratory system is made aside from pneumonia and the common cold. When the unhappy John Hector McFarlane burst into No. 221B Baker Street, Holmes commented on the "obvious facts that you are a bachelor, a solicitor, a Freemason, and an asthmatic." (Norw 415) Even the usually dense Doctor Watson understood for once the bases for these snap judgments—"the untidiness of attire, the sheaf of legal papers, the watch-charm, and the breathing," which are not described in any detail. McFarlane's attack may well have been brought on by the violent emotion of imminent arrest for the murder of Mr. Jonas Oldacre. Somewhat surprising to our modern view was Holmes' potentially harmful offer of a cigarette to the gasping McFarlane.[864] But, Conan Doyle cannot be faulted. In his day tobacco smoke was recommended to ward off an attack.[696i]

A skin disease is also mentioned in only one Canonical story. Unlike the asthma incident it is a basic ingredient of the plot. James M. Dodd sought Holmes' aid in finding Godfrey Emsworth, his former army comrade of the Boer war (in which Conan Doyle had also participated). While inquiring about him at his parents' home, he looked out at the night and saw Godfrey. (Blan 712)

> *He was deadly pale—never have I seen a man so white. I reckon ghosts may look like that; but his eyes met mine, and they were*

> *the eyes of a living man. He sprang back when he saw I was looking at him, and he vanished into the darkness.*

James searched the grounds the next day and found a lodge in which he caught a glimpse of Godfrey; but his father arrived and, in a rage, ordered James off his property.

Holmes, by a series of deductions, eliminated all possibilities except that Godfrey was kept in seclusion because he had contracted leprosy in South Africa. (Blan 720) In Holmes' own words "when you have eliminated all which is impossible then whatever remains, however improbable, must be the truth." (Blan 720) The truth was that Godfrey after being wounded in battle, staggered into a leper hospital, the nature of which was unknown to himself, and slept overnight in a leper's bed. "Not one of them was a normal human being. Everyone was twisted or swollen or disfigured in some strange way." (Blan 718) And when he developed "bleaching of the skin," one of the findings in leprosy, the incorrect diagnosis was made by a surgeon—Mr. Kent. "Mottled in patches over this darker [sunburned] surface were curious whitish patches which had bleached his skin." (Blan 717) This pure white, depigmented lesion of the skin in leprosy is usually preceded by erythema (reddening) and accompanied by anesthesia (loss of feeling). These were not described as being present in Godfrey.[N103]

Holmes, always prepared, had brought along Sir James Saunders, a specialist in tropical medicine, for a second opinion. His verdict was so unexpected that Godfrey's mother fainted. (Blan 721)

> *It is not leprosy. A well-marked case of pseudo-leprosy or ichthyosis, a scale-like affection of the skin, unsightly, obstinate, but possibly curable, and certainly non-infective.*

Ichthyosis is a rough, dry skin with white scales, having a "fish-skin" appearance. Sir James suggested a possible cause of Godfrey's ichthyosis. (Blan 721)

> *Are we assured that the apprehension, from which this young man has no doubt suffered terribly since his exposure to its contagion, may not produce a physical effect which simulates that which it fears?*

This indicates a noteworthy appreciation by Conan Doyle of the possible effects of the mind on the physical body (psychosomatic), although there is no evidence that ichthyosis itself has such a relationship.

There has been some disagreement by recent commentators with Sir James' (and thereby Conan Doyle's) diagnosis of ichthyosis.[53] As well they might! Most cases of ichthyosis are inherited and present from birth or appear during childhood.[559] Those cases that do begin in adulthood may appear when a drug, not known until recently, is taken, and when hypothyroidism or a malignant process such as Hodgkin's disease is present. There is no evidence in the story that any of the foregoing applied to Godfrey.

Suggested alternative diagnoses have been vitiligo (loss of skin pigment in otherwise healthy individuals),[54] pityriasis alba (slight scaling and loss of pigment over the cheeks),[826] and scleroderma (a hardening of the skin).[121] At any rate, Doctor Kent who had "the ordinary knowledge of the educated medical man" made a grievous error in diagnosing leprosy. (Blan 721) Conan Doyle, who wrote this adventure about 35 years after he left practice, retained sufficient medical knowledge to use very effectively the similarities and differences between leprosy and other skin diseases.[N104]

Godfrey's exposure to leprosy occurred during the Boer war in South Africa where leprosy does occur.[5] Although Conan Doyle was in Africa at that time, he makes no mention of leprosy in his autobiography[375] or his history of the Boer War.[316] He does use this disease, however, as the basis for "The Blighting of Captain Sharkey."[353] Sharkey's pirate ship, *Happy Delivery,* had captured the good ship *Portobello* and murdered her passengers except for the beautiful Inez Ramirez whom he fancied. She was discovered to have leprosy and was cast off in a boat with Sharkey by his rebellious crew.[N105]

The large amount of commentary on skin diseases is considerably out of proportion to the small number found in the *Canon.* In comparison, little has been said of the two diseases of metabolism and the several instances of accidental trauma. Jephro Rucastle, who engaged Miss Violet Hunter as governess for an uncertain reason, was "A prodigiously stout man with a very smiling face, and a great heavy chin which rolled down in fold upon fold over his throat." (Copp 116) Conan Doyle also depicted Holmes' older brother Mycroft, "the most indispensable man in the country," (Bruc 433) as being "a much larger and stouter man than Sherlock. His body was absolutely corpulent. . . ." (Gree 593) The potential ill effects of marked obesity are not mentioned.

Another metabolic disease was treated more seriously, and rightly so. Mr. John Turner, another villain-hero, committed the murder of Charles McCarthy, "a devil incarnate," for which the son had been accused. "I am a dying man . . . I have had diabetes for years. My doctor says it is a question whether I shall live a month. Yet I would rather die under my own roof than in a gaol." (Bosc 149) After Holmes tracked him down, he provided his own brand of justice by promising to keep the confession secret unless needed to save the son.

Watson's description of John Turner was not specific for diabetes. (Bosc 149)

> *His slow, limping step and bowed shoulders gave the appearance of decrepitude . . . his face was an ashen white, while his lips and the corners of his nostrils were tinged with a shade of blue. It was clear to me at a glance that he was in the grip of some deadly and chronic disease.*

And it was such a malignant disease before the discovery of insulin by Banting and Best in 1921.[940] In the same year that Conan Doyle published "The Boscombe Valley Mystery," Osler's renowned medical textbook stated that "Personally, I have never seen recovery from a case of true diabetes [mellitus]."[696j]

The ashen white face of the unfortunate Mr. Hunter may have been due to the anemia which can occur in many chronic illnesses, and perhaps aggravated by the stringent enforced diet that was the only treatment before the modern era. One possible explanation for the tinge of blue is the interference with oxygen exchange in the lungs by chronic infection to which diabetics are quite susceptible.[119] Because of this he is unlikely to have had a childhood onset of diabetes which would have been fatal long before maturity.

Not as inevitably fatal are the several instances of noncriminal trauma in the Sherlockian works. Jonathan Small, who was later to be cursed by stolen treasure, was swimming in the Ganges at the age of 18 when:

> *A crocidile took me, just as I was half way across, and nipped off my right leg as clean as a surgeon could have done it, just above the knee. With the shock and the loss of blood, I fainted, and should have drowned if Holder had not caught hold of me and paddled for the bank. (Sign 674)*

It is a wonder that he survived at all, given the severance of the major arteries of the thigh, and the distance to go for help. At least the incident later provided Holmes with the clue of the wooden leg footsteps.

Another animal-related injury, but far less serious, was the bite on the ankle of Sherlock Holmes by the bullterrier of his college friend, Victor Trevor. (Glor 108) Although he was "laid by the heels for ten days," he was indeed fortunate to escape both infection and tetanus which were often fatal in the era before antibiotics and vaccines.

One result of trauma induced by humans against each other was noticed by Holmes in Victor Trevor's father. "You have boxed a great deal in your youth. . . . It is your ears. They have the peculiar flattening and thickening which marks the boxing man." (Glor 109) The recognition of increased fibrous tissue of the ear due to repeat blows in boxing is not surprising for an author who exhibited considerable enthusiasm for this sport. Conan Doyle not only wrote six short stories[343] and much of one novel[295] about boxing but also participated actively as a young man.

"Trauma" to the mind with resulting fainting is a much more frequent occurrence than accidental physical trauma in the *Canon,* Campbell[121] having found 21 instances. A prime example is the rich American, Hatty Doran, who "fainted dead away" when she read in a newspaper story that Frank Moulton, to whom she was secretly married, had been killed by Apache Indians. (Nobl 296)[N106] She had another emotional shock when she saw him shortly after marrying a noble bachelor, Lord Robert St. Simon. But, this time she disappeared instead of fainting. Conan Doyle, in this instance as in many others, used the act of fainting to represent acute emotional stress and, of course, to heighten an already dramatic event.

Another dramatic faint due to emotional shock occurs when Mary, the cousin of Arthur Holder, thinks that he was the one who stole three jewels from the beryl coronet entrusted to his father, the banker. (Bery 289) "Mary was the first to rush into my room, and at the sight of the coronet and of Arthur's face, she read the whole story, and, with a scream, fell down senseless on the ground." It took a far more gruesome sight to make Horace Harker, the reporter, faint—the discovery on his doorstep of the body of the criminal, Pietro Venucci, with "a great gash in his throat." (SixN 576)

Fainting was a prominent feature of genteel society in Conan Doyle's day, occurring in young women with emotional illness—the so-called mid-Victorian drawing room swoon.[523] The episodes of sudden, transient loss of consciousness in the *Canon* are, however, best categorized as vasodepressor syncope (the common faint), which can be caused by sudden fear, anxiety, or pain. Dilatation of blood vessels results in a sufficient fall in blood pressure to cause unconsciousness. Conan Doyle does not "clutter" such dramatic occurrences with description of the accompanying manifestations of pallor, nausea, sweating, pupil enlargement, yawning, increased breathing, and slow pulse.[523]

The emotional shock resulting in such a dramatic event is not always of a dire nature. Thus, Mrs. Emsworth fainted at Sir

James Saunders' diagnosis of a benign skin disease, ichthyosis, rather than the dreaded leprosy. (Blan 721) Even the stoic Doctor Watson fainted when Holmes removed his disguise as a white-haired, wizened book collector, to reveal himself several years after his apparent tragic plunge over Reichenbach Falls. (Empt 332-333)

> *I moved my head to look at the cabinet behind me. When I turned again Sherlock Holmes was standing smiling at me across my study table. I rose to my feet, stared at him for some seconds in utter amazement, and then it appears that I must have fainted for the first and the last time in my life. Certainly a grey mist swirled before my eyes. . . .*

Although much has been made of the unlikelihood of Watson, the old soldier, fainting, Conan Doyle did appreciate the fact that vasodepressor syncope, unlike swooning, is not restricted to females—13 of the 21 Canonical faints occurred in men.

Much more serious and prolonged than the swoon or the simple faint was the curious endemic of brain fever in the *Canon,* occurring at least five times by name and twice by description. In all instances its onset was triggered by an exceptionally severe emotional shock. Thus, when the temperamental Rachel Howells, the second housemaid of Reginald Musgrave, was thrown over by Brunton the handsome butler, she "had a sharp touch of brain fever, and goes about the house now . . . like a black-eyed shadow of her former self." (Musg 129) From the description this could well be a melancholic depression due to disappointment in love.

Of possibly more serious import were the nine weeks of brain fever endured by Percy Phelps, Watson's old schoolmate, which began when he learned of the loss of a document, a secret treaty between England and Italy, which had been entrusted into his care by his uncle, Lord Holdhurst. (Nava 168, 170, 177) The symptoms given are a marked weakness and pallor, hardly enough on which to make a definitive diagnosis. Another attribute of the Holmesian brain fever was its potentially fatal nature. Miss Alice Rucastle's father kept on worrying her to sign away her inherited money and kept her away from suitors. The constant stress resulted in "brain fever, and for six weeks [she] was at death's door." (Copp 131)

No symptoms are given at all for Miss Sarah Cushing whose hatred for her former lover, James Browner, led to his murdering his wife Mary and her lover. We are told that her brain fever began with the arrival of a packet from Browner. (Card 203) Another dimension of brain fever occurred in the wife of the apparently murdered Colonel Barclay. No information could be gotten from Mrs. Barclay, an eyewitness, because she "was temporarily insane from an acute attack of brain fever." (Croo 230) The insanity is used by Conan Doyle as a plot device to force Holmes to solve the case by his own deductive powers and wits, rather than by the direct account of a witness.

Not labeled as brain fever, but surely a typical example, was the case of Sir Henry Baskerville. As a result of the staggering information that the woman he loved was the wife of the villain, Stapleton, and of the extreme stress of grappling with the hideous hound, "he lay delirious in a high fever." (Houn 103) He only fully recovered after a trip around the world. Another example of brain fever may be that of the second Mrs. Ferguson who took to her room with a high fever after discovering the harm done to her baby by her stepson. (Suss 469) From these seven patients we can characterize the Holmesian disease "brain fever" as one which follows quickly on a severe emotional shock, which exhibits weight loss, weakness, palor, and high fever, and which has a protracted course. Most patients recover, but insanity or death is possible.

To track down the exact nature of brain fever from these paultry clues would greatly tax even a medical Holmes such as Doctor Thorndyke. But, some have tried. Van Liere has suggested that Doctor Watson [sic] used this term loosely in the *Canon* for extreme nervous exhaustion, although this would not explain the rapid onset.[894] Brenner prefers a psychiatric category, such as a reactive psychosis.[96] The term has recently been applied by Casamajor[129] to a disease characterized by convulsions and various paralyses in children. This is certainly different from Conan Doyle's brain fever.

Conan Doyle has been criticized for using a vague and medically meaningless term such as brain fever. If so, then so should other writers of 19th century fiction who used the same term. Examples include Brontë (Catherine Linton in *Wuthering Heights,* 1847), Flaubert (Emma Bovary in *Madame Bovary,* 1857), and Meredith (Lucy Feverel in *The Ordeal of Richard Feveral,* 1859).[719] Such widespread usage indicates that brain fever was a generally accepted medical condition in the 19th century.[N107] The history of the term has been delineated by Audrey Peterson.[719] It was derived from terms phrensy and phrenitic which were used in the 18th century for inflammations of the brain (encephalitis) and its covering layers (meningitis).[662] In fact, a current dictionary defines brain fever as synonymous with meningitis.[847a] Before the 20th century, concepts of fever in general were vague.[577] It was attributed to various causes, including infection, fatigue, excessive mental activity, and especially severe emotional shock.[719] And so brain fever became associated with extreme shock. As a final vindication of Conan Doyle and other literary figures of the 19th century, an 1892 textbook of medicine[696k] described fever as occurring in an occasional case of hysterical reaction. The writers of fiction took advantage of a contemporary disease of the psyche that had a sudden onset and a long duration to enhance the dramatic effect of their fiction.

Evidently less serious, but at times difficult to separate from descriptions of brain fever, is the nervous breakdown. John Turner, a landowner in Boscombe Valley, was described by Doctor Willows as being "a wreck, and . . . his nervous system is shattered." (Bosc 141) There is no indication that such a chronic nervous condition might make one more susceptible to brain fever. It was noted, however, that Rachel Howells, a victim of this disease, was "of an excitable Welsh temperment." (Musg 129) Most likely there is a continuum of increasing severity from an unstable emotional personality to nervous breakdown to brain fever. Also related was hysteria,[889] as exemplified by the banker, Alexander

Holder, who came to consult Holmes about the mutilated beryl coronet. He "could not get his words out, but swayed his body and plucked at his hair . . . beat his head against the walls." (Bery 283)

Other psychological aberrations are not used in as dramatic fashion as brain fever in the Canonical writings. Four incidents of insanity are included, not counting Professor Presbury who "appears to be a case for an alienist [psychiatrist]. The old gentleman's cerebral processes were disturbed by the love affair."(Cree 756) Mrs. Barclay's insanity on the death of her husband was stated to be a manifestation of brain fever. (Croo 230)

Two other occurrences of insanity are called monomania by Conan Doyle—monomania in the sense of psychotic thinking being confined to one idea or group of ideas.[847b] Monomania was recognized long before Conan Doyle's time, being called partial moral mania.[502] Victor Hatherley, the engineer, much to his regret, considered the woman who warned him to "get away from here before it is too late!" (Engr 217) to be a monomaniac. Doctor Watson gave his medical opinion, wrong as usual, that the destroyer of statues of Napoleon suffered from monomania. (SixN 574)

> *There is the conditon which the modern French psychologists have called the* idée fixe, *which may be trifling in character, and accompanied by complete sanity in every other way. A man who read deeply about Napoleon . . . might conceivably . . . under its influence be capable of any fantastic outrage.*

Conan Doyle had read deeply in the literature of Napoleon in preparation for his historic novels and short stories, but fortunately remained unscathed. Some Sherlockian enthusiasts might disagree because he considered these works much superior to his Sherlock Holmes stories.

Another case of insanity was that of Mme Henri Fournaye, of Creole origin and extremely excitable nature, who murdered her husband, a prime suspect in the disappearance of a very sensitive diplomatic letter. (Seco 312) The motive was frenzied jealousy, leading to "mania of a dangerous and permanent form." The inclusions of insanity in only four of 56 short stories and four novels which are permeated with crime is surprising. Perhaps crimes committed because of insanity do not lend themselves as well to the type of ratiocination for which Holmes is so famous.

Another psychologic disorder in the *Canon* is hypochondriasis. The only example is a rather severe case of such imaginary ill health. On hearing that Watson was a doctor, Thaddeus Sholto immediately reacted. (Sign 625)

> *'A doctor, eh?' cried he, much excited. 'Have you your stethoscope? Might I ask you—would you have the kindness? I have grave doubts as to my mitral valve, if you would be so very good. The aortic I may rely upon, but I should value your opinion upon the mitral.' I listened to his heart, as requested, but was unable to find anything amiss, save, indeed, that he was in an ecstasy of fear, for he shivered from head to foot.*

This is a striking description of hypochondriasis with its intimations of masochism and the superficial knowledge of medical terms. It indicates Conan Doyle's superb understanding of patients with imaginary ills who both fear and hope that these are actually present.

Hypochondriasis is quite different from malingering, which denotes nonpsychotic and self-induced disease. Sherlock Holmes was a master of such deception. In "The Reigate Squires" he feints a seizure in order to prevent Inspector Forrester from revealing a clue to a suspect. (Reig 337) Watson "had suspicions at times that he was really finding himself faster than he pretended, even to me." (Illu 684) Holmes even released newspaper reports that he had erysipelas, a streptococcal skin infection. The purpose was to deceive his attackers. The most extreme example is Holmes' depiction of a dying man, expert enough to delude loyal Watson and to trap Culverton Smith, the poisoner. (Dyin 450) Such malingering is the conscious adoption of signs and symptoms of disease in order to gain an end.[31] For Holmes it was the solving of crime; for others it may be an attempt to gain sympathy or drugs.[30] For Conan Doyle it provided the plot for one of his most successful detective stories.[N108]

Another attempt at malingering was related to Mr. Blessington (nee Sutton), a former member of the Worthington bank gang, who established the brilliant but impecunious Doctor Percy Trevelyan in practice, in return for three-quarters of the profit. (Resi 270) Another member of the gang attempted to gain entrance to his dwelling by faking an attack of catalepsy—a hysterical condition in which the limbs became fixed in any position they are placed.

> *I [Trevelyan] was shocked to see that he was sitting bolt upright in his chair, staring at me with a perfectly blank and rigid face. He was again in the grip of his mysterious malady.* (Resi 271)

Conan Doyle used the term for the rigid condition of individuals affected by *The Poison Belt.*[360] Rigor mortis might have been the more accurate term.

The doctor was completely fooled even though he had written a monograph on obscure nervous lesions and had done research on catalepsy. But Holmes, who often exhibited more medical knowledge than even specialists, recognized "A fraudulent imitation, Watson, though I should hardly dare to hint as much to our specialist. It is a very easy complaint to imitate. I have done it myself." (Resi 274) One suspects that Conan Doyle's purpose was to enhance the stature of Holmes rather than satirize physicians.

Not strictly abnormal psychology, but certainly harmful in interpersonal relationships, was the emotional tie between the criminal Stapleton and his wife. (Houn 111)

> *There can be no doubt that Stapleton exercised an influence over her which may have been love or may have been fear, or possibly both, since they are by no means incompatible emotions.*

This very elemental closeness between love and hate in human psychology is well recognized today. It is another example of Conan Doyle's perceptiveness.

In addition to "nervous" diseases that are primarily psychological, Conan Doyle described several conditions that have a physical basis in the brain. The most serious and dramatic one was the cerebrovascular accident, either a hemorrhage into the substance of the brain or a localized area of dead tissue (infarct) due to blockage of its blood supply. He used two terms—apoplexy, which indicates sudden hemorrhage into the brain, and stroke, which indicates sudden paralysis from either cause.

It appeared initially that Colonel Barclay had been murdered. But, Holmes' shrewd investigations tracked down the deformed "crooked man," a rival for the prettiest girl in the regiment, whom Barclay believed he had murdered years before. The sudden sight of him was too much for the Colonel. (Croo 236)

> *. . . at the sight of me he looked as I have never seen a man look before, and over he went with his head on the fender. But he was dead before he fell. I read death on his face. . . . The bare sight of me was like a bullet through his guilty heart.*

The trauma to the back of the head caused by the fender was reason enough to suggest murder. But, at the inquest "The medical evidence showed conclusively that death was due to apoplexy." (Croo 237)

Of further interest is Conan Doyle's description of the contortion of the dead Colonel's face—"It had set . . . into the most dreadful expression of fear and horror which a human countenance is capable of assuming." (Croo 230) This is reminiscent of Sir Charles Baskervilles' "almost incredible facial distortion—so great that Dr. Mortimer refused at first to believe that it was indeed his friend and patient who lay before him." (Houn 12) This was attributed to dyspnoea and death from cardiac exhaustion. In both instances such facial contortions are quite unlikely in the nonfiction world, but intensify the dramatic fictional events.

Another case of cerebrovascular accident came to Holmes' attention through "the only friend I made during the two years that I was at college." (Glor 107) Victor Trevor's father, a wealthy landowner and Justice of the Peace, reacted strangely on reading an apparently innocuous letter. (Glor 114)

> *My father read it, clapped both his hands to his head, and began running round the room in little circles like a man who has been driven out of his senses. When I [Victor] at last drew him down*

> *on to the sofa his mouth and eyelids were all puckered on one side, and I saw that he had a stroke. Dr. Fordham came over at once . . . but the paralysis has spread, he has shown no sign of returning consciousness, and I think that we shall hardly find him alive.*

The clapping of his hands to his head is indicative of the sudden onset of severe headache which sometimes accompanies brain hemorrhage.[206] Conan Doyle was also aware of the poor prognosis that is associated with increasing paralysis and prolonged loss of consciousness.[N109]

The brain hemorrhages of both Barclay and Trevor occurred dramatically at a time of sudden and severe emotional shock. In other instances in the *Canon* this resulted in brain fever. The different effect may have been due to the older ages of these two victims with consequent weakened arteries (arteriosclerosis) and hypertension, which are the usual causes of apoplexy. Also blood pressure can rise precipitously with severe emotion.

There remain for consideration two somewhat less ominous diseases of the nervous system. One of these afflicted the six-year old son of Jephro Rucastle, who was described to Holmes by his new governess as being:

> *. . . small for his age, with a head which is quite disproportionately large. His whole life appears to be spent in an altercation between savage fits of passion and gloomy intervals of sulking. Giving pain to any creature weaker than himself seems to be his one idea of amusement . . . mice, little birds and insects. (Copp 123)*

The very large head could well represent hydrocephalus (water in the brain) caused by enlargement of the ventricles because of obstruction to the outflow of cerebrospinal fluid which is produced by their lining. The obstruction can be due to infection at any age, but in a six-year-old child is more likely the result of a malformation present at birth.

Holmes extrapolated from the cruel disposition of the boy to the supposition that it was derived from that of his parents. In hydrocephalus, however, pressure on the brain substance by the enlarging ventricles can affect the disposition although not necessarily in a malevolent fashion. In an account of the condition contemporary with the story it is stated that "The mental condition is variable; the child may be bright, but, as a rule, there is some grade of imbecility. . . . Even when extreme, the mental facilities may be retained."[696m] It is likely that Conan Doyle was aware of the association of hydrocephalus with mental changes. More likely he described the disproportionately large head to introduce an element of the grotesque and not as a specific disease entity.

One further disease of the nervous system is the so-called St. Vitus dance, characterized by involuntary, irregular contractions of muscles. Mr. Melas, a Greek interpreter, described Wilson Kemp—"a man of the foulest antecedents" (Gree 605)—as an older man whose "lips and eyelids were continually twitching, like a man with St. Vitus's dance. I could not help thinking that his strange, catchy little laugh was also a symptom of some nervous malady." (Gree 599) In this instance Conan Doyle is using an affliction to heighten the loathsomeness of a character.

Reference to St. Vitus dance was also used for a different purpose—the reason why Watson was able to purchase an established practice for a small sum, which Conan Doyle was unable to do. (Stoc 153)

> *Old Mr. Farquhar . . . had at one time an excellent general practice but his age, and an affliction of the nature of St. Vitus dance from which he suffered, had very much thinned it. The public, not unnaturally, goes upon the principle that he who would heal others must himself be whole. . .*

The term St. Vitus dance has a long history, extending back to medieval times when there were "epidemics" of the dancing mania. It was characterized by complete loss of control with frenzied dancing until collapse.[498] It was variously considered as caused by the devil or the bite of the venomous spider, tarantula.[639b] The dance was named after St. Vitus a martyred youth (A.D. 303) who prayed that all who commemorated him should be protected from the dancing mania. There is little doubt, from today's perspective, that the cause was mass hysteria.[825, 901]

By the time Conan Doyle practiced medicine the term was used for an affliction of the nervous system, most likely a manifestation of rheumatic fever. It was also called Sydenham's chorea and acute chorea (jerky movements).[696n] Although it occurs primarily in children, Conan Doyle described it in the two elderly men. More likely causes of tremor in old age would be Parkinson's disease, senile chorea, or Huntington's chorea.[96] The last is inherited and appears between the ages of 35 and 45 years.[676] In all fairness, however, he did not diagnose their afflictions as St. Vitus dance but "like" and "of the nature of" this disease.

The *Canon* contains one possible reference to a physiologic attribute of the brain. Because of the use of the term "brain wave" it has been suggested that Holmes [sic] had knowledge of the discovery of electric currents of the brain. This phenomenon was reported by Caton in 1875;[131] he did not, however, use the word wave. In current general dictionaries it is defined as "electrical potentials or impulses given off by brain tissue,"[847e] but is not listed in medical dictionaries.[863] "Brain wave" was originally used to indicate a telepathic message and now a sudden inspiration or bright thought.[455] The context in which the term was used by Conan Doyle is indicative of the latter. "One more coruscation [flash of light], my dear Watson. Yet another brain-wave. Had the volume been an unusual one he would have sent it to me." (Vall 474)

The largest category of diseases in the Holmesian works is that of infections. This should come as no surprise, given the orientation of many of Conan Doyle's scientific writings and the extensive epidemics in Victorian England of such communicable diseases as smallpox, cholera, measles, and tuberculosis.[5] And these were all the more terrifying because of the uncertainty as to their basic nature and the lack of specific therapy, with consequent high rates of complications and death.

The best known infectious disease in the *Canon* is of a very uncertain if not dubious nature. It occurs in one of the two Holmesian tales that have a medical condition as the major theme of the plot—"The Dying Detective," the other story being "The Blanched Soldier" who was diagnosed as a leper. Holmes was successful in attempting to deceive both Watson and Culverton Smith, the poisoner. (Dyin 440)

> *He was indeed a deplorable spectacle . . . it was that gaunt, wasted face staring at me from the bed which sent a chill to my heart. His eyes had the brightness of fever, there was a hectic flush upon either cheek, and dark crusts clung to his lips; the thin hands upon the coverlet twitched incessantly, his voice was croaking and spasmotic.*

It would take a consumate master of disguise, as was Holmes, to produce such an appearance; a superb writer to provide the graphic description; and an experienced physician to include the clinical details. Conan Doyle was all of these. More evidence of the dependency of this adventure on medical knowledge are the techniques used by Holmes in achieving his ends. (Dyin 450)

> *Three days of absolute fast does not improve one's beauty, Watson. For the rest, there is nothing which a sponge may not cure. With vaseline upon one's forehead, belladonna in one's eyes [to dilate them], rouge over the cheek-bones, and crusts of beeswax round one's lips, a very satisfying effect can be produced.*

This accounting is a fascinating admixture of the medical and the theatrical.[N110]

The question has been asked many times as to which tropical disease Conan Doyle had in mind. In truth, the description is not specific for any particular one, being applicable to anyone dying of an infectious disease. Holmes' diagnosis, "a coolie disease from Sumatra," (Dyin 440) is of little help, except as a clue leading to determination of what diseases occur in Sumatra, one of the greater Sunda Islands of Indonesia, being located near the Malay Peninsula and Java.

One disease relatively common in Sumatra is scrub typhus (Tsutsugamushi disease), a disease caused by a rickettsial organism and spread by the bite of a mite. It is distributed widely in southern Asia and the western Pacific regions.[639a] L'Etany[608] has traced two other names applied by Holmes to scrub typhus—Black Formosa Corruption, a name similar to one used by some for the disease, and Tapanuli fever, Tapanuli being located in Sumatra. If this is so it indicates an extensive knowledge of tropical diseases and of geography on the part of Conan Doyle.

Scrub typhus has many features in common to most severe and potentially fatal infectious diseases. There are several specific features that are not alluded to—an ulcer with a black scab at the site of the bite of the mite and a rash of the trunk and extremities.[933]

How Holmes was to have acquired this exotic, tropical disease is uncertain. His faithful housekeeper, Mrs. Hudson, intimated to Watson that "He has been working at a case . . . in an alley near the river." (Dying 439) But, this disease is unheard of in the Western hemisphere where the specific mite is absent, aside from infected individuals arriving from endemic areas before the onset of clinical symptoms. Much more likely on the Thames water front would have been typhoid or possible cholera. Perhaps Conan Doyle did not have a specific tropical disease in mind but combined his fertile imagination with his medical knowledge to provide the basis for a gripping tale. Ober[684] disagrees, stating that "Doyle was too sound a doctor . . . not to have had some disease clearly in mind when he wrote it." In any case, by 1913, 22 years after he left practice, he was much more an author than a doctor.

Two other infectious diseases in the *Canon* are also spread by insects from human to human as is scrub typhus, but by mosquitoes instead of mites. Major John Sholto, who was bribed by Jonathan Small with the Agra treasure to gain his freedom, had "suffered for years from an enlarged spleen" and had a bottle of quinine, both hallmarks of the malarial patient. (Sign 627, 628) Small, himself, was exposed to malaria as a prisoner on the island of Andaman in the Bay of Bengal. (Sign 673)

> *Twenty long years in that fever-ridden swamp, all day at work under the mangrove tree, all night chained up in the filthy convict-huts, bitten by mosquitoes, racked by ague [malaria]. . . . That was how I earned the Agra treasure. . . .*

Malaria is not referred to in other Sherlockian stories and in only one other work, "The Horror of the Heights,"[359] in which a blood stain in the log of a vanished aviator contained malarial parasites. Of interest is the association by Conan Doyle of mosquito bites with malaria in this story. The parasite of malaria was discovered in the blood by Sir Ronald Ross ten years previously.[516] Its transmission by mosquitoes (of the species *Anopheles*), however, was only suspected before 1890 and not proved until 1898. If the close apposition of the phrases "bitten by mosquitoes" and "racked by ague" is not fortuitous, then Conan Doyle was indeed familiar with the frontiers of medical knowledge in his last few years of practice.

Although not caused by a parasite but by a virus, yellow fever is also spread by a mosquito, but of a different species (*Aedes*) than malaria.[928] In the *Canon* there are only two references to this tropical disease. Rodger Baskerville, the black sheep of the family, died of yellow fever in Central America, thus clearing the way for Henry to assume the family title. (Houn 16) Mrs. Munro's first husband, the black American John Hebron, had died of yellow fever in Atlanta. (Yell 579) In both instances Conan Doyle invoked this disease to explain the death of characters in order to further the plot line.

He was quite accurate in locating yellow fever in 19th century America.[188] Highly virulent epidemics occurred in the southeastern United States.[815] Particularly prominent were those which involved Civil War camps.[848] More important historically was endemic yellow fever which devastated the builders of the Panama Canal in Central America, from early attempts beginning in 1880[682] until the discovery of its mosquito transmission about 1900 by Walter Reed.[49] It is quite possible that Conan Doyle placed Rodger Baskerville in Central America because he knew of its experience with yellow fever.

Conan Doyle had a much more direct and personal experience with two further infectious diseases that occur in the *Canon*—typhoid and tuberculosis. Typhoid is mentioned twice in *A Study in Scarlet*[244] which was published 13 years before he treated typhoid victims during the Boer War in Bloemfontein. Doctor Watson, after his encounter with the Jezail bullet: (Stud 143)

> *. . . was struck down by enteric fever [typhoid], that curse of our Indian possessions. For months my life was despaired of, and when at last I came to myself and became convalescent, I was so weak and emaciated that a medical board determined that not a day should be lost in sending me back to England.*

This was indeed a severe case of typhoid and validated Watson's indolence before meeting Holmes. His first stop from India was Portsmouth, Conan Doyle's practice site. Watson then "gravitated" to London as did Conan Doyle.

In the same story the justification for two houses in Lauriston Gardens being empty was

> *. . . on account of him that owns them who won't have the drains seed to, though the very last tenant what lived in one of them died o' typhoid fever. (Houn 176)*

This is similar to the mention of inadequate drains and typhoid in the non-Canonical story, "The Curse of Eve."[286] Although the typhoid bacillus had been isolated only three years before, in 1884,[114a] the spread of the disease by unsanitary water and sewage systems had been recognized long before.[631a] In fact Britain was in advance of other major countries of the western world in its level of sanitation by the mid-19th century. Conan Doyle was obviously well aware of the implications. The only other reference to typhoid in the *Canon* is as the cause of death of the very beautiful wife of John Douglas who was horribly murdered. (Vall 497)

Tuberculosis had a very special meaning for Conan Doyle because it was the cause of the death of his first wife in 1906. A similar event occurred to Godfrey Staunton, the crack three-quarter of the Cambridge rugger team who mysteriously disappeared so that news of his marriage would not become known and result in his disinheritance. But, alas, his wife, who was " as good as she was beautiful, and as intelligent as she was good," died of consumption of the most virulent kind." (Miss 490)

In "The Final Problem" Watson was lured away to leave Holmes alone for his near fatal confrontation with Moriarity at Reichenbach Falls. The bait was a supposed English lady in the last stage of comsumption who had a sudden hemorrhage. (Fina 314) The association between these Falls and tuberculosis was poignant for Conan Doyle. It was on a tour of Switzerland in 1892 that he visited this site and that his wife Louise exhibited tuberculosis.[375aa] Because of pain in her side and a cough Louise was examined by "the nearest good physician."

> *To my surprise and alarm he told me when he descended from the bedroom that the lungs were very gravely affected, that there was every sign of rapid consumption and that he thought the case a most serious one with little hope, considering her record and family history, of a permanent cure.*

This was eight years after her brother had died of the same disease while under Conan Doyle's care.

Conan Doyle moved his wife, his home, and two children to Davos in the High Alps of Switzerland in 1893. Davos was a fashionable health resort, especially for tuberculosis, in the latter half of the 19th century. This was a decade after the isolation of the tubercle bacillus, and over 50 years before the first effective antibiotic.[400] The only hope appeared to be exposure to fresh, clean air.[879] The sojourn in Davos appeared to be successful because Louise survived until 1906. It also provided Conan Doyle with two highlights in his life—the killing off of Sherlock Holmes, at least temporarily, and the introduction of "ski-running" into Switzerland.[N111]

In contrast to these tropical diseases, several other infectious diseases are mentioned almost in passing. Victor Trevor's sister had "died of diphtheria while on a visit to Birmingham." (Glor 108) Death was undoubtedly related to the effects of the bacterial toxin on the heart. The bacillus for diphtheria was isolated in 1884, when Conan Doyle was still in practice.[696a] Fortunately, Joseph Bell, one of the sources for Holmes' characteristics, survived an episode of diphtheria in 1864.[634] Another bacterial infection of the throat, and very dangerous as was diphtheria in the preantibiotic era, is quinsy, a severe inflammation of the tonsils. Hosmer Angel, Mary Sutherland's fiance who had mysteriously disappeared, "had the quinsy and swollen glands when he was young . . . and it had left him with a weak throat and a hesitating, whispering fashion of speech." (Iden 409) The peculiar voice suggests involvement of the vocal cord by spreading infection. It also helps to characterize a very shy individual. But Hosmer Angel (James Windibank, the stepfather of Mary Sutherland) had merely *faked* these afflictions, so he could disguise his voice and thus fool the near-sighted Mary Sutherland. (Iden 415) This is actually another instance of malingering.

An epidemic of unspecified nature was the reason given by Stapelton, the villainous relative of the Baskervilles, for moving to the moors. It had shut down his school after three of the boys had died. (Houn 50) Possibilities include measles, smallpox, or diphtheria.

A reference is also made in the *Canon* to another infectious disease, tetanus, which can be very deadly. The term was not used as we use it today, for a bacterial disease, but for tetany, a violent rigid contraction of muscles of various causes including tetanus. Tetanus bacillus was isolated in 1889, one year before this mystery was published.[696a]

In the case of Bartholomew Sholto it was the result of poisoning by a strychnine-like substance. Conan Doyle's graphic description applies to either. Most dramatic was "that ghastly, inscrutable smile upon his face," (Sign 635) due to muscle contraction.

> *. . . all his limbs were twisted and turned in the most fantastic fashion. The muscles are hard as a board. . . . They are in a state of extreme contraction, far exceeding the usual* rigor mortis *[stiffening of muscles after death] . . . this distortion of the face, this Hippocratic smile, or '*risus sardonicus,*' as the old writers called it. . . . (Sign 635, 639)*

As usual, Holmes' medical knowledge was sufficient to recognize the condition and its cause, and Watson concurred.

There is one final condition in the *Canon* which is difficult to classify under any of the specific categories yet discussed.[76] Chronic alcoholism was even more rampant in the last few centuries than it is today.[768] Henry Baker, who had lost his hat and his bird when assaulted, had "a touch of red in nose and cheeks, with a slight tremor of his extended hand." (Blue 458) John Openshaw's uncle Elias had emigrated to America and later received the death sign of the K.K.K. "He was . . . very foul-mouthed" and ". . . drank a great deal of brandy." (Five 392–393) Also crude, as are all of the Sherlockian male drunkards, was the manservant Toller who prevented Miss Alice from escaping from her greedy father. (Copp 128) Loathsome was Mrs. Ronder's husband, the lion-tamer, who was a "Ruffian, bully, beast—it was all—written on that heavy jowled face. . . . For he was terrible at all times, and murderous when drunk."(Veil 459)

Somewhat more serious was the case of Captain Peter Carey, who had been murdered by a steel harpoon driven through his chest.

> *The man was an intermittent drunkard, and when he had the fit on him he was a perfect fiend. (Blac 400) On the Tuesday [he] was in one of his blackest moods, flushed with drink and as savage as a dangerous wild beast. (Blac 401)*

As dangerous was the double murderer, Jim Browner, who "would always take drink when he was ashore, and a little drink would send him stark, staring mad." (Card 199) Possibly as despicable, was Sir Eustace Brackenstall. According to his wife, Sir Eustace

> *. . . was a confirmed drunkard. To be with such a man for an hour is unpleasant. Can you imagine what it means for a sensitive and high-spirited woman to be tied to him for day and night? It is a sacrilege, a crime, a villainy to hold that such a marriage is binding. I say that these monstrous laws of yours will bring a curse upon the land. . . . (Abbe 493)*

One result was bruises upon her arm.[N112]

Conan Doyle's depictions of these last three alcoholics show none of the sympathy he evoked for the widower, Sir John Bollamore, in his non-Holmesian short story, "The Japanned Box."[307] He did show some sympathy, however, for another Canonical alcoholic.

Lady Beatrice Falder lived with her brother Lord Robert Norberton who "never goes near her. And she takes it to heart. She is brooding and sulky and drinking, Mr. Holmes—drinking like a fish." (Shos 633) Conan Doyle had some appreciation that emotional stress can contribute to alcoholism.

In Conan Doyle's decade of practice chronic alcoholism was considered by many to be a weakness of character and even a trait inherited from dissipated parents;[739] but today it is recognized as a disease with psychological and metabolical contributions. Excessive drinking of alcohol had been a problem in Great Britain for many ages.[480] In the 19th century it resisted even legislative attempts at control—bills for establishment of asylums for alcoholics being defeated.[628] Throughout history alcohol in itself has also been recognized as a therapeutic agent,[439] and was so used by Conan Doyle frequently in the Holmesian stories, along with a multitude of other remedies.

Several conclusions can be made from this review of diseases in Conan Doyle's detective fiction. He not only was generally knowledgeable about diseases but also had an understanding of newly developing advances. This knowledge was not limited to Britain but also included the Near East and the Far East. In the early stages of development of modern psychiatry he understood the effects of emotional stress on the psyche and the body.

As an author he introduced diseases in his fiction liberally and for various purposes. In only two stories did the plot revolve around a specific disease. More frequent uses were to create mood, to enhance a characterization, and to explain the death of a minor character. Examples are Colonel Barclay's episodes of deepest gloom; (Croo 227) the deafness of Mrs. Allen the housekeeper (Vall 496) and of the mother of William the murdered coachman; (Reig 334) and the scorbutic (scurvy) Shinwell Johnson, one of Holmes' informants. (Illu 677) Holmes' loss of interest when a mystery was over was compared by Watson to that of "An abstruse and learned specialist" when confronted with the commonplace measles. (Abbe 495) Spinal meningitis was considered by a veterinarian to be the cause of paralysis of the spaniel, but Holmes knew better. (Suss 468) Not to be forgotten is the increase in stature of Holmes by his exhibition of more and more astute medical knowledge than that of Doctor Watson.

Above all, the myriad of references to disease provide much of the detail that enhances the realism and the fascination of the *Canon*. In doing so Conan Doyle has also provided a panorama of 19th century concepts of disease, one which indicates a transition period with retention of some elements of the slowly fading nonrational era and incorporation of the rapidly developing scientific era. It remains to be seen if the same orientation is obtained from a review of the Canonical drugs.

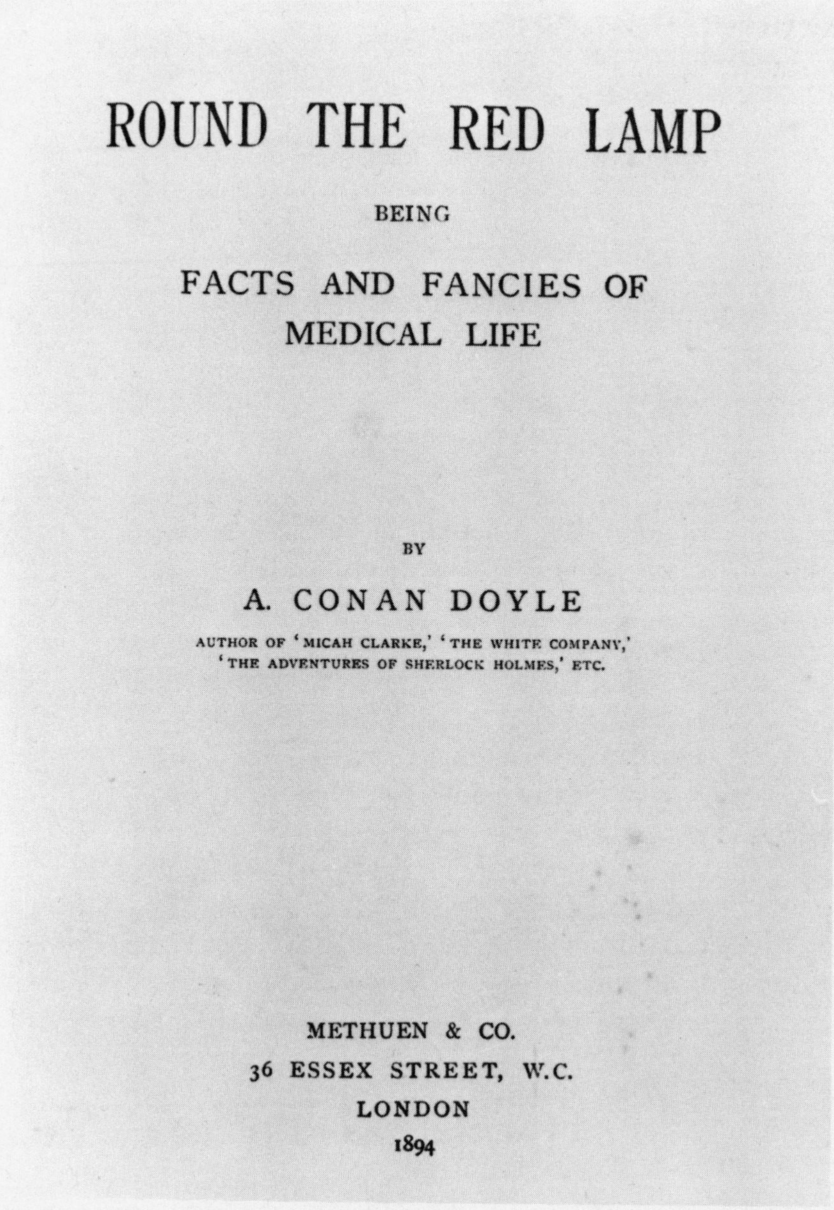

ROUND THE RED LAMP

BEING

FACTS AND FANCIES OF
MEDICAL LIFE

BY

A. CONAN DOYLE

AUTHOR OF 'MICAH CLARKE,' 'THE WHITE COMPANY,'
'THE ADVENTURES OF SHERLOCK HOLMES,' ETC.

METHUEN & CO.
36 ESSEX STREET, W.C.
LONDON
1894

Figure 18. Title page of the 1894 collection of Conan Doyle's short stories which relate to medicine.

THE STARK MUNRO LETTERS

BEING A SERIES OF SIXTEEN LETTERS WRITTEN BY J. STARK MUNRO, M.B., TO HIS FRIEND AND FORMER FELLOW-STUDENT, HERBERT SWANBOROUGH, OF LOWELL, MASSACHUSETTS, DURING THE YEARS 1881-1884

EDITED AND ARRANGED BY

A. CONAN DOYLE

AUTHOR OF "MICAH CLARKE," ETC., ETC.

LONDON
LONGMANS, GREEN, AND CO.
1895

Figure 19. Title page of Conan Doyle's semiautobiographical novel about his early medical practice days, published in 1895.

6

DRUGS AND DETECTION

CANONICAL DRUGS

During the last few decades of the 19th century, when Conan Doyle practiced medicine and Sherlock Holmes detection, a mixture of the old and the new was also seen in the treatment of disease. The centuries-old bloodletting had finally phased out, only to be replaced by spurious systems related to the new science and technology such as magnetism and electricity. At the same time more rational methods of treatment were being introduced.

The most striking improvement in treatment occurred with drug therapy. Finally a strong reaction developed against the massive overdosing indulged in by many physicians for centuries. Doctor Cullingworth of Bradfield used such massive doses that Stark Munro was "afraid that a succession of coroners' inquests may check [his] career."[293q] Such a reaction tended to go to the opposite extreme, as exemplified by the development of homeopathy which taught that the more dilute the drug, the more effective it was. More extreme, but to make a point, was the suggestion by Oliver Wendell Holmes, one of Conan Doyle's physician and author heroes, "that if the whole materia medica, as now used, could be sunk to the bottom of the sea, it would be all the better for mankind,—and all the worse for the fishes."[538]

Oliver Wendell Holmes also wrote that "Old theories, and old men who cling to them, must take themselves out of the way as the new generation with its fresh thoughts and altered habits of mind comes forward to take the place of that which is dying out."[539] The question arises as to whether Conan Doyle belonged to the old or the new. The review of his concepts and knowledge of diseases suggests more the latter than the former. An assessment of the drugs referred to in the Holmesian stories will help us further to evaluate the professional caliber of Doctor Arthur Conan Doyle.

Several drugs and chemicals are referred to including alkaloids, ammonia, amyl nitrate, belladonna, chloroform, cocaine, curare, ether, hormones, morphine, opium, prussic acid, snake venon, and strychnine.[890] In addition, there are several poisons, but these are generally uncertain in nature. It is unlikely that this number of drugs and their variety can be found in any other series of detective stories. They fall into five categories of use:[770]

1. For treatment—as ammonia and brandy to revive someone who has fainted, amyl nitrate for catalepsy, and morphine for pain.
2. For simulating disease—as when Holmes placed belladonna in his eyes to produce dilated pupils, simulating those of a dying person in "The Dying Detective."
3. For poisoning—as curare in "The Sussex Vampire" to poison a baby, as strychnine in *The Sign of Four*, as carbon monoxide in "The Retired Colourman," and a variety of less well-kown poisons.
4. For inducing anesthesia—as ether and chloroform.
5. For addiction—as morphine, opium and cocaine.

A favorite medicament in the *Canon*, alcohol, is not strictly speaking a drug.[892] Watson used brandy and ammonia to revive

Mr. Melas, the Greek interpeter, after being poisoned with burning charcoal. (Gree 604) The resultant carbon monoxide could cause a cherry red color of the skin and rapid death from asphyxia if in high concentration.[755] Modern treatment consists of giving oxygen, artificial respiration, and fresh air, which Holmes provided by throwing open the window. Watson's therapy, however, appeared to be as successful. "I had the satisfaction of seeing him open his eyes, and of knowing that my hand had drawn him back from the dark valley in which all paths meet." (Gree 604)

Brandy was even administered by Inspector Lestrade to revive Sir Henry Baskerville after his encounter with the giant hound. (Houn 101) Another lay person, Hilton Soames of the College of St. Luke's, also used brandy to bolster his servant, Bannister, after the scholarship examination had been tampered with. (3Stu 370) Another instance was Watson's use of brandy to revive "Dr. Thorneycroft Huxtable, M.A., Ph.D. etc." who had collapsed from sheer exhaustion after entering 221B Baker Street. (Prior 607)

The *Canon* abounds with other examples of alcohol, usually brandy, given as a stimulant. James Ryder, an attendant at the Cosmopolitan Hotel, was given brandy when accused of stealing the Countess of Morcar's fabulous blue carbuncle. (Blue 464) Scott Eccles was given a brandy and soda on Holmes' request by Watson when he learned of the death of Mr. Garcia, his host. (Wist 240) Brandy was poured down the throat of Percy Phelps who was beginning to faint from the sudden shock of recovering the lost naval treaty. (Nava 189) A much more dire need for brandy was that of Ian Murdoch who was collapsing from severe pain of traumatic skin lesions. (Lion 786) Brandy for pain was also given to the engineer who had his thumb cut off by an axe. (Engr 210) And brandy was needed even for Watson when he was suddenly confronted by the supposedly dead Holmes. (Empt 333)

Alcohol in various forms has been considered since Biblical days as a cure for many of man's ailments. Most prominent has been its use as a stimulant, as in the Canonical works. Most modern pharmacologists, however, consider it more a depressant of the central nervous system.[479a] Even in 1907, there were some doubts. "Alcohol in the form of whisky or brandy is much used in shock or collapse. . . . Its value is strongly asserted by some authorities and disputed by others."[517] Conan Doyle's use of alcohol as a direct stimulant is, however, still accepted as valid by most lay people and some physicians. It is likely that the ammonia given to Mr. Melas was more responsible than the brandy for his revival. (Gree 604) Spirits of ammonia was accepted as a stimulant in 1893 when this story was published.[179] With the numerous episodes of fainting in the *Canon* it is surprising that this is the only time it is mentioned.

Another inhalant used once by Watson is amyl nitrite. Doctor Trevelyan, the expert in nervous diseases, went to get a bottle of it for a patient with supposed catalepsy. "I had obtained good results in such cases by the inhalation of nitrite of amyl." (Resi 272) Why this drug should be given for a manifestation of hysteria is uncertain. It dilates blood vessels as does nitroglycerin, both being organic nitrites.[479d] Conan Doyle, the physician, used nitroglycerin on a patient with an actual disease of the nervous system, tabes dorsalis, because of his theory that it was due to constriction of blood vessels.[240] Such an action of organic nitrites was known when Conan Doyle was a medical student.[673]

Another drug, belladonna was used by Holmes on himself to dilate his pupils in simulating a dying man. (Dyin 450) Belladonna is a category of alkaloids whose effect on the pupil was well-known in the latter part of the 19th century.[754a] Quinine, mentioned as a remedy for malaria, (Sign 628) has an even older history. Its efficacy in treating malaria was known in the 17th century in the form of the bark of the cinchona tree which contains quinidine.[516a]

Much more unusual and dramatic therapy was that taken by the aging Professor Presbury who desired to become younger because of a love affair. (Cree 765) The abrupt change in his behavior and appearance was noted by Holmes to occur every ninth day. He theorized that "the Professor takes some strong drug which has a passing but highly poisonous effect." (Cree 761) The substance was indeed strong, being the serum of the "Langur . . . a crawler and a climber . . . the great black-faced monkey of the Himalayan slopes. . . .'' (Cree 765) Presbury had obtained it from Lowenstein of Prague who was ''striving in some unknown way for the secret of rejuvenescence and the elixir of life.''

The serum, presumably hormonal, was anything but an elixir of life. Its effect were grotesque at best.

> *He was crawling Mr. Holmes-crawling. . . . (Cree 755) His face was convulsed and he grinned and gibbered at us in his senseless rage. . . . (Cree 759) Thick and horny [knuckles] in a way which is quite new in my experiences. . . . (Cree 762) From branch to branch he sprang, sure of foot and firm of grasp. . . . (Cree 763)*

The emotional and physical brutalization of man by a drug is a familiar theme in literature. The outstanding example is *The Strange Case of Dr. Jekyll and Mr. Hyde* [851] written by Robert L. Stevenson in 1886, 37 years before Conan Doyle's short story. But, Doctor Jekyll did not have a Sherlock Holmes to save him from suicide. Conan Doyle, of course, did not believe in such a nonexistant substance any more than did Stevenson.[891]

Conan Doyle's notice of rejuvenation may also have been due to the work of Brown-Séquard (1817-1894), a French physiologist.[468j] Around 1890 Brown-Séquard injected himself with extracts of sex organs. Even though he felt more youthful as a result, he still died at his appointed time as all men must. Controlled studies using water instead of extracts have also produced subjective feelings of improvement. Even in the decade when ''The Creeping Man'' was published (the 1920s) medical fadism and quackery included transplanted monkey glands as well as extracts for rejuvenation.[910d]

Most drugs have the potential to be used for purposes other than treatment of disease. In the *Canon* there are many examples of harmful use, including addition, subduing individuals, and poisoning. Morphine, a potentially addictive drug, was given to Holmes by Sir Leslie Oakshott for pain after being attacked by ruffians; (Illus 683) and to Baron Gruner who had vitriol (sulfuric acid) thrown in his face by Kitty Winter whom he had "ruined." (Illus 688) "The vitriol was eating into it [face] everywhere and dripping from the ears and the chin. One eye was already white and glazed. . . . They [his features] were blurred, discolored, inhuman, terrible." Doctor Watson provided immediate emergency treatment. "I bathed his face in oil, put cotton wadding on the raw surfaces, and administered a hypodermic [injection] of morphia."

The only suggestion of morphine addiction occurs when Watson asked Holmes rather sardonically if it was to be morphine or cocaine, and Holmes replied, cocaine. (Sign 610) Conan Doyle provides no other indication that Holmes may also have been addicted to morphine, although this substance is mentioned in four of the Canonical works. Isa Whitney, the man with the twisted lip, was addicted to opium, as evidenced by a yellow, pasty face, drooping eyelids, and pin-point pupils. (Twis 368) Thaddeus Sholto, the hypochondriac, may have smoked opium in a hookah to calm his nerves. (Sign 626) More nefarious uses of opium were also recounted by Watson. Miss Burnet, who was part of a plot to murder the bloodthirsty dictator of San Pedro, was drugged by opium put in her food. (Wist 254) "Her pupils were dark dots in the center of the broad grey iris." Similarly, Hunter, the watchman for the horse Silver Blaze, was drugged by sprinkling powdered opium in his curried mutton. (Silv 267–269)

The uses and dangers of morphine and opium were well recognized before the Holmes and Watson chronicles. Morphine was isolated in 1803 by Serturner, but not acknowledged as an addictive agent until 70 years later.[754] Opium has a much older history, beginning long before the 1st century A.D. The addictive nature of opium was established by the time Conan Doyle graduated from medical school. A treatise on the subject,[550] published in 1881, considered that "The habitual use of opium is a disease, and a formidable one."

Cocaine is of more recent vintage than opium. It was responsible for the stimulant action of coca leaves chewed by the Incas, and was isolated as a chemical in 1859 by Nieman.[675] It soon became considered as a wonder drug in Europe.[647] America was

not exempt. For example, William Hammond, who had served as the Surgeon General, made a presentation to the Medical Society of Virginia in 1887 extolling its virtues and denying its addictive nature.[508] Although its addictive nature was suspected, Freud advocated its use for many physical, emotional, and nervous ailments.[464] Today's society may look askance at the habitual use of cocaine by a detective, but there was little negative public reaction in the last quarter of the 19th century. In fact it was widely and easily obtainable, and used in snuff, candies, gargles, ointments, and Coca-Cola until into the 20th century.

In 1890, the last year of Conan Doyle's general practice, cocaine was considered as a therapeutic agent. It was recommended as a "nerve stimulant and local anaesthetic, largely for temporary destruction of sensibility in superficial parts."[74] Usually a 4% solution was given subcutaneously. Even double such a dose given intravenously is used by some addicts.

It has been suggested that Conan Doyle picked up his knowledge of cocaine when in Vienna to study ophthalmology for a few months in 1891.[860] At that time it was being used as a local anesthetic for the eye. The first reference to Holmes' use of cocaine, however, was in *The Sign of Four*,[257] published in 1890, a year before. The characteristics exhibited by Holmes indicate a knowledge of the behavioral effects of cocaine usage.[593] Thus, Conan Doyle dramatically and accurately used cocaine to depict its stimulant effect on the mental processes of Sherlock Holmes, and to provide another fascinating aspect for his character. It is not known if Conan Doyle used cocaine in his practice. There is no existent evidence that he ever used it on himself.

Much, if not too much, has been made of a relationship between Conan Doyle and Freud, based only on their common interest in cocaine, even though with one it was for fiction, and with the other, for science.[675] One can forgive an excellent novel on the subject, such as *The Seven-Per-Cent Solution*[653] by Nicholas Meyer, except when it is analyzed on the basis of the historical reality of the *Canon*.[505] It is even more difficult to accept the Freudian psychoanalytic extrapolations of Rosenberg.[782] For example, he considers "The Red-Headed League" to contain "a parable of fantasized pederastic rape that is thwarted by Sherlock Holmes." Because a pawnbroker's shop is mentioned, the intent (conscious or unconscious) was to provide a Freudian symbol—"the balls and cross-sections of penis that hang in front of the shop." The appeal of Holmes is so strong that some of his cases 'and peculiarities, such as the use of cocaine, has generated both novels and psychoanalysis of one of the first proponents of its clinical use.

Cocaine, however, is not as prominent a feature in the 60 Canonical stories as might be expected from the large amount of commentary. The first suggestion that Holmes might be taking an addictive drug is given by Watson in the first published story. (Stud 153)

> *I have noticed such a dreamy, vacant expression in his eyes, that I might have suspected him of being addicted to the use of some narcotic, had not the temperance and cleanliness of his whole life forbidden such a notion.*

Watson was soon to be disillusioned. In the next published story of the *Canon*, but set seven years after the first one, Holmes indicates his use of a 7% solution of cocaine, (Sign 610) which is not an impossible quantity. Jack Tracy has found references to the drug by name in only five stories and implied use in three others.[874] Of significance is that the specific name was used in stories published between 1890 and 1893, whereas the more general allusions were between 1904 and 1913. Freud himself had lost his enthusiasm for it about the mid-1890s.[583] It was shortly thereafter, around the turn of the century, that public attitudes to cocaine changed from general acceptance to enlightened rejection. For example, in 1903 cocaine was removed from Coca-Cola, and within a few years its availability in the United States restricted by law to prescriptions.

That Holmes was a cocaine addict has been questioned by some. Miller[658] has stated that "the facts [sic] are all against it;" to be countered by Grilly[492] who stresses that the depiction of its effects on Holmes is "accurate and consistent with what is presently known about cocaine." Another mythical denial of the fictional reality of his addiction is that it resulted from receiving cocaine for dental problems.[483] With even less basis in the *Canon* is the conclusion that Holmes was not an addict but was actually "pulling Watson's leg."[627,689] Conan Doyle may have depicted Watson as somewhat dull, but not to the degree that he could be so completely misled after living in close and prolonged contact with Holmes. And would the master detective expend so much time and energy over the years on a mere prank?

The objection that he was not an addict but a "user" because there are no cocaine addicts,[124] can also be easily dispensed with in short order. It is true that cocaine users do not develop a physical basis for their craving. But, there is a very strong psychological craving which also constitutes an addiction.[479c] Conan Doyle does provide Holmes with specific symptoms suggestive of episodes of chronic cocaine use, such as prolonged sleep, general fatigue, lassitude, and depression. (Scan 346)

Such unfounded extrapolations from a work of fiction, especially when written on the assumption that the characters are real, contribute little to an assessment of the knowledge of the author. There is no doubt that Conan Doyle intended to depict Holmes as a cocaine addict in the earlier stories. In doing so he added significantly to the realism of the characterization of his detective. The adoration resulting from his literary skills has led to a hero-worship that reacts against any blemish on his character.

Another matter of concern of Holmesian aficionados was his use of a hypodermic syringe for injection of cocaine. The inconsistency appears to be that, although the syringe was first invented in 1853 by Pravaz, it was not used for cocaine until 1891 by Schleich of Berlin.[677] In fact, seven years prior to this, in 1884, William Halsted, the renowned American surgeon, was injecting himself with cocaine solution in a syringe to test its value as a local anesthetic.[173] Many such investigations were being conducted at this time in America, with at least the one known "accidental" addiction—that of Halsted. Conan Doyle's first reference to cocaine injected by a hypodermic syringe, one year before Schleich's publication, suggests a knowledge of such prior use in America.

Conan Doyle was also quite aware of the detrimental effects of cocaine well before general recognition at the turn of the century. In the second adventure, published in 1890, Watson admonished Holmes to quit its use before his mental faculties deteriorated. (Sign 610–611)

> *Count the cost! Your brain may, as you say, be roused and excited, but it is a pathological and morbid process, which involves increased tissue change, and may at last leave a permanent weakness. You know, too, what a black reaction comes upon you. Surely the game is hardly worth the candle. Why should you, for a mere passing pleasure, risk the loss of those great powers with which you have been endowed?*

The truth of Watson's warning on the harmful effects of cocaine is even more evident today than it was a hundred years ago.[18] It also indicates that Conan Doyle's knowledge of cocaine and its addictive powers was well in advance of that of most practitioners of his time.

One commentary on the use of cocaine by Sherlock Holmes has no substantiation whatsoever. It has been alleged that Conan Doyle himself used the drug. Extensive research on the subject by Cox[182] has revealed that this myth has been spread by completely unfounded statements in stories on cocaine in *Newsweek* and the *Pittsburgh North Star* (1977). As Cox stresses, the basis for such a supposed fact is not given. Undoubtedly Conan Doyle's skills in achieving the aura of reality in the *Canon* have lead to the impression that he had personal experience with cocaine.

There was another drug in the *Canon* that is involved in addiction—nicotine in the form of tobacco. The references to Holmes' pipes are so numerous as to indicate a tobacco addict.[873] Its most effective use is to heighten the unconventionality of Holmes. Watson visited him when he was "smoking his before-breakfast pipe, which was composed of all the plugs and dottles left from his smokes of the day before, all carefully dried and collected on the corner of the mantelpiece." (Engr 211) That Conan Doyle was aware of the stimulant action of nicotine is evident by his designation of the perplexing case of the Red-Headed League as a "three-pipe problem." (RedH 429) While considering the problem of the man with the twisted lip, Holmes consumed an ounce of shag pipe tobacco in one night. (Twis 381)[N113]

It is not known if Conan Doyle was aware of the many possible harmful effects of tobacco usage on health. Reactions of Watson to Holmes' smoking, however, indicate a general awareness. After an all-night session of ratiocination and smoking, Watson complains that "it was the acrid fumes of strong, coarse tobacco which took me by the throat and set me coughing." (Houn 18) Holmes' reactions to the curious death of Miss Brenda Tregennis were characteristic. "I think, Watson, that I shall resume that course of tobacco-poisoning which you have so often and so justly condemned." (Devi 514) Such negative statements about tobacco were not as common or universal in Victorian society as they are in society today. Medical textbooks of the 1890s did refer to effects such as palpitations of the heart and aggravation of preexisting heart disease.[696o] It was known that irritation could cause cancer,[489] but there was not general knowledge of the relationship between pipe smoking and cancer of the lip and tongue.[N114]

Conan Doyle himself smoked a pipe. Carr's biography contains three photographs showing him with a pipe; in only one is it actually in his mouth.[125g] As these pictures are obviously carefully posed, the presence of a pipe may be as a prop for effect and not indicative of a heavy smoker. Also two photographs show Conan Doyle with cigars, in one instance holding one while meeting with James Payn in 1897,[125h] and in the other smoking one while in his automobile during the Anglo-German car race of 1911.[862d] One suspects that he was an intermittent smoker.

Another category of drugs is nonaddictive, but can have serious effects on the human body. In the Holmesian writings anesthetic agents were used by criminals and by Holmes alike to gain various ends. One instance is that of Mrs. Maberly, who was the widowed mother of a diplomat who died of pneumonia after he had sent her a damaging manuscript. In order to destroy the manuscript, concerned parties broke into her house and chloroformed her. (3Gab 729) They obviously did not give her enough as she soon recovered while they were at work and raised an alarm.

Holmes used chloroform when disguised as Altamont—an English hating Irish-American spy working for the German espionage agent von Bork. Holmes captured von Bork and retrieved secret British Naval documents by forcibly holding a chloroformed sponge over his face. (Last 799) ". . .he was gripped at the back of his neck by a grasp of iron, and a chloroformed sponge was held in front of his writhing face."

A more dramatic anesthetic event was related to the disappearance of Lady Frances Carfax. (Lady 669) In order to obtain her jewels, thieves placed her in a coffin with her head smothered in cotton wool soaked in chloroform. The lid was then screwed shut. Holmes and Watson arrived in the nick of time. Watson revived Lady Carfax by two means—artificial respiration and the injection of ether. Using one anesthetic agent to overcome the effects of another is rather startling because both are depressants of the central nervous system.[594] Ether, however, may have been used by subcutaneous injection as a cardiac stimulant during the 19th century.[873a]

The use of chloroform as a major device in the plots of these three Sherlockian adventures is dramatic, but certainly not indicative of any sophistication of medical knowledge on the part of Conan Doyle. Chloroform was first used as an anesthetic in 1847, and for delivery of Queen Victoria in 1853, 50 years before these stories were published.[573] Conan Doyle cannot lay claim to the first use of chloroform in criminal fiction nor in fact. Twenty-five years before the first Holmesian chloroform episode Hume had used this plot device for a murder in a hansom cab.[551] In actuality, chloroform had been used by real criminals in 1850, during an epidemic of robberies in London. ". . .two notorious women used it to render a Mr. Jewett, a solicitor. . . unconscious. He woke to find himself stripped of his clothing and valuables, lying on a filthy bed in a wretched lodging."[868] The chloroform crimes depicted by Conan Doyle, although over a half-century later, were more gripping and suspenseful.

As suspenseful and perhaps more poignant was the use of curare as a poison rather than a drug. Mr. Ferguson's teenage son, Jacky, wounded his little stepbrother in the neck with a small arrow dipped in it. Ferguson's second wife, from Peruvia, prevented her baby's death by sucking the poison out of the arrow wound, but was thereby suspected of being a vampire. (Suss 473) Fortunately, curare is inactive when taken by mouth,[479d] as Conan Doyle was undoubtedly aware. Puzzling, however, is the prolonged paralysis of the hind-legs of a spaniel which persisted for four months after the dog was pierced by a dart poisoned with curare. (Suss 468) The animal should have died quickly or recovered completely. But fiction has its liberties, especially for enigmatic clues.

Such a use of curare is not fanciful, for it has a long history as a South American arrow poison. Death is due to paralysis of skeletal muscles.[479d] In Conan Doyle's time curare had no clinical application. Its use as a muscle relaxant for general anesthesia began in the 1930s. Before that time it was an exotic poison that added a mysterious element from an alien world to Conan Doyle's mysteries.

Another substance identified as an arrow poison is featured in yet another story. Jefferson Hope revengefully poisoned Drebber (who had broken the innocent heart of sweet Lucy Ferrier) with a South American alkaloid arrow poison which was instantly effective by mouth. (Stud 227) This could not be curare, which is active only on injection. Allen suggests that it may have been an Erythrina alkaloid that is active by mouth[13] but not used clinically. Conan Doyle further exploited the use of this questionable poison for dramatic effect. Hope gave Drebber the choice between two pills, one harmless and the other deadly, but both identical in appearance.

> *A spasm of pain contorted his [Drebber] features; he threw his hands out in front of him, staggered, and then, with a hoarse cry, fell heavily upon the floor. . . . He was dead! (Stud 228)*

Sherlock Holmes' expert knowledge of poisons was fully established in this first published adventure. "Having sniffed the dead man's lips, I detected a slightly sour smell, and I came to the conclusion that he had had poison forced upon him." (Stud 232) Conan Doyle earlier in the story commented, through Stamford, on Holmes as a researcher into poisons. (Stud 149)

> *Holmes is a little too scientific for my tastes—it approaches to cold-bloodedness. I could imagine his giving a friend a little pinch of the latest vegetable alkaloid, not out of malevolence, you understand, but simply out of a spirit of inquiry in order to have an accurate idea of the effects.*

Holmes did carry out such an experiment with the alkaloid arrow poison that had killed Drebber, but not on a human. He gave a pill found in the murderer's room to a poor little terrier who was in chronic pain. ". . .it gave a convulsive shiver in every limb, and lay as rigid and lifeless as if it had been struck by lightning. (Stud 194)[N115] This description is more compatible with strychnine than with curare, the muscle relaxant. Nonetheless, Conan Doyle's poison of questionable nature served to introduce Holmes as a forensic expert and to establish a facet of his character.

Strychnine is another drug that can be used for poisoning. In the *Canon*, however, it was suggested as a prescription by Watson for Thaddeus Sholto, out of desperation at his

> *. . .pouring forth interminable trains of symptoms, and imploring information as to the composition and action of innumerable quack nostrums . . . I recommended strychnine in large doses as a sedative. (Sign 631)*

In actuality strychnine would not sedate but cause convulsions, stiffness of muscles, and death. Doctor Watson (and thereby Doctor Conan Doyle) has been considered ignorant because of this recommendation, or at best confused by the nearness of Miss Morstan.[121] More likely it was Conan Doyle's sense of humor reacting to his own creation, the extreme hypochondriac.[N116] Death due to poisoning by a thorn containing a drug identified only as having strychnine-like action occurred to Bartholomew Sholto. (Sign 639) The use and effects of strychnine as a poison were well recognized when this story was published in 1890.[671] Four prostitutes were murdered with strychnine by Thomas Neil Cream in 1892, when Conan Doyle was living in London.[40]

Another type of poison is found in "The Speckled Band," this time venom from a snake rather than a plant poison. The murder instrument, used by Doctor Roylott on his stepdaughter Julia

Stoner, was a snake identified by Holmes as a swamp adder, "the deadliest snake in India." (Spec 261) Considerable energy has been spent in trying to relate Conan Doyle's fictional snake to an actual one. For example, Boswell has suggested that the snake was Russel's viper because it is speckled by three rows of black rings and by chocolate brown spots, as described for the swamp adder.[88]

As must happen to many villains, even if physicians, the snake turned on Doctor Roylott himself. Holmes exclaims: (Spec 261)

> *He had died within ten seconds of being bitten. Violence does in truth, recoil upon the violent, and the schemer falls into the pit which he digs for another.*

The moralizing may be acceptable, but rapid death is not. Snake bites do not produce such an instant effect, and on the average have only a 40% death rate.[755a] But what a dramatic conclusion to a spine-chilling story!

Another toxic poison from a biologic source was the villain in "The Lion's Mane," a name given to a huge jellyfish, because, in Holmes' own words, it "did indeed look like a tangled mass torn from the mane of a lion." (Lion 787) In this adventure Fitzroy McPherson, a young science master, met a rapid, painful, and mysterious death while swimming in the ocean. (Lion 777)

> *He was obviously dying. Those glazed sunken eyes and dreadful livid cheeks could mean nothing else . . . he uttered two or three words . . . "the lion's mane". . . . His back was covered with dark red lines as though he had been terribly flogged by a thin wire scourge.*

He also recognized that McPherson's dog, which died later on the same spot, was the victim of the same poison. "The body was stiff and rigid, the eyes projecting, and the limbs contorted. There was agony in every line of it." (Lion 784) The deaths were puzzling until Holmes recognized *Cyanea capillata*, a jellyfish species which can grow to six feet across and occurs in the cold waters of the Northern Hemisphere.[451]

One difficulty with this adventure is that stings from jellyfish of this species are not generally known to cause death.[906] Van

Liere,[893] therefore, has suggested that the culprit was a Portugese man-of-war, contact with which can cause anaphylactic shock (reaction to foreign protein) due to a nervous system toxin. But this would require sensitization from a previous sting. At any rate death from this sea creature is also considered uncommon. Perhaps Conan Doyle used the wrong type of jellyfish because stings of some species can result in death, although mostly in Australian waters.[172] Petty differences of opinion as to the fictional sea monster do not, however, detract from his graphic descriptions of the consequence of contact with poisonous aquatic life.

Even more controversial than the identity of the lion's mane or the swamp adder is that of the devil's foot root. It was used by Mortimer Tregennis to murder his sister, and in turn on him by Doctor Leon Sterndale, an explorer and lion hunter, who took the law into his own hands. It is described as a root "shaped like a foot, half human, half goat-like." (Devi 524) When burnt it produced a toxic smoke that maddens and kills. Again there is controversy as to its counterpart in the nonfiction world. Suggested has been an Asiatic plant, rauwolfia, because in large doses it can cause nightmares.[13] Cooper provides a somewhat more likely prospect, an African ordeal drug and the smoking of prepared hemp which can cause insanity.[162] Perhaps, Conan Doyle heard of these during his visit as ship's surgeon to the west coast of Africa in 1881–1882.

Several other suggestions have been made as to the nature of the devil's foot root. Mescaline is an alkaloid found in the peyote cactus. It has been used in Mexico and the southwestern United States as a hallucinogen.[570] More recently an African poison, the ordeal bean (Calabar), has been proposed because of its content of eserine.[746] Its appearance is similar to the devil's root foot. Conan Doyle may have become aware of this substance during his visit to Old Calabar in 1882,[375j] and through the studies done on the Calabar bean by Christison, the Edinburgh professor.[138]

Of more compelling interest was the burning of the devil's root foot by Holmes in order to ascertain its nature. The effect on both Holmes and Watson was dramatic and almost fatal.

> *At the very first whiff of it my brain and my imagination were beyond all control . . . Vague shapes swirled and swam amid the dark cloud-bank, each a menace and a warning of something coming, the advent of some unspeakable dweller upon the threshold, whose very shadow would blast my soul. A freezing horror took posession of me. I felt that my hair was rising, that my eyes were protruding, that my mouth was opened, and my tongue like leather . . . I tried to scream and was vaguely aware of some hoarse croak which was my own voice, but distant and detached from myself. (Devi 520)*

Isaac Asimov[32] has pointed out the similarity of these effects of the fumes of devil's foot root to that of LSD, discovered a half century later. These symptoms are also similar in American Indians who for several centuries have used the hallucinogenic drug peyote for religious purposes.[84] This is indeed chemical science fiction come true! But even more gripping is the tale of victims with faces twisted in horror as a result of terrifying fumes from an exotic African root, shaped like a devil's foot.[N117.]

The burning of another substance was used for poisonous purposes. An attempt was made on the life of Mr. Melas, the Greek interpreter, by exposure to carbon monoxide from burning charcoal. (Gree 604) It is rather surprising that, when Holmes threw open the door, "there reeked a horrible, poisonous exhaltation, which set us gasping and coughing" for it is a colorless, odorless, nonirritant gas.[755] Of interest is that another victim of carbon monoxide poisoning did not survive. He was described as in the last stage of emaciation, having been starved by his captors. (Gree 604) Thus, he would be quite anemic, making him more susceptible to carbon monoxide poisoning. This gas combines with hemoglobin of the blood, making it incapable of carrying oxygen. Therefore, the less hemoglobin the quicker death because all of it is inactivated by carbon monoxide. It is quite unlikely that Conan Doyle was aware of this specific chemical effect of burning charcoal. "Charcoal-vapor" was a recognized cause of death when this story was published. Carbon monoxide was listed as carbonic oxide, but its effect on hemoglobin had not yet been discovered.[865]

Poisoning by carbon monoxide was accomplished by old Amberley in a different manner. Coal-gas, used for heating and illumination before the safer methane, is an excellent source.[865f] He used it to murder his wife and her physician lover. (Reti 555)

> *That end [of the pipe] is wide open . . . by turning the outside tap the room could be flooded with gas. With door and shutters closed and the tap full on I would not give two minutes of conscious sensation to anyone shut up in that little chamber.*

Such gas, however, has been used as much or more for suicide than for murder.[755c]

Two poisons of unspecified nature are mentioned in the *Canon*, both used in suicide attempts. Anna Coram, who was betrayed by her husband, a Russian revolutionist, successfully committed suicide after being exposed as accidentally killing his secretary. (Gold 366) "Too late! . . . I took the poison before I left my hiding-place. My head swims! I am going." The poison was not likely cyanide, which has a much more rapid effect; nor was it a nervous system depressant, which would not have allowed her to talk until the end. Cyanide was known as being extremely poisonous even in the Victorian Era.[754b]

Cyanide may have been in the white pellet which Holmes forced out of the mouth of Amberley who attempted suicide after being accused of the murder of his wife and her supposed lover. (Reti 553) Holmes used persuasion rather than force on Mrs. Eugenia Ronder, who was veiled because her face had been horribly mutilated by a lion. He detected something in the woman's voice which attracted his attention. (Veil 461)

> *'Your life is not your own . . . Keep your hands off it.'*
> *'What use is it to anyone?'*
> *'How can you tell? The example of patient suffering is in itself the most precious of all lessons to an impatient world.'*
> *The woman's answer was a terrible one. She raised her veil and stepped forward into the light. . . .*

It was horrible . . . Two living and beautiful brown eyes looking sadly out from that grisly ruin did but make the view more awful.

Holmes' success at preventing her suicide was evident when he received a small blue bottle. Its contents had the pleasant almondy odor of prussic acid. This poison has long been recognized as acting almost the instant it is swallowed, with loss of consciousness and convulsive breathing.[865b]

All in all, Conan Doyle had a fair knowledge of poisons for his era, but greatly enhanced by his fertile imagination. In doing so he committed several pharmacological errors, of which only some were due to the state of the art of his day. The others would indicate imperfections in detailed knowledge of poisons which one might expect in a general practitioner. Poisons are also a feature of modern detective stories, but contain many inaccuracies of effect.[14]

A general practitioner would have more exposure to and knowledge of crime by more violent methods. The *Canon* does contain more instances of murder by traumatic means, than by poisoning. But, both are illegal acts which result in disease or injury to the body and thus come under the heading of forensic medicine.

FORENSIC MEDICINE AND THE CANON

Forensic (legal) medicine is defined, in its broadest sense, as "the application of medical knowledge to questions of civil and criminal law."[847c] The term includes many areas, such as medical ethics, drug dependency, industrial injuries, unexplained deaths, and death from accident, suicide, or murder.[447] Another category, forensic science, is related to forensic medicine when it involves material from humans or characteristic traces, such as footprints and fingerprints.

Conan Doyle provided Holmes with a somewhat spotty expertise as a forensic scientist in the nonmedical area. His ability to differentiate between zinc and copper filings and to identify glue only under the microscope (Shos 630) could not be done in his time, nor in ours, if ever.[32] Similarly his ability to differentiate between "the ashes of any known brand either of cigar or of tobacco" (Stud 173) is beyond the realm of science.[541] Conan Doyle, however, had the ability to use the trappings of science for dramatic effect. (Nava 169)

> *'You come at a crisis, Watson,' said he. "If this [litmus] paper remains blue, all is well. If it turns red, it means a man's life.' He dipped it into the test-tube, and it flushed at once into a dull, dirty crimson. 'Hum! I thought as much!' he cried. . . . He turned to his desk and scribbled off several telegrams. . . .*

Conan Doyle, through Holmes and Watson, also exhibited some knowledge of ballistics. William Kirwan, the coachman murdered by his employees, was shot "at a distance of something over four yards. There was no powder-blackening on his clothes." (Regi 343) Such a relationship was well known in his day.[865c] In the shooting death of Mr. Cubitt there were no powder markings on his hands or on his dressing gown. (Danc 537) The bullet that killed Ronald Adair "mushroomed out, as soft-nosed bullets will." (Empt 331) Such knowledge of bullets is not surprising in one who took as much interest in war as did Conan Doyle.[N118] No mention is made, however, of identification of bullets by bore markings, a ballistic technique which was developed during the last decade of the 19th century.[830]

Of much more credit to the practicality of Conan Doyle's imagination is the application of variations in typescript for identification of the typewriter used to type a letter. (Iden 414) "It is a curious thing . . . that a typewriter has really quite as much individuality as a man's handwriting." This was published in 1891, 21 years after the first practical typewriter was invented in 1867, and before such a technique was used in any actual case.[909,N119] Thus, James Windibank, who tried to retain control of his step-daughter's income, became the first individual, fictional or otherwise, to be incriminated by a typewriter.

Conan Doyle was also quite familiar with the uniqueness of handwriting, and occasionally it was of considerable help. For example, Holmes recognized the coded warning of a planned murder as being in the hand of Porlock, a member of Moriarity's gang. (Vall 471) "The Greek 'e' with the peculiar top flourish is distinctive." He also noted the same peculiarity in the disguised hand of the addresses of the pearl-box. (Sign 619) Holmes deduced that the letter sent to Watson by his old school friend was dictated as it was in a woman's hand. (Nava 169) There might be some validity to this, but only in very broad generalities.

Conan Doyle was on even shakier ground when Holmes implicated the Cunninghams for the murder of their coachman on the basis of inherited similarities between the handwriting of the son and father. (Reig 345) We must look, however, to a non-Sherlockian story by Conan Doyle to find a clear cut, legitimate example of the identification of the culprit by handwriting. The removal of jewels from "The Jew's Breastplate"[306] was discovered to be done by Professor Andreas on the basis of similarities between an anonymous letter of warning and a personal letter from him. "Look at the *c* in 'congratulate' and the '*c*' in committed. Look at the capital *I*. Look at the trick of putting in a dash instead of a stop!" Handwriting, unlike typescript, can be forged, although identification can be avoided by printing. (RedC 692)

But even printing did not daunt Holmes. Its form and the incorrectness of spelling on the cardboard box led to the conclusion that the ears were sent to Miss Cushing by a male of limited education. (Card 197) Even the word RACHE printed in blood on a wall by the dying Stangerson yielded information. (Stud 174)

> *The A, if you noticed, was printed somewhat after the German fashion. Now, a real German invariably prints in the Latin character, so that we may safely say that this was not written by one, but by a clumsy imitator who overdid his part.*

This is symbolic of the value of combining close observation with detailed knowledge.

FOOTPRINTS IN THE CANON

In the area of forensic medical science Sherlock Holmes was given expertise in identifying human materials and imprints. There is frequent reference to footprints, either as a discussion of their value, or as their actual use in investigations at the scene of a crime. Tracy has listed 29 such events.[873b] Conan Doyle was quite aware of the value of making casts of footprints. Holmes shows Watson "my monograph upon the tracing of footsteps, with some remarks upon the uses of plaster of Paris as a preserver of impresses." (Sign 612) Student Conan Doyle may well have noted the reference to this technique by P.H. Watson in Doctor Bell's surgical manual of 1878.[56] In a mystery by Freeman published 40 years later, *The Touchstone*,[462] Doctor Thorndyke used wax rather than the usual plaster.

Holmes used footprints for various deductions, in addition to estimating height from the length of stride. On a sounder basis are his observations at the scene of the murder of Drebber. (Stud 174)

> *Patent-leathers and Square-toes came in the same cab, and they walked down the pathway together as friendly as possible—arm-in-arm in all probability. When they got inside . . . Patent-leathers stood still while Square-toes walked up and down. I could read all that in the dust.*

Holmes was quite impressed with the very small footsteps found in the room of the murdered Bartholomew Sholto, which proved to be that of Tonga, "a little Andaman Islander." (Sign 685)

Holmes disagreed with the interpretation that Sir Charles Baskerville's footprints indicated that he was walking on tiptoe. (Houn 20) "He was running, Watson—running desperately, running for his life, running until he burst his heart and fell dead." Another example of close observation of footprints resulted in the identification of John Turner, who murdered Charles McCarthy, the blackmailer. (Bosc 148) "The impression of his right foot was always less distinct than his left. He put less weight upon it. Why? Because he limped—he was lame.'' This is a further example of Conan Doyle's creative imagination. He did not, however, invent such a use of footprints, although he popularized their importance in criminology. In 1844 there is a record of the imprint of a boot leading to the conviction of the murderer of an elderly woman.[814]

Conan Doyle also introduced humor into the *Canon* in one reference to footprints. After the escape of Holmes and Watson from watching the murder of the blackmailing Charles Augustus Milverton by a noblewoman, Lestrade of Scotland Yard came to consult with the master detective. (Chas 570)

> *'We have their footmarks, we have their description; it's ten to one that we trace them. The first fellow was a bit too active, but the second was caught by the under-gardener, and only got away after a struggle. He was a middle-sized, strongly built man—square jaw, thick neck, moustache, a mask over his eyes.'*
>
> *'That's rather vague,' said Sherlock Holmes.*
>
> *'Why, it might be a description of Watson!'*
>
> *'Its true,' said the Inspector with much amusement.*
>
> *'It might be a description of Watson.'*

It is surprising that the *Canon* does not have more such humor in light of the amount in other works, such as *Round the Red Lamp*,[281] and of Conan Doyle's own personal sense of humor. Perhaps, it was not quite as appropriate for murder stories.

THE CANONICAL THUMBPRINT

In only one instance was a fingerprint used for identification in the *Canon*. But it was Inspector Lestrade who used it, and not Holmes, to identify the culprit of the apparent murder of Jonas Oldacre as John McFarlane. Most surprising was the lukewarm response of Holmes to Lestrade's question that ''you are aware that no two thumb-marks are alike?'' (Norw 425) ''I have heard something of the kind.'' This was not ignorance on Holmes' part, but knowledge that the thumbmark was not on the wall when he first examined the scene of the crime. And, here Conan Doyle again displayed his creativity. Jonas Oldacre, who had created false evidence of his own murder to cheat his creditors,

> *. . .got McFarlane to secure one of the seals [of packets] by putting his thumb upon the soft wax. . . . It was the simplest thing in the world for him to take a wax impression from the seal, to moisten it in as much blood as he could get from a pinprick and to put the mark upon the wall. . . . (Norw 430)*

Another mention of fingerprints appears in the *Canon*. Holmes explained that the corner of a note had been torn off because "There was evidently some mark, some thumb-print, something which might give a clue to the person's identity." (RedC 693) It is not really surprising that Conan Doyle did not make further use of fingerprints to solve crimes. They are so specific that they can obviate much need for the type of ratiocination that makes Holmes so fascinating. This use of fingerprints by Inspector Lestrade in a story published in 1903 is in accord with historical facts. After at least a century of study of fingerprints, they became firmly established by Galton's publication in 1892 of a workable classification.[467] The system was officially adopted by Scotland Yard in 1901.[868a] Not quite as accurate is Freeman's *The Red Thumb Mark* of 1907.[461] The plot is based upon the unheard of forgery of a thumbprint by use of a gelatine stamp. Conan Doyle, however, was quite aware of the fact that fingerprints were unique for each individual, and could not be forged in spite of the relative impreciseness of early classifications.[N120]

THE TEST FOR BLOOD

Examination of substances from the human body itself is much more limited in the Holmesian chronicles than that of its imprints. There is only one mention of this area of forensic medicine. It occurred in the chemical laboratory of St. Bartholomew Hospital, as Stamford approached Holmes to introduce him to Watson. (Stud 150)

> *At the sound of our steps he glanced around and sprang to his feet with a cry of pleasure. 'I've found it! I've found it . . . I have found a reagent which is precipitated by haemoglobin, and by nothing else. . . . Why, man, it is the most practical medico-legal discovery for years. Don't you see that it gives us an infallible test for blood stains.*

This episode is extremely useful, aside from any scientific merit. It immediately establishes a basic part of Holmes' personality. In recording Watson's less than lukewarm response ('Indeed!' I murmured), it also sets up a rather dull and slow-witted, but very effective foil for Holmes.

There have been numerous recountings, discussions, and analyses of this integral event in the first Canonical story. Most, playing the game of the historical reality of the "Master," exult in this triumph.[28] However, Isaac Asimov, the skeptic, again questions Holmes' (and thereby Conan Doyle's) knowledge of chemical procedures.[32] The statement that a drop of blood into a litre of water results in a dilution of no more than one in a million is inaccurate—it is more like one in only 50,000.

A more basic problem relates to the fact that this revolutionary practical test is not referred to again in any of the 60 adventures, even though there are numerous references to bloody footsteps, (RedC 700) thumbprints, (Norw 425) walls, (Stud 170) and stains. (Seco 314) Evidently Holmes accepted these on the basis of color. A possible explanation for Conan Doyle's apparent neglect is that, as for fingerprints, an infallible test for blood would detract from Holmes' powers of observation and reasoning.

Conan Doyle was, however, quite familiar with the standard guaiacum blood test of his day. (Stud 150)

> *The old guaiacum test was very clumsy and uncertain . . . the microscopic examination for blood corpuscles is valueless if the stains are a few hours old. . . . [A suspect's] linen or clothes are examined and brownish stains discovered upon them. Are they blood stains, or mud stains, or rust stains, or fruit stains, or what are they?*

He did not refer to another contemporary test, that is, spectral analysis of suspect material to look for the characteristic absorption band of hemoglobin.[865d] Holmes was apparently not concerned about animals as the possible sources of blood.

Although Holmes does not use his remarkable test for blood in any specific cases, Conan Doyle does refer to a scientific investigation of a blood stain in a non-Canonical work. In the "Horror of the Heights,"[359] published in 1913, a manuscript was identified as most likely that of the missing aviator, Mr. Joyce-Armstrong. Stains on the last page and the outside cover were

> *. . .pronounced by the Home Office [Scotland Yard] experts to be blood—probably human and certainly mammalian. The fact that something closely resembling the organism of malaria was discovered in this blood, and that Joyce-Armstrong is known to have suffered from intermittent fever, is a remarkable example of the new weapons which modern science has placed in the hands of our detectives (page 552).*

Modern science, unfortunately, cannot identify malarial organisms in such circumstance. They would be destroyed after release from blood cells which soon disrupt after leaving the blood vessels unless quickly treated with fixative solution.[926] Conan Doyle was correct in stating that human and mammalian blood could be distinguished from that of other animals, such as birds and reptiles, which have nuclei in their red blood cells. This episode is yet another example of the effective meld of his knowledge of medicine with his ability to write engaging mysteries.

THE BODY AFTER DEATH

In the specific cases of the adventures, Holmes was actually more interested in studying murder victims with his naked eye than with scientific technology. Thus, bruises of the skin take on a special importance in respect to Holmes' dedication to his profession—so much so that, as Watson is informed by Stamford, he has taken "to beating subjects in the dissection-rooms with a stick . . . to verify how far bruises may be produced after death."(Stud 149) Considerable force is required to produce even a small bruise after death.[806]

In attributing this to Holmes, Conan Doyle was emulating one of his medical school teachers. Christison, in 1829 studied the effect of violence on the body after death of a large dog, a female 33 years of age and a 38-year-old male.[137] He concluded that blows inflicted after death do not result in some features seen after blows before death—swelling, yellow margin, and clots of blood in adjacent tissues. These observations by Christison, and then presumably by Holmes, were well accepted by the mid-19th century[502a] and are still used 150 years later as the basis for distinguishing between ante-mortem and post-mortem bruises.[755b] The only significant modern addition is microscopic examination of the bruise for the presence of white blood cells, which would not be present if incurred after death.[N121] As in the instance of the test for hemoglobin, the study of bruises did not enter into any of the cases. Both, however, gave Holmes the aura of a forensic research scientist.

Somewhat similar to bruises after death, but due to gravity rather than a blow, is the pooling of blood in the skin of the lowest-lying parts of the body. This so-called livor mortis was observed by Holmes in the body of the asphyxiated butler, Richard Brunton. He had been locked in an air-lighted chamber and died with his forehead down upon the edge of a box containing old coins. (Musg 136)

> *The attitude had drawn all the stagnant blood to his face, and no man could have recognized that distorted, liver-coloured countenance.*

Such livid discoloration is more intense when death is due to asphyxiation as in the case of Brunton.[816] As so often occurs in the *Canon*, a medical description does not play a role in solving the crime, but contributes greatly to the sense of horror.

Another result of death is stiffening of the muscles. Conan Doyle recognized that the extent of this "rigor mortis" is determined by the length of time after death. Stangerson, who had been stabbed, "was quite dead, and had been for some time, for his limbs were rigid and cold." (Stud 191) Similarly, Watson opined that Blessington, who had been hanged, "has been dead about three hours, judging by the rigidity of the muscles."(Resi 276)

Holmes was given sufficient medical knowledge by Conan Doyle to determine that the stiffening of the body of poisoned Bartholomew Sholto was "in a state of extreme contraction, far exceeding the usual *rigor mortis*." (Sign 693) Also astute was his realization of one significance of the note in the hand of the dead Mrs. Gibson who shot herself and tried to implicate Miss Dunbar.(Thor 598)

> *'Clutched, you say?'*
>
> *'Yes, sir; we could hardly open the fingers.'*
>
> *'That is of great importance. It excludes the idea that anyone could have placed the note there after death in order to furnish a false clue. . . .'*

Knowledge of rigor mortis, unlike livor mortis, was used by Conan Doyle as an important observation in solving two crimes.

FORENSIC PATHOLOGY

One further important area of forensic medicine is forensic pathology, the study of the actual diseases and wounds that occur under circumstances having legal implications. Information gained can assist in determining the nature of the environmental factor or weapon used, the way in which the damage was inflicted, the physical relationship between the victim and the agent at the time of occurrence, and the individual characteristics of the agent, human or otherwise. In the Holmesian mysteries wounds are produced mostly by trauma resulting from criminal intent. Three categories of weapons are used for murder in the *Canon*—blunt weapons, knives, and firearms.

Seven instances of a blow to the head inflicted to commit murder and four accidental ones are reported. All were to the head, and quite lethal. The resultant trauma is not described in any gory detail but in general terms. Conan Doyle uses a variety of terms for the end results.

> *. . .head had been beaten in by repeated blows . . . of some heavy and blunt instrument. (Bosc 136) . . . struck from immediately behind, and yet was upon the left side. (Bosc 148)*
> *. . . skull had been shattered by a blow from a poker, delivered from behind. (Stoc 166)*
> *. . . head had been smashed to pulp by heavy blows of a sandbag or some such instrument, which had crushed rather than wounded. (Wist 243)*
> *. . . head was badly crushed. (Bruc 434)*
> *. . . bone was crushed but there was not great external injury . . .(Bruc 439) a short life-preserver [weighted stick]. (Bruc 451)*
> *. . . back of his head crushed in and deep claw marks across his scalp. (Veil 456) . . . a club . . . leaden head . . . five long steel nails. (Veil 459)*
> *. . . head was knocked in . . . with his own poker. (Abbe 492)*
> *. . . a frightful blow upon the head which had crushed in part of his skull. (Prio 618)*

Conan Doyle, fortunately, had sufficient restraint to avoid more sensational details, such as splattered brains, which would have repulsed his readers. In only one instance, that of the murder of McCarthy, were the characteristics of the wound used by Holmes to track the killer. "The blow was struck from immediately behind, and yet was upon the left side. Now, how can that be unless it were by a left-handed man?" (Bosc 148) This is an intriguing assumption, but one would have expected useful interpretations of head wounds in more than one of these seven murder cases studied by the master detective.

Also reported are several nonhomicidal examples of death due to head injury. Joseph Openshaw "had fallen over one of the deep chalk-pits . . . lying senseless, with a shattered skull.'' (Five 396) Although the jury ruled death from accidental causes, Holmes thought otherwise because of the murder of his brother Elias and his son John. Conversely, murder was at first suspected in the death of Colonel Barclay who had ''a ragged cut, some two inches long, at the back part of his head,'' apparently caused by a club found nearby the body. (Croo 229) The accidental nature was not determined by Holmes, but by evidence from the crooked man whom he traced. The cut was caused by striking the fender (fire-place guard) while falling after an attack of apoplexy. (Croo 236–237) Conan Doyle was well aware that circumstances can deceive as evidenced by his real life cases of Edalji and Slater.

Two further examples of violent but nonhomicidal head injury and death appear in the *Canon*. Seldon, the escaped convict, fell over a sheer cliff while being chased by the gigantic hound. (Houn 86–87)

> *So grotesque was the attitude [contortion] that I could not for the instant realize that that moan had been the passing of his soul . . . The gleam of the match which he [Holmes] struck shone upon his clotted [with blood] fingers and upon the ghastly pool which widened slowly from the crushed skull of the victim.*

The accidental nature of Straker's death was not quite as apparent. (Silv 267)

> *His head had been shattered by a savage blow from some heavy weapon, and he was wounded in the thigh, where there was a long, clean cut, inflicted evidently by some very sharp instrument. It was clear, however, that Straker had defended himself vigorously against his assailants, for in his right hand he held a small knife, which was clotted with blood up to the handle. . . .*

This is an excellent example of Conan Doyle's skills as a mystery writer. The almost ''airtight'' case for murder proves to be, by Holmes' investigations, due to a kick from the steel horseshoe of Silver Blaze, and the cut by his own knife as he fell. For both Seldon and Straker, death was well deserved, as it was for some of Conan Doyle's murder victims.

One murder was committed by a blow to another area of the body, the abdomen. ". . .Drebber received a blow from the stick, in the pit of the stomach perhaps, which killed him without leaving any mark." (Stud 190) This is not farfetched. Such a blow can rupture the spleen or liver and cause severe hemorrhage into the abdominal cavity;[502b] a fact of which an experienced physician such as Doctor Conan Doyle would be well aware. In his day, sudden death with no obvious lesions was considerd to occur with blows to the upper abdomen.[865e]

The cases of knife wounds are fewer than those of head blows in the Holmesian chronicles. A newspaper story reported that Edwardo Lucas, the blackmailer, had been "stabbed to the heart" by a curved Indian dagger. (Seco 308) Holmes, himself, examined the body of Joseph Stangerson, son of a Mormon elder. "The cause of death was a deep stab in the left side [of the chest], which must have penetrated the heart." (Stud 191–192) The coughing up of blood that occurs with lung lacerations in stab wounds would not be expected if death is sudden as was Stangerson's.[502c] Medical knowledge is evident in that the heart lies largely in the left side of the chest.

More such knowledge is displayed in the murder of young Willoughby Smith, Professor Coram's secretary, who was killed in error by the professor's wife. (Gold 353)

> *. . .blood was pouring from the under side of his neck. It was pierced by a very small but very deep wound, which had divided the carotid artery.*

It has long been recognized that knife wounds to the upper part of the throat are very dangerous.[502d] A more forensic description was provided not by Holmes but by Detective Hopkins. "The stab was on the right side of the neck and from behind forwards, so it is almost impossible that it could have been self inflicted." (Gold 356)

The knifing of the throat of Giuseppe Gorgiano, a leader of the Red Circle, is noteworthy for the terse but graphic description of the result. (RedC 700)

> *In the middle of the floor of the empty room was huddled the figure of an enormous man, his clean-shaven, swarthy face grotesquely horrible in its contortion, and his head encircled by a ghastly crimson halo of blood, lying in a broad wet circle upon the white woodwork.*

The description is also an excellent one of techniques used by Conan Doyle in creating interest, that of contrasting images—empty room/enormous body, clean-shaven face/grotesquely horrible, halo of blood/white woodwork.

One further knife-inflicted wound is that of Pietro Venucci, a member of the Mafia, who had his throat slashed. The body was found by a reporter, Hoarce Harker, on his doorstep. (SixN 576)

> *. . .there was the poor fellow, a great gash in his throat and the whole place swimming in blood. He lay on his back, his knees drawn up, and his mouth horribly open. I shall see him in my dreams.*

A slashed throat is much more gruesome than a stab wound, and expected more from members of criminal cults than from individual murderers.

In addition to the eleven violent deaths by head blows and the five by knives, there are six by firearms. Handguns fired into the chest and through the heart were responsible for the death of William Kirwan, the coachman, (Reig 332) and Hilton Cubitt, a squire. (Danc 536) Multiple shots were fired into the shirt front of Charles Augustus Milverton by a noblewoman whose life he had ruined by blackmail. (Chas 569)

> *The woman stood with her hand buried in her bosom, and the same deadly smile on her thin lips.*
>
> *'You will ruin no more lives as you ruined mine . . . I will free the world of a poisonous thing. Take that, you hound, and that!—and that!—and that!. . .*
>
> *Then he staggered to his feet, received another shot, and rolled upon the floor.*
>
> *'You've done me,' he cried, and lay still.*

Noteworthy is that this is the only instance of Conan Doyle descending to the level of the melodrama (and almost to that of the soap opera). It is also one of the several times that Conan Doyle gave his cold, calculating detective one of his own attributes—a kindly heart that responds to an injustice. For Holmes let the noblewoman escape.

Two individuals were murdered by being shot in the head, the result more gruesome than being shot in the heart. The Honorable Robert Adair's head "had been horribly mutilated by an expanded revolver bullet through the head" (Empt 330) fired by Moriarity's chief of staff, Colonel Sebastian Moran. Even more terrible was the shotgun blast in the face which blew the head of Ted Baldwin "almost to pieces." (Vall 485) This was another instance of retribution, the weapon being his own and discharged while in a struggle to murder Birdy Edwards, a Pinkerton detective. Another shot to the head was suicidal on the part of Maria Gibson, and staged to implicate the governess, Miss Dunbar, as a murderess. (Thor 590)

Not mentioned in the *Canon* is the close study of wounds, either by knife or bullet. A major feature of modern forensic pathology is the distinction between the small, funnel-shaped entrance wound and the larger, irregular exit wound.[641] This was well recognized and described by 1845.[502] Such detail might be expected from Conan Doyle's scientific detective whose mainstay was careful and minute observation.

One other weapon of violent death was the harpoon. Captain Peter Carey (Black Peter) had it thrust through his chest when he refused to be blackmailed by Patrick Cairns. He was found in his cabin, transfixed by his own harpoon that he kept from his whaling days: (Blac 401)

> *. . .his face twisted like a lost soul in torment and his great brindled beard stuck upwards in his agony. Right through his broad chest a steel harpoon had been driven, and it had sunk deep into the wood of the wall behind him. He was pinned like a beetle on a card.*

Conan Doyle kept such a harpoon on his study wall as a memento of his seven months as ship's surgeon on an Arctic whaler.[43]

LESS VIOLENT MEANS OF DEATH

Less gruesome but still fatal are the three instances of drowning reported in the *Canon*. Elias Openshaw's death by drowning in a "little green-scummed pool" (Five 394) was considered as suicide by the jury. His nephew, John, thought otherwise, but in turn drowned in the Thames, an event that was considered accidental by the police. (Five 402) The third drowning was of Edwards, the Pinketon detective who was lost overboad from a ship on its way to Cape Town. (Vall 573) Holmes was convinced that it was murder. Not described are the changes in appearance of the body that occur with drowning. Conan Doyle is absolved of such neglect because his detecive did not have the opportunity to examine these corpses.

Also appearing to be suicide at first was the murder of Blessington, a former member of the Worthington Bank Gang, who was hanged by his cohorts in such a way as to suggest suicide. (Resi 276)

> *The neck was drawn out like a plucked chicken's, making the rest of him seem the more obese and unnatural by the contrast. He was clad only in his long night-dress, and his swollen ankles and ungainly feet protruded starkly from beneath it.*

Holmes quickly indicated murder because of considerable evidence that others had been in the room.

With no violence, but equally fatal was the asphyxiation of Richard Brunton, the butler. His greed had led him to enter the deep chamber in the ground which contained the coins and crown of Charles II. (Musg 136) His equally greedy conspirator, Rachel Howells, closed the chamber with a flagstone and death ensued from want of air. (Musg 138) Another criminal death is that of

John Ferrier, who was killed for not adhering strictly to Mormon doctrine. (Stud 219) The means by which he was murdered is not given, but violence is implied.

WATSON'S PERSONAL WOUND

There remains one wound in the *Canon* to discuss. This incident is almost as well known as those involving the assassinated American Presidents—Lincoln[600] and Kennedy.[913] In brief, it was during the battle of Maiwand in Afghanistan[841] that Watson was "struck on the shoulder by a Jezail bullet, which shattered the bone and grazed the subclavian artery." (Stud 143) It was not likely the severely damaging dum-dum bullet, which was used extensively by the British but not the enemy during the Afghan campaign.[830] The result was observed by Holmes as a stiff left arm held in an unnatural manner. (Stud 162) Another reference is to "the Jezail bullet which I had brought back in one of my limbs." (Nobl 281) Because of anatomical relationships, the shattered bone had to be the clavicle in order to also graze the subclavian artery.[19] This is one of the large arteries which carry oxygenated blood from the left side of the heart via the aorta to the upper limbs.

There is a controversy because of another reference to the wound, which has driven Sherlockians to extensive and occassionally outlandish solutions. Watson "sat nursing my wounded leg. I had had a Jezail bullet throught it some time before . . . ." (Sign 611) It would be simple and fair to give Conan Doyle his due and accept "the two bullet theory."[519] But many ingenious attempts have been made to justify one bullet only. Thus, he may have been bent over a patient when shot; or shot from below while squatting over a cliff to answer a call of nature;[92] or even misrepresenting the site of the bullet which was located in an embarrassing location, the groin.[935]

Several other suggestions are more rational. The bullet may have ricocheted off the bone, grazed the artery, left the body at an acute angle, and then entered the leg.[46] More intriguing is the proposal that the bullet ricocheted downward, traveling under the skin of the chest and abdomen to reach the leg.[837] This is reminiscent of Conan Doyle's own experience during the Boer War with a soldier who had a bullet that traveled under the skin of the abdomen for some distance.

One more sophisticated suggestion is that the Jezial bullet actually entered the subclavian artery and was carried along by the blood stream. Such embolization would carry the bullet till it stopped at a site where the artery narrows to less than the diameter of the projectile. Garzon[469] found reports of 29 patients with such an injury. In Watson's case, if the bullet entered the subclavian artery it would be carried in the direction of the blood flow into the arm. Within the realm of possiblity, the bullet may have entered the subclavian artery toward its origin from the aorta, and with sufficient force to be carried to the lower extremities.[809] Such an event has been described in a soldier during the Korean War.[603]

The saga of the Jezail bullet is not done. Van Liere[899] has proposed that, in grazing the subclavian artery, it caused a blood clot which obstructed the artery with resultant drop in pressure of blood in the vertebral artery (subclavian steal syndrome) resulting in decreased blood supply to Watson's brain. Surely we need no other explanation for his occasional dullness and forgetfulness than Conan Doyle's need of a foil for his detective.

As a final orientation, a Jezail bullet is also mentioned in a non-Sherlockian story, *The Mystery of Cloomber*,[249] published in 1888, two years after the first reference to Watson's wound. The British General, Heatherstone, bared his chest to John Easterling, F.R. C.P. Edin. (p. 61)

> *. . .and showed me a puckered region over the heart. 'That's where the Jezail bullet of a hillman went in. You would think that was in the right spot to settle a man; and what does it do but glance upon a rib, and go clean round and out at the back, without so much as penetrating what you medicos call the pleura. Did ever you see such a thing?'*

Conan Doyle did see such passage of a bullet within the skin eleven years later during the Boer War. Such precognition in fiction has generated no plaudits for the author, in comparison to the frenetic reaction to Watson's wound. Also ignored has been Watson's other bullet wound, acquired in the thigh from the revolver of the notorious American criminal, Evans. (3Gar 653)

FORENSIC MEDICINE AND CONAN DOYLE

It would be unjust to base a full assessment of Conan Doyle's forensic knowledge on the Canonical stories which were written for literary effectiveness. Of course, considerable evidence shows that he was familiar with some uses of science in this area. The most striking examples relate to changes in the body after death—livor mortis and rigor mortis. Other examples are the study of handwriting and footprints for identification. Conan Doyle's major contribution was the first mention of identifying a specific typewriter by its typescript.

Beyond these the *Canon* is somewhat of a disappointment in respect to the forensic medical sciences. Fingerprints, which were well established then, are referred to only a few times, and analysis of blood stains only once. Only twice are the physical characteristics of the many wounds used to provide clues in solving crimes—the direction of a knife stab, and the absence of powder burns on a bullet wound. One misses the use in specific cases of differences between bullet entrance and exit wounds, of the telltale marks of suicidal wounds, of the detailed examination of bullets, and of chemical analysis of poisons. All these were well known in Conan Doyle's time[865] and before.[502]

Instead we are presented with a "master detective" who is given a partial scientific orientation, some of which he seldom uses in his cases. Much of the data he used for arriving at a solution of a murder came from the environment and oral testimony rather than from the human body. At this he was superb, but as a reasoning detective, and not as one who used scientific medical testing extensively. Edwards[429f] has suggested that such separation between laboratory skills and their application was Conan Doyle's satire on the overly academic University of Edinburgh. Such deliberate orientation of all 60 Canonical works may be too much extrapolation for the motivation of a superb story teller.

But surely we are asking too much for a work of fiction to be a textbook of forensic science and pathology. The image of the scientific Sherlock Holmes as "The Father of Forensic Pathology"[28] is grossly exaggerated by devotees; and so much so that the literary skills of the author are overlooked at best, when not negated. In fact it is the intrinsic humaneness, the understanding of elemental human emotions, and the realistic psychological insights that provide considerable appeal and are a truer measure of the stories and the man—Conan Doyle.

MEDICAL ATTRIBUTES OF SHERLOCK HOLMES

Further orientation to the medical Conan Doyle can be obtained by examination of the personal attributes of Sherlock Holmes. Some instances in which he was even more adroit than Doctor Watson have been discussed. In fact, at times he appears to direct Watson's practice of medicine. Detective Hopkins was told that "the doctor has a prescription containing hot water and a lemon which is good medicine on a night like this." (Gold 352) At other times he practices medicine without a license. Holmes informed an eavesdropping maid, Susan, that "you breathe too heavily for that kind of work . . . wheezy people may not live long, you know. . . . Paregoric is the stuff." (3Gab 726) Here is the diagnosis (asthma), the prognosis (long range), and the treatment (an opium drug) in one fell swoop!

Further medical expertise was exhibited by Holmes. He was capable of completely fooling Watson in his portrayal of a dying man, (Dyin 450) and of a fit. (Reig 344) He recognized an attempt at faking catalepsy by a criminal trying to gain access to a house, a pretense not even obvious to a specialist in neurology. (Resi 274)

Holmes was not beneath such deception himself for the illegal purpose of entering Irene Adler's house under false pretenses, by acting as a severely injured man. (Scan 363) Such realistic theatrics require a consumate knowledge of medicine.

Conan Doyle endowed Holmes with still other facets of his own medical proficiency. Most instances occur in the first story, *A Study in Scarlet*,[244] published when he was in the midst of medical practice. Young Stamford described Holmes as "well up in anatomy" and "a first-class chemist." (Stud 148) Thus, "his hands were invariably . . . stained with chemicals" (Stud 153) and his knowledge of chemistry was considered to be "profound." (Stud 156) This was not proved in the rest of the *Canon*. It was, in fact, a little less than one would expect of a practicing physician in Conan Doyle's day.

The adventures did substantiate in part the listing of Holmes' knowledge of anatomy as "accurate, but unsystematic," and of botany (drugs) as "variable. Well up in belladonna, opium and poisons generally." (Stud 156) He may well have dabbled "with poisons a good deal," (Stud 151) but did no chemical tests for identification in specific cases of poisoning. And neither would a practitioner such as Conan Doyle.

The *Canon* does contain some interesting examples of increase in size of parts of the body. Holmes recognized the thickening of ears, due to the stimulation of fibrous tissue growth, that occurs with repeated blows in boxers. (Glor 109) Of course, even a non-physician oriented to boxing would recognize this condition. Holmes himself was stated by Watson to be "one of the finest boxers of his weight that I have ever seen." (Yell 575) More medical is Holmes' description of the crippled crooked man. "Surely your medical experience would tell you, Watson, that weakness in one limb is often compensated for by exceptional strength in the others." (Twis 376) The wording of this description of compensatory hypertrophy is also an example of Holmes' disdain for Doctor Watson's medical acumen.

Of interest is Conan Doyle's understanding of the basic premise of statistics. (Sign 666)

> *. . . while the individual man is an insoluble puzzle, in the aggregate he becomes a mathematical certainty. You can, for example never foretell what any one man will do, but you can say with precision what an average individual number will be up to. Individuals vary, but percentages remain constant.*

Statistics were in use in medicine at least a century before this story. [468i] This is one basis for the labeling of Holmes as a social scientist by Truzzi. Surely we can claim no less for Conan Doyle.[880]

More fascinating is Conan Doyle's characterization of the personality of the ''master detective'' Holmes. There are many indications that Holmes was not a stable, well-adjusted individual. At the onset of his relationship with Watson he admits to excessive episodes of depression. ''I get in the dumps at times, and don't open my mouth for days on end.'' (Stud 151) At best it is an ''ennui.'' (RedH 438) At worst he is ''prey to the blackest depression'' especially after prolonged and exhaustive investigations. (Reig 331) It has been suggested that Holmes' cold attitude to some individuals was a deliberate satire on the indifference shown to patients at Edinburgh.[424g] As likely, or more so, it is the result of Conan Doyle's attempt to enhance Holmes' image as a ''thinking machine.''

As with so many other items in the Sherlockian stories, a considerable explanatory literature has arisen. At one extreme is the interpretation that Holmes is ''nothing but a genius who has a lazy streak and needs the stimulation of a congenial task to get him going.''[900] At the other extreme is a diagnosis of a paranoid manic-depressive disorder.[33] More kind is the label of neurasthenia.[704] This is a susceptibility to nervous debility and exhaustion from overwork or prolonged mental strain.[847d] From a review of the entire *Canon*, it is evident that all three such psychological diagnoses apply to Holmes at various times.

The concept of neurasthenia was well developed when Conan Doyle practiced medicine,[696p] although not so precisely as for the concept of the manic-depressive personality. No doubt Conan Doyle used his observation of the marked ''ups and downs'' exhibited by hard-working overachievers to enrich the figure of Holmes;

and such behavior has contributed to his fascination for many readers. Although Conan Doyle was extremely active and productive all of his life there is no extant evidence that he was "prey to the blackest depression" for any significant period of time.

Due to ennui and depression, Holmes was prone to taking stimulants in excess. During a one-day period, while contemplating the mystery of the Baskerville hound, he admitted to Watson that "My body has remained in this arm-chair; and has, I regret to observe, consumed in my absence [of his "spirit"] two large pots of coffee and an incredible amount of tobacco." (Hound 18) His addiction to caffeine was considerably less than that to nicotine as judged by the numerous references in the *Canon* to the latter.

The more serious and best known addiction of Holmes was to cocaine, one of its effects being mental stimulation. According to his own statement, he used cocaine for stimulation when he had few challenges because "I abhor the dull routine of existence. I crave for mental exaltation." (Sign 611) Such a motivation is consistent with the diagnosis of Holmes' personality as manic-depressive.[33] Holmes seemed to realize that his addictions had negative features, because he grinned at Watson's suggestion that he was a "self-poisoner by cocaine and tobacco." (Five 399)

Holmes was not under the complete control of cocaine. When challenged, "He had risen out of his drug-created dreams, and was hot upon the scent of some new problem." (Scan 347) That Conan Doyle understood the addictive psychology, unlike many of his time, is well demonstrated by Watson's description of Holmes' weaning from cocaine. (Miss 475)

> *For years I gradually weaned him from that drug mania which had threatened once to check his remarkable career. Now I knew that under ordinary conditions he no longer craved for this artificial stimulus; but I was well aware that the fiend was not dead, but sleeping.*

This is, indeed, a forecast of the modern view that true addiction is never "cured' but only controlled.

Evidently cocaine was the only addictive drug taken by Holmes. There is a reference to opium by Holmes, but only in a jocular manner. When found by Watson in an opium den during an investigation, Holmes teased him for imagining "that I have added opium-smoking to cocaine injections." (Twis 371) Opium dens were numerous in Victorian London[69] and readily available even after the restrictions of the Pharmacy Act of 1860.[70] Conan Doyle, like his peers, had an appreciation of the addictive nature of opium.[718] He was in advance of his time in the depiction of Holmes' habitual use of cocaine.

References to other aspects of Holmes' health are scanty. It is remarkable that he was "capable of greater muscular effort" in light of the fact that he "seldom took exercise for exercise's sake." (Yell 575) That his "diet was usually of the sparsest" (Yell 575) would be of concern for vitamin deficiency, capsulated vitamins not being available until much later. But in spite of such lack of preventative health measures, Holmes was seldom physicially ill. Perhaps an occasional "glass of port after dinner" (Glor 109) (Sign 662) produced sufficient relaxation to prevent psychosomatic diseases related to stress.

The one possible instance of disease was related by Billy, Holmes' page, to Doctor Watson. "I'm frightened for his health. He gets paler and thinner, and he eats nothing." (Maza 735) This was not related to a physical ailment, but to the intensity of his involvement in solving the puzzling robbery of the Crown diamond. Again, this relates to the abnormal but intriguing psychology of Sherlock Holmes as depicted by Conan Doyle.

HOLMES THE REASONER

Holmes exhibited yet another characteristic that is essential for any practicing physician. Conan Doyle would have been well aware of the need for reasoning in arriving at clinical diagnoses. There have been several discussions on the similarity of such a process between the work of the detective and that of the doctor.

They both have a short time to arrive at a decision,[20] both need clear logical reasoning,[501] and both put together pieces of observation.[552] Moreover "To the diagnostician . . . [illness] is a mystery story in which he is the detective."[887]

But, is the logical process similar in these two diverse professions—one seeking the name of a criminal and the other that of an illness? Holmes basically synthesized facts and reasoned "backwards" from effect to cause, (Stud 231) as physicians appear to do.[527] Holmes is not the "spectacular diagnostician"[589] he is considered to be by some, at least in the sense of sound reasoning processes in specific applications. He considers a "bad habit" to be when "one forms provisional theories [hypotheses] and waits for time or fuller knowledge to explode them." (Suss 467–468) Of 217 such inferences found by Kress in the *Canon* only 28 were tested.[591] This would never do for clinical diagnostics.

In fact, studies have shown that physicians do generate hypotheses early on.[426] These are based on the complaints of the patient and the initial physical examination.[633] After such a tentative diagnosis the physician then tests this first diagnostic hypothesis by more focused examination of the patient and by appropriate x-rays and tests. If testing the hypothesis proves it wrong, then another is made based on the additional data and tested in turn. One of the numerous aphorisms of Holmes states that "It is a capital mistake to theorize before you have all the evidence." (Stud 166) How does one know when he has all the evidence? Without an initial hypothesis the physician (and the detective) would be nonfocused and forced to collect every possible item of information—an endless and futile task.[N122]

There is an even more famous Canonical maxim that bears upon diagnostic reasoning. ". . .when you have excluded the impossible, whatever remains, however improbable, must be the truth." (Beryl 299) This must have been one of Conan Doyle's favorite sayings because he repeated it twice in *The Sign of Four*,[244] and even in a non-Sherlockian story, "The Lost Special,"[301] with only minimal changes in wording. Again, there is difficulty in medical application. When the impossible is eliminted, several or many improbable or even probable diagnoses may be left. This is not a criticism of Conan Doyle. It is a disagreement with some commentators who consider Holmes' modus operandi as equivalent to medical reasoning. After all, Conan Doyle created a master sleuth who ferrets out criminals, and not a physician who must quickly develop a tentative diagnosis as the basis for selecting further investigation. What Holmes and a good physician *do* have in common is the patience and the skill for detailed observation, of not only looking but also seeing, in combination with extensive knowledge and experience. Watson remarks to Holmes, "You have an extraordinary genius for minutiae." (Sign 612) Holmes' extrapolations from his article "The Book of Life" are rather fanciful although quite effective. "From a drop of water . . . a logician could infer the possibility of an Atlantic or a Niagara without having seen or heard of one or the other." (Stud 159)

MISCELLANEOUS MEDICAL MATTERS

There remain several other matters to complete the study of the medical texture in the large yet detailed canvas of the Sherlockian stories. One category of individual that received little attention is that of the medical student. He is restricted to one adventure, and only in a cameo fashion. Inspector Lestrade suspected that it was three former lodgers, medical students, who sent Miss Cushing the two ears, presumably from the dissecting rooms. (Card 195) The students undoubtedly had a grudge against her for getting rid of them "on account of their noisy and irregular habits." (Card 195) Holmes came to their rescue by observing that the ears had not been fixed in perservative as they would be in an anatomy laboratory. (Card 197) Nonetheless, the image of the medical student was that of a rowdy in the mid-Victorian era.[720e] It began to improve by the time Conan Doyle entered the University of Edinburgh in 1876.

Several comments are made on the practice of medicine, aside from the specifics of that of Doctor Watson. The very healing aura of the physician contributed to the fact that the engineer felt like "another man since the doctor bandaged [thumb stump] me." (Engr 212) The practice of medicine also has its lures and traps. "Dr. Ray Ernest . . . was frequently in the house [of old Amberley], and an intimacy between him and Mrs. Amberley was a natural sequence." (Reti 547) This is contrary to the dictates of the centuries old Hippocratic Oath,[406] but not unheard of even today.

Some annoyance was expressed by the American Senator and Gold King, J. Neil Gibson, when Holmes pressed him for details as to his relationship with his young female employee. "You're like a surgeon who wants every symptom before he can give his diagnosis." (Thor 594) Holmes had a more sympathetic attitude toward the medical profession. When Watson questioned his minimal gain from continuing his investigation of a complex mystery, he replied patiently

> *'It is Art for Art's sake, Watson. I suppose when you doctored you found yourself studying cases without thought of a fee?'*
>
> *'For my education, Holmes.'*
>
> *'Education never ends, Watson. It is a series of lessons, with the greatest for the last. This is an instructive case.' (RedC 697)*

Conan Doyle undoubtedly felt such challenges when he practiced medicine.

There remains one other association with the practice of medicine—hospitals. Three of the well known London hospitals have their moment in the *Canon*. Charing Cross Hospital was featured briefly as the initials C.C.H. on the cane of Doctor Mortimer who had left the hospital to go into country practice. (Houn 5) It was in King's College Hospital that Doctor Percy Trevelyan did research on catalepsy, (Resi 269) but to little avail in recognizing a faked case.

Somewhat more prominence was given to St. Bartholomew's Hospital, one of the oldest in London, being found in 1123.[731] It was at "Barts" that Conan Doyle chose to have Stamford introduce Watson to Holmes. (Stud 149) He described one area of the hospital in some detail. (Stud 149-150)

> *. . .we ascended the bleak stone staircase and made our way down the long corridor with its vista of whitewashed wall and dun-coloured doors. Near the further end a low arched passage branched away from it and led to the chemical laboratory . . . a lofty chamber, lined and littered with countless bottles. Broad, low tables were scattered about, which bristled with retorts, test-tubes, and little Bunsen lamps with their blue flickering flames.*

And there was Holmes! Adjectives such as stone, long, dun-coloured, lofty, and blue, along with the chemical paraphernalia helped to endow Holmes with the mantle of the cold and calculating scientific detective.

Conan Doyle's relationship to criminology was more than the writing of crime fiction. He determined the innocence of actually convicted individuals such as Edalji and Slater. He also published in 1901 detailed analyses of three murders under the general title of "Strange Studies from Life." The cases were real, but names were changed to protect living relatives.

William Godfrey Youngman,[317] who had the insanity of jealousness and a colossal selfishness, was accused of killing his two brothers, his fiancée, and his mother for insurance. His defense was that his mother had killed the others and then he stabbed her in retribution. Conan Doyle concluded "The man was guilty seems to admit no doubt, and yet it must be admitted that circumstantial evidence can never be absolutely convincing."

In the instance of George Vincent Parker,[318] his "moral sense was more vitiated than any case he had seen"—in other words he was a psychopath. A letter from Mary Grover breaking off their engagement resulted in an extreme state of nervous excitement with convulsive twitching necessitating morphine. He stabbed her in the neck and severed the carotid artery. Parker's execution was commuted to a life sentence when he began to show signs of madness. Conan Dyole editorialized that there are two causes of murder: "the lust of money and the black resentment of a disappointed love."

Less clear cut was "The Debatable Case of Mrs. Emsley"[319] for whose murder George Mullins, the plasterer, was hung. The circumstances and items of evidence are reminiscent of the Holmesian murders. Her head had been crushed, there was a footprint outlined in blood, and a boot fitted the imprint. Conan Doyle's conclusion was "that, though Mullins was very likely guilty, the police were never able to establish the details of the crime, and that there was a risk of a miscarriage of justice when the death sentence was carried out."

These three case studies of actual murders reveal Conan Doyle at his best. The narrative style alone is captivating. He not only analyzed the details of the crimes in a logical manner but also showed a human understanding of and concern for the individuals involved—criminal and victim alike. He understood the rules of evidence and the danger of circumstantial grounds. Thus, Conan Doyle was undoubtedly a sounder student of crime than his creation.

CONAN DOYLE, THE MEDICAL CANON AND POSTERITY

The Sherlock Holmes works have evoked two contrasting reactions. On the one hand is the critical literary analysis that labels the works as popular literature, as tales rather than stories,[457] and as somewhat wanting in the quality of writing.[661] The renowned mystery writer, Dorothy Sayers, generalizes that "The detective story does not, and . . . never can attain the loftiest of literary achievement. Although it deals with the most desperate effects of rage, jealousy and revenge it rarely touches upon the heights and depths of human passions."[563c] In the case of the *Canon* an attribute such as a "superb narrative technique" is considered as somehow not really "literature."[457] Even Conan Doyle himself did not regard his mysteries as literature, especially in comparison with his historical novels.

In spite of such negation of the *Canon* as literature (or perhaps because of it), the Sherlockian chronicles have become one of the best known works of fiction. According to Ousby "It seems possible that Sherlock Holmes is the most famous character in English literature."[703] The sales have continued at a high level for almost a century after the publication of the first story.[213] Numerous restaurants and hotels in various countries have been named after elements in the *Canon*. Pastiches are being published in ever increasing numbers. And the appeal is as much, if not more, to the well educated and the intellectual. One example is Paul Ehrlich, the famous medical scientist who made many advances in the field of infectious diseases, and who kept a signed portrait of Conan Doyle in his study.[640]

Part of the appeal of the stories is the effective creation of atmosphere. T.S. Eliot has commented that "in the Sherlock Holmes stories the nineteenth century is always romantic, always nostalgic, and never silly."[921] The image of "two men dashing through the fog-veiled streets of London in a hansom cab is for many *the* impression of the nineties."[40] And yet fog appears in less than one-sixth of the Holmes stories. Its softening of the harsh realities of life evokes a feeling of romance and of the eternal. "We can picture him [Watson] riding along in his hansom—the lights of which shine dimly through the fog—rattling over the cobblestones of the old London streets, carrying on the tradition of his noble profession."[897]

Sherlock Holmes has not gone unnoticed by forensic pathologists in Britain. Sir Bernard Spilsbury was called a real-life Sherlock Holmes, much to his annoyance.[445] More laudatory are comments by Sir Sidney Smith in the chapter on "Dr. Bell and Sherlock Holmes" in his autobiography.[828]

> *To-day criminal investigation is a science . . . . This was not always so and the change owes much to the influence of Sherlock Holmes.*

As stated in a recent book on forensic science, "Forensic experts look, Sherlock Holmes-fashion, for 'occupational' marks on the body."[830] The combination of Conan Doyle's fertile imagination resulted in the transfer of Doctor Bell's diagnostic acumen from the medical arena to the forensic field for the enrichment of both readers and criminology.

The acceptance of Conan Doyle' main character has increased even to the point of uncritical adulation. Literally hundreds of clubs are devoted to the "master"[196] and dedicated to the "higher criticism" of his activities. Part of such acceptance of the historical reality of Sherlock Holmes, at least in game if not in name, is due to the extensive amount of detail provided for both the hero and his world.[842]

It is this myth, played to its fullest, that has obscured the serious study of any merits, literary or otherwise, of the stories.[535] The so-called "Sherlockian scholarship" extolls the virtues of the hero and analyzes contradictions in the adventures. And these are published not only in the numerous journals devoted to the "master" but also in medical ones.

It has been recognized that the Canonical works are "intensely medical in nature—and uniquely so,"[597] and that their success, in part, is related to Conan Doyle's medical training.[626] This becomes quite evident when the works are reviewed on the basis of assessment rather than a listing of its medical content. The interpretations from such a review are variable, and in part a reflection of the knowledge and interests of Conan Doyle. There is good understanding of infectious diseases in which he took a considerable interest. His empathy for individuals is evident with some of the victims of crime and even some of the more worthy culprits, as it was with the victims of disease in his medical writings, both fictional and factual.

Outstanding is Conan Doyle's appreciation of the psychology of cocaine addiction. In particular, he applied psychological concepts, a new science for his time, in many of the plots.[556] He did, however, tend to consider that a propensity for crime was inborn, as did many Victorians. Recent genetic studies concerning the XXY genotype personality tend to validate this theory in part only.

Conan Doyle's knowledge of drugs, as seen in the *Canon*, is adequate. His appreciation of chemistry is below that of his time, although probably adequate for a practitioner. He did demonstrate a detailed and excellent knowledge of the chemistry needed for developing exposed film in his essays on photography.[475] Analysis of the much vaunted Canonical forensic medical science, however, leads to disappointment. The scientific master sleuth did not use much scientific testing in resolving the crimes on which the stories are based. But, let us not forget that Conan Doyle was writing fiction, not a textbook. The intrusion of much specific testing would interfere with the flow of events and the demonstration of ratiocination. The frequent sprinkling of medical terms and conditions throughout do not intrude on the story-line. It contributes by evoking the fascination that most people have with the mystique of the medical world.

Guthrie has stated that "I would counsel students to study Sherlock Holmes," both for his "clear logical reasoning" and for the "subtle difference between seeing and observing."[501] Holmes' method of reasoning is, however, contrary to the early hypothesis generation so necessary for clinical diagnosis. It is the close attention to observation, the thinking while seeing, that is the hallmark of Holmes and also must be that of the physician.[552] This, perhaps, is why the *Canon* is of special appeal to the dermatologist, whose specialty requires extremely close attention to the details of skin lesions.

The Holmesian stories are of medical importance for several other reasons. They do provide some orientation to medical knowledge and practice during the last few decades of the 19th century. This does not apply to doctors as such because all except Watson are briefly used to further the plot-line. Even the more detailed character of Watson is biased by his use as a contrasting foil for the brilliant Holmes.

Recently Fitzgerald and Tierney have highlighted what could well be the major medical contribution of the *Canon* for our time—bedside diagnosis.[438] In the present era of multitudinous technology, the major emphasis in diagnosis is on physiological, radiological, and laboratory testing; with the frequent neglect of even the most elemental visual observation of the patient. Sherlock Holmes did not use testing much in his profession, but he accomplished wonders by looking and seeing. The medical profession today could well rededicate itself to this time-honored method of investigation; it is one which can "solve" the majority of clinical diagnostic problems at little cost. This, then, is the message that Conan Doyle has sent us from the past.

That there is much of Conan Doyle in the *Canon* is obvious, as is true in the works of many authors. This applies to his two main characters as well. He was displaying his own patriotism when Holmes told Von Bork, the captured German spy, that "you have done your best for your country, and I have done my best for mine, and what could be more natural?" (Last 802) Holmes also echoed his views in referring to "amateur sport, which is the best and soundest thing in England." (Miss 476) In his life he exhibited some of the traits he ascribed to Watson—loyalty, chivalry, and honesty. Much has been made of Conan Doyle's debt to Jospeh Bell, by himself as well as others. But, he was himself an acute observor. His medical short stories contain many incisive observations and descriptions of both the physical and psychological attributes of patients.

In summary, then, Conan Doyle's Holmesian works have contributed more than just popular entertainment to humanity. His mythical detective played a major role in turning public interest to scientific crime detection.[80] Above all the *Canon* integrated various fundamental aspects of human existence. Conan Doyle combined primeval reactions to ghastly wounds and dastardly deeds with a sprinkling of science, a larger dose of human rationality, a detailed delineation of contrasting characters, a practicum of medical knowledge, and a seasoning of basic human concerns. It is a signal credit to Conan Doyle that his writings have become timeless classics with characters that have transcended the printed page to become living, breathing human beings for so many readers. The literary creations have overshadowed the creator, but Conan Doyle continues to live because of them.

DOCTOR CONAN DOYLE RECONSIDERED. . .

Three years after Conan Doyle was captured on film for posterity with the Jack Connolly 1927 interview, he experienced increasingly frequent and severe chest pains.[525e] He required oxygen, undoubtedly due to his failing heart. His sons were sent for cylinders, much as Professor Challenger sent Malone and Summerlee in preparation for *The Poison Belt.*[360] Conan Doyle met his last adventure with an equanimity he did not give to the Professor. He departed this life quietly, his last concern being for his wife Jean.[1251]

And what a legacy he left!—A lifetime filled with such a variety of activities that the sum total leaves one incredulous, if not breathless.[936] Several months before he died Conan Doyle drew a sketch which summarized his life. As "The Old Horse"[383] Conan Doyle depicted himself pulling the wagon of the "Life Work Carriage Co.," piled high with 23 boxes labeled with the affairs of his life and leaving a trail of its events. At the pinnacle of the wagon load is equipment for various sports. Remarkable is that an amateur sportsman could excel in such a diversity of sports as billiards, cricket, boxing, golf, bowling, soccer, and skiing. Phenomenally, the same individual was also a successful crusader for the unjustly accused, a patriot who changed world opinion in favor of his homeland, a war historian, and advocate of divorce where necessary and one of the leaders of the spiritualism movement.[648,N123]

Even without the aforementioned, he made significant contributions to humanity as an author. Unusual is the fact that his reputation as a writer was acknowledged with honors during his lifetime, unlike many authors who are appreciated more after death than before. He was knighted for writing his enormously influential pamphlets and a book on the British position in the Boer War. He was honored at the Encaenia of 1908 at Oxford, along with other notables such as the Prince of Wales, Sir Thomas Lipton (international merchant), Sir Hall Craine (writer), Eugene Sandow (physical culturist), and Lord Curzon (statesman).[761]

The greatest literary recognition Conan Doyle received was an honorary doctorate (LL.D.) from his Alma Mater.[486] The Laureation Address was given on April 7, 1905, by Professor Sir Ludovic J. Grant, Bart, Dean of the Faculty at Law. This brief address provides a succinct account of the far-ranging variety and appeal of Conan Doyle's fiction.

> *If the chief function of the novelist be to entertain his reader, Sir Arthur yields place to no comtemporary writer of fiction. Some may prefer his historical romances, with their brilliant studies of distant days. . . . Over others his tales of modern hazard and adventure may exercise a stronger spell . . . [or] the trail of some latter-day mystery of the very Argus of detectives. . . . Let us not forget that he has proved himself no less capable as a writer of serious history . . .*

Interestingly, three medical men received honorary degrees along with Conan Doyle—William Watson Cheyne, Professor of Surgery; Augustus D. Waller, Professor of Physiology; and John Hughlings Jackson, the neurologist who established the use of the ophthalmoscope for diagnosing brain diseases.[407] It is a moot question as to whether or not Conan Doyle would have been so honored for work in medicine if he had not left his primary profession. He might have contributed much in this area if he had applied to it some of the energy used to propogate his religion—spiritualism.[337] Such an assumption is not mere speculation. Conan Doyle did show evidence of a great aptitude for the analysis and understanding of the medical research of his time. His medical writings are few in comparison with the sheer bulk of his literary efforts. They are sufficient, however, to make one appreciate not only the lucid and yet engaging scientific literary style but also the farsighted insights into their significance for the future.

The myths of Watson's lowly "literary agent" and of the unsuccessful physician are negated by a study of the record itself. He did see few patients, but only during the first six months of establishing a practice de novo. The fact that within a year he was "making a living" is indicative of skills as a general practitioner.[N124] The extant evidence strongly suggests that he left the practice of medicine not because he was a failure, but because he was so successful that it interfered with his writing. Even as a medical student "the general aspiration towards literature was tremendously strong upon me."[375h]

Conan Doyle's potentiality for achieving medical renown is better documented in his scientific medical writings. This is especially evident in publications relating to infectious diseases. He strongly supported prophylactic measures for smallpox by compulsory vaccination, in spite of considerable public opposition, and for typhoid by inoculation, in spite of the recalcitrant military hierarchy. Conversely, he was the first to caution against the overwhelming and world-wide acceptance of tuberculin as a cure for tuberculosis in 1890. Conan Doyle based his conclusion on a carefully reasoned consideration of its clinical effects and of pathological changes in lung tissue.

Remarkable was Conan Doyle's grasp of the significance of the newly emerging science of medical bacteriology. As a general practitioner, in 1883, he wrote that bacteria were undoubtedly the cause of many human diseases—this, at a time when only a few were so demonstrated. He also predicted the eradication of bacterial diseases several generations in the future—as has occurred recently for smallpox.

Medical training and experience continued to influence Conan Doyle's activities after he changed his profession to that of full-time writer.[171] Many of his causes were related to needs for physical and psychological well being. He supported daylight saving time because sunlight would contribute to health. His campaign against the spread of venereal disease by prostitution was based more on the need to prevent disease than on moral issues. He supported vivisection, if done humanely, because of its major contributions to the amelioration of human disease and suffering. Even in his all-pervading dedication to spiritualism he applied medical concepts, such as the study of the pulse during a trance.

Nor can his literary output be separated from his medical orientation, which permeated many of his works. The blustering, egocentric professors Challenger,[357] Ainslee Grey[256] and von Baumgarten[239] were drawn from his medical teacher, Rutherford, and his medical confrere, Budd. Many commentaries pertain to the derivation of the name of his master sleuth, Holmes. It has been suggested that the source was Oliver Wendell Holmes, physician, writer and anatomist, although Conan Doyle himself has stated that "I don't know how I got that name."[856] Nonetheless, the attributes of Sherlock Holmes are based on two physicians—Joseph Bell, the surgeon, and Conan Doyle, the general practitioner.

Much prominence has been given to the medical aspects of the Holmesian *Canon*, mostly adulatory and nonevaluative. A critical analysis reveals, however, variability in the caliber of medical knowledge. Conan Doyle's appreciation of poisons was no better than can be expected from a generalist of his time. His orientation to alcohol and cocaine addiction was beyond the limits of both the cultural environment and the medical concepts of his time. The emphasis on infectious diseases in his scientific writings is reflected in the inclusion of numerous such afflictions in the *Canon*.

The intimate mix of medicine and literature is evident in Conan Doyle's non-Sherlockian fiction. It contains approximately 100 doctors found not only in the essentially medical short stories but also throughout his historical novels, science fiction, adventures, and sport stories. More important than numbers is the caliber of the medical orientation in both the *Canon* and in his other fiction.[821]

> *The many brief but accurate descriptions of the symptoms of specific pathological conditions indicated that Doyle was an accurate observer for they often have a vividness in formal textbook accounts.*

One further relevant characteristic of Conan Doyle is his humaneness—his concern for human beings both collectively and as individuals. He frequently rose to the defense of oppressed groups, such as the natives of the Congo, and to that of the underdog, such as Edalji and Slater. There is also documentation of his concern for his patients during both the "adventure in that romantic period" of practice[856] and during the Boer War. The orientation to psychiatric conditions in his fiction is generally one of sympathy; and to eccentric characters, such as Budd and Challenger, it is one of amused tolerance. Part of his acceptance of spiritualism was the inconceivability of so many human lives extinguished forever by the horror of World War I.

Conan Doyle's fervent support of divorce reform arose from intense concern for the mental and physical suffering of a spouse inextricably linked to a cruel or psychopathic mate. And yet he remained intensely loyal in his own marriages. His first wife, Louise, was afflicted with chronic tuberculosis for a dozen years before her death. Indeed "he was ethical and compassionate" in his two professions of doctor and writer, and his manifold public activities, and in his private life.[705]

All in all, Conan Doyle's life and activities suggest the designation of "Renaissance Man"—one who is knowledgeable about and engages in many different areas of human endeavor.

> *Doctor, whaler, athlete, writer, speculator, dramatist, historian, war correspondent, spiritualist. . . . Generous personality, his virtues had always something of the fresh vigor of the amateur, keen, open-minded, flexible, imaginative.*[664]

In Conan Doyle's own, and humbler words of 1907 "There's hardly anything that doesn't interest me."[856]

"If he was not great what was he?" has recently been asked.[115] The answer has been obscured for at least 90 years after the publication of the first Holmesian story. The reputation of Conan Doyle has not merely languished—it has suffered greatly because of the success of his creation. His realistic characters have resulted in accolades rarely accorded directly to fictional individuals. For example, plaques commemorating Sherlock Holmes, with no mention of his creator, are located in St. Bartholomew Hospital, where Holmes and Watson first met, and at Reichenbach Falls where Holmes seemingly plunged to his death.[576]

Conan Doyle is responsible in good part for his own obscurity. In the words of his wife Jean, written several years after his death:[390]

> *He loved building up his fictional characters with all their little idiosyncrasies, their strengths and weaknesses, so that they became like living personalities to him, and this is why, in the minds of so many of his readers also, they are like familiar friends . . . one of the reasons why he was able to make his characters so very real was that he was able to imbue them, all unknown to himself, with parts of his own character and personality.*

Quite recently there has been some awakening of interest in Conan Doyle, aside from his arch rival, Sherlock Holmes. In 1980, the 50th anniversary of his death, a large collection of non-Sherlockian short stories was published.[693] The following year there were collections of his science fiction works[840] and of those set in Edinburgh.[421] The year, 1982, saw two further collections—essays on photography,[475] and some previously uncollected stories[474]—as well as a biography of his Edinburgh days.[424] In 1983 the long-awaited comprehensive bibliography of Conan Doyle appeared.[488]

The emerging interest in Conan Doyle in his own right is still only a faint glimmer compared to the enormous volume of commentary on his Victorian sleuth. Yet, there are now signs that such interest may be subverted. This concern has been expressed in a review by Booker.[86]

> *The same kind of lunacy [trivial detail about Holmes] now seems to be spreading out to encompass Holmes' creator as well . . . obscuring it [his reputation] under a mountain of batty, inconsequential trivia.*

This statement is undoubtedly an exaggeration, but should serve as a warning that even a great forest can be camouflaged by excessive emphasis on the details of its leaves.

In any event, we suggest that Conan Doyle might have been a "great" physician if circumstances and motivation had been right. He had an excellent knowledge of his profession and was generously endowed both with sympathy and imagination. Conan Doyle's reputation as physician and medical writer, now awaits further appreciation. His body, in the meantime, rests in the cemetery of a 13th century Norman Church in Minstead. It is located in the New Forest of Hampshire, an area which he loved and which he used as the site for his own favorite novels, *The White Company* and *Sir Nigel*. On the grave is a cross etched with words from a poem by his friend Robert Louis Stevenson,[850] "Steel-true and blade-straight," a phrase which was also used in his book on spirit photography.[373]

The imagery of Conan Doyle's epitaph is fitting. It characterizes the man and his activities—the lustrous writer, the righteous champion of the underdog, the faithful husband, the stalwart sportsman, the loyal citizen, the lucid medical luminary, and the humane physician.

Figure 20. Conan Doyle with other members of the medical staff of the Langman Hospital, Bloemfontein, South Africa, 1900. (Photograph used with permission from Hodder & Stoughton Ltd., London.)

Figure 21. Conan Doyle writing at Bloemfontein (1900).

SECTION NOTES

SECTION ONE NOTES

1. Conan Doyle's birthplace no longer stands. Its location on the south side of Picardy Place is now a traffic interchange.[773] The house was standing, however, in 1963 when visited by Rosenblum.[783]

   Eleven Picardy Place is one of a group of four similar buildings, with two storeys above the street floor and an upper storey like an attic with dormer windows. . . . Its highest storey is below the level of the topmost storey of the other buildings, and on the left side, as you face it . . . there is a projection of an adjacent building which contains shops.

   The building had a plaque reading "Creator of Sherlock Holmes /ARTHUR CONAN DOYLE/ was born here 22nd May 1859." A new plaque is now located on the north side of Picardy Place on the wall of the Abercaig Hotel. Added to the information is "at No. 11 Picardy Place Formerly Opposite Here."

   Another reminder that Conan Doyle was born in Picardy Place is a bar at the corner with Broughton. It was renamed the "Conan Doyle" (in large gold letters) in 1979.[773] A statement in the menu would in itself, be a fitting summation of his life—"Conan Doyle for Quality and Service."

2. Research by Edwards[424a] indicates that Doctor Waller was six years older than Conan Doyle. He began living with the family in 1875, a year before he graduated and Conan Doyle entered the Universtiy of Edinburgh. His vigorous personality made an impression on many. He carried on a small consulting practice out of the Conan Doyle home and had an extramural lectureship in pathology. He gained his M.D. with a thesis in 1881. His inclination to research is evidenced by refusal in 1877 of a license to perform vivisection.[463] It did not stop him, however, from writing articles on pathology.
3. Also described in Joseph Bell's manual is Mr. Holmes' procedure for amputation of the hip.[56a]
4. The *Edinburgh Medical and Surgical Journal* is not to be confused with the *Edinburgh Medical Journal* which began publication in 1855 with volume one.
5. Conan Doyle's sojourns in Birmingham were commemorated by a plaque, placed in 1958 on the house of Doctor Hoare. It stated that "Arthur Conan Doyle Lived Here 1878-1879." The house is no longer standing, having been replaced by an automobile distributorship. Another plaque, however, has been erected on the new building.[773] It contains the following message.

   Birmingham Civic Society
   SIR ARTHUR
   CONAN DOYLE
   Creator of Sherlock Holmes
   lived here
   1878-1881

   The wording gives the false impression that he was in continuous residence during these years, and gives no indication that he was there in a medical capacity.
6. The "University of Philadelphia" was one of about 20 diploma mills which were established to take advantage of State legislation which required a medical degree for licensing.[506] The one in Philadelphia was run by "unscrupulous

medical merchants . . . John Buchanan, William Payne and Rev. T. Miller.'' It must not be confused with the earliest bona fide medical school in the United States, the Medical College of Philadelphia, established in 1768 by University of Edinburgh graduates.[562]

7. Joseph Conrad, a literary contemporary of Conan Doyle, was also a member of a ship's crew on a voyage to Africa eight years later, in 1889.[448] Both had a severe illness. Conrad's was probably dysentery and resulted in lifelong chronic illness. There was no lasting effect on the robust Conan Doyle. The two authors were acquainted with each other, Conrad having entertained Conan Doyle in 1904.[683] For the former, the sea experience was the seminal basis for his literary output. For the latter, it was his medical school experiences.
8. This letter is part of the Berg Collection at the New York Public Library.[385] Its descriptive outline states that it was written to Mrs. Hoare. Dame Jean Conan Doyle is of the opinion that the letter was written to her father's mother, especially because of the closing ''Ever Yr. loving son'' (personal communication).
9. The highly unusual Doctor George Budd is not to be confused with another Doctor Budd, John Wreford, of Plymouth who died in 1873.[473] His methods were also quite unconventional and recollected in articles in *Doidge's Western Counties' Illustrated Annual* (Plymouth) between 1880 and 1889. The two Plymouth Budds were evidently not related.[724]
10. Although Doctor Budd's article on white corpuscles is listed in Budd's entry in the Medical Directory of 1882 as being in the *Lancet* it could not be found in issues of this journal from 1876 to 1882 or in the *Index Medicus* and the *Surgeon General's Catalogue*. . . .
11. Doctor George T. Budd, Jr. was sufficiently unusual to warrant a brief account. He was the son of Doctor William Budd (1811-1880) of Bristol who, in turn, was one of seven sons of Mr. Samuel Budd (surgeon), all of whom entered the medical profession.[494] William Budd attained wide recognition as an

outstanding physician.[144, 398] George Jr. was named after his uncle, Doctor George Budd (1808-1882) of London.[822] After graduating from the University of Edinburgh in 1880 George Jr. started practice in Bristol basing it on that of his father William who had died the same year. Shortly before Conan Doyle left on his African trip in 1881 he visited Bristol on George Jr.'s request for advice. "He had started in great style, hoping to rally the remains of his father's patients, but his money had run out, he was dunned by his tradespeople, there were no patients, and what was he to do?"[375i] Conan Doyle advised that he should make a composition with his creditors. Shortly thereafter George Jr. moved to Plymouth, became a rapid success, and sent for Conan Doyle as an assistant. Doctor Budd may have been the "black sheep" of his medically oriented family, but he certainly had considerable potential. For example, in 1880 he had at least six items published in the *British Medical Journal.* There were papers on amyloid[104,106] and gout,[110] a memorandum on lung tubercles,[105] and letters on incontinence of urine,[107] Esmarch's bandage,[108] and elementary pathology.[109] Perhaps this was a manifestation of Budd's extraordinary mental energy which was soon diverted to building a practice in Plymouth.

12. In *The Stark Munro Letters*[293a] the trip is described as being by rail and the city is called Birchespool.
13. Henry VIII's flagship, the *Mary Rose,* remained relatively well preserved in the fine silt of the sea channel off Southsea. On October 10, 1982, 437 years after it sank, its skeleton was lifted out of the water to become another major tourist attraction of Southsea located next to the *HMS Victory.*[757] Conan Doyle would have been enthralled!
14. The crude (all ages) death rate in Southsea in 1882 of 14.73 per 1,000 population compares with that of England and Wales a hundred years later of 12 per 1,000.[937] The closeness of these figures (in spite of the marked differences in culture, hygiene, and medical knowledge) is evidence of the relatively healthy state of this sea resort and port chosen by Conan Doyle for his medical practice.

15. The physician per population ratios are comparable in that the 53 surgeons and physicians listed for 1882[133] were all engaged in general practice, as specified for the 1978 figure.[428] Other possible variables may invalidate a meaningful comparison. For example, there can be differences in cultural orientations for using medical services, in number and types of available health support personnel, and in the availability of specific therapeutic agents.
16. In *The Stark Munro Letters*[293] Conan Doyle's home, 1 Bush Villas, is called 1 Oakley Villas. Some time after he left Southsea the house was renamed Doyle House in commemoration of his practice there.[375l] The house was destroyed in the German fire raid on Portsmouth, January 10, 1941.[415] There is some question as to whether it bore a plaque stating that it was the "birthplace" of Sherlock Holmes.[449]
17. Well before the 18th century in England all categories of licensed doctors functioned as general practitioners, including surgeons, physicians, and apothecaries.[762] Receiving degrees in both medicine (M.B.) and surgery (C.M.) on graduation, as did Conan Doyle, is still common.
18. Conan Doyle himself was quite encouraged by the development of his practice. In his December letter to Doctor Hoare[385c] he stated that "Things look rather brighter." "My affairs would seem desperate to men who have not gone through what I have in the last five months—but to me they seem promising."
19. Some idea of Doctor Conan Doyle's fees can be obtained from several letters which were donated anonymously in 1963 to the Portsmouth Medical Society Postgraduate Center, located on the grounds of St. Mary's Hospital.[388]

W. Chapman
91 Cottage Grove

To A Conan Doyle, M.D. CM
Physician

To attendance upon the late Mrs. Chapman

Feb. 3.6.7.9.10.14.16.19.21.23.25.26.28,

March 1.2.3.4.5.7.8.9.11.12.14.16.17.18.
19.21.23.25.28.30

April 1.4.5.6.7.

(36 visits = 16 bottles medicine –
one consultation)

£7 . . 11 . . 6.

---

with Dr. Conan Doyle's compliments
June 18.87

March Quarter

W. Chapman, Esq.
100 Margate Road

To A Conan Doyle, M.D. CM

Physician

To attendance upon child
Dec. 20.21.24.27.28.29.31.
Jan. 1.2.5.
Received with thanks £*2 . . 2 . . 0.*
A. Conan Doyle
Mar 21st/89
with Dr. Conan Doyle's Compliments

---

20. George Alfred W. Drayson, FRAS, was both a patient and a friend of Doctor Conan Doyle. He had served in India, South Africa, and Canada. Like the doctor, he was a prolific writer. His works included reminiscences, textbooks on astronomy and military science, and various articles.[842] Drayson's major influence on Conan Doyle was as a committed spiritualist. In addition, his works on satellites of Uranus and rotations of

the earth may have been the stimulus for Conan Doyle to credit astronomical studies to Sherlock Holmes' arch enemy Moriarity.[361]

21. Southsea has a long history of Eye and Ear Institutions.[679] In 1821 a Dispensary was established for indigent persons afflicted with eye and ear complaints. The Hospital was opened in 1884 and had five rooms and three beds. Doctor Vernon Ford was one of the first two medical officers. The hospital remained at its original site for 57 years until 1941 when it was severely damaged in the German fire bomb raid which also destroyed 1 Bush Villas. In 1970, after several moves, its services were transferred to the Queen Alexandra Hospital in Cosham as an Ophthalmic Unit.
22. Conan Doyle had another specific connection with Vernon Ford. In 1896, six years after leaving Southsea, he returned for a visit and purchased a property at 53 Kent Road with a down payment of £500 and a mortgage of £1,300.[604] The mortgage was paid in full in 1901. The reason for the purchase is not known, but there may be some significance in the fact that Vernon Ford was a tenant in the building. Conan Doyle let the property in 1912 at £83 per year and used it as security to borrow £730 in 1913 at an interest rate of £5 (.7% per year). He sold the property in 1919 for £1,900, £100 more than the purchase price 23 years previously.
23. Phrenology began in 1870 with the theory of the Austrian Franz Gall that the brain consists of 27 separate organs which control the various moral, sensual and intellectual traits of the individual.[468a] The size of each organ is proportional to the extent of each trait, as manifested by protuberances on the surface of the skull. In 1896 Arthur Conan Doyle had his head examined by a phrenologist as part of a demonstration. Stern[849] has recently republished the resultant analysis.

> *We would direct the attention of our readers to the breadth of the head, especially the frontal lobe, which indicates the faculties above mentioned [cleverness]. They will also per-*

> *ceive the massive jaw, the breadth of chin, the powerful nose, the keeness of the eye and a fullness of the arch of the eye, all of which are indications of power which help in such a work [detective fiction] undertaken by this writer.*

Such conclusions would not be difficult to make by anyone familiar with Conan Doyle, even without the opportunity to palpate his head.

24. Witchcraft has a long history in England.[534] In the middle ages witches were considered instruments used by the Devil to destroy Christendom. During the 17th century there were many trials for women accused of witchcraft and many were found guilty and hanged. Penal laws against witches were done away with by an Act of 1736. But the belief persisted. Eccentric individuals continued to be abused as witches and sometimes murdered well into the present era.

25. Conan Doyle commented in his *Through the Magic Door*[338] on the trials and horrors of exposure in the Arctic. The statement is the epitome of the Victorian ideal of manliness which Conan Doyle also applied to sports and to war.

> *The episode of those twenty-odd men lying upon that horrible bluff, and dying one a day from cold and hunger and scurvy, is one which dwarfs all our puny tragedies of romance. And the gallant starving leader giving lectures on abstract science in an attempt to take the thoughts of the dying men away from their sufferings—what a picture!*

26. The Liberal Party of Great Britain, of which the Liberal-Unionists were a segment, held to certain principles such as trust in rationality, faith in the idea of progress, and belief in individualism. Conan Doyle certainly exemplified these attitudes. The Liberal-Unionists broke from the main party because of dislike for Gladstone's plan for Home Rule of Ireland.[609] Conan Doyle ran for a Parliament seat in the British elections of 1900 and 1905 under the banner of the Unionists.[125c] One seat was a Radical stronghold in the city of

his birth and the other, several border counties. He lost both times. By 1911 Conan Doyle had changed his views on Home Rule sufficiently to write a strong letter in its support.[351]

27. Conan Doyle's nonmedical writings during his Southsea days are referenced in increasingly comprehensive and complex bibliographies of Locke (1928),[614] Reece (1975),[753] Goldscheider,[482] and Green and Gibson.[488]

Short Stories	*Year*	*Number*
	1883	8
	1884	6
	1885	5
	1886	3
	1887	2
	1888	3
	1889	5
	1890	7
	1891	1
Novels	1887-1891—one book published each year	

It is apparent that the volume and variety of his writing was somewhat variable throughout the length of his stay in Southsea. Of particular interest is *The Captain of the Polestar* subtitled "Being an Extract from the Singular Journal of John M'Alister Ray, Student of Medicine."[225] It is set in the ice fields of the Arctic, as was Conan Doyle's voyage as a student.

28. In 1885 Claude Clarke Claremont was official Medical Officer at the Royal Portsmouth Hospital, having formerly been a House Surgeon at Sheffield and then House Physician at the Seaman's Hospital in Greenwich.[845] He was a prominent member of the Portsmouth Literary and Scientific Society. When Conan Doyle left he took over his position as joint Honorary Secretary.[844] He was president in 1904-05. Doctor Claremont died in 1910 or 1911.

29. It is not certain whether Conan Doyle's stay in Southsea was commemorated by a plaque on his house before it was de-

stroyed by bombing during World War II.[449] Quite recently, on November 18, 1982, a plaque was placed on Bush House which is on the same site.[542] It reads as follows:

> *Doctor Arthur Conan Doyle, M.D. practiced from 1882 until 1890 at No. 1 Bush Villas which formerly stood on this site. It was here the first Sherlock Holmes story was written.*

As the plaque was erected by the Sherlock Holmes Society of London, it is not surprisng that its central portion contains a profile of Conan Doyle's detective.

30. About one half mile to the west of Conan Doyle's office there is another eye hospital on Maryleborne Road. This is the Western Ophthalmic Hospital, established in 1856.[141] A search of old records has failed to yield Conan Doyle's name.[140] Figures are available for the number of ophthalmologists practicing in Britain in 1891.[875] In London there were only 99 and surely less than this ten years earlier. This would not constitute an overwhelming competition for Conan Doyle in a city with a population of several million.
31. Although there is no plaque at #2 Devonshire Place commemorating Conan Doyle's practice site, there is one on his former house at No. 12 Tennyson Road.

SIR
ARTHUR
CONAN DOYLE
1859-1930
creator of
Sherlock Holmes
lived here
1891-1894

It is a circular plaque, one of many put up by the Greater London Council to commemorate outstanding historical figures who lived in London. Conan Doyle is in good company. Some other physicians so recognized are Sigmund Freud, John Hunter, John Keats, Joseph Lister, and Somerset Maugham.[793]

32. Modern views on the causes of the Boer War are more balanced.

> *War broke out between British and Boers in 1899, ostensibly over the grievances of the 'outlanders' but really as the climax to a long story of Kruger's truculent intransigence and of British jostling in her imperial expansion.*[869]

33. Some disagreement exists as to the number of beds in the Langman field hospital. It is given as 100 in the *Time* story,[911] but as 50 by Conan Doyle in his various writings. In *The Great Boer War* he did refer to it as a half hospital.[316a] One of the two trains with the field hospital equipment was lost. Conan Doyle soon discovered it and reclaimed its contents for the hospital.
34. The *Daily News* of April 16, 1900,[312] had a story in which Conan Doyle states that the field hospital is "to go straight up to Bloemfontein." The field hospital actually left Capetown on March 26. The story was delayed by the three-week journey between Capetown and England.
35. Conan Doyle described a more dramatic surgical case in his autobiography.[375s] A shrapnel bullet had fractured a cervical vertebra of a Dutch military attache during the battle of Sannasport on March 31, 1900.[192] The result was paralysis. He was taken to Bloemfontein by British ambulance and operated on by Watson Cheyne of London on April 10, a week after Conan Doyle's arrival.

> *He had cut down on the bone with a free incision and was endeavoring with a strong forceps to raise the broken arch of bone, when an amazing thing happened. Out of the great crimson cleft there rose a column of clear water 2 feet high, feathering at the top like a little palm tree. . . . Charles Gibbs . . . said that the cerebrospinal fluid . . . had been greatly stimulated and increased by the pressure of the broken bone. . . . The forceps had punctured a small hole in the sheath and then the fluid had been pressed through. . . . Perhaps the release was too sudden, for the patient died shortly after he was removed from the table.*[375s]

Doctor Conan Doyle had learned about the dangers of sudden decompression of increased intraspinal pressure.

36. Conan Doyle's attempt to enter into the comic opera field involved D'Oyly Carte. Two accounts are provided in biographies of Gilbert and Sullivan.

> *Sullivan [in 1891] had rejected a proposal by D'Oyly Carte that he should team up with two rising young novelists, J.M. Barrie and Conan Doyle, who had contracted a script called 'Jane Annie.'*[34]

In spite of this rejection D'Oyly Carte did produce the work.

> *His [D'Oyly Carte] recent productions at the Savoy—Sullivan and Grundy's* Haddon Hall *and* Jane Annie, *a play by J.M. Barrie and Conan Doyle with music by Ernest Ford— had not done very well.*[524]

Conan Doyle did actually appear in the June 12, 1906, production of Gilbert and Sullivan's "Trial by Jury." He was one of several celebrities who acted as the Jury.

37. Conan Doyle was not the only physician who raised his voice against rampant prostitution. In 1899 Dr. William Hammond, retired Surgeon-General of the U.S. Army, pointed out that "military men of all ranks . . . have in every age of the world evinced a marked tendency to become the victims of female blandishments . . . of the fair sex both of high and low life."[510] During World War I, Sir William Osler delivered the Annual Oration of the Medical Society of London on "The Campaign against Syphilis."[700] Unlike Conan Doyle, he dealt more with manifestations, complications, and early treatment than with remonstrations against prostitutes.

38. The Edalji case was not the only one in which Conan Doyle rose to the defense of an accused. He unsuccessfully opposed the execution in 1916 of Sir Roger Casement who had supported the German cause in Ireland.[862b] More successful were his efforts on behalf of Oscar Slater, a German Jew, who had been sentenced to hard labor for life for the murder with a hammer of an old woman in 1909. Conan Doyle reviewed all

the evidence (a la Sherlock Holmes), satisfied himself as to Slater's innocence and characteristically wrote a book on the subject.[356] Slater was not released until after 18 years of imprisonment. Both in this case and that of Edalji, Conan Doyle fought the prejudice of society against foreigners. In Slater's and Casement's convictions Conan Doyle ignored his own biases against gambling and loose living (Slater) and homosexuality (Casement). Conan Doyle's sense of injustice was greater than his sense of impropriety!

39. Captain Leckie is buried in the Frameries Communal Cemetery, 5 kilometers Southwest of Mons (Register B202:Plat 1, Row B, Grave 1).[11]
40. Gelsemium sempervirens (Carolina jessamine) has also been called gelseminum, as by Conan Doyle.[216] It is a woody perennial evergreen vine found particularly in the south, and used as an ornamental climbing vine. Gelsemium is one of the most poisonous of plants, with a high concentration of toxic alkaloid, gelsemine.[78] Gelsemine is a potent antagonist of nicotinic acetylcholine receptors, both centrally and peripherally.
41. As a drug, gelsemium was prepared by soaking one part of the root to four parts of alcohol.[760] It was sold as packets containing the root cut in pieces varying from two to eight inches in length and ⅓ to ¾ of an inch in diameter.[536]
42. Although one of Conan Doyle's teachers, Doctor Bennett, had first described leucocythemia in 1845,[59] it was Rudolf Virchow who concluded, in 1847, that it was not a secondary suppuration of the blood but a separate disease entity which he labeled as leukemia.[807]
43. Gout may have been present in prehistoric man but the evidence is not specific. Changes in the joint itself are similar to those of osteoarthritis. It is deposits of urates (tophi) in the surrounding soft tissues that are characteristic, and these are not usually preserved on ancient bones. They are, however, sometimes preserved in Egyptian mummies,[100] and some of these do contain tophi. Descriptions by Hippocrates[722] and by Anna Camnema[120] were clinical in nature.

44. Psoriasis, like gout, can have an increased urinary excretion of uric acid. This should not be taken as a sign of gout, unless specific joint and soft tissue changes of gout are also present.[26]
45. The inheritance of gout is not a clear-cut subject. A family history of gout is obtained in 6% to 18% of gouty patients, but with persistent questioning as high as 75%.[565] The delineation is made difficult by overlapping of other types of hyperuricemia with the "classical" presentation of gout, and several reported patterns of inheritance—x-linked, autosomal dominant, and multifactoral.
46. William Murrel (1853–1912) was a member of the Royal College of Physicians, Senior Physician at Westminster Hospital and Assistant Physician to the Royal Hospital for Diseases of the Chest.[827] He engaged in self-experimentation, as did Conan Doyle, by taking nitroglycerin to determine its effects.[673] Only then did he give the drug to others. Whereas Murrel used 10 grains, Conan Doyle took up to 40 grains (minums). The "official" dosage is one half to two grains.[905]
47. Sophistry is "a subtle, tricky, superficially plausible but general fallacious method of reasoning."[624] One suspects that Holmes (Conan Doyle) at times used "a specious argument for displaying ingenuity in reasoning." Nevertheless it is to Conan Doyle's credit that he "used the process of observations and the inductive deductive phase of the reasoning employed by all excellent clinicians when he fashioned the character and exploits of Sherlock Holmes."[82]
48. The terms inoculation and vaccination have the same meaning, although the former is no longer used for a procedure that develops immunity. Before 1798 the placing of smallpox virus into the skin, as by Lady Montagu, was called inoculation.[48] About 40 years after Jenner's first use of cowpox virus, the terms vaccination and vaccine came into use. They are derived from the Latin word for cow, "vacca." At first they were restricted to smallpox vaccination, but in 1881 Pasteur proposed that they be used for any prophylactic immunization.

49. In spite of such opposition there was a rapid spread of smallpox vaccination throughout the world.[781] For example, smallpox vaccination was introduced into the United States by Doctor Benjamin Waterhouse in 1800, only four years after Jenner's discovery.[77] But reaction against it continued, and by some very prominent individuals. For example, George Bernard Shaw scathingly satirized vaccination, as he was to do for many matters relating to physicians.[91] In the preface to his play of 1913, "The Doctor's Dilemma,"[810] he claimed that Jenner had rejected the efficacy of smallpox vaccination, but it was carried forward as a craze by the public.
50. Typhoid fever was one of the great scourges of the past in both war and peace. It was especially prevalent along the West Coast of Africa where Conan Doyle may have picked up the bacillus in 1892.[128] Typhoid fever was probably quite prevalent in ancient Greece and Rome.[5] It was not, however, clearly delineated from typhus fever until the mid-19th century.[175]
51. Alleyne Kingsley, Conan Doyle's second child and first son, was born in November 1892, about two years after his father had left general practice. Some of his education was in Europe, as was his father's, studying at Lausanne and Hanover.[125d] He attended Eton and then passed the preliminary examination in general education in June and September 1911. He entered St. Mary's Hospital Medical School on October 12, 1911.[211] According to its records he successfully completed three and a half of the five years. He then left without qualifying in the fall of 1914.[211] In 1915 he enlisted as a private and was assigned to Egypt where he worked his way up to the rank of Acting Captain in the First Hampshires. Carr has stated that Kingsley joined the Royal Army Medical Corps, but this is contrary to Conan Doyle's own account.[375w] Kingsley was then assigned to the Western front, where he was seriously injured during the battle of Somme. He was considerably weakened and returned to London. According to his record card he enrolled again at St. Mary's Hospital Medical School, receiving credit

for at least January and February 1918.[211] However, he fell prey to the great influenza epidemic of that year and died of pneumonia on October 28. It was a great blow for Conan Doyle to lose his first son, and especially one who shared his interest in medicine and his love of sports. For years thereafter he communicated with Kingsley through mediums at seances.[525b]

52. Conan Doyle may not have been aware that Jean Paul Marat (1743–1793) had been a medical practitioner before his involvement in the French revolution. He was born in Switzerland and attended the universities of Toulouse and Bordeaux.[685] He arrived in London about 1765 and practiced medicine with neither medical license or degree. He wrote an essay on diseases of the eye. In 1775 Marat was awarded an M.D. degree from the University of St. Andrews on the recommendation of two physicians. At about this time he lived for two years in Conan Doyle's home town, Edinburgh. In 1787 Marat moved to France as the physician to the bodyguard of the King's brother. It was here that he became involved in the French revolution by writing pamphlets.[23] This involvement was to lead not only to a high position but also to death by the knife of Charlotte Corday. Death occurred while he was sitting in his medicinal bath, necessitated by severe skin disease. Marat's skin was covered with blisters and open, suppurating sores, accompanied by fever, headaches and severe pains in his arms and legs.[209] Suggested diagnoses have been syphilis, eczema, scabies, seborrheic keratosis, pemphigoid, and dermatitis herpetiformis.[450] Whatever the cause, his disease, as suggested by Conan Doyle, may have been the cause, in part, of the torture and death of many.

53. The disease that caused Napoleon's death is not as much a mystery as that of Marat's skin disease, but is still controversial. Napoleon died in St. Helena on May 5, 1821. Autopsy was reported to have revealed a carcinoma of the stomach, the same disease that killed his father and his paternal grandfather.[763] Also evident was feminization of the body, possibly glandular in origin. But, as with many famous individuals,

the exact cause of death remains disputed. The bloody and corroded mucosa of the stomach has also been interpreted as due to a large dose of calomel or to arsenic poisoning.[417] To support this latter supposition, a recent analysis of hairs removed shortly after death showed a high content of arsenic.[442] This, however, has been countered by the suggestion that the hairs may have been removed long after burial, or that the arsenic came from the earth. A more recent study of another sample of his hair, removed before burial, revealed a normal level of arsenic.[608A] Thus, Conan Doyle could well have been correct in suggesting that a slowly growing gastric cancer greatly affected his career. It has also been suggested that Napoleon's ability for decision making was considerably hampered by painful hemorrhoids.[176]

SECTION TWO NOTES

54. There are various types of works on "Literature and Medicine:"
    a. Quotations: these are very short selections, usually of one page or less, and often selected as sayings, aphorisms, or homilies. An example is Coope's *The Quiet Art. A Doctor's Anthology*.[161]
    b. Excerpts: these are usually selections of several pages, often included because of their humorous, tender, or moving nature. An example is Corcoran's *A Mirror up to Medicine*.[167] It includes four excerpts from Conan Doyle's medical fiction, under headings of "Gratitude," "My First Patient," "A Lady," and "The Surgeon Talks."
    c. Segments: these are significant parts including chapters or major sections, chosen often for dramatic, moral or ethical impact. An example is Davenport's *The Good Physician*.[187]
    d. Reprints: these are reproductions of entire works, usually short stories, novelettes, or complete essays, on a variety of nonscientific medical themes. An example is Ceccio's *Medicine in Literature*[132] which contains Conan Doyle's medical short stories "The Doctors of Hoyland"[274] and "The Curse of Eve."[286] Cousin's *The Physician in Literature*[177] includes these two and also "A Medical Document."[288]

e. Bibliographies: listings of writings that have a major medical orientation or include references to medicine. An example is Trautmann's *Literature and Medicine*[877] which lists the above three medical short stories by Conan Doyle and "The Third Generation,"[284] as well as "The Croxley Master"[309] and the Sherlock Holmes stories.

f. Commentaries: articles which discuss various aspects of the area, including descriptions, analyses, and rationales. An example is *Literature and Medicine*,[742] volume one of which was published in 1982.

55. Conan Doyle probably coined the phrase "cleanliness-and-cold-water school."[127] Joseph Lister used this method from 1860 until 1865. He then developed his carbolic acid method in response to Pasteur's demonstration of the relationship between bacteria and infection.

56. His views on divorce were oriented toward considerations of the quality of life.[817]

> *The divorce laws are so arranged at present that divorce is practically impossible for a poor man, that people are tied without hope of release to lunatics, drunkards, and criminals, and great numbers . . . are separated by law, and yet are not free to marry again—a fact which cannot be conducive to public morality.*

57. The latter part of the 19th century was a period of turmoil and transition in respect to higher education for women. There was concern that such intellectual activity would affect their reproductive organs, not to mention a decrease in their femininity and the danger to their health.[118] Medical education for women was strongly opposed by Christison,[424d] and advocated by Simpson,[811] both renowned faculty members of the University of Edinburgh. Although there is little prejudice or restriction in our enlightened era to female physicians, they are still markedly unrepresented in important groups such as committees of the British Medical Association.[632]

58. Donaldson's[207] exhaustive measurements of the brains of three scholars in 1928 concluded that the extent of cortex (of

the cerebrum) in the scholars was greater in the frontal area than in others, much as Doctor Grey had implied in his comparison of men and women. There is little support today, however, for such views. Quite different from anything else Conan Doyle wrote is the description in 1888 of his study on intellect.[246] He compiled a listing of men who attained eminence in various "intellectual walks of life," and their birth places. His native country (Scotland) had the highest ratio of men of distinction, 1 in 22,000, his adopted country (England), 1 in 30,000, the country of his family roots (Ireland), 1 in 49,000 and Wales, 1 in 58,000. Of 235 born Londoners of distinction only 12 were medical men. He concluded "that, with a few notable exceptions, music, poetry, and art reach their highest development in the south, while theology, science, and engineering predominate in higher latitudes." One wonders what specific criteria Conan Doyle used for selecting men of distinction.

59. Colchicum, with its active ingredient, colchicine, has been recognized as a specific treatment for gout since the 6th century.[165a] Today, it is still the most frequently used drug for gout.[125b] "Clouding" of the brain, as mentioned by Conan Doyle, is not usually listed as one of its side effects.

60. Homeopathy was the invention of Samuel Hahnemann (1775–1843) a German physician. Oliver Wendell Holmes, one of Conan Doyle's heroes, delivered two critical and scathing lectures on homeopathy, in 1842.[537] He attacked its espoused basic principles. Diseases are cured by agents capable of producing symptoms resembling those found in the disease under treatment; the more diluted a medicinal substance the more efficacious; seven-eighths of all chronic diseases are produced by a Psora (an itch). In the United States, several homeopathic schools were established.[784a] The Hahnemann Medical College of Philadelphia was founded in 1867 and still exists, although the last vestiges of homeopathy were removed from its curriculum in the 1940s.

61. Porphyria has been suggested as the cause of the periods of madness of George III.[620] Thus, it may have contributed to Britain's loss of the American colonies, an event that Conan

Doyle hoped to see rectified. The porphyria afflicting both George III and Doctor Cameron was most likely of the hepatic variety, which has a dominant inheritance and begins in middle age. It has an acute intermittent type which is associated with psychotic episodes.[654]

62. The reference to a relationship between sewage and the spread of typhoid was made in 1894, six years before Conan Doyle's experience with the epidemic in Bloemfontein. Thus, he was already knowledgeable on the subject before entering the Boer War.
63. Evident stressful events in Conan Doyle's life included his attempts to find a practice, controversy over religion with his family, the break with Budd, the first six months in Southsea, the prolonged fatal illness of his first wife, and the deaths during WWI of a son, a brother, and a brother-in-law. Yet, he exhibited considerable zest, resiliency, and self-confidence which overcame all tribulations. In addition, his acceptance of spiritualism, much as one would any religion, provided considerable support.
64. The abnormality of Sir Francis' teeth was undoubtedly the unusual notched, peg-shaped appearance of the incisors, first described by Sir Jonathan Hutchinson (1826–1913) in 1861, a professor at the Royal College of Surgeons in London.[468f]
65. The intrauterine spread of syphilis from one generation to another has long been recognized. The first mention of congenital syphilis was in 1565.[854] There is a suspicion that Henry VIII had syphilis because none of his three children produced a child—one was deaf, one had a flattened bridge of the nose, and another an unusual skin rash—all of which can be caused by congenital syphilis.[780a] In our modern era, in spite of antibiotics, congenital syphilis is not unknown, there being 1,903 cases reported in the United States in 1970.[780b]
66. Conan Doyle's rejection of the Christian beliefs of his family occurred about the time of graduation from medical school. "I found that the foundations not only of Roman Catholicism but of the whole Christian faith, as presented to me in nine-

teenth century theology, were so weak that my mind could not build upon them.''[375y] Related, is Sir Francis' objection to Doctor Selby's attempt at consolation by reference to the Pope's words on the subject of the unknown ways of God. ''Words, words, words! You sit comfortably there in your chair and say them—and think them too, no doubt. You've had your life. But I've never had mine . . . ah, it's such a mockery and a make belief.'' Conan Doyle also included theological dissertations in *The Stark Munro Letters*.[293e] For example, ''Even the most material of modern minds would flinch at depicting the Diety as ordering wholesale executions, and hacking kings to pieces upon the horns of altars.''—not to mention inflicting congenital syphilis on the innocent.

67. Doctor Selby did not recommend the use of mercury which was the major therapeutic agent for syphilis from the 16th to the early 20th century.[780c] Nothing was lost, because it had little effect on syphilis, but extensive side effects such as necrosis of bone, loosening of teeth, nephritis, hepatitis, and excess salivation.[194] Only with the introduction of Salvarsan (arsphenamine) by Ehrlich in 1909,[640] did a specific agent become available, to be followed by penicillin in about 40 years.

68. ''The Los Amigos Fiasco'' was first published in 1892 in the *Idler* magazine.[269] In this version, John Murphy Stonehouse, the narrator, is a journalist. In its reprinting in *Round the Red Lamp*, however, the narrator is a nameless medical practitioner. The story line is otherwise identical except for being strengthened by the active involvement of the narrator physician in the proceedings, unlike the journalist.

69. ''Electric'' therapeutic devices were of several kinds.[910c] Electric belts were made of leather which contained a series of metal disks which were supposedly activated by the warmth of the body. Electric metal batteries made of copper and zinc disks were worn around the neck with a chain just long enough so that the metal would rest against the heart, where

its supposed electrical energy would be imparted to this organ. Electric rings were made of a combination of metals which supposedly released a constant curative current of electricity on contact with acid sweat. The ring was worn on the third finger of the left hand because of a belief that this digit contained a vessel which goes directly to the heart. Electric insoles contained a strip of zinc for one shoe and of copper for the other, presumably generating an electric current from the former to the latter. We may well deride our forebearers for such delusions, but even in our own age of strict federal control of therapeutic devices, we have some such idiosyncrasies.

70. Stimulation of the phrenic nerve by electricity would require implantation of electrical nodes at its site. The result would be rather frightening contractions of the diaphragm which it innervates. In 1784, Galvani discovered the contractile effect of electricity on muscles of frog legs.[468g] But, utilization of electricity in the treatment of disease had begun about 40 years before by many, including Benjamin Franklin.

71. In *The Parasite*[280] there is reference to a book on "animal magnetism," which was Mesmer's hypothetical basis for his treatment method. Gradually mesmerism merged into the large mass of systems that promised to cure diseases. These were characterized by absence of objectivity in determining efficacy and by each being promoted as a treatment for all diseases. At best they probably did no more harm than the aggressive polypharmacy and blood-letting which were indulged in by some physicians before the age of objective-scientific medicine. Hypnotism is used today, of course, as a mode of treatment, not of physical disease, but of various mental states, including addiction to smoking and avoidance of pain.[459] The latter has a long history,[468h] being described by John Elliotson (1791–1868) in 1843, in a pamphlet on "Numerous Cases of Surgical Operations Without Pain in the Mesmeric State." Elliotson was president of the Royal Medical and Chirurgical Society of London, but resigned because of disputes over his work. James Esdaile (1808–1859) reported in 1846, on the use of hypnotism for 261 painless

operations on Hindu convicts. But, he found that the more self-contained Europeans were not especially susceptible to hypnotism, unlike the impressionable Hindus. Today, the use of hypnotism for prevention of pain is limited, possibly for the same reason.

72. Samuel Warren (1807–1877) was yet another physician/writer. He studied medicine at Edinburgh, graduating in 1827, but went on to study law.[558] His *Passages from the Diary of a Late Physician* was written between 1829 and 1837.[914] The "Diary" consists of an account of early struggles. Each of the subsequent ones is concerned with a single patient. Diseases are similar to those included by Conan Doyle—cancer, tuberculosis, apoplexy, syphilis, insanity, gout, asthma, and catalepsy. Of interest is Chapter X, in which is described an episode of grave robbing in order to perform an autopsy on a patient whose relatives had refused such a procedure. These stories are not as effective as those in *Round the Red Lamp* because of their length, verbosity, and lack of vividness.

73. Lowell is an actual city in northeastern Massachusetts, near the New Hampshire border. It is the birthplace of Abbott McNeil Whistler, and was originally a major textile center.[617] Charles Dickens mentioned the city in his *American Notes*.[200] How Conan Doyle obtained the name Lowell is uncertain. He did travel in the United States in the late autumn of 1894. "I visited every town of any size between Boston in the north and Washington in the south, while Chicago and Milwaukee marked my western limit."[375aa] *The Stark Munro Letters,* however, was first published in serial form from October 1894 to November 1895.[292] Perhaps Conan Doyle encountered Lowell, (Mass.) while studying the United States map before his departure. His familiarity with American geography is evident from the number of related place names in the Sherlock Holmes stories.[454]

74. Conan Doyle expressed through Cullingworth his concern for protection of soldiers by a "patent portable bullet-proof shield."[293dd] Ten years later he refined his views to include a helmet and more.

> . . . *why should it not be supplemented by steel shoulder-guards, since the helmet might actually guide the bullets down on to the shoulders? And why not a plastron [plate armor] over the heart? . . . I experimented with my own service rifle upon steel plates. . . .*[375gg]

Other suggestions, for the saving of lives of naval personnel, have been widely adopted—swimming ''collars'' and collapsible boats. Conan Doyle also was the first to suggest special badges for the wounded in Britain.[513]

75. The word genetics was first used by the English biologist William Bateson in 1905.[135] It was much later, in the fourth to the sixth decades of the 20th century, that the identification of the genetic material, DNA was made.[547]
76. In the 18th century a widespread theory of preformation stated that the spermatozoon contained a developed animalcule.[680] But, the equal importance of the ovary in embryonic development, as indicated by Conan Doyle, was gradually recognized.
77. The scientific study of heredity began with an Augustinian monk, Gregor Johann Mendel (1822–1884). In 1865, he published the results of hybridization of peas.[446] Conan Doyle could not have been aware of this work because it lay unheeded in an obscure journal until discovered about 1900.
78. The descriptive nature of the names given by Conan Doyle to some of his characters is reminiscent of Charles Dickens. Tom Dimsdale is indeed a failing student. Who else but Doctor Winter would be old and ''Behind the Times''?
79. Rugby football was one of the many sports in which Conan Doyle was active. His involvement began as a medical student.

> . . . *I played for a short time as forward in the Edinburgh University team, but my want of knowledge of the game was too heavy a handicap.*[375bb]

He also played on teams in Portsmouth while a practitioner and in Bloemfontein during the Boer War. It was there that ''a foul from a man's knee buckled two of my ribs and brought my games to a close.''

80. *Religio Medici* is also the title of a book written by the 17th century English physician Sir Thomas Browne (1605–1682) in 1643.[699] Unlike Conan Doyle's brief poem, Browne's opus was an attempt to reconcile scientific skepticism with the Christian faith.
81. A flavor of some of Conan Doyle's other 88 poems may be obtained from the following verses of his poem "Sir Nigel's Song," included in *Songs of the Road*.[354]

> *A Sword! A Sword Ah, give me a sword!*
> *For the world is all to win.*
> *Though the way be hard and the door be barred*
> *The strong man enters in.*
> *If chance or Fate still hold the gate*
> *Give me the iron key,*
> *And turret high, my plume shall fly*
> *Or you will weep for me.*

82. Also set in West Africa is Joseph Conrad's *Heart of Darkness*.[159] Many of his stories deal with the theme of civilized man faced with the mysteries of contemporary primitive societies.[917] Two of Conan Doyle's stories have a similar encounter, *The Lost World*,[357] and "The Fiend of the Cooperage," but there is no comparison with the literary and psychologic qualities of some of Joseph Conrad's works.
83. The medical school in Montpellier, a city in southern France, has a long history, originating about the 11th century.[741]
84. The "obsonic" index undoubtedly refers to the "opsonic" index which was developed by Almroth Wright as a measurement of phagocytic ability, and scathingly satirized by Bernard Shaw.[810]
85. Conan Doyle became quite an automobile enthusiast, obtaining his first car in 1908. He had a serious accident when his auto ran up a high bank, threw him out, and then turned over on him. It is described verbatim in both *Memories and Adventures*[375hh] and "Some Recollections of Sport."[342] Fortunately, he was not killed or even injured. He entered "my little 16 horse-power landaulette" in the 1911 International

Road Competition held in Germany.[375ii] It was at this time that he recognized the German danger.

86. These descriptions of insanity were written by Conan Doyle at the time Freud was developing his concepts of mental disease.[12] The modern classification of symptoms of mental disease had begun in the 1830s and 1840s with the works of Wilhelm Griesinger (1817–1868) of Berlin.[805]
87. Bloodletting is the therapeutic removal of blood from the body. It had been used for a thousand years to release the supposed excess of humors proposed by Hippocrates as a cause of many diseases.[695] Methods used were application of leeches, creating a vacuum in a cup on the skin, and draining elbow veins.[518] It was widely practiced in 18th century America and Britain. For example, four pints of blood were removed from George Washington in a 24-hour period before his death from croup.[803]
88. The general public was not well protected from experimental therapy in the 19th century. The use of "new" drugs such as Datura would not be permitted today in the United States because of the stringent regulations and requirements of the Federal Drug Agency.
89. The accuracy and realism of *The Lost World*[357] so enthused a group of Americans that they set sail for Brazil to explore the Amazon and its tributaries.[47] Since Conan Doyle's prehistoric romance there have been various books and movies on the same theme.
90. H. G. Wells was seven years younger than Conan Doyle, being born in 1866 in Bromley just outside of London.[625] He spent several months as a boy employed in a draper shop in Southsea. In Conan Doyle's *Memories and Adventures*[375] he acknowledges that he may have seen Wells ". . . indeed I must have often entered the draper's shop in which he was employed at Southsea, for the proprietor was a patient of mine."[375u] They first met formally in 1905, in Rome, where they spent some time together in a group of British visitors which included E. W. Hornung, Conan Doyle's brother-in-

law.[125] They evidently maintained contact. According to Carr, H. G. Wells wrote letters to Conan Doyle congratulating him on his novel *A Duet* and upon his knighthood.[125j,k] Both agreed on the suffrage movement, but Wells did not enter into the fray as did Conan Doyle.

> *I do my best to avoid the present suffrage agitation because it overaccentuates all those sexual differences I want to minimize and shakes my faith in the common humanity of women.*[625]

They disagreed, however, on the fate of the traitor, Roger Casement. Wells refused to sign Conan Doyle's petition for his pardon.[683d] A more fundamental disagreement related to spiritualism, which Wells denied completely. To Conan Doyle this represented a major failing.[375u]

> . . . *he has never shown any perception of the true meaning of the psychic, and for want of it his history of the world* . . . *seemed to me to be a body without a soul* . . . *I remember discussing the matter with him* . . . *in Rome* . . . *but apparently my words had no effect.*

This was about 12 years before Conan Doyle's full and public acceptance of spiritualism.[367]

SECTION THREE NOTES

91. Conan Doyle suggested that the gentleman had disappeared voluntarily from his London Hotel because he had withdrawn all his money from the bank (although other possibilities suggest themselves). Because he left the hotel near midnight he was likely trying to conceal himself. A study of railway timetables revealed a train to Edinburgh and Glasgow, which he had likely taken.[57] Such was suggested by Conan Doyle and later proved true. Was this reasoning plus intuition or extrasensory perception?
92. Conan Doyle had several actual experiences with cryptograms. He was sent a puzzling diagram purported to refer to the location of a treasure-laden ship which was wrecked on the South African coast in 1782.[366] From the various hieroglyphics he suggested a location, but its validity has not been explored. Of more immediate practical value was a cipher he used to send news to a prisoner of war in Germany. The cipher was contained in one of his books sent to the prisoner. It consisted of "little needle-pricks under the various printed letters until I had spelled out all the news."[375cc]
93. A further comparison of Doctor Thorndyke and Mr. Holmes is of interest. Freeman wrote that he "was not based on any

person, real or fictitious.''[208a] ''As he was a man of acute intellect and sound judgment, I decided to keep him free from eccentricities.'' The result was an interesting, but relatively flat characterization—but still more interesting than Poe's Dupin. Thorndyke dealt with a more complex cipher in ''The Moabite Cipher,'' than did Holmes in ''The Dancing Men.''

94. At least four Holmesian encyclopedias can be of considerable use for anyone desiring to analyze Conan Doyle's 60 Sherlock Holmes tales.

> Who's Who in Sherlock Holmes[113] *by S. R. Bullard and M. L. Collins is an alphabetical listing and a brief orientation to each proper name in the* Canon. *It is the only one that cites specific pages.*
>
> The Sherlock Holmes Companion[512] *by M. & M. Hardwick includes a listing of proper names and plots of each story. The solutions to the mystery are not provided, however.*
>
> Sherlock Holmes Esq. and John H. Watson, M.D.[710] *by O. Park is also a ''Who's Who,'' but contains other items, such as very short plot summaries.*
>
> The Encyclopedia Sherlockiana[873] *by J. Tracy is more comprehensive and provides more detail on many items, some of which are related to medicine.*

95. In the past 15 years there has been increased recognition that the study of anthropology is of importance in the education of physicians.[691]

96. Acetone is one specific member of a class of substances known collectively as ketones. A knowledgeable chemist would not confuse the two. Acetone as a substance was known as early as the 17th century.[709]

97. The basic laws of inheritance were first worked out by an Augustinian monk, Gregor Johann Mendel (1822–1884), in 1865.[198] These did not become noticed until 1900,[446a] well after Conan Doyle's medical education.

98. Conan Doyle did recognize the possibility that the environment itself might corrupt a child. He provided an analogy with dogs.

> *A dog reflects the family life. Whoever saw a frisky dog in a gloomy family, or a sad dog in a happy one? Snarling people have snarling dogs, dangerous people have dangerous ones. And their passing moods may reflect the passing moods of others. (Cree 752)*

99. Ophthalmology was recognized as a special field of medical practice long before Conan Doyle's time. The first public eye hospital was opened as the "Royal London Ophthalmic Hospital" in 1805.[134]

100. *The Sign of Four* was published in 1890 and dated by Baring-Gould as having taken place in 1888.[41] The latest treatise may have been *A Manual of General Pathology* by Payne, first published in 1888,[712] but this was an American work. The first pathology book written originally in the English language was Matthew Baillie's *Morbid Anatomy*[35] first published in 1793 and the last English edition in 1838.[765]

101. The diagnosis of Marfan's syndrome has been applied to some historical figures solely on the basis of their excess height. Abraham Lincoln has been so labeled, although he had none of the other stigmata—dislocated lens of the eye, hyperflexible joints, long and tapering fingers, and a family history of such abnormalities.[601] The syndrome was described by Antonin Bernard Jean Marfan (1858–1942), a French pediatrician, in 1896.[802]

102. Syphilitic aneurysms of the aorta are now a rarity because of the availability of antibiotics which destroy the spirochetes. Few physicians before the 20th century recognized syphilis as a possible cause.[194a] Osler's textbook of 1892, however, lists syphilis along with alcohol and overwork.[696h] It is not apparent whether or not Conan Doyle knew of this association.

103. Leprosy is not very contagious, contrary to former belief, and a one night's exposure is not very likely to transmit the disease. Leprosy has been known since Biblical times.[631] Between the 13th and 16th centuries it decreased in incidence and then disappeared from all but the peripheral parts of Europe. It advanced, however, in Central and South America, East India, Pacific islands, and Africa,[5a] where Godfrey had his frightening encounter.

104. Although only two specific skin diseases exist in the entire *Canon,* there are several published papers on dermatology and Sherlock Holmes.[826] One discusses the need for the Sherlockian method of keen observation and attention to details in the diagnosis of skin diseases.[201] Another applies his method to a session of a fictional skin-disease clinic.[582]

105. The development of dermatology as a specialty in Britain was hindered by considerable opposition from general physicians, which excluded specialists from larger hospitals.[778] Therefore, they developed their own hospitals dedicated to diseases of concern for their specialty. By the time Conan Doyle opened his ophthalmology office in London (1891) there were five skin hospitals in that city as compared to two eye hospitals. The Dermatological Society of London, the first one of its kind in Britain, had been founded nine years earlier.[779]

106. Conan Doyle, in this story as elsewhere, expressed a very positive attitude toward the United States.[595]

> *It is always a joy to me to meet an American Mr. Moulton, for I am one of those who believe that the folly of a monarch and the blundering of a Minister in fargone years will not prevent our children from being some day citizens of the same world-wide country under a flag which shall be a quartering of the Union Jack with the Stars and Stripes. (Nobl 798)*

He expressed a similar, but not as extravagant a view on being interviewed before leaving London in 1914 for a visit to the United States and Canada.[154] "Personally I regard the United States as a country with the most remarkable destiny the world has ever known.''

107. Brain fever was not only a diagnosis popular with the lay public and fiction writers of the Victorian era. For example, some cases of infection with Trichinosis in slaves of the Old South were probably diagnosed erroneously as brain fever.[795] More generally, it was believed that mental and emotional stress could produce actual congestion of the brain. William Alexander Hammond, M.D. (1828–1900), who was Surgeon General of the U.S. Army for two years, made a presentation on ''Cerebral Hyperemia, the Result of Mental Strain'' to the New York Neurological Society, in 1877.[571] It was published as late as 1895.[509]

108. The assumption of factitious illness was given the name ''Münchausen's Syndrome'' in 1951.[29] The name is derived from Karl von Münchhausen (1720–1797), a German Baron who told extraordinary and false tales about his life as a soldier.[672] A significant characteristic of this syndrome, as illustrated so well by Holmes, is the dramatic and emergency nature of the feigned illness.[678]

109. There is some disagreement as to the peculiar manifestion of running around in small circles. Carter[126] suggests that it was not hemorrhage but thrombosis of the posterior inferior cerebellar artery with involvement of the medulla resulting in severe vertigo. Brenner,[97] a neurologist, argues that lesions of the lateral medulla do not result in loss of consciousness unless there is extension to involve the pontine tegmentum bilaterally. At any rate it is indeed an attention getting occurrence.

110. Conan Doyle did have direct connections with the theater. He wrote several plays that were produced. The first was ''Jane Annie,''[44] a play written in rough draft by his literary friend, J.M. Barrie, and completed by Conan Doyle when Barrie's health failed.[375u] In 1897 he wrote the script of a play about Sherlock Holmes. It eventually reached the prominent actor, William Gillette, who rewrote the entire play with

Conan Doyle's permission.[824] Conan Doyle cabled that he could "marry Holmes or murder him or do anything he liked with him."[125f] The results were a different play than the original, and the generally accepted portrait of Holmes as played by Gillette.[840] Another Conan Doyle play was staged shortly after the opening of Gillette's play in 1889. "Halves," his stage adaption of a novel about two brothers by James Payn, an English Novelist, followed. Like "Jane Annie" it was not a success.[525c] He also wrote other plays based on his fiction, including "Brigadier Gerard," "The Tragedy of the Korosko"—(The Fires of Fate), "Rodney Stone"—(The House of Temperley), and, his most successful play, "The Speckled Band."[110d] Doyle's skills as a dramatist contributed to the theatrical aspects of Holmes, the detective.

111. The illness of his wife was responsible for the introduction by Arthur Conan Doyle of skiing in Davos which is in the Grisons canton of eastern Switzerland.[277] By his own account:

> . . . *I can claim to have been the first to introduce skis into the Grisons division of Switzerland, or at least to demonstrate their practical utility as a means of getting across in winter from one valley to another.*[375ee]

He is undoubtedly referring to what today is called cross-country skiing. More recently, two articles in the *London Times* have given him credit for introducing skis in general in Grisons.[158,823] A letter to the editor, however, objected that it was a Colonel Napier who was the first to ski in Davos.[599] Nonetheless Conan Doyle did much to promote the expansion of this healthy sport.

112. The statement by Sir Eustace's wife reveals her utter anguish at being irrevocably tied to an alcoholic. (Abbe 493) It also reveals Conan Doyle's views on the subject, which he is expressing through her. This story was published in 1927, 18 years after his almost equally forceful pamphlet on "Divorce Law Reform."[344] Once Conan Doyle assumed a cause he did so with apparent total acceptance, commit-

ment, and energy. Fortunately, he did not use his Sherlock Holmes adventures as a vehicle for other crusades, except for one phrase, "window-breaking Furies," (Last 794) which may refer to the suffragettes whom he detested. He exhibited considerable restraint in not including any references to spiritualism in the 13 Canonical stories he wrote after 1916, when he totally accepted and committed himself to this cause.

113. Holmes had a variety of pipes including ones made out of clay, of the root of the brier (briar), and of cherrywood.[873] But, he had a greater number of pipes than these, as evidenced by Watson's observation of his mantelpiece. "A litter of pipes, tobacco-pouches, syringes, pen-knives, revolver cartridges and other *débris* was scattered over it." (Dyin 442) The number was such that they were also found in "the coal-shuttle, which contained . . . the pipes and tobacco." (Maza 735) Probably one of the few types of pipes which Holmes did not have was the one which has become his symbol. The pipe with a curved stem was introduced by William Gillette in portraying Holmes.[99] He found that he could speak better on stage with the bowl beneath the level of his mouth. The calabash with its Meerschaum bowl [520] is now famous because of its supposed connection with the famous detective.

114. The harmful effects of smoking are now well know, including cancer of the lung, heart attacks, and chronic lung disease.[946] Fortunately, for Holmes, pipe smokers are at lower risk than cigarette smokers. But, today smoking has become a cause célèbre for nonsmokers.[169] Reaction such as Watson's to the fumes generated by Holmes' pipe has become raised to a societal and even legal level. In addition to the discomfort, innocent bystanders may have increased levels of carbon monoxide in their blood.[418] For a heavy smoker as was Holmes it was difficult to stop even for a friend for several reasons. There was no great pressure from his society, the serious health problems had not been clarified as yet, and it can be a manifestation of tension to which he was often exposed.[529] It is now generally agreed that the heavy

smoking habit can have both pharmacological and psychological bases.[799] Conan Doyle may not have been aware of its addictive nature, but he appreciated its stimulant effect (due to nicotine) which Holmes found necessary in grappling with complex problems.[584]

115. The *A Study in Scarlet*[244] which contains this account of animal experimentation was published in 1887, a year after Conan Doyle strongly objected to a speech by a clergyman against vivisection for scientific research.[904]

116. Strychnine was long thought to be a useful drug. Today it is considered not to have any therapeutic value.[479e]

117. The victims of the devil's foot root had faces "twisted into the same distortion of terror . . . as though he had died in a very paroxysm of fear." (Devi 517–518) Such distorted facial features are present after death in several of Conan Doyle's characters. The cause appears to be varied. Charles Baskerville, who died of his long-standing heart condition while trying to escape the hound, had an "incredible facial distortion." (Houn 12) This must be due to fear because "Men who die from heart disease, or any sudden natural cause, never by any chance exhibit agitation upon their features." (Stud 232) Bartholomew Sholto who was poisoned by a strychnine-like substance did have such facial distortion. (Sign 639) Severe contortions of the human face add to the fearful but awe-inspiring aura of Conan Doyle's mysteries. An exception was Jefferson Hope whose face had a placid smile after death due to a ruptured aneurysm, possibly because he had had his revenge. (Stud 230) The most detailed description is that of the body of Enos J. Drebber. (Stud 168)

> *On his rigid face there stood an expression of horror, and, as it seemed to me, of hatred, such as I have never seen upon human features. This malignant and terrible contortion, combined with the low forehead, blunt nose, and prognathous [jutting] jaw, gave the dead man a singularly simous and ape-like appearance.*

These details also create a repulsion for the individual who was later revealed as the murderer of John Ferrier and the abductor of his daughter. Such facial expressions after death have a much higher incidence in the world of fiction than in ours. A facial expression of terror is depicted in a book of drawings of 1806 by a famous surgeon, Sir Charles Bell, but this was from a living model and not a dead one.[615]

118. Arthur Conan Doyle showed considerable interest in firearms. In 1901, after returning from the Boer War, he organized a rifle club at his Undershaw home, "but it is really an attempt to engraft the commando system on British soil."[878] With the onset of World War I he helped organize the Crowborough Company of the Sixth Royal Sussex Volunteer Regiment.[375ff] As a private he drilled with rifle and bayonet. He also proposed bulletproof armour for soldiers.[375gg]

119. Conan Doyle may have obtained a typewriter in 1890, before leaving Southsea. On August 13 he wrote a letter to Mrs. George A. Sala, evidently in response to an enquiry about purchasing a typewriter.[251] "My getting a machine is rather in the nature of an experiment. I am myself a dabbler in letters. . . if you are willing to divide the respective sums named and make $10 I shall be happy to send my cheque."

120. Mark Twain also used a thumbprint as a plot device, considerably before Conan Doyle's account in 1903. (Norw) In *Life on the Mississippi,*[145] published in 1883, a dying man told the story of the brutal murder of his wife and two children by soldiers in disguise. One had left a thumbprint on a bloodied manuscript. The old man disguised himself as a fortune teller who read fortunes from prints of thumbs using red paint and white paper.

> *. . . there was one thing about a person that never changed, from the cradle to the grave—the lines in the ball of the thumb; . . . these lines were never exactly alike in the thumbs of any two human beings. . . . I pored over those*

> *mazy red spirals, with that document which bore the right-hand thumb and fingermarks of that unknown murderer, printed with the dearest blood-to me-that was ever shed on this earth.*

He of course finds the culprit, and with somewhat more facility than Sherlock Holmes.

121. Christison also examined the body of Margery Campbell, who had been suffocated by Burke to sell for anatomical study. He found blood on the sheath of the spinal cord. He considered it as occurring after death, because he produced the same lesion in another corpse by bending the head forcefully down on the chest.[520f]

122. The formulation of an initial hypothesis is also of basic importance in scientific research. Most experiments are carried out with the purpose of testing an hypothesis.[72] It stimulates the development of new experiments and observations. Without a hypothesis, research would be aimless and nondirective. Only when a research hypothesis has been "proven" under all circumstances can it be elevated to a theory.

123. On the basis of information from Dame Jean Conan Doyle (personal communication Aug. 15, 1983) and listings in the *Medical Directory 1930* (86th Annual Issue, London, J. & A. Churchill, 1930) the three "Veterinarians of the Old Horse" were: Matthew Lovell Mackintosh "our local G.P.;" John Parkinson (cardiologist) "[who] must also have been a doctor in London, possibly also a specialist;" and Cecil Webb-Johnson (associated with the National Hospital for Diseases of the Heart, London) "[who] was the London specialist."

124. In a BBC radio interview on February 9, 1982, Dame Jean Conan Doyle had the following comments on her father as a physician. "It is true he had a lot of time on his hands as a doctor because he tried to build up a practice from scratch . . . I never thought he was a failed doctor. Of course he was a failure from a financial point of view, but I am sure he was a very good GP. He cared for people very much. I'm sure that many of his patients were not required to pay."

APPENDICES

APPENDIX A

Medical Chronology of Doctor Arthur Conan Doyle

BIRTH

May 22, 1859	11 Picardy Place, Edinburgh

EARLY EDUCATION (1865–1876)

1865–1867	Day School, Edinburgh
1868–1869	Hodder Preparatory School, Lancashire, England
1870–1875	Stonyhurst Jesuit College, Lancashire, England
1875–1876	Stonyhurst Branch School, Feldkirch, Austria

MEDICAL SCHOOL YEARS (1876–1881)

October, 1876	Entered Edinburgh Medical School
Summer, 1878	Student Assistant to Dr. Richardson, Sheffield, and Dr. Elliot, Shropshire

APPENDIX A

Summer, 1879	Student Assistant to Dr. Hoare, Birmingham
September, 1879	First Medical Publication (Gelseminum)
October, 1879	First short story (The Mystery of Sasassa Valley)
1880	Ship's Surgeon on Arctic Whaler *Hope* for 7 months
1880	Student Assistant to Dr. Hoare, Birmingham
August, 1881	Graduated as Bachelor of Medicine and Master of Surgery

MEDICAL PRACTICE YEARS (1881–1891)

September, 1881	Medical Assistant to Dr. Hoare, Birmingham
Oct. 22, 1881–Jan. 14, 1882	Ship's Surgeon on the cargo boat *Mayumba* to the Gold Coast of Africa
Feb.–Apr., 1882	Medical Assistant to Dr. Hoare, Birmingham
May–June, 1882	Medical Assistant to Dr. Budd, Plymouth
July, 1882	Began own practice in Southsea, Portsmouth
July, 1885	M.D. degree from University of Edinburgh
August, 1885	First marriage, Louise Hawkins
1887	First Sherlock Holmes Story (A Study in Scarlet)
1889	First novel (*Micah Clarke*)
1889	First child born, Mary
November, 1890	Trip to Berlin to investigate Koch's tuberculin cure
December, 1890	Left general practice in Southsea
Jan. 5–Mar. 9, 1891	Attending eye lectures at the Krankhaus in Vienna, Austria
April 6, 1891	Eye specialist at 2 Devonshire Place in London
May 4, 1891	Onset of Influenza
June, 1891	Gave up medical career for full-time writing

THE VERSATILE CONAN DOYLE (1891–1929)

1892	Birth of first son, Kingsley
1893–1895	Travels to America, Switzerland
1894	*Round the Red Lamp* (medical short Stories)
1895	*Stark Munro Letters*—(autobiographic novel)
1896	An Egyptian interlude
Feb. 28–July 11, 1900	Senior physician, Boer War, at Langman Hospital, Bloemfontein, South Africa
1901	Lost election for seat in Parliament

Aug. 9, 1902	Knighted by Edward VII
1906	Death of first wife
1907	Second marriage, Jean Leckie
1908	LL.D. conferred by the University of Edinburgh
1908	Honored at the Encaenia, Oxford
1912	Birth of last child, Jean
1916	Visited three war fronts in France and Italy
1918	First publication on Spiritualism (*The New Revelation*)
1920	Beginning of world-wide speaking tours on spiritualism—Africa, Australia, Canada, France, Scandinavia, United States
1924	Autobiography, *Memories and Adventures*
1927	Last Sherlock Holmes Stories, Filmed interview

DEATH (1930)

October, 1929	Woke up with chest pain while on tour in Copenhagen
July 7, 1930	Died at his home (Windlesham), Crowbrough, Sussex
July 11, 1930	Buried on the grounds of Windlesham
1940	Death of wife, Jean
1955	Bodies of Conan Doyle and his wife were moved to Minstead, Hampshire in the graveyard of its 13th century church, near one of his homes (Bignell Wood)

APPENDIX B

Medical Writings of Doctor Arthur Conan Doyle—By Category

A. Nonfiction

1. M.D. Thesis—Tabes Dorsalis — 1885
2. Letters to Editors
    - a. Gelseminum — 1879
    - b. Leucocythaemia — 1882
    - c. Contagious Disease Act — 1883
    - d. American Medical Diplomas — 1884
    - e. Gout — 1884
    - f. Compulsory Vaccination (3) — 1887
    - g. The Consumption Cure — 1890
    - h. Chloroform — 1897
    - i. Conan Doyle in ''Luck'' — 1900
    - j. The Case of Edalji (5) — 1907
    - k. Soldiers in London (2) — 1907
    - l. Guinea Pig or Man — 1910
    - m. (Pulse Rate in Trance) — 1923

n. (Vital Signs in Trance) 1927
o. The Prenatal State 1927

3. Journal Articles
   a. Life and Death in the Blood 1883
   b. Dr. Koch and his Cure 1890
   c. Enteric Fever in South Africa 1900
   d. The Romance of Medicine 1910
4. Forewords for Books
   a. *Exercise,* by Sandow 1907
   b. *Alloquia,* by Marinus 1928
5. Obituary—Captain Malcolm Leckie 1915
6. Chapters of Books
   Memories and Adventures 1924
   Chapter III Recollections of a Student
   Chapter VI My First Experience in Practice
   Chapter VII My Start at Southsea
   Chapter IX Pulling up Anchor
   Chapter X The Great Break
   Chapter XVI The Start for South Africa
7. Doggerel
   Marginalia in *The Essentials of Materia Medica and Therapeutics* 1877

B. *Fiction*

1. Short Stories
   a. Crabbe's Practice 1884
   b. The Great Keinplatz Experiment 1885
   c. The Surgeon of Gaster Fell 1890
   d. In *Round the Red Lamp*
      A Physiologist's Wife 1890
      A Straggler of '15 1891
      Lot No. 249 1892
      The Los Amigos Fiasco 1892
      The Case of Lady Sannox 1893
      Behind the Times 1894
      His First Operation 1894
      The Third Generation 1894
      A False Start 1894

The Curse of Eve 1894
Sweethearts 1894
A Question of Diplomacy 1894
A Medical Document 1894
The Doctors of Hoyland 1894
The Surgeon Talks 1894

e. The Retirement of Signor Lambert 1898

2. Novels
   a. *The Parasite* 1894
   b. *The Stark Munro Letters* 1895
3. Poetry—in *Songs of the Road* 1911
   Religio Medici
   Darkness
4. Chapters of Books
   The Firm of Girdlestone 1890
   Chapter V Modern Athenians
   Chapter VI A Rectorial Election
   Chapter VII England Versus Scotland
   Chapter VIII A First Professional
   Chapter IX A Nasty Cropper

Medical Writings Of Doctor Arthur Conan Doyle—References By Year

1877

1. Marginalia in *The Essentials of Materia Medica and Therapeutics,* by A. B. Garrod, 6th ed., London, Longmans, Green, 1877.

1879

2. Letter to Editor: Gelseminum as a Poison: *British Medical Journal,* 2:483, 1879 (Sept. 20).

1882

3. Letter to Editor: Notes on a Case of Leucocythaemia: *Lancet,* 1:490, 1882 (Mar. 25).

1883

4. Life and Death in the Blood: *Good Words,* 24:178–181, 1883.
5. Letter: (Contagious Disease Act): *Med. Times & Gazette,* June 16, 1883, pp. 671–672.

1884

6. Letter to Editor: The Remote Effects of Gout: *Lancet,* 2:978–979, 1884 (Nov. 29).
7. Crabbe's Practice: *The Boy's Own Paper,* Christmas, 1884, pp. 54–57.
8. Letter to Editor: American Medical Diplomas: *Evening News* (Portsmouth), Sept. 23, 1884, p. 2, col. 4.

1885

9. *An Essay Upon the Vaseomotor Changes in Tabes Dorsalis* and on the Influence which is Exerted by the Sympathetic Nervous System in that Disease, being a Thesis presented in the Hope of Obtaining the Degree of Doctorship of Medicine of the University of Edinburgh, M.D. Thesis, U. of Edinburgh, handwritten, unpublished, 1885, 88 pages.
10. The Great Keinplatz Experiment: *Belgarvia Magazine,* V. 52, July 1885.

1887

11. Letter to Editor: Compulsory Vaccination: *Evening Mail* (Portsmouth) July 15, 1887.
12. Letter to Editor: Compulsory Vaccination: *Portsmouth Times,* July 16, 1887.
13. Letter to Editor: Compulsory Vaccination: *Hampshire County Times,* July 27, 1887.

1890

14. Letter to Editor: The Consumption Cure: *The Daily Telegraph* (London), Nov. 20, 1890, p. 3.
15. Dr. Koch and His Cure: *The Review of Reviews,* 2:552–556, 1890.
16. A Physiologist's Wife: *Blackwood's Magazine,* 148: 339–351, 1890 (Sept.) (also in Item 26, pp. 120–155).

17. The Surgeon of Gaster Fell: *Chambers' Journal,* 67:770–890, 1890 (December).
18. *The Firm of Girdlestone,* Chapters V, VIII, IX: London, Chatto & Windus, 1890.

1891

19. A Straggler of '15: *Harper's Weekly,* 35:205–207, 1891 (Mar.) (dramatized as the Story of Waterloo, 1907). (also in Item 26, pp. 20–45).

1892

20. Lot No. 249: *Harper's Magazine,* 86:525–544 (Sept.). (also in Item 26, pp. 281–294).
21. The Los Amigos Fiasco: *The Idler,* 2:548–557, 1892 (Dec.). (also in Item 26, pp. 281–294).

1893

22. The Case of Lady Sannox: *The Idler*, 4:331–342, 1893 (Nov.). (also in Item 26, pp. 156–173).

1894

23. *The Parasite*: London, A. Constable & Co., 1894.
24. The Doctors of Hoyland: *The Idler*, 5:227–238, 1894 (April). (also in Item 26, pp. 295–315).
25. Sweethearts: *The Idler*, 5:451–457, 1894 (June). (also in Item 26, pp. 109–119).
26. *Round the Red Lamp being Facts and Fancies of Medical Life*, London, Methuen & Company, 1894.
27. Behind the Times in *Round the Red Lamp* pp. 1–8
28. His First Operation in *Round the Red Lamp* pp. 9–19
29. The Third Generation in *Round the Red Lamp* pp. 46–64
30. A False Start in *Round the Red Lamp* pp. 65–88
31. The Curse of Eve in *Round the Red Lamp* pp. 89–108
32. A Question of Diplomacy in *Round the Red Lamp* pp. 174–199 (dramatized, 1907)
33. A Medical Document in *Round the Red Lamp* pp. 200–219
34. The Surgeon Talks in *Round the Red Lamp* pp. 316–328

1895

35. *The Stark Munro Letters* Being a Series of Letters Written by J. Stark Munro, M.D. to his Friend and Former Student,

Herbert Swanborough, of Lowell, Massachusetts During the Years 1881–1884: London, Longmans, Green and Company, 1895, 346 pages.

1896

36. (Chloroform): in The Queen's Reign, Its Most Striking Characteristic and Most Beneficient Achievement: *The Temple Magazine*, 1:709–712, 1897.

1898

37. The Retirement of Signor Lambert: *Pearson's Magazine*, 6:720–725, 1898.

1900

38. Conan Doyle in "Luck". Surgeons to the Front. Heroism of Tommy Atkins. Hospital Stories: *Daily News*, April 16, 1900, p. 8.
39. The War in South Africa. The Epidemic of Enteric Fever at Bloemfontein: *British Medical Journal*, 2:49–50, 1900 (July 7)

1907

40. Foreword in *The Construction and Reconstruction of the Human Body. A Manual of the Therapeutics of Exercise*, by E. Sandow, London, John Bale, Sons and Danielson, Ltd. 1907, pp. ix–xi.
41. Letter to Editor: The Question of Eyesight: *Daily Telegraph*, Jan. 15, 1907, p. 9, col. 7.
42. Letter to Editor: Edalji Case: *Daily Telegraph*, Jan. 16, 1907, p. 9, col. 7.
43. Letter to Editor: The Edalji Case: *Daily Telegraph*, Jan. 18, 1907, p. 9, col. 7.
44. Letter to Editor: The Edalji Case: *British Medical Journal*, 1:173, 1907 (Jan. 19).
45. Letter to Editor: the Case of George Edalji. A Question for Ophthalmologists: *Lancet*, 1:189, 1907 (Jan. 19).

1910

46. Letter to Editor: Guinea Pig or Man: *Daily Express*, Jan. 11, 1910, p. 4, col. 5.
47. The Romance of Medicine: *St. Mary's Hospital Gazette*, 16:100–106, 1910 (October).

1911

48. Religio Medici: in *Songs of the Road*, London, Smith, Elder & Co., 1911, pp. 82–85.
49. Darkness: in *Songs of the Road*, London, Smith, Elders & Co., 1911, pp. 91–92.

1915

50. Obituary. Captain Malcolm Leckie, D.S.O., R.A.M.C.: *Guy's Hospital Gazette*, 29:3–4, 1915.

1917

51. Letter to Editor: Soldiers in London: *The Times*, Feb. 6, 1917.
52. Letter to Editor: Soldiers in London: *The Times*, Feb. 10, 1917.

1923

53. Letter to Editor: Pulse-Rate in Trance: *J. Amer. Soc. Psychical Res.*, 17:274–375, 1923.

1924

54. *Memories and Adventures*, Chapters III, VI, VII, IX, X, XVI: London, Hodder & Stoughton, 1924.

1927

55. Letter to Editor: The Affairs of Hulham House: *Light*, June 11, 1927.
56. Letter to Editor: The Pre-Natal State: *Light*, Nov. 19, 1927.

1928

57. Preface: in *Alloquia. Experiences and some Reflections of a Medical Practitioner* by D. Marinus, London, C.W. Daniel Co., 1928, pp. 7–8.

APPENDIX C

The University of Edinburgh Connection

Table 1
University of Edinburgh Medical Faculty 1876–1881*

John Hutton Balfour	Botany	1876–1879
Alexander Crum Brown	Chemistry	1876–1881
Sir Robt. Christison, Bart.	Materia Medica	1876–1877
Prof. Dickson	Botany	1879–1881
T. R. Fraser	Materia Medica	1878-1881
Thomas Laycock	Practice of Physic	1876–1877
	Chemical Medicine	1876–1877
Joseph Lister	Clinical Surgery	1876–1878
Douglas Maclagan	Clinical Medicine	1876–1881
	Medical Jurisprudence	1879–1881
William Rutherford	Institutes of Medicine	1876–1881
W. R. Sanders	Clinical Medicine	1876–1881
	General Pathology	1876–1881

Table 1 (Cont.)
*University of Edinburgh Medical Faculty 1876–1881**

James Spence	Surgery	1876–1881
Sir James Young Simpson	Dis. of Women & Children	1876–1881
	Midwifery	1876–1881
Sir Thomas Grainger Stewart	Practice of Physic	1877–1881
Sir Charles Wyville Thomson	Natural History	1876–1881
Sir William Turner	Anatomy	1876–1881

*As listed in the Edinburgh University Calendars from 1876 to 1881. Doctor Joseph Bell is not listed in the University Calendars because he was one of the extra-academic teachers.

Table 2
*Conan Doyle's Grades at the University of Edinburgh**[876]

Preliminary	French	S
	German	D
	Moral Philosophy	S
April, 1878	Botany	S +
	Natural History	S +
	Chemistry	S
	Chemical Testing	B
April, 1879	Anatomy	S
	Institutes of Medicine	S
	Materia Medica	B
	Pathology	S +
June, 1881	Surgery	S
	Midwifery	S
	Practice of Physic	B
	Medical Jurisprudence	S
	Clinical Surgery	S –
	Clinical Medicine	S

* B = better than average
S = satisfactory (average)
D = pass but below average

APPENDIX D

Doctors in the Fictional Works (non-Sherlockian)

Table 1
Doctors in the Medical Short Stories

Althaus, von	Anatomy Prof.	The Great Keinplatz Experiment
Archer	Surgeon	His First Operation
Barton	G.P.	Crabbe's Practice
Baumgarten, Alexis von	Physiology Prof.	The Great Keinplatz Experiment
Bellingham, Edward	Medical Student	Lot 249

APPENDIX D

Table 1 (Cont.)
Doctors in the Medical Short Stories

Brown, Fraser	Alienist	The Surgeon of Gaster Fell
Browne, Anthony	Laryngologist	His First Operation
Cameron, J., Sr.	G.P.	The Surgeon of Gaster Fell
Cameron, Jr.	Surgeon	The Surgeon of Gaster Fell
Crabbe, Thomas Waterhouse	G.P.	Crabbe's Practice
Davidson	G.P.	Crabbe's Practice
Doctor	G.P.	A Straggler of '15
Doctor	G.P.	Sweethearts
Foster, Theodore	G.P.	A Medical Document
Grey, Ainslie	Physiology Prof.	A Physiologist's Wife
Hargrave	Surgeon	A Medical Document
Hartmann, Fritz von	Medical Student	The Great Keinplatz Experiment
Hastie, Jephro	Medical Student	Lot 249
Hayes	Surgeon	His First Operation
Hobson	G.P.	Crabbe's Practice
Horton	G.P.	The Doctors of Hoyland
M'Namara	Surgeon	A Surgeon Speaks
Manson, Charles	Psychiatrist	A Medical Document
Markham	G.P.	Crabbe's Practice
Miles	G.P., Obstetrics	The Curse of Eve
Murphy	Pathologist	His First Operation
Narrator	G.P.	The Los Amigos Fiasco
Narrator	G.P.	Sweethearts
Narrator	G.P.	Behind the Times
O'Brien	Physiology Prof.	A Physiologist's Wife
Patterson	G.P.	Behind the Times
Peterson	Plastic Surgeon	His First Operation
Peterson, Plumtree	G.P.	Lot 249
Prichard	G.P. & Obstetrics	The Curse of Eve
Ripley, James	G.P.	The Doctors of Hoyland
Selby, Horance	Venereologist	The Third Generation
Smith, Abercrombie	Medical Student	Lot 249
Smith, Verrinder	G.P.	The Doctors of Hoyland
Stoddard	Ophthalmologist	His First Operation
Stone, Douglas	Surgeon	The Case of Lady Sannox

APPENDIX D

Table 1 (Cont.)
Doctors in the Medical Short Stories

Walker, James	Neurologist	The Surgeon Talks
Wilkinson, Horace	G.P.	A False Start
Winter	G.P.	Behind the Times

Table 2
Doctors in the Medical Novels

Cullingworth, Sr.	G.P.	The Stark Munro Letters
Cullingworth, Jr.	G.P.	The Stark Munro Letters
Dimsdale, Sr.	G.P.	The Firm of Girdlestone
Dimsdale, Thomas	Medical Student	The Firm of Girdlestone
Gilroy, Austin	Physiology Professor	The Parasite
Garraway, Jack	Medical Student	The Firm of Girdlestone
Horton	G.P.	The Stark Munro Letters
Munro, Sr.	G.P.	The Stark Munro Letters
Munro, Stark	G.P.	The Stark Munro Letters
Peterson	G.P.?	The Stark Munro Letters
Porter	G.P.	The Stark Munro Letters
Wilson,	Psychology, Professor	The Parasite

Table 3
Doctors in the Nonmedical Short Stories

Angus,	G.P.	The Nightmare Room
Armitage, Robert	Medical Student	John Barrington Cowles
Atherton, J.H.	G.P.	The Horror of the Heights
Baker, Solomon	Medical Student	Our Derby Sweepstakes
Bannerman	Research	Hilda Wade VII
Benger	G.P.	An Exciting Christmas Eve
Cousins	G.P.	The Lonely Hampshire Cottage
Cowles, John Barrington	Medical Student	John Barrington Cowles
Doctor	Prison Surgeon	My Friend the Murderer
Doctor	Ship's Surgeon	De Profundis
Doctor	London physician	De Profundis
Gaster, Octavius	Ship's Surgeon	The Winning Shot
Hamilton	G.P.	The Beetle Hunter

Table 3 (Cont.)
Doctors in the Nonmedical Short Stories

Hardacre	G.P.	The Brown Hand
Hardcastle, James	G.P.	The Terror of Blue John Gap
Hewett, Jack	House Surgeon	The Brown Hand
Holden, Sir Dominick	Surgeon, Pathologist	The Brown Hand
Jackson, J. S.	Jephson's partner	J. Habakuk Jephson's Statement
Jephson, Joseph Habakuk	Consultant	J. Habakuk Jephson's Statement
Lana, Aloysuis Xavier	G.P.	The Black Doctor
Langemann	Medico-jurist	The Silver Hatchet
Larousse	Physician	The Governor of St. Kitts
Latour, Henry	Medical Student	The Cabman's Story
Lawrence, Hugh	Medical Student	Uncle Jeremy's Household
Linchmere, Lord	Retired	The Beetle Hunter
MacDonald, Archie	Student, G.P.	Our Midnight Visitor
Mayby	G.P.	Hilda Wade VII
Medical Man	Hospital	Recollections of Captain Wilkie
Mercer	Professor	The Pot of Caviare
Messinger	Mesmerist	John Barrington Cowles
Middleton	G.P.	The King of the Foxes
Montgomery, Robert	Medical Student	The Croxley Master
Oldacre	Miner's Doctor	The Croxley Master
Picton	Psychiatrist	The Terror of Blue John Gap
Ray, John M'Alister	Medical Student	The Captain of the Polestar
Schleissinger	Army Surgeon	The Silver Hatchet
Severall	Medical Officer	The Fiend of the Cooperage
Sinclair	G.P.	The Silver Mirror
Smith, Kavanagh	Chest Physician	J. Habakuk Jephson's Statement
Stable, 'Baldy'	Fleet Surgeon	The Blighty of Sharkey
Stephanus	Greek Physician	An Iconoclast
Stube, T. E.	M.D.	Selecting a Ghost

APPENDIX D

Table 4
Doctors in the Nonmedical Novels

Atkinson	Surgeon	The Land of Mist
"Brodie"	Staff Surgeon	The Mystery of Cloomber
Challenger	Professor	The Lost World
Chirurgeon	War Surgeon	Micah Clarke
Easterling, John	G.P.	The Mystery of Cloomber
Felkin	Spirit Doctor	The Lost World
Fellow Royal College	Surgeon	Beyond the City
Haw, Sr.	G.P.	The Doings of Raffle Haw
Horscroft	G.P.	The Great Shadow
Horscroft, Jim	Student & Graduate	The Great Shadow
Jackson	Practitioner	Micah Clarke
Jordon	G.P.	A Duet
Letour, Achille	Medical Graduate	Refugees
Maupuis	Metaphysician	The Land of Mist
Physician	Practitioner	The White Company
Proudie	Quack	Beyond the City
Prussian	Surgeon	Brigadier Gerard at Waterloo
Purdie	Surgeon	The Great Shadow
Robinson	?	The Land of Mist
Scotton, Ross	Neurologist	The Land of Mist
Walker, Balthayer	G.P.	Beyond the City

APPENDIX E

Medicine in the Canonical Writings

Table 1 *Doctors*
Table 2 *Specialties*
Table 3 *Diseases*
Table 4 *Drugs and Poisons*
Table 5 *Forensic Science*
Table 6 *Violent Deaths*
Table 7 *Holmes and Medicine*
Table 8 *Medical Miscellanea*

PAGE NUMBERS contained in Table 1 and following (i.e., Illus *685*) refer to: Baring-Gould, W. S.: *The Annotated Sherlock Holmes,* 2 Vols., 1967.[41]

APPENDIX E

Key to the Story Names
***From: DeWaal, R. D.:* The International Sherlock Holmes, *1980 p. 14.*[197]**
(dates of publication have been added)

		*	*Year*
Abbe	Abbey Grange	2	1904
Bery	Beryl Coronet	2	1892
Blac	Black Peter	2	1904
Blan	Blanched Soldier	2	1926
Blue	Blue Carbuncle	1	1892
Bosc	Boscombe Valley Mystery	2	1891
Bruc	Bruce-Partington Plans	2	1908
Card	Cardboard Box	2	1891
Chas	Charles Augustus Milverton	2	1904
Copp	Copper Beeches	2	1892
Cree	Creeping Man	2	1923
Croo	Crooked Man	2	1893
Danc	Dancing Men	2	1903
Devi	Devil's Foot	2	1910
Dyin	Dying Detective	1	1913
Empt	Empty House	2	1903
Engr	Engineer's Thumb	2	1892
Fina	Final Problem	2	1893
Five	Five Orange Pips	1	1891
Glor	Gloria Scott	1	1893
Gold	Golden Pince-Nez	2	1904
Gree	Greek Interpreter	1	1893
Houn	Hound of the Baskervilles	2	1902
Iden	Case of Identity	1	1891
Illu	Illustrious Client	2	1925
Lady	Lady Frances Carfax	2	1911
Last	His Last Bow	2	1917
Lion	Lion's Mane	2	1926
Maza	Mazarin Stone	2	1921
Miss	Missing Three-Quarter	2	1904
Musg	Musgrave Ritual	1	1893
Nava	Naval Treaty	2	1893
Nobl	Noble Bachelor	1	1892
Norw	Norwood Builder	2	1903
Prio	Priory School	2	1904
RedC	Red Circle	2	1911
RedH	Red-Headed League	1	1891

APPENDIX E

Key to the Story Names (Cont.)

		*	*Year*
Reig	Reigate Squires	1	1893
Resi	Resident Patient	1	1893
Reti	Retired Colourman	2	1927
Scan	Scandal in Bohemia	1	1891
Seco	Second Stain	1	1904
Shos	Shoscombe Old Place	2	1927
Sign	Sign of the Four	1	1890
Silv	Silver Blaze	2	1892
SixN	Six Napoleons	2	1904
Soli	Solitary Cyclist	2	1904
Spec	Speckled Band	1	1892
Stoc	Stockbroker's Clerk	2	1893
Stud	Study in Scarlet	1	1887
Suss	Sussex Vampire	2	1924
Thor	Thor Bridge	2	1922
3Gab	Three Gables	2	1926
3Gar	Three Garridebs	2	1925
3Stu	Three Students	2	1904
Twis	Man with the Twisted Lip	1	1891
Vall	Valley of Fear	1	1915
Veil	Veiled Lodger	2	1927
Wist	Wisteria Lodge	2	1908
Yell	Yellow Face	1	1893

* Number of Volume in *The Annotated Sherlock Holmes*

Table 1
Doctors

Watson, John	G.P.	
alias (Hill Barton)		Illus 685
education, medical		Stud 143
experience		Stud 143, 145; Reig 331
expertise		Dyin 441, 450; Blue 458; Miss 475
health		Stud 143, 148, 153
practice		Blue 458; Sign 642; Houn 32; Bosc 134; Stoc 153, 154; Nava 179 Engi 209; Scan 347; Iden 413, 428; Croo 225, 226; Fina 306; Gold 350;

Table 1 (Cont.)
Doctors

		Norw 414; Illu 675; Maza 737; Cree 758, 761
reading		Sign 620; Stoc 153; Gold 350
wound		Sign 611, 620; Stud 143
Other Doctors		
Agar, Moore	Harley Street Consultant	Devi 508
Ainstree	Tropical Disease Specialist	Dyin 441
Anstruther	G.P.	Bosc 134
Armstrong, Leslie	Consultant	Miss 483, 485
Barnicot	G.P.	SixN 573
Beacher	G.P.	Engi 223
Bennet, Trevor	A medical degree	Cree 753, 764
Doctor	G.P.	Devi 512, 513
Ernest, Ray	G.P.	Reti 546, 547, 553
Farquhar	G.P.	Stoc 153
Ferrier	G.P.	Nava 176, 177
Fisher, Penrose	Consultant	Dyin 441
Fordham	G.P.	Glor 114
Horsom	G.P.	Lady 667
Jackson	Research Attendant G.P.	Croo 226
Kent, Mr.	Surgeon	Blan 717
Lownstein	Endocrinology Prof.	Cree 765
Meek, Sir Jasper	Harley Street Consultant	Dyin 441
Morphy	Comparative Anatomy Professor	Cree 753
Mortimer, James	Surgeon	Houn 3, 4, 5, 6, 7, 36
Oakshott, Sir Leslie	Surgeon	Illu 683
Palmer	Dr.	Spec 257
Presbury	Physiology Professor	Cree 751, 752, 753, 755
Pritchard	Dr.	Spec 257
Richards	G.P.	Devi 510
Roylott, Grimesby	G.P.	Spec 243, 245, 246, 257, 261
Saunders, James	Dermatology Consultant	Blan 719

Table 1 (Cont.)
Doctors

Somerton	Indian Medical Services	Sign 682
Stamford, young	G.P.	Stud 145
Sterndale	(Explorer) G.P.	Devi 516, 517
Starr, Lysander	(Mayor)	3Gar 646
Surgeon, local	Surgeon	Danc 536
Surgeon, ship	Surgeon	Glor 119, 121
Trevelyan, Percy	Nervous Diseases	Resi 267, 268
Verner	G.P.	Norw 414
Willows	G.P.	Bosc 141
Wood	G.P.	Vall 485

G.P. = General Practitioner

Table 2
Specialties

Anatomy	
femur	Shos 635
preservatives	Card 197
skull size	Blue 454; Houn 7; Fina 304
Anesthesia	Lady 669; 3Gab 729; Last 799
Anthropology	
ancient	Houn 7, 12, 13, 22, 48, 52, 54, 55, 73, 74; Devi 509; 3Gar 647
physical	Bosc 148; Stud 173; Sign 612, 615
Chemistry	
acetone	Copp 121
acids	Sign 635
baryta (barium)	Iden 413
Bunsen burner (lamp)	Nava 169; Stud 149; Sign 635
carbuncle	Blue 457
carbolic acid	Card 197
coal-tar	Empt 337
desk	Empt 345
guaiacum test	Stud 150
hemoglobin	Stud 150

Table 2 (Cont.)
Specialties

hydrocarbon	Sign 662
hydrochloric acid	Iden 413
litmus paper	Nava 169
pipette	Nava 169; Stud 150
prussic acid	Veil 461
reagent	Stud 150
rectified spirits	Card 197
retort	Nava 169; Copp 120; Sign 635; Stud 149
stains	Empt 345; Stud 153; Scan 349
test tube	Stud 150; Sign 635; Copp 120
vitriol (sulphuric acid)	Blue 457; Illu 688
Dentistry	Empt 346
Dermatology	Blan 719, 720, 721
Forensic	
Bertillon, Monseur	Houn 7
Dupin (Poe)	Stud 162
Holmes (Conan Doyle)	Houn 8
Lecoq (Gaboriau)	Stud 162
Genetics	
art skill	Gree 590
black skin	Yell 588
criminal	Fina 303; Empt 347
cruelty	Houn 91; Copp 129
handwriting	Regi 535
physical	Card 202
racial	Yell 588
Mental Disease	
alienist	Cree 156
psychologist	SixN 574
Neurology	Resi 268
Ophthalmology	
cataract knife	Silv 271
Pathology	Sign 620; Houn 5, 12; Resi 269

APPENDIX E

Table 3
Diseases

Addiction	
alcohol	Blue 344, Five 292; Copp 128; Veil 459; Card 199
cocaine	(see Table 7)
opium	Twis 368, 371; Sign 630
Ear & Eye	
blindness	Empt 344
cataract	Empt 330
deafness	Vall 496; Reig 344
short-sighted	Gold 356; Iden 406, 409
Exhaustion, absolute	Prio 607
Extremities	
clubfoot	Musg 124
gout	Miss 478
limp	Bosc 149; Houn 29
loss	Sign 627, 674; Beryl 293; Illus 682
rheumatism	Lady 656
slipped knee-cap	Miss 480
Heart	
aneurysm aorta	Stud 223, 224, 230
"broken"	Chas 568; 3Gab 725
failure	Houn 12; Shos 633, 641; Sign 627, 628, 629
rheumatic	Lion 177
valvular	Sign 625, 626
"weak"	Glor 110; Resi 270
Infections	
black Formosa corruption	Dyin 441
coolie disease	Dyin 440, 441, 443, 445, 448, 450
diphtheria	Glor 108
epidemic	Houn 50
malaria	Sign 627, 628, 673
measles	Abbe 495
meningitis	Suss 468
quinsy	Iden 409

Table 3 (Cont.)
Diseases

Tapanuli fever	Dyin 441
tetanus	Sign 635, 639
tuberculosis	Fina 314; Miss 490
typhoid	Stud 143, 176; Vall 497
yellow fever	Houn 16; Yell 588
Liver	
jaundice	Glor 119
Metabolic	
diabetes	Bosc 149
obesity	Copp 116; Gree 593
scurvy	Illu 677
Nervous System	
apoplexy	Croo 237
brain fever	Musg 128, 129, 130, 131; Nava 168; Copp 131; Card 203; Croo 230; Houn 103
fainting	Nobl 296; Bery 289; Empt 332, 333; Blan 721; SixN 576; Glor 109
*hydrocephalus	Copp 123
St. Vitus dance	Stoc 152; Gree 599
stroke	Glor 114
Psychiatric	
alcoholism	Abbe 493; Blac 400; Blue 458; Card 199; Copp 128; Five 192, 193; Shos 633; Veil 459
catalepsy	Resi 271, 272
depression	Croo 277
epileptic	Stud 196
*hysteria	Bery 283
*hypochondriasis	Sign 625, 626, 630, 631
insanity	Seco 312; Engr 216; Reig 334; SixN 574; Cree 756; Thor 588
malingering (valetudinarian)	Reig 337; Dyin 440–449; Illus 684
monomania (idée fixe)	SixN 574
nervous breakdown	Bosc 141
*psychosomatic	Blan 721

APPENDIX E

Table 3(Cont.)
Diseases

Respiratory	
asthma	Norw 415
cold	Stoc 154
pneumonia	3Gab 724
Skin	
erysipelis	Illus 684
ichthyosis	Blan 721
leprosy	Blan 719, 720
scabby (scabies)	Vall 550
Spine	
curvature	Vall 504
lumbago	Cree 755
twisted	Suss 466; Croo 236
Trauma (noncriminal)	
amputation	Sign 673
boxer's ears	Glor 109
dog bite	Glor 108; Cree 764
hack (skin gash)	Miss 480

* Term not used in *Canon* but based on interpretation of descriptions.

Table 4
Drugs and Poisons

Drugs	
Alcohol	Gree 604; Blue 464; Lion 786; Nava 189; Houn 101, 103; 3Stu 370; Prio 607; Engr 210; Empt 333; Wist 240
Ammonia	Gree 604
Amyl Nitrite	Resi 272
Anthropoid serum	Cree 764
Belladonna	Dyin 456
Caffeine	Wist 255
Carbolized bandages	Engr 211
Castor oil	Sign 431
Chloroform	Lady 669; 3Gab 729; Last 799

Table 4 (Cont.)
Drugs and Poisons

Cooling medicine	Sign 657
Curare	Suss 473
Ether	Lady 669
Hormone	Cree 761, 762, 763, 764, 765
Iodoform	Sign 349
Laudanum	Twis 368
Lemon	Gold 352
Morphine	Stud 153; Illu 683, 688; Cree 764
Opium	Twis 368, 371; Sign 630, 676; Wist 254; Silv 267, 268, 269
Paregoric	3Gab 726
Quinine	Sign 628
Silver nitrate	Sign 349
Strychnine	Sign 631
Poisons	
Alkaloid	Stud 149, 168, 172, 227, 228, 231, 232
Aqua tofana	Stud 184
Carbon Monoxide	Gree 604; Reti 555
Devil's Foot (Radix pedis diaboli)	Devi 524
Jellyfish (Cyanea capillata)	Lion 777, 786, 787
Snake	Spec 261
Strychnine-like	Sign 639
Prussic Acid	Gold 366, Reti 553; Veil 461

Table 5
Forensic Science

"Ballistics"	Reig 343; Empt 330, 331; Danc 537; Nobl 281; Stud 143, 162; Sign 611
Blood Identification	Stud 150
Prints, Animal	
cows	Prio 617
dog	Lion 784; Houn 14
horses	Prio 629
mongoose	Croo 231

Table 5 (Cont.)
Forensic Science

Prints, Human	
footprints	Sign 612, 629, 537, 685; Stud 167, 174; Houn 20; Bosc 148; Chas 570; Vall 494; Blac 401; Prio 620 RedC 700; Norw 423; Resi 277; Beryl 297; Croo 231 Danc 538; Engr 223; Wist 243, 248; Lion 778; Nava 185; Soli 393; Vall 487, 494, 502
handprint	Lion 778
knee print	Lion 778
thumb-print	Sign 617; Norw 425, 430; RedC 693
Prints, Tire	Prio 617, 618
Post-Mortem	
livor mortis	Musg 136
rigor mortis	Stud 191; Resi 276; Sign 635, 639; Thor 598
Skin	
bruises	Stud 149; Black 399; Houn 103

Table 6
Violent Deaths

MURDER		
Knife		
Gorgiano	RedC 700	(neck)
Lucas	Seco 307, 308	(heart)
Smith	Gold 352, 353, 356	(neck)
Stangerson	Stud 190, 192	(heart)
Firearms		
Adair	Empt 329, 330	(head)
Baldwin	Vall 481, 485, 518, 519	(head)
Crabbe	Vall 564	(?)
Cubitt	Danc 535, 536	(heart)
Kirwan	Reig 332	(heart)
Larbey, Mrs.	Vall 560	(?)
Milverton	Chas 569	(chest)

Table 6 (Cont.)
Violent Deaths

Blows to Head		
Brackenstall	Abbe 492	(poker)
Garcia	Wist 240, 243	(sandbag)
Heidigger	Prio 618	(stick)
McCarthy	Bosc 136, 148	(heavy stone)
Ronder	Veil 456, 459	(clawed club)
West	Bruc 434, 439, 451	(life-preserver)*
Workman	Stoc 166	(poker)
Drowning		
Douglas	Vall 574	(Atlantic)
Openshaw, Elias	Five 394	(pool)
Openshaw, John	Five 402	(Thames)
Miscellaneous		
Blessington	Resi 276, 278	(asphyxia)
Brunton	Musg 136, 138	(asphyxia)
Corey	Blac 400, 401	(harpoon)
Drebber	Stud 190	(stomach blow)
Ferrier	Stud 219, 221	(?)
Hyam	Vall 529	(?)
James, Billy	Vall 529	(?)
Jenkins, brother	Vall 560	(?)
Jenkins, elderly	Vall 560	(?)
Milman	Vall 529	(?)
Nicholson family	Vall 529	(?)
Stendals	Vall 560	(blown up)
Van Shorst	Vall 529	(?)
SUICIDE		
Gibson	Thor 590, 598, 605	(shot in head)
ACCIDENTAL		
Barclay	Croo 299	(struck head)
Openshaw, Joseph	Five 396	(fall)
Seldon	Houn 86, 87	(fall)
Straker	Silv 262, 267, 281	(horse kick)

*weighted stick

APPENDIX E

Table 7
Holmes and Medicine

Illnesses	
faked	Resi 274; Reig 337, 344; Scan 363; Dyin 439, 440, 441, 444, 456; Sign 660; Prio 620
starvation	Maza 735
strain	Reig 331
Knowledge of Medicine	
anatomy	Stud 148, 156
botany	Stud 156
chemistry	Stud 148, 153, 156
ears	Card 202, 203; Glor 109
hypertrophy	Twis 376
poisons	Stud 151
Life Style	
alcohol	Glor 109; Sign 662
cocaine	Stud 153; Scan 346; Twis 371; Yell 575; Sign 610, 611, 688; Miss 475; Five 399
coffee	Houn 18
exercise	Yell 575
manic-depressive	Stud 151; Reig 331; RedH 438
smoking	Glor 107; Twis 381; Dyin 449; Houn 17, 18; Devi 514; Engr 211; RedH 429; Five 399

Table 8
Medical Miscellanea

Army Medical Department	Stud 143
Hospitals	
Base Hospital, Peshawur	Stud 143
Broadmoor Asylum	Reti 554
Charing Cross	Houn 5, 6, 7
King's College	Resi 269
Leper Hospital, Buffelsspruit	Blan 718
St. Bartholomew	Stud 145, 149
Medical Health Officer	Houn 5

Table 8 (Cont.)
Medical Miscellanea

Medical Institutions	
Museum, College of Surgeons	Houn 36
Swedish Pathology Society	Houn 5
Medical Journals	
British Medical J.	Stoc 39; Blan 720
J. Psychology	Houn 5
Lancet	Houn 5; Blan 720
Medical Practice	Engr 212; Reti 547; Thor 594; RedC 697; Devi 508
Medical Schools	
Edinburgh University	Engi 233
London University	Stud 143; Resi 268
Medical Students	Card 195, 199
Medical Terminology	
arteries	Stud 143
atavism	Houn 5
bones	Houn 22; Bosc 142
cannula	Cree 754
carotid	Gold 353; Cree 764
condyle	Shos 635
dolichocephalic	Houn 7
dropsy	Shos 633
dyspnea	Houn 12
ears	Card 202, 203
epithelial scale	Shos 630
femur	Shos 635
heart valves	Sign 625, 626
heredity	Gree 590
hypodermic syringe	Sign 610; Cree 764
jaundice	Glor 199
livor	Musg 136
maxillary curve	Houn 22
obesity	RedH 419
occipital bone	Bosc 142
parietal bone	Bosc 142
parietal fissure	Houn 7
pinna	Card 202
plethoric	Sign 640; Chas 564
prognathus	Stud 168
pulse	Prio 607

Table 8 (Cont.)
Medical Miscellanea

rigor mortis	Sign 639
risus sardonicus	Sign 639
scorbutic	Illu 677
subclavian artery	Stud 143
supraorbital	Houn 7, 22
Other	
bodkin (used as lancet)	Stud 150
bath chair (wheelchair)	Gold 352
crutch, aluminum	Musg 127
microscope	Shos 630; 3Gar 647; Stud 150
nurses	Musg 131; Nava 170, 177; Devi 513
stethescope	Scan 349

REFERENCES

1. Abbott ME: History of Medicine in the Province of Quebec: Montreal, McGill U Press 1932
2. Abercrombie GH: John H. Watson, M.D.: Medical Digest Part 1, 20(10):63–67; Part 2, 20(11):54–56; Part 3, 20(12): 43–46, 1975
3. Abram HS: Conan Doyle Looks at Medicine: Medical Times 99:106–114, 1971
4. Ackerknecht EH: Rudolph Virchow, Doctor, Statesman, Anthropologist: Madison, U Wisconsin Press 1953 pp 105–118
5. ______ History and Geography of the Most Important Diseases: NY, Hafner Pub Co 1965 p 41, a. pp 109–117
6. ______ Great Doctors and Scientists as Freemasons: Clio Med 17:145–156, 1982
7. (Adams RD), Holmes KK: Symptomatic Neurosyphilis *in* Harrison's Principles of Internal Medicine 9th ed, KJ Isselbacher et al Eds, McGraw-Hill Co 1980 p 720
8. Admission Records of the Portsmouth Lunatic Asylum, 1882–1890: Portsmouth, City Records Office
9. Aitchison J: Letter to Editor: Daily Telegraph (London), Jan 14, 1907 p 10

10. ______ Letter to Editor: Daily Telegraph (London), Jan 17, 1907 pp 9–10
11. Alder C: Letter to Dr. Devloo: Maidenhead, Commonwealth War Graves Commission Feb 16, 1983
12. Alexander FG, Selesnick ST: The History of Psychiatry: An Evaluation of Psychiatric Thought and Practice from Prehistoric Times to the Present: NY, Harper & Row Pub 1966
13. Allen FA: Devilish Drugs Part One: Sherlock Holmes J 3:12–14, 1957
14. ______ Devilish Drugs Part Two: Sherlock Holmes J 3:11–12, 1958
15. Althaus J: Diseases of the Nervous System. Their Prevalence and Pathology: London, Smith, Edler & Co 1877
16. ______ On Sclerosis of the Spinal Cord: London, Longmans & Co 1885
17. Altman LK: Auto-experimentation. An Unappreciated Tradition in Medical Science: N Engl J Med 286:346–352, 1972
18. Andersen K: Crashing on Cocaine: Time Mag 121:22–31 Apr 11, 1983
19. Anderson JE: Grant's Atlas of Anatomy: 7th ed, Baltimore, Williams & Wilkins 1978, Figs 1–77, 1–79
20. Anderson PC: Murder in Medical Education: JAMA 204: 119–123, 1968
21. Anderson RGW, Simpson ADC: Edinburgh and Medicine. A Commemorative Catalogue of the Exhibition held at the Royal Scottish Museum, Edinburgh, June 1976–January 1977: Edinburgh, Royal Scottish Museum 1976
22. Annual Meeting Notes: Sir Arthur Conan Doyle: Br Med J 2:192, 1913
23. Appleyard OB: Jean-Paul Marat (1743–1793). Revolutionary and Doctor of Medicine: Practitioner 206:826–835, 1971
24. Arctic Exploration: Hampshire Post (Portsmouth), Dec 7, 1883
25. The Arctic Seas: Portsmouth Times, Dec 5, 1883
26. Arnold WJ: Hyperuricemia and Gout: *in* Current Therapy. Latest Approved Methods for the Practicing Physician, HF Conn Ed, Phila, WB Saunders 1980 pp 430–432

27. Arnstein F: The "Adventures" of Arthur Conan Doyle: Armchair Detective 3:166–169, 1970
28. Aronson ME: Sherlock Holmes, Father of Forensic Pathology: Trans Stud Coll Physicians Phila 4th series, 45:258–261, 1978
29. Asher R: Munchausen Syndrome: Lancet 1:339–341, 1951
30. ______ Malingering: Sherlock Holmes J 4:54–58, 1959
31. ______ Malingering: Trans Med Soc London, 75:34–44, 1959
32. Asimov I: The Problem of the Blundering Chemist: Sci Digest 88:8–17, 1980
33. Astrachan BM: The Cyclical Disorder of Sherlock Holmes: JAMA 196:142, 1966
34. Bailey L: The Gilbert and Sullivan Book: London, Cassell & Co 1952
35. Baillie M: The Morbid Anatomy of Some of the Most Important Parts of the Human Body: London, Johnson & Nicol 1793
36. Baker M: The Strange and Curious Case of Charles Altmount Doyle: *in* The Doyle Diary, NY, Paddington Press 1978 p xiv
37. Baker Street J 10:58, 1960
38. Ball D: Sir Arthur Conan Doyle 1859–1930: Practitioner 215: 359-368, 1975
39. Barber G: Equiping the Surgery. XI.—The Doctor's Bag: Practitioner 179:621–626, 1957
40. Bargainnier EF: Fog and Decadence: Images of the 1890's: J Popular Culture 12:19–29, 1978
41. Baring-Gould WS, Ed: The Annotated Sherlock Holmes. The Four Novels and the Fifty-Six Short Stories Complete by Sir Arthur Conan Doyle: 2nd ed, 2 Vols, NY, Clarkson N Potter Inc. a. II 335, b. I 606–609, 1967
42. Barnfield JE: Letter to Cdr. G. S. Stavert MBE, MA, RN (Ret'd): Feb 26, 1982
43. Barr R: Real Conversations.—V. A Dialogue Between Conan Doyle and Robert Barr: McClure Mag 3:503–509, 1894
44. Barrie JM, Doyle AC: Jane Annie; or The Good Conduct Prize. A New and Original Comic Opera: London, Chappell & Co 1893

45. Bates HR: Sherlock Holmes and Syphilis: Can Med Assoc J 113:815, 1975
46. ______ Dr. Watson and the Jezail Bullet: Va Med Bull 103:828–829, 1976
47. Batory DM: A Look Behind Conan Doyle's "Lost World": Riverside Quart 6:268–271, 1977
48. Baxby D: Jenner's Smallpox Vaccine. The Riddle of Vaccine Virus and its Origin: London, Heinemann Educational Books 1981
49. Bean WB: Walter Reed. A Biography: Charlottesville, U Press Virginia 1982
50. Beaumont W: Experiments and Observations on the Gastric Juice and the Physiology of Digestion: Plattsburgh, FP Allen 1833
51. Beaven DW: Morals and Ethics in Medical Research: NZ Med J 81:519–524, 1975
52. Beecher HK: Experimentation in Man: 169:461–478, 1959
53. Beerman H: A Few Remarks about the Blanched Soldier: Baker Street J 23:148–155, 1973
54. ______ Sherlock Holmes and Medical History: Trans Stud Coll Physicians Phila 45:243–248, 1978
55. Behbehani AM: The Smallpox Story. Man Finally Defeats an Old Adversary: J Kans Med Soc 81:447–456, 474, 1980
56. Bell J: A Manual of the Operations of Surgery: 3rd ed Edinburgh, MacLachlan & Stewart 1878, a. pp 130–132
57. ______ The Adventures of Sherlock Holmes: Bookman (London), Dec 1892 pp 79–81
58. Bendiner E: Elementary My Dear Doctor Doyle: Hosp Pract 17:180–212, 1982
59. Bennet JH: Case of Hypertrophy of the Spleen and Liver, in which Death Took Place from Suppuration of the Blood: Edinburgh Med Surg J 64:413–423, 1845
60. Bergonzi B, Ed: H.G. Wells, A Collection of Critical Essays: Englewood Cliffs, NJ, Prentice-Hall Inc 1976
61. Berlin Correspondent: The German Empire: Daily Telegraph (London), Aug 4, 1890 P 3
62. ______ The German Empire: Daily Telegraph (London), Aug 5, 1890 p 5

63. ______ Medical Congress at Berlin. Important Statement: Daily Telegraph (London), Aug 6, 1890 p 5
64. ______ The Consumption Cure: Daily Telegraph (London), Nov 11, 1890 p 3
65. ______ The Consumption Cure: Daily Telegraph (London), Nov 12, 1890 p 7
66. ______ The Consumption Cure. Dr. Koch's Paper: Daily Telegraph (London), Nov 15, 1890 p 3
67. ______ The Consumption Cure: Daily Telegraph (London), Nov 17, 1890 p 5
68. ______ The Consumption Cure. First English Patient: Daily Telegraph (London), Nov 18, 1890 p 5
69. Berridge V: East End Opium Dens and Narcotic Use in Britain: London J 4:3–28, 1978
70. ______ Professionalization and Narcotics: The Medical and Pharmaceutical Professions and British Narcotic Use 1868–1926: Psychol Med 8:361–372, 1978
71. Bertillon A: Does "Raffles" Exist or, The Myth of the Gentleman Burglar: Strand Mag 46:465–471, 1923
72. Beveridge WIB: The Art of Scientific Investigation: 3rd ed Melbourne, William Heinemann 1957 pp 46–52
73. Bigelow ST: In Defence of Joseph Bell: Baker Street J 10 ns:207–212, 1960
74. Billings JS: The National Medical Dictionary: Vol I, Phila, Lea Brothers & Co 1890 pp x, 294
75. Black DC: Doyle's Drug Doggerel: Baker Street J 31:90–103, 1981
76. Blacker H: Drink in Fiction. The Adventures of Sherlock Holmes: J Alcoholism 9:20–30, 1974
77. Blake JB: Benjamin Waterhouse and the Introduction of Vaccination: Phila, U Penn Press 1957
78. Blaw ME, Adkisson MA, Levin D, Garriott JC, Tindall RSA: Poisoning with Carolina Jessamine (Gelsemium sempervirens [L.] Ait): J Pediatr 94:998–1001, 1979
79. Bleiler EE: Introduction: *in* The Best Dr. Thorndyke Detective Stories, NY, Dover Pub 1973

80. Block EB: Science vs Crime. The Evolution of the Police Lab: San Francisco, Cragmont Pub 1979 p 9
81. Bloor DU: The Rise of the General Practitioner in the Nineteenth Century: J R Coll Gen Pract 28:288–291, 1978
82. Bodansky O: Physicians Who Abandoned Medicine for Literature: John Keats, Arthur Conan Doyle, Arthur Schnitzler and Somerset Maugham: Proc Virchow Pirquet Med Soc 32:13–22, 1978
83. Bond H: Sherlock Holmes in Toronto: Wilson Library Bull 54:505–507, 1980
84. Bonn RS: Radix Pedis Diaboli: Baker Street J 18:90–93, 1968
85. Book Review: Fiction. The Stark Munro Letters by A. Conan Doyle: Speaker (London), Sept 14, 1895
86. Booker C: Baker Street Disease: Sunday Telegraph (London), Dec 12, 1982 p 14
87. Borough of Portsmouth Lunatic Asylum. The Third Annual Report of the Committee of Visitors, Being the Report for the Year 1882: Portsea, Hollbrook & Sons 1883
88. Boswell R: Dr. Roylott's Wily Fillip with a Proem on Veneration of Vipers: Baker Street J 1:307–311, 1946
89. Böttiger LE: The Murderer's Vade Mecum: Br Med J 285:1819–1821, 1982
90. Bouchier IAD: Some Experiences of Ship's Surgeons During the Early Days of the Sperm Whale Fishery: Br Med J 285: 1811–1813, 1982
91. Boxill R: Shaw and the Doctors: NY, Basic Books Inc 1969
92. Brain P: Dr. Watson's War Wounds: Lancet 2:1354–1355, 1969
93. Brain R: Diseases of the Nervous System: 5th ed, London, Oxford U Press 1955 pp 434–436
94. Bramwell B: The Diseases of the Spinal Cord: Edinburgh, MacLachlan & Stewart 1882
95. Bramwell B: The Edinburgh Medical School and its Professors in My Student Days (1865–1869): Edinburgh Med J 30:133–156, 1923

96. Brenner RP: Holmes, Watson and Neurology: J Clin Psychiatry 41:202–205, 1980

97. Brinvillers, Marie-Madeleine-Marguérite d'Aubray, marquise de (1630–1676): 15th ed Vol II Micropaedia, Encyclopaedia Britannica, Chicago, U Chicago 1974 p 273

98. British Medical Association: Hampshire Times (Portsmouth), June 19, 1886 p 6

99. Brook G: Sherlock Holmes's Pipe: Baker Street J 10:152-154, 1960

100. Brothwell D, Sandison AT, Eds: Diseases in Antiquity. A Survey of the Diseases, Injuries and Surgery of Early Populations: Springfield, Ill, Charles C Thomas Pub 1967 p 369

101. Brown I: The Strange Career of Conan Doyle: Hist Med 4:3–4,6, 1972

102. Bruce D: Recent Researches into the Epidemiology of Malta Fever: J R Army Med Corps 8:225–235, 1907

103. The Bruce-Partington Night: Sherlock Holmes J 3:17–18, 1956

104. Budd G Jr: Amyloid Degeneration: Br Med J 1:659, 1879

105. ______ Why Does Tubercle Frequent the Apex of the Lung?: Br Med J 1:242, 1880

106. ______ Amyloid Degeneration: Lancet 1:322–324, 1880

107. ______ Treatment of Incontinence of Urine: Br Med J 2:536, 1880

108. ______ The Use of Esmarch's Bandage: Br Med J 2:648, 1880

109. ______ A Note Upon Elementary Pathology: Br Med J 2:837, 1880

110. ______ Gout: Br Med J 2:972, 1880

111. ______ Clinical Memorandum. Gout: Br Med J 1:13, 1881

112. Budd, George T., 1 Durnford-St., Plymouth: Medical Directory 1882, 38th Annual Issue, London, J A Churchill 1882 p 415

113. Bullard SR, Collins ML: Who's Who in Sherlock Holmes: NY, Taplinger Pub 1980

114. Bullock W: The History of Bacteriology: London, Oxford U Press 1938, a. p 237, b. pp 259, 157
115. Burgess A: Baker St Immortal: Sunday Observor (London), Dec 5, 1982
116. Burkitt DP: Etiology of Burkitt's Lymphoma—An Alternative Hypothesis to a Vectored Virus: JNCI 42:19-28, 1969
117. Burnett JC: Vaccinosis and Its Cure by Thuja: London, Homeopathic Pub Co 1884
118. Burstyn JN: Education and Sex: The Medical Case Against Higher Education for Women in England 1870-1900: Proc Am Philisoph Soc 117:79-89, 1973
119. Cahill GF Jr: Diabetes Mellitus: *in* Cecil Textbook of Medicine 15th ed. PB Beeson, W McDermott, JB Wyngaarden Eds, Phila, WB Saunders Co 1979 pp 1969-1989
120. Camnena A: The Alexiad of Anna Camnena: trans by ERA Sewter, Harmondsworth, Middlesex, Penguin Books 1969
121. Campbell M: Sherlock Holmes and Dr. Watson. A Medical Digression: London, Guy's Hosp Gazette Committee, 1934 p 4
122. Campbell M: Sir Arthur Conan Doyle, L.L.D., M.D. Born May 22, 1859. A Biographical Note: Br Med J 1:1341-1342, 1959
123. Caplan RM: The Circumstances of the Missing Biographer or Why Watson Didn't Narrate These Four Sherlock Holmes Stories: J Am Acad Dermatol 6:1112-1114, 1982
124. Carey EF: Holmes, Watson and Cocaine: Baker Street J 13 n s: 176-181, 195, 1963
125. Carr JD: The Life of Sir Arthur Conan Doyle: London, John Murray 1949 pp 21-35, a. pp 43-45, b. p 55, c. pp 169, 209-212, d. pp 236-276, e. pp 334-337, f. p 147, g. pp 144, 257, 289, h. p 129, i. p 297, j. p 140, k. p 198, 1. pp 336-337
126. Carter, HS: Medical Matters in the Sherlock Holmes Stories: From the Records of John H. Watson, M.D.:

Glasgow Med J 28:414–426, 1947
127. Cartwright, FF: Antiseptic Surgery: *in* Medicine and Science in the 1860s, FNL Paynter Ed, London, Wellcome Inst Hist Med 1968 pp 87–88
128. ______ Disease and History. The Influence of Disease in Shaping the Great Events of History: NY, Thomas Y Crowell Co 1972 p 138, a. pp 70–73
129. Casamajor L: Brain Fever: JAMA 147:1443–1446, 1952
130. Cash P: Medical Men at the Siege of Boston: Phila, Am Philosoph Soc 1973 pp 7–8
131. Caton R: The Electric Currents of the Brain: Br Med J 5:278, 1875
132. Ceccio J: Medicine in Literature: NY, Longman Inc 1978
133. Chamberlain's Portsmouth including Portsea, Southsea, Landport, and District: Portsmouth, G Chamberlain 1881–1882
134. Chance B: Clio Medica. Opthalmology: NY, Hafner Pub Co 1962
135. Charcot LM: Lectures on the Diseases of the Nervous System Delivered at La Salpêtrière: 2nd series, trans by G. Sigerson, London, New Sydenham Soc 1881
136. Chargaff E: How Genetics Got a Chemical Education: *in* The Origins of Modern Biochemistry. A Retrospect on Proteins, NY Academy Sci 325:345–360, 1979
137. Christison R: IV. Murder by Strangling, with Some Remarks on the Effects of External Violence on the Human Body after Death: Edinburgh Med Surg J 31:236–250, 1829
138. ______ On the Properties of the Ordeal Bean of Old Calabar: Monthly J Med 20:815–820, 1855
139. Clark B: The Pathological Holmes: *in* The Best of the Pips, NY, The Five Orange Pips of Westchester County 1955 pp 107–114
140. Clark CR: Letter to A.E. Rodin: Mar 9, 1983
141. ______ Personal Communication to A.E. Rodin: June 17, 1982
142. Clark JD: A Chemist's View of Canonical Chemistry: Baker Street J 14 n s: 153–155, 1964

143. Clarke E: History of British Medical Education: Br J Med Educ 1:7–15, 1966
144. Clarke WM: William Budd, M.D., F.R.S. "In Memoriam": Br Med J 1:163–166, 1880
145. [Clemens S] Twain M: Life on the Mississippi: NY, Harper & Bros Pub 1911 pp 239–240
146. Cohen, Lord of Birkenhead: Medical Education in Great Britain and Ireland 1868–1968: Practitioner 201:179–193, 1968
147. Colebrook L: Almroth Wright. Provocative Doctor and Thinker: London, Heinemann 1954
148. Coles R: William Carlos Williams. A Writing Physician: JAMA 245:41–42, 1981
149. Collins ET: History of Moorfield's Eye Hospital: London, K Lewis & Co 1929 pp 217–219
150. Colvin S, Ed: Letters and Miscellanies of Robert Louis Stevenson: NY, Charles Scribner Sons 1905 pp 341–342, 357–358, 359–360, 425–426
151. Commission of Three, Press Comments: Daily Telegraph (London), Jan 14, 1907 pp 9–107
152. Compulsory Vaccination: An Act Further to Extend and Make Compulsory the Practice of Vaccination: Med Times Gaz 7 n s: 222–223, 1853
153. Comric JD: The History of Scottish Medicine: 2nd ed, London, Bailliere, Tyndax & Cox 1932
154. Conan Doyle, On Way to U.S. Tells his Plans: NY American, May 21, 1914
155. Conan Doyle Says: 'Let the Militants Die of Starvation': NY American, May 28, 1914 p 5
156. Conan Doyle: Spectator, July 12, 1930 p 42
157. Conan Doyle: Nation, 131:86 July 23, 1930
158. Conan Doyle on Skis. Learning the Hard Way at Davos: Times (London), Jan 5, 1959 p 12
159. Conrad J: The Heart of Darkness: Edinburgh, Blackwood 1899
160. Coope J: Mania Sakhalinosa. An Episode in the Life of Dr. Anton Chekhov: Med Hist 23:29–37, 1979

161. Coope R: The Quiet Art. A Doctor's Anthology: Edinburgh, E & S Livingstone 1952
162: Cooper P: The Devil's Foot: Pharmaceut J 197:657–658, 1966
163. Cooperman EM: Marfan's Syndrome and Sherlock Holmes: Can Med Assoc J 112:423, 1975
164. Cope Z: Sherlock Holmes and the Doctors: Med Illustrated 3:227–229, 1949
165. Copeman WSC: A Short History of the Gout and the Rheumatic Diseases: Berkeley, U California Press 1964 p 5, a. p 12
166. ______ The Evolution of the Clinical Method in English Medical Education: Proc R Soc Med 58:887–894, 1965
167. Corcoran AC: A Mirror Up to Medicine: Phila, JB Lippincott Co 1961
168. The Cost of Medical Education: Lancet 2:588–590, 1895
169. Council on Scientific Affairs: Smoking and Health: JAMA 243:179–781, 1980

Courtney JF: The Medical History of Napoleon . . . see reference 176

Cousins N: The Physician in Literature . . . see reference 177

170. Craig PC: Memoirs of Sherlock Holmes. Through the Eyes of an Ophthalmologist: Trans Acad Ophthalmol Otolaryngol 25:42–43, 1972
171. Cromwell A: Dr. Conan Doyle and His Stories I.—A Pen Portrait of the Author: Windsor Mag 4:367–368, 1896
172. Crone HD, Keen TEB: Chromatographic Properties of the Hemolysin from the Cnidarian *Chironex Fleckeri:* Toxicon 7:79–87, 1969
173. Crowe SJ: Halstead of Johns Hopkins. The Man and His Men: Springfield, Ill, Charles C Thomas 1957 p 29
174. Cule J: A Doctor for the People. 2000 Years of General Practice in Britain: London, Update Books 1980 pp 103–110
175. Cunha BA: Typhoid Fever, the Typhus Like Disease. Historical Perspective: NY State J Med 82:321–324, 1982

176. Courtney JF: The Medical History of Napoleon Bonaparte: Resid & Staff Physc, April 52–57, 1970
177. Cousins N: The Physician in Literature: Phila, WB Saunders Co 1982
178. Curjel HEB: Doctors in the Works of Sir Arthur Conan Doyle, M.D.: Practitioner 204:423–426, 1970
179. Curtis RH: Triumph Over Pain. The Story of Anesthesia: NY, David McKay Co 1972
180. Curtis W: Southsea. Its Story: Alresford, Hants, Bay Tree Pub Co 1978
181. Cutler RE, Glatte H, Dowling JT: Effects of Hyperthyroidism on the Renal Concentrating Mechanism in Humans: J Clin Endocrinol 27:453–460, 1967
182. Cox JR: Did Sir Arthur Conan Doyle Use Cocaine?. A Study in Research: Baker St Misc No 14, June 1978 p 11–17
183. Cox S: Indirections for Those Who Want to Write: Boston, David R Godine 1981 p 87 (reprint pb)
184. Darwin F ED: Charles Darwin's Autobiography: NY, Henry Schuman, 1950 pp 19–20
185. D'AP: Spence, James (1812–1882), Surgeon: Vol 18 DNB, S Lee Ed, London, Smith Elder & Co 1909 pp 743–744
186. Dauber LG: Dickens and Doctors. Physicians in Fiction of Charles Dickens: NY State J Med 81:1522–1526, 1981
187. Davenport WH Editor: The Good Physician. A Treasury of Medicine: NY, Macmillan Co 1962
188. Davison WC: Walter Reed, 1851–1902: *in* Yellow Fever in Galveston, C Leake Ed, Austin, U Texas Press 1951 pp 108–110
189. Daylight Savings Bill: Times (London), June 17, 1908 p 7
190. Death of Dr. Budd of Stonehouse: Western Morning News (Plymouth), Feb 3, 1889 p 4
191. deCamara MP, Hayes S: Sir Arthur Conan Doyle's Sherlock Holmes: The Novels: NY, Simon & Schuster, Monarch Notes 1977
192. DeJong C: Die Operasie opendie Dood van Luitenant M.J. Nix: S Afr Med J 58:950, 1978

193. Delafield F, Prudden TM: A Handbook of Pathological Anatomy and Histology: 3rd ed, NY, William Woods Co 1889
194. Dennis CC: A History of Syphilis: Springfield, Ill, Charles C Thomas Pub 1962 p 111, a. p 93
195. The Departure of Dr. A. Conan Doyle: Hampshire Times (Portsmouth), Dec 20, 1890 p 4
196. DeWaal RD: The World Bibliography of Sherlock Holmes and Dr. Watson. A Classified and Annotated List of Materials Relating to Their Lives and Adventures: NY, Bramhall House 1974 pp 464–470
197. ______ The International Sherlock Holmes: Hamden, Conn, Archon Books 1980 p 14
198. Dewald GW: Gregor Johann Mendel and the Beginning of Genetics: Mayo Clin Proc 52:513–518, 1977
199. Dewhurst J: Royal Confinements. A Gynaecological History of Britain's Royal Family: NY, St Martin's Press 1980 pp 176–187
200. Dickens C: American Notes . . .: London, Macmillan 1893
201. Dirckx JH: Medicine and Literature. Sherlock Holmes and the Art of Dermatologic Diagnosis: J Dermatol Surg Oncol 5:191–196, 1979
202. ______ Doctor Watson's Brothers: Pharos, Summer 1981 pp 24–27
203. Discussion on Hydrophobia: Portsmouth Times, Apr 17, 1886 p 5
204. Dobell C: Anthony Van Leeuwenhoek and his "Little Animals.": London, Constable & Co 1932
205. Dobson J, Walker RM: Barbers and Barber-Surgeons of London: Oxford, Blackwell Scientific Pub 1979 pp 53–56
206. Dollery CT: Cerebral Hemorrhage: *in* Cecil Textbook of Medicine 15th ed. PB Beeson, W McDermott, JB Wyngaarden Eds, Phila, WB Saunders Co 1979 p 1206
207. Donaldson HH, Canavan MM: A Study of the Brains of Three Scholars. Granville Stanley Hall, Sir William Osler, Edward Sylvester Morse: J Comp Neurol 46:1–94, 1928

208. Donaldson N: In Search of Dr. Thorndyke. The Story of R. Austin Freeman's Great Scientific Investigator and His Creator: Bowling Green, OH, Bowling Green U Popular Press 1971, a. p 65
209. Dotz W: Jean Paul Marat. His Life, Cutaneous Disease, Death and Depiction by Jacques Louis David: Am J Dermatopathol 1:247–250, 1979
210. The Double Life of William Carlos Williams, M.D.: MD 26:103–5, 109–110, 114–5, 118, 123, 1982
211. Doyle AAKC: Record Cards: London, St Mary's Hosp Med School, file 83, folio 67, 1911–1918
212. Doyle A (Adrian) C: Sherlock Holmes's Identity. Conan Doyle Himself: Times (London), Oct 28, 1943 p 2
213. ______ Letter: Daily Telegraph (London), Oct 8, 1955
214. ______ Sir Arthur Conan Doyle. Centenary 1859–1959: London, John Murray 1959 p 29
215. ______ To The Editor: Sherlock Holmes J 6:96, 1963
216. Doyle A (Arthur) C: Gelseminum as a Poison: Br Med J 2:483, 1879
217. [______]The Mystery of Sasassa Valley: Chambers' J 568, Sept 1879
218. ______ The American's Tale: London Society, Extra Christmas No 1880 pp 44–48
219. ______ The Gully of Bluemansdyke: London Society, Christmas 1881 pp 23–37
220. ______ Bones, the April Fool of Harvey's Sluice: London Society, Apr 1882 p 391
221. ______ Our Derby Sweepstakes: London Society May 1882 p 417
222. ______ On the Slave Coast with a Camera: Br J Photogr 29:185–187, 220–223, 1882
223. ______ Notes on a Case of Leucocythemia: Lancet 1:490, 1882
224. ______ Letter to Blackwell Magazine, Mar 24, 1882: National Library of Scotland, Blackwood Collection, Letters D-GL, M.S. 4431, 1882

225. ______ Captain of the Pole Star: Temple Bar Mag (London) 67:33 Jan 1883
226. ______ Gentlemanly Joe: All the Year Round, 31:299, Mar 31, 1883
227. [______] The Week-Topics of the Day: Med Times & Gazette, June 16, 1883 pp 671-672
228. ______ Selecting a Ghost. The Ghosts of Goresthorpe Grange: London Society, Dec 1883 p 681
229. ______ The Silver Hatchet: London Society, Christmas No 1883 pp 25-35
230. ______ An Exciting Christmas Eve or, My Lecture on Dynamite: Boy's Own Paper, Christmas 1883 p 15
231. ______ Life and Death in the Blood: Good Words 24:178-181, 1883
232. ______ J. Habakuk Jephson's Statement: Cornhill Mag 49:1, Jan 1884
233. ______ John Barrington Cowles. The Story of a Medical Student: Cassell's Sat J, Apr 12, 19, 1884 p 433-435, 461-463
234. ______ The Cabman's Story: Cassell's Sat J, May 17, 1884
235. ______ Easter Monday with the Camera: Br J Photogr 31:330-332, 1884
236. ______ Southsea: Three Days in Search of Effects: Br J Photogr 30:359-361, 1883
237. [______] American Medical Diplomas: Evening News (London), Sept 23, 1884, p 2
238. ______ The Remote Effects of Gout: Lancet 2:978-979, 1884
239. ______ The Great Keinplatz Experiment: Belgravia Mag (London) 57:52-65, 1885
240. ______ An Essay Upon the Vasomotor Changes in Tabes Dorsalis and on the Influence Which is Exerted by the Sympathetic Nervous System in that Disease: Unpublished Thesis, U of Edinburgh, April 1885
241. ______ Uncle Jeremy's Household: Boy's Own Paper 9:233, 249, 271, 279, 299, 318, 329 Jan 8-Feb 19, 1887

242. ______ Compulsory Vaccination: Evening Mail (Portsmouth), July 15, 1887
243. ______ Compulsory Vaccination: Hampshire County Times, July 27, 1887
244. ______ A Study in Scarlet. The Remeniscences of John H. Watson, M.D.: Beeton's Christmas Annual, No 29, 1887
245. ______ The King of the Foxes: Windsor Mag 8:123 July 1898
246. ______ On the Geographical Distribution of British Intellect: Nineteenth Century 24:184–195, 1888
247. ______ My Friend the Murderer: *in* Mysteries and Adventures, London, Walter Scott 1889
248. ______ Micah Clarke: London, Longmans, Green & Co 1889
249. ______ The Mystery of Cloomber: London, Ward & Downey 1888
250. [______] The Ring of Thoth: Cornhill Mag 61:46–61 Jan 1890
251. ______ Letter to Mrs. Sala: San Marino, CA, Huntington Library, HM 7962 Folder LF, Aug 13, 1890
252. ______ The Consumption Cure: Daily Telegraph (London), Nov 20, 1890 p 3
253. ______ Dr. Koch and His Cure: Review of Reviews 2:552–556, 1890
254. ______ A Pastoral Horror: People, Dec 21, 1890
255. ______ The Surgeon of Gaster Fell: Chambers' J 7: 770–773, 787–790, 802–805, 819–822, 1890
256. ______ A Physiologist's Wife: Blackwood Mag 148: 339–351, 1890
257. ______ The Sign of the Four: Lippincott's Monthly Mag 45:147–223, 1890
258. ______ The Firm of Girdlestone: London, Chatto & Windus 1890, Chapters 5, 8, 9, a. p 32, b. Chapter 7
259. ______ Our Midnight Visitor: Temple Bar (London), Feb 1891 p 223
260. ______ The Boscombe Valley Mystery: Strand Mag 2:401–416 Oct 1891

261. ______ A Sordid Affair: People, Nov 29, 1891
262. ______ The Doings of Raffles Haw: London, Cassell & Co 1892
263. ______ A Straggler of '15: Harper's Weekly 35:205–207, 1891
264. ______ Beyond the City; the Idyl of a Suburb: London, Good Words, Christmas No 1891 pp 1–51
265. ______ The White Company: Cornhill Mag, Jan-Dec 1891
266. ______ Lot No. 249: Harper's Mag, 85:525–544 Sept 1892
267. ______ The Adventure of Silver Blaze: Strand Mag 4: 645–660, 1892
268. ______ The Great Shadow: Arrowsmith's Christmas Annual 1892
269. ______ The Los Amigos Fiasco: Idler Mag 2:548–557, 1892
270. ______ The Adventures of Sherlock Holmes: London, Newnes 1892
271. ______ My First Book. VI.-Juvenilia: Idler Mag 2:632–640, 1893
272. ______ The Case of Lady Sannox: Idler Mag 4:331–342, 1893
273. ______ The Refugees. A Tale of Two Continents: London, Longmans 1893
274. ______ The Doctors of Hoyland: Idler Mag, 5:227–238, Apr 1894
275. ______ Before My Bookcase: Great Thoughts, May 5–June 30, 1894
276. ______ De Profundis: McClure's Mag 3:513–518 Nov 1894
277. ______ An Alpine Pass on "Ski": Strand Mag 8:657–661 Dec 1894
278. ______ Crabbe's Practice: The Boy's Own Paper, Christmas 1884 pp 54–57
279. ______ Sweethearts: Idler Mag 5:451–457, 1894
280. ______ The Parasite. A Novel: London, Archibald Constable 1894
281. ______ Round the Red Lamp Being Facts and Fancies of Medical Life: London, Methuen & Co 1894

282. ______ Behind The Times: *in* Round the Red Lamp, London, Methuen & Co 1984 pp 1-8
283. ______ His First Operation: *in* Round the Red Lamp, London, Methuen & Co 1894 pp 9-19
284. ______ The Third Generation: *in* Round the Red Lamp, London, Methuen & Co 1894 pp 46-64
285. ______ A False Start: *in* Round the Red Lamp, London, Methuen & Co 1894 pp 65-88
286. ______ The Curse of Eve: *in* Round the Red Lamp, London, Methuen & Co 1894 pp 89-108
287. ______ A Question of Diplomacy: *in* Round the Red Lamp, London, Methuen & Co 1894 pp 174-199
288. ______ A Medical Document: *in* Round the Red Lamp, London, Methuen & Co 1894 pp 200-219
289. ______ The Los Amigos Fiasco: *in* Round the Red Lamp, London, Methuen & CO 1894 pp 281-294
290. ______ The Surgeon Talks: *in* Round the Red Lamp, London, Methuen & Co 1894 pp 316-328
291. ______ The Recollections of Captain Wilkie: Chambers' J, 12:40-42, 57-59, Jan 19, 26, 1895
292. ______ The Stark Munro Letters: Idler Mag Vols 6-8, Oct 1894-Nov 1895
293. ______ The Stark Munro Letters: London, Longmans, Green & Co 1895, a. pp 207-231, b. pp 232-243, c. pp 289-295, d. pp 265-267, e. pp 40-48, f. p 288, g. p 159, h. pp 313-315, i. p 297, j. pp 52-55, k. p 14, l. p 109, m. p 12, n. pp 62-63, p. p 66, q. pp 163-164, r. pp 337-345. s. pp 1-14, t. pp 200-201, u. p 252, v. p 21, w. p 259, x. p 84, y. p 101, z. pp 153-157, aa. pp 221-224, bb. pp 102-104, cc. p 95, dd. pp 23-24; ee, p 140
294. ______ The Stark Munro Letters: reprinted Bloomington, Ind, Gaslight Pub 1982
295. ______ Rodney Stone: London, Smith, Elder & Co 1896
296. ______ The Queen's Reign. Its Most Striking Characteristic and Most Beneficient Achievement: Temple Mag 1:709, 1897

297. ______ The Governor of St. Kitts: McClure's Mag 9:565–573, May 1897
298. ______ Life on a Greenland Whaler: Strand Mag 13:16–25, 1897
299. ______ Uncle Bernac. A Memory of the Empire: London, Smith, Elder & Co 1897
300. ______ The Story of the Beetle Hunter: Strand Mag 15: 603–612 June 1898
301. ______ The Story of the Lost Special: Strand Mag 16: 153–162 Aug 1898
302. ______ The Story of the Sealed Room: Strand Mag 16: 243–250 Oct 1898
303. ______ The Story of the Black Doctor: Strand Mag 16: 372–382 Oct 1898
304. ______ The Retirement of Signor Lambert: Pearson's Mag 6:720–725, 1898
305. ______ The Tragedy of the Korosko: London, Smith, Elder & Co 1898
306. ______ The Story of the Jew's Breastplate: Strand Mag, 17:123–134, March 1899
307. ______ The Story of the Japanned Box: Strand Mag, 17:3–11, Jan 1899
308. ______ The Story of the Brown Hand: Strand Mag 17:499–508, May 1899
309. ______ The Croxley Master: Strand Mag, Oct–Dec 1899 pp 363, 484, 615
310. ______ A Duet: London, Grant Richards 1899
311. [______] XII-The Episode of the Dead Man Who Spoke: *in* Hilda Wade by Grant Allen, Strand Mag 19:217–224 February 1900
312. ______ Surgeons to the Front. Heroism of Tommy Atkins. Hospital Stories: Daily News, April 16, 1900 p 8
313. ______ The Leather Funnel: McClure's Mag 20:17–25, Nov 1902
314. ______ The War in South Africa. The Epidemic of Enteric Fever at Bloemfontein: Br Med J 2:49–50, 1900

315. ______ A Glimpse of the Army: Strand Mag 20:345–354, 1900
316. ______ The Great Boer War: London, Smith, Elder & Co 1900, a. p 370–371, b. p 13, c. p 528
317. ______ Strange Studies from Life I.—The Holocoust of Manor Place: Strand Mag 21:252–258 March 1901
318. ______ Strange Studies from Life II.—The Love Affair of George Vincent Parker: Strand Mag 21:363–370 April 1901
319. ______ Strange Studies from Life III.—The Debatable Case of Mrs. Emsley: Strand Mag 21:483–489 May 1901
320. ______ The War in South Africa. It's Cause and Conduct: London, Smith, Elder & Co 1902, a. p 74, b. p 84–85
321. ______ The Hound of the Baskervilles: London, Newnes Co 1902
322. ______ Brigadier Gerard at Waterloo: Strand Mag, Jan pp 3–13, Feb pp 123–134, 1903
323. ______ How the Brigadier Lost His Ear: *in* the Adventures of Gerard, London, George Newnes 1903 pp 1–48
324. ______ Adventures of Gerard: London, George Newnes 1903
325. ______ The Adventure of the Priory School: Strand Mag 27:122–140 February 1904
326. ______ Prescription for Captain Hay Doyle, RA.: Sherrington, Norfold 1904
327. ______ The Great Brown-Pericord Motor: Pictorial Mag, 23:273–277, Jan 1905
328. ______ An Incursion into Diplomacy: Cornhill Mag 94: 744–754, 1906
329. ______ Sir Nigel: London, Smith, Elder & Co 1906
330. ______ The Case of Mr. George Edalji. Special Investigation by Sir A. Conan Doyle Part I: Daily Telegraph (London), Jan 11, 1907 p 5
331. ______ The Case of George Edalji. Part 2: Daily Telegraph (London), Jan 12, 1907
332. ______ Letter to the Editor: Daily Telegraph (London), Jan 15, 1907 p 9

333. ______ The Edalji Case: Daily Telegraph (London), Jan 16, 1907 p 9
334. ______ The Edalji Case: Daily Telegraph (London), Jan 18, 1907 p 9
335. ______ The Edalji Case: Br Med J 1:173, Jan 17, 1907
336. ______ The Case of George Edalji: A Question for Ophthalmologists: Lancet 1:189 Jan 19, 1907
337. ______ Foreword: *in* Sandow, E., The Construction and Reconstruction of the Human Body, London, John Bale Sons & Danielson 1907 pp ix–xi
338. ______ Through the Magic Door: London, Smith, Elder Inc 1907 p 233, a. p 1, 2, b. pp 272
339. ______ The Pot of Caviare: Strand Mag 35:243–250 Mar 1908
340. ______ The Silver Mirror: Strand Mag 36:123–128 Aug 1908
341. ______ The Fiend of the Cooperage: *in* Round the Fire Stories, London, Smith, Elder & Co 1908
342. ______ Some Recollections of Sport: Strand Mag 38: 271–281, 1909
343. ______ The Croxley Master and Other Stories of Ring and Camp: NY, George H Doran 1909
344. ______ The Divorce Law Reform: Union 1909
345. ______ The Crime of the Congo: London, Hutchinson & Co 1909
346. ______ Introduction: *in* Great Britain and the Congo by ED Morel, London, Smith, Elder & Co 1909 pp xi–xvi
347. ______ The Terror of Blue John Gap: Strand Mag 40:131–141, Aug 1910
348. ______ Guinea Pig or Man?: Daily Express (London), Nov 1, 1910 p 4
349. ______ The Romance of Medicine: St. Mary's Hospital Gazette 16:100–106, 1910
350. ______ The Romance of Medicine: Lancet 2:1066–1068, 1910

351. [______] Sir Arthur Conan Doyle. Why he is Now in Favor of Home Rule: London, Liberal Pub Dept, Leaflet 2399 Sept 26, 1911
352. ______ An Inconoclast: *in* The Last Galley, London, Smith, Elder & Co 1911
353. ______ The Blighting of Sharkey: *in* The Last Galley, London, Smith, Elder & Co, 1911 pp 154–172
354. ______ Songs of the Road: London, Smith Elder & Co 1911
355. ______ "Licensed to Kill": Cartoon in Bookman (London), 43:108, Nov 1912
356. ______ The Case of Oscar Slater: London, Hodder & Stoughton 1912
357. ______ The Lost World: London, Hodder & Stoughton 1912
358. ______ How it Happened: Strand Mag 46:304–307, Sept 1913
359. ______ The Horror of the Heights Which Includes the Manuscript Known as the Joyce-Armstrong Fragment: Strand Mag 46:551–562 Nov 1913
360. ______ The Poison Belt: London, Hodder & Stoughton 1913
361. ______ The Valley of Fear: Strand Mag 48–49:(serialized), Sept 1914–May 1915
362. ______ Obituary. Captain Malcolm Leckie, D.S.O., R.A.M.C.: Guy's Hospital Gazette 29:3–4, 1915
363. ______ Soldiers in London: Times (London), Feb 6, 1917
364. ______ Soldiers in London: Times (London), Feb 10, 1917
365. ______ His Last Bow: The War Service of Sherlock Holmes: Stand Mag 54:226–236 Sept 1917
366. ______ Some Personalia About Mr. Sherlock Holmes: Strand Mag, 54:531–535, Dec 1917
367. ______ The New Revelation or What is Spiritualism: London, Hodder and Stoughton 1918
368. ______ The Nightmare Room: Strand Mag 62:545–549, Dec 1921
369. ______ The Bully of Brocas Court: Strand Mag 62: 381–388, Nov 1921
370. ______ The Poems of Arthur Conan Doyle. Collected Edition: London, John Murray 1922

371. ______ Pulse-Rate in Trance: J Am Soc Psychical Res 17:374-375, 1923
372. ______ Our American Adventure: London, Hodder & Stoughton [1923] pp 55, 69-70
373. ______ The Case for Spirit Photography: NY, George H Doran Co 1923 p 38
374. ______ The Adventure of the Three Garridebs: Colliers Mag, Oct 25, 1924 pp 5-7, 36-37
374A. ______ The History of Spiritualism: London, Doran 1926, Vol 2 p 182
375. ______ Memories and Adventures: London, Hodder & Stoughton 1924 p 22, a. pp 23-25, b. p 27, c. Chapter 4, d. pp 58-59, e. p 24, f. pp 24-25, g. p 28, h. p 29, i. p 57, j. pp 47-57, k. p 60, l. pp 61-65, m. pp 65-70, n. pp 81-82, p. pp 72-82, q. pp 87-91, r. pp 92-97, s. pp 152-200, t. p 210, u. pp 253-259, v. pp 215-221, w. pp 342-362, x. pp 238-239, y. pp 31-33, z. p 66, aa. p 120-125, bb. pp 276-277, cc. p 338, dd. p 99, ee. p 291, ff. pp 332-333, gg. p 341-2, hh. pp 287-288, ii. pp 313-315, jj. p 55
376. ______ The Land of Mist: London, Hutchinson 1926
377. ______ My Religion: *in* My Religion, A Bennet et al. London, Hutchinson & Co. [C. 1926] pp 33
378. ______ The Affairs of Hulham House: Light, 47:281, June 11, 1927
379. ______ The Pre-Natal State: Light, 47:573, Nov 19, 1927
380. ______ Filmed Interview, 1927. Sir Arthur Conan Doyle: Davenport, Eastin Phelan Corporation, *in* Blackhawk Film Digest Catalog, Spring 1981 p 94
381. ______ Pheneas Speaks. Direct Spirit Communications in the Family Circle Reported by Arthur Conan Doyle: London, Psychic Press 1927
382. ______ Foreward: *in* D Marinus, Alloquia, London, CW Daniel Co 1928 pp 7-8
383. ______ The Old Horse. Cartoon Sketch: Winter 1929
384. ______ The End of Devil Hawker: Sat Evening Post (Phila), Aug 23, 1930
385. ______ Letters to Dr. Reginald Hoare and Family, 28 letters, 1881-1921: *in* Berg Collection, NY Public Library, a. No. 4, Folio 5 Edinburgh 1881; b. No. 3, Folio 5 Plymouth

1882; c. No. 9, Folio 3 Southsea 1882; d. No. 5, Folio 3 Southsea, July 24, 1890; e. No. 2, Folio 3 Southsea 1889 or 90; f. No. 7, Folio 3 Southsea Nov 30, 1890; g. No. 8, Folio 3 Southsea, Dec 15, 1890; h. No. 2, Folio 5 Masongill, Vienna (no date); i. No. 7, Folio 5, 2 Wimpole Street (1891); j. No. 8, Folio 5 Nov 20, 1890; k. No. 1, Folio 2 (1881)

386. _____ Letters to Mrs. Charlotte Thwaites Drummond, Edinburgh: ten letters, 1881 to 1888, John Hench Collection, Worcester, Mass
387. _____ Letters to Mrs. Charlotte Thwaites Drumond Edinburgh: *in* Hench Collection, University of Minnesota, Minneapolis, a. to Dearest Mam 1882, b. to Dear Mam 1882
388. _____ Four Letters to Mr. Chapman 1887–1890: Postgrad Inst, Portsmouth Med Soc, St Mary's Hosp, Portsmouth, 1963
389. Doyle, Dame JC: Letter to A. Rodin: July 21, 1981
390. Doyle, Lady [J] C: Conan Doyle was Sherlock Holmes: Pearson's Mag 78:574–577 Dec 1934
391. Dreisbach RH: Handbook of Poisoning: 10th ed, Los Altos, Lange Med Pub 1980 pp 214–215
392. Dr. A. Conan Doyle: The Crescent (Portsmouth), Sept 28, 1888
393. Dr. A. Conan Doyle: Portsmouth Times, Dec 13, 1890 p 5
394. Dr. Conan Doyle on His Medical Career: St James Gazette, Oct 6, 1893
395. Dr. Conan Doyle on the War: Times (London), Nov 13, 1900 p 10
396. Dr. Koch's Remedy For Tuberculosis: Br Med J 4: 1200–1201, 1890
397. Dr. Reginald Ratcliff Hoare, F.R.C.S. Edin.: Br Med J 1:989, 1898
398. Dr. William Budd: Br Med J 1:102–103, 1880
399. Dubos RJ: Louis Pasteur. Free Lance of Science: Boston, Little Brown & Co 1950
400. Dubos R, Dubos J: The White Plague. Tuberculosis, Man and Society: Boston, Little, Brown & Co 1952, a. pp 7–8
401. Dudgeon JA: Immunization in Times Ancient and Modern: J R Soc Med 73:581–586, 1980

402. ______ Development of Smallpox Vaccine in England in the 18th and 19th Centuries. Br Med J 2:1367–1372, 1963
403. Dubovsky H: Koch's Remedy For Tuberculosis: S Afr Med J 47:1609–1614, 1973
404. Dunglison R: Medical Lexicon. A New Dictionary of Medical Science: 3rd ed, Phila, Lea & Blanchard 1842 pp 215, 468
405. EBS, DBH: Simpson, Sir James Young (1811–1870), physician: Vol 18 DNB, S Lee Ed,· London, Smith Elder & Co 1909 pp 272–273
406. Edelstein L: The Hippocratic Oath, Text, Translation and Interpretation: Baltimore, Johns Hopkins Press 1943
407. The Edinburgh University Calendar 1876–77: Edinburgh, James Thin Pub 1876
408. ______ 1877–78: Edinburgh, James Thin 1877
409. ______ 1878–79: Edinburgh, James Thin 1878
410. ______ 1879–80: Edinburgh, James Thin 1879
411. ______ 1880–81: Edinburgh, James Thin 1880
412. ______ 1881–82: Edinburgh, James Thin 1881
413. ______ 1882–83: Edinburgh, James Thin 1882
414. ______ 1886–87: Edinburgh, James Thin 1886 p 193
415. The Editor: Where Sherlock Holmes First Came to Life. Conan Doyle's Eight Years in Southsea: Evening News (Portsmouth), Feb 10, 1949
416. Editorial: Author Physicians—Dr. Conan Doyle: NY Med J, Aug 14, 1920 pp 226–227
417. Editorial: The Cause of Napoleon's Death: Can Med Assoc J 85:1402, 1961
418. Editorial: Passive Smoking: Forest, Gasp, and Facts: Lancet 1:548–549, 1982
419. Edwards E: Sir Arthur Conan Doyle—Lover of the New Forest: Hampshire, Feb 1974 pp 29–31
420. Edwards OD: Burke and Hare: Edinburgh, Polygon Books 1980
421. Edwards OD Ed: The Edinburgh Stories of Arthur Conan Doyle: Edinburgh, Polygon Books, 1981
422. Edwards OD: Dr. Jekyll and Mr. Holmes. A Study in Lothian Cultural Imperialism: Lothian Regional Council 1982

423. ______ Personal Communication, May 1982
424. ______ The Quest for Sherlock Holmes: Edinburgh, Mainstream Pub Co 1983 p 47, a. pp 148–176, b. p 180, c. p 288, d. p 193, e. p 22, f. p 199, g. p 200
425. Electrocution: 15th ed Vol III Micropaedia, Encyclopaedia Britannica, Chicago, U Chicago 1974 p 835
426. Elstein AS, Shulman LS, Sprafka SA: Medical Problem Solving. An Analysis of Clinical Reasoning: Cambridge, Mass, Harvard U Press 1978 p ix
427. Entralgo PL: Doctor and Patient: trans from French by F Partridge, NY, McGraw-Hill Book Co 1969 pp 136–146
428. Eurohealth Handbook, 1980: White Plains, NY, Robert S. First Inc, Sept 1980
429. The Eye and Ear Infirmary. Annual Meeting: Hampshire Telegraph and Sussex Chronicle, Mar 30, 1889 p 6
430. Eye and Ear Infirmary: Portsmouth Times, Sept 7, 1890 p 6
431. Fabricant ND: Sherlock Holmes as an Eye, Ear, Nose and Throat Diagnostician: Eye Ear Nose Throat Monthly 36: 523–526, 1957
432. Fantastic Voyage: Twentieth-Century Fox Film Corp 1966
433. Fiction. Round the Red Lamp Being Facts and Fancies of Medical Life: Speaker (London), Dec 1, 1894 p 605
434. Fiction. The Stark Munro Letters: Speaker (London), Sept 14, 1895
435. Finch E: The Centenary of the General Council of Medical Education of the United Kingdom 1858–1958 in Relation to Medical Education: Ann R Coll Surg Engl 23:321-331, 1958
436. Fisher RB. Joseph Lister 1827–1912: NY, Stein & Day Pub 1977 p 218
437. Fitz R: A Belated Eulogy: To John H. Watson, M.D.: Am J Surg 31 n s: 584–589, 1936
438. Fitzgerald FT, Tierney LM: The Bedside Sherlock Holmes: West J Med 137:169–175, 1982
439. Fleming A: Alcohol the Delightful Poison. A History: NY, Dell Pub Co 1975 pp 116–117

440. Flexner A: Medical Education in the United States and Canada. A Report to the Carnegie Foundation for the Advancement of Teaching: Bull No 4, NY, Carnegie Foundation 1910
441. Ford WW: Clio Medica. Bacteriology: NY, Paul B Hoeber Inc 1939
442. Forshufvrid S, Smith H, Wassen A: Arsenic Content of Napoleon I's Hair Probably Taken Immediately After His Death: Nature 192:103–105, 1961
442A Hart ED: Conan Doyle as Rheumatologist: Ann Rheum Dis 41:437–438, 1982
443. Ivy AC: The History and Ethics of the Use of Human Subjects in Medical Experiments: Science 108:1–5, 1948
444. Jackson GG. The Common Cold: *in* Cecil Textbook of Medicine 15th ed. PB Beeson, W McDermott & JB Wyngaarden Eds, Phila WB Saunders Co 1979 pp 230–233
445. Jackson R: Coroner. The Biography of Sir Bentley Purchase: London, George G Harp & Co 1963
446. Jacob F: The Logic of Life. A History of Heredity: trans by BE Spillmann, NY, Pantheon Books 1973 pp 202–204, a. p 219
447. JDJH: Medical Jurisprudence: 15th ed, Vol 11 Macropaedia, Encyclopaedia Britannica, Chicago, U Chicago 1974 pp 812–815
448. Jean-Aubry G: The Sea Dreamer: A Definitive Biography of Joseph Conrad: trans by Helen Sebba, Garden City, NY, Doubleday & Co 1957 pp 149–176
449. JGO: Portsmouth Vignettes: No. 3—Dr. Doyle of "Bush Villa," Southsea: Portsmouth Reader, Oct 1947 pp 52–54
450. Jelinek JE: Jean-Paul Marat. The Differential Diagnosis of his Skin Disease: Am J Dermatopathol 1:251–252, 1979
451. Jellyfish: 15th ed, Vol V Micropaedia, Encyclopaedia Britannica, Chicago, U Chicago 1974 pp 539–540
452. J.G.O.: Portsmouth Vignettes No. 7—Arthur Conan Doyle—The Years of Struggle: Portsmouth Reader, Apr 1949 pp 19–22

453. Foster M: A Textbook of Physiology: Phila, Henry C Lea's Son 1880
454. Foster R: United States Place Names and Sherlock Holmes: Trans Stud Coll Physicians Phila 4th series, 45:249–251, 1978
455. Fowler HW: A Dictionary of Modern English Usage: 2nd ed, NY, Oxford U Press 1965 p 63
456. Fowler NO: Diseases of the Aorta: *in* Cecil Textbook of Medicine 15th ed. PB Beeson, W McDermott, JB Wyngaarden Eds, Phila, WB Saunders Co 1979 pp 1294–1297
457. Fowles J: A Study in Scarlet: New Statesman, Nov 26, 1976 pp 751–752
458. Francis D: Portsmouth Old and New: Portsmouth, EP Pub 1975 p 15
459. Frankel FH: Hypnosis—Both Poetry and Science: Lancet 2:1391–1393, 1982
460. Freeman JN: Gelsemium: Lancet 2:475, 1873
461. Freeman RA: The Red Thumb Mark: London, Collingwood Bros 1907
462. ______ Touchstone: *in* Dr. Thorndyke Investigates, London, U London Press 1930
463. French RD: Antivivisection and Medical Science in Victorian Society: Princeton, Princeton U Press 1975 table 1 p 186
464. Fülöp-Miller R: Triump Over Pain: trans by E & C Paul, NY, Literary Guild of America, 1938
465. Gaboriau E: The Mystery of Orcival: NY, Lovell 1883
466. ______ The Lerouge Case: NY, Caldwell n.d. (c. 1885)
467. Galton F: Fingerprints: London, Macmillan & Co 1892
468. Garrison FH: An Introduction to the History of Medicine: 4th ed, Phila, WB Saunders Co 1929 p 757, a. p 539, b. p 612, c. p 597, d. p 744, e. pp 446–447, f. p 597, g. pp 327–328, h. p 427–428, i. p 410–411, j. p 553–554 (reprinted 1960)
469. Garzon A, Gliedman ML: Peripheral Embolization of a Bullet Following Perforation of the Aorta: Ann Surg 160: 901–904, 1964

470. Gear JHS: The Anglo-Boer War of 1899–1902: Enteric Fever and Captain Maxwell Louis Hughes: Adler Museum Bull 7:10–13, 1981
471. General AW Drayson: Portsmouth Times 1889
472. George Meredith. Lecture by Dr. Conan Doyle: Hampshire Telegraph, Nov 24, 1888
473. Gibson A: The Remarkable Dr. Budd: Western Morning News (Plymouth), Sept 6, 1963
474. Gibson JM, Green RL Eds: The Unknown Conan Doyle, Uncollected Stories: London, Secker & Warburg 1982
475. ______ The Unknown Conan Doyle. Essays on Photography: London, Secker & Warburg 1982
476. Gilbert WM Ed: Edinburgh in the Nineteenth Century: Edinburgh, J & R Allan 1901
477. Gillard RD: Sherlock Holmes—Chemist: Educ in Chem 13:10–11, 1976
478. Gillray J: The Cow Pock: Colored etching, Chicago, Art Institute 1808
479. Gilman AG, Goodman LS, Gilman A: Goodman and Gilman's The Pharmarologic Bases of Therapeutics: 6th ed, NY, Macmillan Pub Co 1980 pp 127–28, a. p 376, b. p 826, c. pp 553–557, d. p 220 e. p 230, 585–587
480. Glatt MM: The English Drink Problem Through the Ages: Proc R Soc Med 70:202–206, 1977
481. Godber G: General Practice, Past and Present: J R Coll Gen Pract 16:175–190, 1968
482. Goldscheider G: Conan Doyle Bibliography. A Bibliography of the Works of Sir Arthur Conan Doyle M.D., LL. D. (1859–1930): Windsor, Privately Published 1977
483. Goodman C: The Dental Holmes: Baker Street J 2:381–393, 1947
484. Goodman LS, Gilman A: The Pharmacologic Basis of Therapeutics: 5th ed, NY, Macmillan Pub Co 1975 p 540
485. Gordan JD: Doctors as Men of Letters. English and American Writers of Medical Background. An Exhibition in the Berg Collection: Bull NY Pub Lib 68:574–601, 1964

486. Grant LJ: Sir Arthur Conan Doyle: *in* Laurentian Addresses Edinburgh University, 1894–1910, Vol II pp 190–191 (unpublished).
487. Green RL: Personal Letter to A. Rodin: Aug 5, 1982
488. Green RL, Gibson JM: A Bibliography of A. Conan Doyle: Oxford, Oxford U Press 1983
489. Green TH: An Introduction to Pathology and Morbid Anatomy: 6th ed, Phila, Lea Brothers & Co 1889 p 132
490. Greene H, Ed; Introduction *in* The Rivals of Sherlock Holmes, NY, Pantheon Books 1970
491. Griffith RE, Maisch JM: Universal Formulary Containing the Methods of Preparing and Administering Officinal and Other Medicines: 3rd ed, Phila, Henry C Lea 1874 p 307
492. Grilly DM: A Reply to Miller's "The Habit of Sherlock Holmes": Trans Stud Coll Physicians Phila, series V, 1:324–327, 1979
493. Groschel DHM, Hornick RB: Who Introduced Typhoid Vaccination. Almroth Wright or Richard Pfeiffer?: Rev Infect Dis 3:1251–1254, 1981
494. GTB: Budd, William (1811–1880), physician: Vol 3 DNB, L Stephen & S Lee Eds, London, Smith Elder & Co 1908 pp 220–221
495. ______ Christison, Sir Robert, M.D. (1797–1882), medical professor: Vol 4 DNB, L Stephen & S Lee Eds, London, Smith Elder & Co 1908 pp 290–291
496. Guerard AJ: Conrad the Novelist: NY, Atheneum 1970 pp 254–255
497. Gunn CB: Leaves from the Life of a Country Doctor: Edinburgh, Moray Press 1935 pp 62–63
498. Guthrie D: A History of Medicine: London, Thomas Nelson & Sons 1945 p 100
499. ______ Sherlock Holmes and the Medical Profession: Baker Street J 2:465–471, 1947
500. ______ Lord Lister. His Life and Times: Edinburgh, E & S Livingstone 1949
501. ______ Sherlock Holmes and Medicine: Can Med Assoc J 85: 996–1000, 1961

502. Guy WA: Principles of Forensic Medicine: 1st Am ed, NY, Harper & Bros 1845 p 309, a. pp 451–453, b. p 489, c. p 487, d. p 485, e. pp 458, f. pp 452–453
503. Hald J & Jacobsen E: A Drug Sensitising the Organism to Ethyl Alcohol: Lancet 2:1001–1004, 1948
504. Hale E: Experiments and Observations on the Communication Between the Stomach and the Urinary Organs, and on the Propensiety of Administering Medicine by Injection into Veins: N Engl J Med Surg 11:163–175, 1822
505. Hall TH: Sherlock Holmes and His Creator: NY, St Martin's Press 1977 pp 16–29
506. Haller JS Jr: American Medicine in Transition 1840–1910: Urbana, U Illinois Press 1981 p 224, a. pp 101–104
507. Hammond M: The Expulsion of the Neanderthals from Human Ancestry: Soc Stud Sci 12:1–36, 1982
508. Hammond WA: Coca. Its Preparation and Their Therapeutical Qualities, with Some Remarks on the So-called Cocaine Habit: Trans Med Soc State VA 1887 pp 212–226
509. ______ Cerebral Hyperemia, The Result of Mental Strain or Emotional Disturbance, the So-called Nervous Neurasthenia: 2nd ed, Washington, Brentano 1895
510. ______ The American Soldier and Venereal Diseases: NY Med J 70:181–187, 1899
511. Hanzlik PJ: Jan Evangelista Purkyne (Purkinje) on Disturbances of the Vision by Digitalis, One Hundred Years Ago: JAMA 84:2024–2025, 1925
512. Hardwick M, Hardwick M: The Sherlock Holmes Companion: NY, Bramhall House 1962
513. ______ The Man Who was Sherlock Holmes: London, John Murray, 1964
514. Harnagel EE: Joseph Bell, M.D.—The Real Sherlock Holmes: N Engl J Med 258:1158–1159, 1958
515. Harrrison B: Separate Spheres. The Opposition to Women's Suffrage in Britain: NY, Holmes & Meier Pub 1978 p 55
516. Harrison G: Mosquitoes, Malaria and Man: A History of the Hostilities Since 1880: NY, EP Dutton 1978, a. p 23

517. Hatcher RA, Wilbert MI: The Pharmacopeia and the Physician: Chicago, Am Med Assoc Press 1907 pp 292–294
518. Heath-Hammond LR, Gelinas CE: A History of Phlebotomy in 18th Century America: Lab Med 13:776–778, 1982
519. Hepburn WR: The Jezail Bullet: Practitioner 197:100–101, 1966
520. Herment G: The Pipe: NY, Simon & Schuster 1955 p 27
521. Herrel JH: Health Care Expenditures. The Coming Crisis: Mayo Clin Proc 55:705–710, 1980
522. Hewitt E: Conan Doyle: The Man: Saturday Review 150:74 July 19, 1930
523. Heyman A: Syncope: *in* Cecil Textbook of Medicine 15 ed. PB Beeson, W McDermott, JB Wyngaarden Eds, Phila, WB Saunders Co 1979 pp 742–745
524. Hibbert C: Gilbert and Sullivan and Their Victorian World: NY, American Heritage Pub Co 1976 p 250
525. Higham C: The Adventures of Conan Doyle. The Life of the Creator of Sherlock Holmes: NY, WW Norton & Co 1976 p 64, a. p 105, b. pp 258–259, c. p 142, d. pp 215–217, e. pp 333–334, f. p 58
526. Hill FD: Gelsemium Sempervirens: Eclectic Med J 4: 353–354, 1852
527. Hitchings JL: Sherlock Holmes the Logician: Baker Street J 1:113–117, 1946
528. Hoare RR: Clinical Memoranda. Gout: Br Med J 2:1014, 1880
529. Hochbaum GM: Psychological Aspects of Smoking with Special Reference to Cessation: Am J Public Health 55: 692–697, 1965
530. Hoehling AA: The Great Epidemic: Boston, Little, Brown & Co 1961 pp 6–7
531. Hoffman NY: The Doctor and the Detective Story: JAMA 224:74–77, 1973
532. Hofmann A: Psychomimetric Drugs. Chemical and Pharmacological Drugs: Acta Physiol Pharmacol Neerl 8:240–258, 1959

533. Hogan JC, Schwartz MD: The Manly Art of Observation and Deduction: J Criminal Law Criminal Police Sci 55: 157–164, 1964
534. Hole C: Witchcraft in England: London, BT Batsford 1947
535. Hollyer C: Arthur Conan Doyle: A Case of Identity: Pacific Quarterly 3:50–61, 1978
536. Holmes EA: Gelsemium Sempervirens: Pharma J Trans 2:521–522, 1876
537. Holmes OW: Homeopathy and Its Kindred Delusions: *in* Medical Essays 1842–1882, Boston, Houghton, Mifflin & Co 1883 pp 1–102
538. ______ Currents and Counter-Currents: *in* Medical Essays 1842–1882, Boston, Houghton, Mifflin & Co 1883 p 203
539. ______ Some of My Early Teachers: *in* Medical Essays 1842–1882, Boston, Houghton, Mifflin & Co 1883 p 430
540. ______ The Complete Poetical Works of Oliver Wendell Holmes: Cambridge ed, Boston, Houghton, Mifflin & Co 1895
541. Holmes S: An Enquiry into the Nature of the Ashes of Various Tobaccos: 2nd ed, Tibet, Privately printed 1893
542. Holmes's First Case Started Here: The News (Portsmouth), Nov 18, 1982 p 7
543. Horn DB: A Short History of the University of Edinburgh 1556–1889: Edinburgh, University Press 1967 pp 3–4, a. pp 56–57, b. p 197
544. Hornung EW: The Amateur Cracksman: NY, Charles Scribner's Sons 1899
545. ______ Raffles. Further Adventures of the Amateur Cracksman: NY, Charles Scribner's Sons 1901
546. Horton-Smith P: The Goulstonian Lectures on the Typhoid Bacillus and Typhoid Fever: London, Churchill 1906
547. Hotchkiss RD: The Identification of Nucleic Acids as Genetic Determinants: *in* The Origins of Modern Biochemistry. A Retrospect on Proteins, NY Academy Sci 325: 321–342, 1979

548. How H: A Day with Dr. Conan Doyle: Strand Mag, Aug 18, 1892 pp 182–188
549. Hoyt EP: The Improper Bostonian. Dr. Oliver Wendell Holmes: NY, William Morrow & Co 1979 p 72
550. Hubbard FH: The Opium Habit and Alcoholism: NY, AS Barnes & Co 1881
551. Hume FW: The Mystery of a Hansom Cab: Melbourne, Kemp & Boyce 1886
552. Hussey HH: Diagnosis by Deduction From a Few Observations: JAMA 235:1884, 1976
553. Hutchinson J: The "Bowman" Lecture on the Relation of Certain Diseases of the Eye to Gout: Lancet 2:901–903, 945–948, 1884
554. Hyde M: Arctic Whaling Adventures: Oxford, Oxford U Press 1955
555. Hypnotism at Southsea. Private Seance by M. Meyer: Evening News (Portsmouth), Feb 9, 1889 p 4
555A Inform: Physician Murderers and Criminals: Forens Sci Int 20:101–106, 1982
556. Iseminger GC: Sherlock Holmes and the Social History of the Victorian Age: North Dakota Quarterly, Spring 1976 pp 51–71
557. Ives AG: British Hospitals: London, Collins 1958 pp 23–24

Ivy AC: The History and Ethics of the Use of . . . see reference number 443

Jackson GG: The Common Cold . . . see reference number 444

Jackson R: Coroner. The Biography of Sir Bentley . . . see reference number 445

Jacob F: The Logic of Life. A History of Heredity . . . see reference number 446

JDJH: Medical Jurisprudence . . . see reference number 447

Jean-Aubry G: The Sea Dreamer . . . see reference number 448

Jelinek JE: Jean-Paul Marat . . . see reference number 450

Jellyfish: 15th ed, Vol 5 Micropaedia . . . see reference 451

J.G.O.: Portsmouth Vignettes No. 3 . . . see reference 449
J.G.O.: Portsmouth Vignettes No. 7 . . . see reference 452

558. TS: Warren, Samuel (1807–1877), author: Vol 20 DNB, S Lee Ed, London, Smith Elder & Co 1909 pp 880–883
559. Johnson M-L: Ichthyosis: *in* Cecil Textbook of Medicine 15th ed. PB Beeson, W McDermott, JR Wyngaarden Eds, Phila, WB Saunders Co 1979 pp 2285–2286
560. Jones HE: The Original of Sherlock Holmes: Collier's Mag 32:14–15, 20 Jan 9, 1904
561. Kavanagh S: Sherlock Holmes was Born in Southsea: Hampshire, The County Mag 5:29, 1965
562. Kaufman M: American Medical Education. The Formative Years, 1765–1910: Westport, Conn, Greenwood Press 1976 pp 18–22
563. Keating HRF Ed: Whodunit? A Guide to Crime, Suspense and Spy Fiction: NY, Van Nostrand Reinhold Co 1982 p 7, a. p 164, b. p 184, c. p 56
564. Keats J: The Complete Poetic Works and Letters of John Keats: Boston, Houghton, Mifflin & Co 1899
565. Kelley, WN: Gout and Other Disorders of Purine Metabolism: *in* Harrison's Principles of Internal Medicine, 9th ed, KJ Isselbacher et al Eds, NY, McGraw Hill Book Co 1980 pp 479–480
566. Kellogg RL: The Holmesian Paradigm of Problem Solving: Lifelong Learning. The Adult Years 1:4–7, 1978
567. Kervran R: Laennec. His Life and Times: trans from French by DC Abrahams-Curiel, NY, Pergamon Press 1960
568. Key JD: Medical Writings of a Literary Physician, Sir Arthur Conan Doyle (1859–1930): Minn Med 61:362–365, 1978
569. ______ Arthur Conan Doyle (1859–1930): Medical Author: *in* Cultivating Sherlock Holmes, BL Crawford Jr, JB Connors Eds, LaCrosse, Wisc, Sumac Press 1978 pp 68–73
570. ______ A Devil Visits Arabela: An Unusual Encounter with Radex Pedis Diaboli: Southwest Heritage 9:21, 25–31, 1979
571. ______ William Alexander Hammond, M.D. (1828–1900): Rochester, Minn, Davies Co 1979 p 69

572. ______ Keeping the Holmes Fires Burning: Mayo Alumnus 17:42–45, 1981
573. Keys TE: The History of Surgical Anesthesia: NY, Dover Pub 1963
574. Killer Executed by Lethal Injection: Journal Herald (Dayton, OH), Dec 7, 1982 p 1
575. King AB: Syphilis of the Spinal Cord: Am J Syph Gonor Vener Dis 26:336–377, 1942
576. King LS: The Medical World of the Eighteenth Century: Chicago, U Chicago Press 1958 p 86
577. King WH: Electro-Therapeutics or Electricity and Its Relation to Medicine and Surgery: NY, AL Chatterton & Co 1889, a. p 199
578. Kinney J, Leaton G: Loosening the Grip. A Handbook of Alcohol Information: St. Louis, CV Mosby Co 1978 pp 41–42
579. Kittle CF: Arthur Conan Doyle: Doctor and Writer (1859–1930): J Kans Med Soc 61:13–18, 1960
580. ______ The Case of the Versatile A. Conan Doyle: U Chicago Mag 547:8–14, 1969
581. ______ Afterword: *in* reprint of "The Stark Munro Letters" by A.C. Doyle, Bloomington, Ind, Gaslight Pub 1982 pp 195–220
582. Klauder JV: Sherlock Holmes as a Dermatologist with Remarks on the Life of Dr. Joseph Bell and the Sherlockian Method of Teaching: Arch Dermat Syphilol 68:363–377, 1953
583. Klawans HL: The Medicine of History from Paracelsus to Freud: NY, Raven Press 1982 pp 19–35
584. Knapp PH, Bliss CM, Wells H: Addictive Aspects in Heavy Cigarette Smoking: Am J Psychiatry 119:966–972, 1963
585. Koch R: Weitere Mitteilunges uber ein Heilmittel gegen Tuberculose: Dtsch Med Wochenschr 16:1029–1032 Nov 15, 1890
586. ______ A Remedy for Tuberculosis: Br Med J (special suppl), Nov 15, 1890

587. ______ Remedy For Tuberculosis: Br Med J 1:125–127, 1891

588. Kofman O: The Changing Pattern of Neurosyphilis: Can Med Assoc J 74:807–812, 1956

589. Kosloske AM: Sherlock Holmes: Spectacular Diagnostician: Marquette Med Rev 29:29–31, 1963

590. Korsch BM, Negrete VF: Doctor-Patient Relationship: Sci Am 227:66–74, 1972

591. Kress PF: Justice, Proof, and Plausability in Conan Doyle and Dashiell Hammett: J Contemp Thought Humanities Arts Social Sci 7:119–134, 1977

592. Krogman WM: Sherlock Holmes as an Anthropologist: Sci Monthly 80:155–162, 1955

593. Labianca DA, Reeves WJ: Sherlock Holmes and His Compulsive Use of Cocaine: A Topic for Coordinated Study: Sci Educ 60:47–52, 1976

594. Labianca DA, Reeves WJ: Drug Synergism and the Case of "The Disappearance of Lady Carfax": Am Notes Queries 16:18–70, 1978

595. Lachtman HL: When Conan Doyle Came to California: Pacific Historian 22:26–37, 1978

596. Lady Doctors. An American Opinion Thereon: Doidges Western County's Illustrated Annual for 1888 (Plymouth), 1888 p 161

597. Lansing DI: Compiler's Commentary on Sherlock Holmes Papers: Trans Stud Coll Physicians Phila, 4th series 45:241–242, 1978

598. Late Local News: Accident in Elm Grove: Evening News (Portsmouth), Nov 2, 1882 p 3

599. La Touche DD: Conan Doyle on Skis: Times (London), Jan 10, 1959 p 7

600. Lattimer JK: Autopsy on Abraham Lincoln: JAMA 193:99–100, 1965

601. ______ Lincoln Did Not Have the Marfan Syndrome. Documented Evidence: NY State J Med 81:1805–1813, 1981

602. Laud Conan Doyle, A Pioneer Spiritualist: NY Times, July 8, 1930 p 4

602A Leblanc M: The Extraordinary Adventures of Arsene Lupin Gentleman-Burglar: trans from French by G Moorehead 1910, Facsimile ed, NY, Dover Pub 1977

603. Le Clerq N, Mueller F: Migratory Arterial Foreign Body: Am J Surg 91:118, 1956

604. Legal Property Records 1896–1919: Portsmouth City Records Office

605. Leishman WB: Antityphoid Inoculation: Glasgow Med J 77:401–411, 1912

606. Lellenberg JL, Lofts WOG: John H(eron) Watson, M.D.: Baker Street J 30 n s: 83–85, 1980

607. Lesky E: The Vienna Medical School of the 19th Century: trans from German by L Williams, IS Levij, Baltimore, John Hopkins U Press, 1976, a. p 445

608. L'Etang H: Some Observations on the Black Formosa Corruption and Tapanuli Fever: Sherlock Holmes J 4:58–60, 1959

608A Levin PK, Hancock RGV, Voynovich P: Napoleon Bonaparte—No Evidence of Chronic Arsenic Poisoning: Nature 299:627–628, 1982

609. Liberal Party in Great Britain: 15th ed, Vol VI Micropaedia, Encyclopaedia Britannica, Chicago, U Chicago 1974 pp 196–197

610. Liebow E: The Firm of Girdlestone, by Arthur Conan Doyle: Baker Street Irregulars, Summer 1981 pp 34–35

611. ______ Dr. Joe Bell. Model for Sherlock Holmes: Bowling Green, Ohio, Bowling Green U Popular Press 1982, a. p 175, b. pp 140–141

612. Lister J: Koch's Treatment of Tuberculosis: Br Med J 4:1372–1374, 1890

613. Local Gossip: Chat (Portsmouth), Mar 29, 1889 p 3

614. Locke H: A Bibliographical Catalogue of the Writings of Sir Arthur Conan Doyle, M.D., LL. D., 1879–1928: Tunbridge Wells, D Webster 1928

615. Loudon ISL: Sir Charles Bell and the Anatomy of Expression: Br Med J 285:1794–1796, 1982
616. ______ Future History: Br Med J 286:501–502, 1983
617. Lowell: 15th ed, Vol VI Micropaedia, Encyclopaedia Britannica, Chicago, U Chicago 1974 p 359
618. Luncheon at Savoy Hotel, 7/11/12 to J.P. Muller, Royal Danish Engineers: Times (London), Nov 8, 1912 p 17
619. Lutzker E: Women Gain a Place in Medicine: NY, McGraw-Hill Book Co 1969
620. Macalpine I, Hunter R: George III and the Mad-Business: London, Penguin Press 1969
621. McCrae J: In Flanders Fields and Other Poems: Toronto, William Briggs 1919
622. McGovern FH: An Oculist Without a Patient: Am J Ophthalmol 37:799–801, 1954
623. Mackay C: Extraordinary Popular Delusions and the Madness of Crowds: reprint 1852 ed, NY, Noonday Press 1932 pp 319–330
624. MacKenzie JB: Sherlock Holmes' Plots and Strategies: Green Bag 14:407–411, 1902
625. Mackenzie N, Mackenzie J: H.G. Wells. A Biography: NY, Simon & Schuster 1973
626. Maclauchlan HS: II-An Appreciation of Dr. Doyle's Work: Windsor Mag 4:369–372, 1896
627. McCleary GF: Was Sherlock Holmes a Drug Addict? Lancet 2:1555–1556, 1936
628. MacLeod RM: The Edge of Hope: Social Policy and Chronic Alcoholism 1870–1900: J Hist Med Allied Sci 22:215–245, 1967
629. MacNalty AS: Conan Doyle: Ann Med Hist 7 n s: 532–537, 1935
630. MacNalty AS: The Prevention of Smallpox: From Edward Jenner to Monckton Copeman: Med Hist 12:1–18, 1968
631. McNeill WH: Plagues and Peoples: Garden City, NY, Doubleday 1976 pp 144–145, a. p 274
632. Macpherson G: All Doctors are Equal: Br Med J 286:3, 1983

633. McWhinney IR: Problem-Solving and Decision-Making in Primary Medical Practice: Proc R Soc Med 65:934–938, 1972

634. Mann RJ, Key JD: Joseph Bell, M.D., F.R.C.S.: "Notes on a Case of Paralysis Following Diphtheria": Pharos 45:27–29, 1982

635. Mannion RA: The Humor of Doyle—An Appreciation: Baker Street J 18:152–155, 1963

636. ______ An Appreciation of our Medical Men of Literature 1. Sir Arthur Conan Doyle: J Indiana State Med Assoc 67:191–193, 1974

637. Manson P: On the Development of Filaria Sanguinis Hominis, and on the Mosquito Considered as a Nurse: J Linnean Soc 14:304–311, 1878

638. Marinus D: Alloquia. Experiences and Some Reflections of a Medical Practitioner: London, CW Daniel Co 1928 pp 36–37

639. Marks G, Beatty WK: Epidemics: NY, Charles Scribner's Sons 1976 pp 173, 221, a. pp 267–268, b. pp 96–99

640. Marquardt M: Paul Ehrlich: NY, Henry Schuman 1951 p 163 seq, a. p 93

641. Marshall TK: Violence and Civil Disturbance: *in* The Pathology of Violent Injury, JK Mason Ed, London, Edward Arnold Pub 1978 p 80

642. Maugham WS: Of Human Bondage: London, William Heinemann 1915

643. Maxfield DK: Watson: Medical Author: Bull Med Lib Assoc 63:345–346, 1975

644. Mayhew H: Those That Will Not Work: Reprinted from 1862 by Peter Quennell, London's Underworld, London, Hamlyn Pub Group 1950 pp 31–32

645. Meade LT, Eustace R: Madame Sara: Strand Mag 24:387–401 Oct 1902

646. Medical Directory for 1890. 46th Annual Issue: London, JA Churchill 1890 p 593

647. Medicinal Baccalaureus: Conan Doyle and Cocaine: *in* John O'London's Letter Box, John O'London's Weekly 34:229, August 11, 1930
648. Merkle JL: "Over There": Arthur Conan Doyle and Spiritualism: Libr Chron U Texas 8:23–37, 1974
649. Menpes M: War Impressions Being a Record in Color by Mortimer Menpes: London, Adam & Charles Black 1901 pp 152–155
650. Merrington WR: University College Hospital and its Medical School: A History: London, Heinemann 1976 p 237
651. Merskey H: Some Features of Medical Education in Great Britain During the First Half of the Nineteenth Century: Br J Med Educ 3:118–121, 1969
652. Metchnikoff O: The Life of Elie Metchnikoff 1845–1916: trans from French, London, Constable & Co 1921 p 120
653. Meyer N: The Seven-Per-Cent Solution Being a Reprint from the Reminiscences of John H. Watson, M.D.: NY, EP Dutton & Co 1974
654. Meyer UA: *in* Harrison's Principles of Internal Medicine 9th ed, K Isselbacher et al Ed, McGraw-Hill Co 1980 pp 494–500
655. Miasma: Vol VI Oxford English Dictionary, Oxford, Clarendon Press 1970 p. 406
656. Miller JM: Poisoning by Antimony: A Case Report: South Med J 75:592, 1982
657. ______ Physicians and Prose: MD State Med J 31:43–47, 1982
658. Miller WH: The Habit of Sherlock Holmes: Trans Stud Coll Physicians Phila, series IV, 45:252–257, 1978
659. Milne AA: New Explorations in Baker Street: New York Times, Mar 9, 1952 pp 10, 20
660. Miscellaneous Wants Etc.: Evening News (Portsmouth), July 1, 1882 p 4
661. Moorman C: The Appeal of Sherlock Holmes: Southern Quarterly 14:71–82, 1976

662. Morgagni JB: The Seats and Causes of Diseases Investigated by Anatomy: facsimile of 1769 English trans by B Alexander, Vol 1, NY, Hafner Pub Co 1960 pp 129–143
663. Morgan AD: Some Forms of Undiagnosed Coronary Disease in Nineteenth-Century England: Med Hist 12:344–358, 1968
664. Morley C: In Memoriam: Sherlock Holmes: Sat Rev Lit, Aug 2, 1930 pp 21–22
665. Morley F: Literary Britain. A Reader's Guide to its Writers and Landmarks: NY, Harper & Row Pub 1980 p 127
666. Morris H: Back View: London, Peter Davies 1960 pp 46–47
667. Mortimer J: Is Disease a Reversion: Jackson Prize for Comparative Pathology, London, Royal College of Surgeons 1883 (unpublished)
668. Moschella SL, Pillsbury DM, Hurley HJ: Dermatology: Vol 1, Phila, WB Saunders Co 1975 p 412
669. Mowan PJ: Conan Doyle Connection: Western Morning News (Plymouth), Jan 10, 1972
670. Moxon W: The Croonian Lectures on the Influence of the Circulation upon the Nervous System: Br Med J 1:491–499, 546–549, 583–586, 628–632, 672–675, 1881
671. Mumby BH: Borough of Portsmouth. Report of the Health of Portsmouth for the Year 1891: Portsmouth, Thomas H Nicholson 1891
672. Munchhausen Karl Friedrich Hieronymus, Freiherr von (1720–1797): 15th Ed, Vol VII Micropaedia, Encyclopaedia Britannica, Chicago, U Chicago 1974 p 99
673. Murrell W: Nitroglycerine as a Remedy for Angina Pectoris: Lancet 1:80–81, 113–115, 151–152, 225–227, 1879
674. Musto DF: Sherlock Holmes and Heredity: JAMA 196:165–169, 1966
675. ______ A Study in Cocaine. Sherlock Holmes and Sigmond Freud: JAMA 204:125–130, 1968
676. Myers PH et al: Maternal Transmission in Huntington's Disease: Lancet 1:208–210, 1983
677. Naganurna K: Sherlock Holmes and Cocaine: Baker Street J 13 n s: 170–175, 1963

678. Nanji AA, Denegri JF: Factitious Illness and Syndromes à la Munchausen: Ann R Coll Physicians Surg (C) 16:33–36, 1983
679. Needham CG: The Portsmouth Eye and Ear Infirmary, 1884 to 1970: Portsmouth Group Hosp Manag Comm 1970
680. Needham J: A History of Embryology: NY, Abelard-Schuman, 1959 pp 205–211, a. p 224
681. Neuburger M: The Historic Past of German Neuropathology: *in* Essays in the History of Medicine, trans by SL Jellife, NY, Medical Life Press 1930 pp 69–84
682. NJP: Panama Canal. History: 15th ed, Vol 13 Macropaedia, Encyclopaedia Britannica, Chicago, U Chicago 1974 p 946
683. Nordon P: Conan Doyle, A Biography: NY, Holt, Rinehart & Winston 1967 p 71, a. p 28, b. p 48, c. p 60–61, d. p 110
684. Ober WB: Conan Doyle's Dying Detective. Problem in Differential Diagnosis: NY State J Med 67:2141–2145, 1967
685. ______ Jean Paul Marat, M.D. (1743–1793). Physician Turned Radical: NY State J Med 71:1125–1135, 1971
686. Obituary: George T. Budd, M.D., C.M. Edin, Plymouth: Br Med J, Mar 16, 1:628, 1889
687. Obituary: Joseph Bell: Edinburgh Med J 7:454–463, 1911
688. Obituary Notes: Conan Doyle is Dead at 71: Publisher's Weekly 118:193–194 July 12, 1930
689. Occasional Correspondent: Was Sherlock Holmes a Drug Addict?: Lancet 2:1555–1556, 1936
690. O'Hara CE, Osterburg JW: An Introduction to Criminalistics. The Application of the Physical Sciences to the Detection of Crime: Bloomington, Indiana U Press 1972 p 110
691. Oliver-Smith A: The Crisis Dyad: Meaning and Culture in Anthropology and Medicine: *in* Nourishing the Humanistic in Medicine, W Rogers & D Barnard Eds, Pittsburgh, U Penn Press 1979 pp 73–93
692. Olmstead JMD, Olmstead EH: Claude Bernard and the Experimental Method in Medicine: NY, Henry Schuman 1952

693. Oppel F, Ed: The Original Illustrated Arthur Conan Doyle: Secaucus, NJ, Castle Books 1980
694. Oral Teaching of the Deaf and Dumb: Times (London), July 17, 1912 p 10
695. Orosz JJ: A Short History of Bloodletting: Artif Organs 5:226–228, 1981
696. Osler W: The Principles and Practice of Medicine: NY, D Appleton & Co 1892 p 962, a. p 703, b. p 287, c. pp 840–845, d. pp 847, 1016, e. p 46, f. p 299, g. pp 655–659, h. pp 671–672, i. p 591, j. p 295–305, k. p 975, m. p 923, n. p 929–942, o. p 649, p. p 501, q. p 252
697. ______ The Master-Word in Medicine: Can J Med Surg 14:333–347, 1903
698. ______ Aequanimitus With Other Addresses to Medical Students, Nurses and Practitioners of Medicine: Phila, Blakiston Co 1904
699. ______ Sir Thomas Browne: *in* An Alabama Student and Other Biographical Essays, London, Oxford U Press 1908 pp 248–277
700. ______ Annual Oration on the Campaign Against Syphilis Delivered before the Medical Society of London, May 14th, 1917: Lancet 1:787–792, 1917
701. ______ Bibliotheca Osleriana: Oxford, Clarendon Press 1929
702. Osol A, Pratt R: The United States Dispensatory: 27th ed, Phila, JP Lippincott Co 1973 p 545
703. Ousby I: Bloodhounds of Heaven: The Detective in English Fiction from Godwin to Doyle: Cambridge, Mass, Harvard U Press 1976 p 140
704. Owen AH: A Psychogram of Sherlock: Med Interface, Feb 1976 p 53–54
705. ______ Doctor Behind the Supersleuth: Br Med J, Oct 1977 pp 33–37
706. Owen RC: Literary Physicians of the Twentieth Century: Prescriber (Edinburgh) 26:218–220, 1932
707. Page HW: May Tabes Dorsalis Sometimes Have a Peripheral Origin?: Brain 568:361–368, 1883

708. Palmer JI: The Consumption Cure: Daily Telegraph (London), Nov 27, 1890 p 2
709. Papaspyros NS: The History of Diabetes Mellitus: 2nd ed, Stuttgart, George Thieme Verlag 1964 p 40
710. Park O: Sherlock Holmes, Esq., and John H. Watson, M.D. An Encyclopaedia of Their Affairs: Chicago, Northwestern U Press 1962
711. Patterson AT: Portsmouth Nineteenth-Century Literary Figures: Portsmouth City Council, Portsmouth Papers, No. 14 Jan 1972
712. Payne JF: A Manual of General Pathology Designed as an Introduction to the Practice of Medicine: Phila, Lea Bros & Co 1888
713. Pearsall R: Conan Doyle. A Biographical Solution: London, Weidenfeld and Nicolson 1977 p 20, a. p 20
714. Pearson H: Sherlock Holmes and 'The Strand': Strand Mag, Aug 1943 pp 44–47
715. ______ Conan Doyle. His Life and Art: London, Methuen & Co 1943 pp 84–93
716. Pellegrino ED: To Look Feelingly—The Affinities of Medicine and Literature: Literature & Med 1:18–22, 1982
717. Personals: When Sir Conan Doyle was Just a Doctor: Literary Digest 29:508 Oct 15, 1904
718. Peters D: The British Medical Response to Opiate Addiction in the Nineteenth Century: J Hist Med Allied Sci 36:455–488, 1981
719. Peterson AC: Brain Fever in Nineteenth-Century Literature: Fact and Fiction: Victorian Studies 19:445–464, 1976
720. Peterson MJ: The Medical Profession in Mid-Victorian London: Berkeley, U California Press 1978, a. p 194, b. pp 91–98, c. p 99, pp 209–216, d. pp 130–131, e. p 40
721. A Philadelphian Journal, "Successful Selling," Which Deals With the Book Trade Records the Following Estimate of Sir A. Conan Doyle's Early Days: Two Worlds, Dec 21, 1923 p 645
722. Phillips ED: Aspects of Greek Medicine: NY, St Martin's Press 1973 p 284

723. Pirrie RR: Nitro-Glycerine Poisoning: Practitioner 88: 259-266, 1912
724. Plymothian: Further Recollections of the Late Dr. Budd: Doidge's Western Counties' Illustrated Annual (Plymouth), 1880 pp 279-283; 1881 pp 327-328; 1886 pp 243-253; Anecdote of Dr. Budd 1888 p 207; Dr. Budd—"Buddism v, Rheumatism 1889 p 155
725. Poe EA: Great Tales and Poems of Edgar Allen Poe: NY, Washington Square Press 1951
726. Portsmouth and District: Death of a Southsea Tradesman: Evening News (Portsmouth), Apr 28, 1888
727. Portsmouth Literary and Scientific Society. The Arctic Seas: Hampshire Telegraph (Portsmouth), Dec 8, 1883
728. [Portsmouth] Literary and Scientific Society, Our: The Hampshire Post, Jan 22, 1886
729. Portsmouth Literary and Scientific Society: Hampshire County Time, Dec 21, 1887 p 5
730. Portsmouth Literary and Scientific Society: The Genius of George Meredith: The Hampshire Post, Nov 23, 1888
731. Power D'A: Clio Medica II. Medicine in The British Isles: NY, Paul B Hoeber Inc 1930 pp 14-16
732. Powers of Justice, Lawyer Opinions, Press Comments: Daily Telegraph (London), Jan 15, 1907 pp 9-10
733. Poynter FNL: Medical Education in England Since 1600: *in* The History of Medical Education, CD O'Malley Ed, Berkeley, U California Press 1970 pp 235-249
734. _____ The Influence of Government Legislation on Medical Practice in Britain: *in* The Evolution of Medical Practice in Britain, FNL Poynter Ed, London, Pitman Medical Pub Co 1981 pp 5-15
735. Presentation to a Southsea Doctor: Evening News (Portsmouth), Sept 16, 1885 p 2
736. President's Commission: Guidelines for the Determination of Death: JAMA 246:2184-2186, 1981
737. Procter W Jr: On Gelseminum Sempervirens or Yellow Jassamin: Am J Pharm 2nd series 18:307-310, 1852

738. Professor Koch's Consumption Cure. Return of Dr. Conan Doyle from Berlin: Evening Mail (Portsmouth), Nov 24, 1890 p 3
739. Pruitt AA: Approaches to Alcoholism in Mid-Victorian England: Clio Med 9:93–101, 1974
740. Pugh M: Electoral Reform in War and Peace: London, Routledge & Kegan Paul 1978 pp 17–28
741. Puschmann T: A History of Medical Education from the Most Remote to the Most Modern Times: London, HK Lewis 1891
742. Rabuzzi KA Ed: Literature and Medicine. Towards a New Discipline: Vol 1, NY, State U NY Press 1982
743. Rae I: Knox the Anatomist: Edinburgh, Oliver & Boyd 1964
744. Ratcliff JD: Yellow Magic. The Story of Penicillin: NY, Random House 1945
745. Ratcliffe SK: Arthur Conan Doyle: New Statesman 35:442 July 12, 1930
746. Ravin JG: The Devil's-Foot Root Identified: Eserine: Baker Street J 32:199–202, 1982
747. Rayfield D: Chekov. The Evolution of His Art: NY, Harper & Row Pub Inc 1975
748. Razzell P: The Conquest of Smallpox. The Impact of Inoculation on Smallpox Mortality in Eighteenth Century Britain: Firle, Sussex, Caliban Books 1977 p 56
749. Recent Novels: The Stark Munro Letters: The Spectator, Oct 26, 1895 p 560
750. Redmond DA: Some Chemical Problems in the Canon: Baker Street J 14 n s: 145–152, 1964
751. ______ Marfan's Syndrome and Sherlock Holmes: Can Med Assoc J 113:19, 1975
752. ______ Sherlock Holmes, A Study in Sources: Kingston, Ont, McGill-Queen's U Press 1982 p 58; a. p 69
753. Reece BR: A Bibliography of the First Appearances of the Writings by A. Conan Doyle: Greenville, SC, Furman U 1975

754. Remington JP: Practice of Pharmacy: 4th ed, Phila, JB Lippincott 1885 p 567, a. p 951, b. p 387
755. Rentoul E, Smith H Eds: Glaister's Medical Jurisprudence and Toxicology: 13th ed, Edinburgh, Churchill Livingstone 1973 pp 565–568, a. p 721, b. p 246, c. p 565
756. Report of the Medical Officer of Health to The Urban Sanitary Authority of the Borough of Portsmouth For the Year ending the 31st day of December, 1882: Portsmouth City Records Office
757. Resurrection: Dayton Journal Herald (Dayton, OH), Oct 12, 1982 p 2
758. Reuter's Agency: The Consumption Cure: Daily Telegraph (London), Nov 14, 1890 p 5
759. Riley RC: The Growth of Southsea as a Naval Satellite and Victorian Resort: Portsmouth City Council, Portsmouth Papers No 16, July 1972 a. p 24
760. Ringer S, Murrell W: Gelseminum Sempervirens: Lancet 1:661–663, 1876
761. Roberts SC: British Universities: London, Collins 1947 p 40
762. ______ The Personnel and Practice of Medicine in Tudor and Stuart England: Med Hist 8:217–234, 1964
763. Robinson JO: The Failing Health of Napoleon: J R Soc Med 72:621–623, 1979
764. Rodin AE: John McCrae, Poet-Pathologist: Can Med Assoc J 8:204–205, 1963
765. ______ The Influence of Matthew Baillie's Morbid Anatomy: Springfield, Ill, Charles C Thomas Pub 1973
766. ______ Humanistic Medicine, William Osler and Medical Education: Ohio State Med J 74:647–649, 1978
767. ______ Autoexperimentation With a Drug by Arthur Conan Doyle: J Hist Med Allied Sci 35:426–430, 1980
768. ______ Infants and Gin Mania in 18th Century London: JAMA 245:1237–1239, 1981
769. ______ Oslerian Pathology. An Assessment and Annotated Atlas of Museum Specimens: Lawrence, Kansas, Coronado Press 1981 pp 51–52

770. ______ The Nature and Significance of Drugs and Poisons in the Sherlock Holmes Canon: Calabash 1:42–49, 1982
771. Rodin AE, Key JD: Arthur Conan Doyle's Thesis on Tabes Dorsalis: JAMA 247:646–650, 1982
772. ______ Assessment and Significance of Arthur Conan Doyle's Medical Writings: South Med J 75:1392–1399, 1982
773. ______ Journal of a Quest for the Elusive Doctor Arthur Conan Doyle (May 12, 1982–June 18, 1982): Rochester, Minn, Davies Co 1982
774. Rodin FH: Eserine. It's History in the Practice of Ophthalmology: Am J Ophthalmol 30:19–28, 1947
775. Roland CG: Sir Arthur Conan Doyle: 50 Years Since the Physician-Author's Death: Can Med Assoc J 123:307–309, 1980
776. Rolleston H: Poetry and Physic: Ann Hist Med 8:1–15, 1926
777. The Romance of Medicine: Times (London), Sept 15, 1910 p 14
778. Rook AJ: Dermatology and 'The Practitioner': 1868–1968: Practitioner 202:5–11, 1969
779. Rook A: Dermatology in Britain in the Late Nineteenth Century: Br J Dermatol 100:3–12, 1979
780. Rosebury T: Microbes and Morals. The Strange Story of Venereal Disease: NY, Viking Press 1971 p 280, a. p 79, b. p 205, c. p 46–48
781. Rosen G: A History of Public Health: NY, MD Publications Inc 1958 pp 188–190
782. Rosenberg S: Naked is the Best Disguise. The Death & Resurrection of Sherlock Holmes: Indianapolis, Bobbs-Merrill Co 1974 pp 150–155
783. Rosenblum M: 11 Picardy Place, Edinburgh. The Birthplace of Sir Arthur Conan Doyle: Baker Street J 13 n s:210–213, 1963
784. Rothstein WG: American Physicians in the Nineteenth Century. From Sects to Science: Baltimore, Johns Hopkins U Press 1972 , a. pp 241–242

785. The Royal Commission: A Report on Vaccination and its Results: Based on Evidence Taken by the Royal Commission During the Years 1889–1897: London New Sydenham Society 1898

786. The Royal Portsmouth, Portsea & Gosport Hospital Thirty-Fourth Annual Report 1882: Portsmouth, Henry Lewis 1883

787. The Royal Portsmouth, Portsea & Gosport Hospital Forty-Second Annual Report 1890: Portsmouth, G Chamberlain 1891

788. Ross R: On Some Peculiar Cells Found in Two Mosquitoes Fed on Malarial Blood: Br Med J 2:1786–1788, 1897

789. Rousseau GS: Literature and Medicine. The State of the Field: ISIS 72:406–424, 1981

790. Ruby L: The Logic of Sherlock Holmes: *in* The Art of Making Sense. A Guide to Logical Thinking, Phila, JB Lippincott Co 1954 pp 225–238

791. Rutherford W: On the Service Rendered to Mankind by Medical Science: A Graduation Address Delivered August 14, 1891: Edinburgh, Oliver & Boyd 1891

792. Saffron R: The Demon Device, by Arthur Conan Doyle: NY, Charter 1981

793. Sakula A: Blue Plaques: London Houses of Medico-Historical Interest: Br Med J 285:1799–1800, 1982

794. Saturday Review 150:35 July 20, 1930

795. Savitt TL: Medicine and Slavery: The Diseases and Health Care of Blacks in Antebellum Virginia: Urbana, U Illinois Press 1978 p 69

796. Saxby JM: Joseph Bell: An Appreciation by an Old Friend: Edinburgh, Oliphant, Anderson & Ferrier 1913

797. Sayers DL: Dr. Watson's Christian Name: *in* Profile by Gaslight, EW Smith Ed, NY, Simon and Schuster 1944 pp 180–186

798. Scarlett EP: The Doctor in Detective Fiction with an Expanded Note on Dr. John Thorndyke: Arch Intern Med 118:180–186, 1966

799. Schuchter S: Pharmacological and Psychological Determinants of Smoking: Ann Intern Med 88:104–114, 1978
800. Scheie HG, Albert DM: Textbook of Ophthalmology: 9th Ed. Phila, WB Saunders Co 1977 p 395
801. Schiller F: Venery, the Spinal Cord, and Tabes Dorsalis Before Romberg: The Contribution of Ernst Horn: J Nerv Ment Dis 163:1–9, 1976
802. Schmidt JE: Medical Discoveries. Who and When: Springfield, Ill, Charles C Thomas Pub 1959 p 32
803. Schwarz AW: Acute Epiglottis and the Death of George Washington: Scalpel & Tongs 26:22–24, 1982
804. Sellers WE: From Aldershot to Pretoria. A Story of Christian Work Among our Troups in South Africa: London, Religious Tract Society 1901 pp 155–158
805. Selling LS: Men Against Madness: NY, New Home Library 1940
806. Senter N: Upon Bruises: Baker Street J 28:225–226, 1978
807. Seufert W, Seufert WD: The Recognition of Leukemia as a Systemic Disease: J Hist Med Allied Sci 37:34–50, 1982
808. Seymour-Smith M, Ed: Novels and Novelists. A Guide to the World of Fiction: London, WH Smith & Sons 1980 p 159
809. Shannon DC: Poor Devil: Pharos, Oct 1978 pp 5–9
810. Shaw B: The Doctor's Dilemma: Baltimore, Penguin Edition 1965
811. Shepherd JA: Simpson and Syme of Edinburgh: Edinburgh, E & S Livingstone 1969 p 224
812. Sheppard F: London 1808–1870: The Informal Wen: Berkeley, U California Press 1971 p 367
813. ''Sherlock Holmes'' Off to the War: Sphere (London), Feb 10, 1900 p 84
814. Shore WD Ed: Crime and its Detection: London, Gresham Pub Co 1938 p 81
815. Siegfried A: Routes of Contagion: trans from French by J Henderson & M Claraso, NY, Harcourt, Brace & World Inc 1960 p 74

816. Simpson K: Forensic Medicine: 8th ed, London, Edward Arnold 1979 p 94, a. p 100–105
817. Sir Arthur Conan Doyle: Strand Mag, Sept 1911 p 270
818. Sir Arthur Conan Doyle. The Creator of "Sherlock Holmes": Times (London), July 8, 1930 p 9
819. Sir Arthur Conan Doyle, M.D.: Br Med J 2:71 July 12, 1930
820. Sir Arthur Conan Doyle in Reminescent Mood. His Varied and Exciting Career as a Doctor. The Inspiration of Sherlock Holmes. Tributes by Graduates of Edinburgh University to the Distinguished Visitor: East African Standard, Mar 9, 1929 p 35
821. Sir Arthur Conan Doyle. Physician, Historical Novelist, Creator of Sherlock Holmes: Clin Excerpts 19:227–234, 1945
822. SJAS: Budd, George, M.D. (1808–1882), professor of medicine: Vol 3 DNB, L Stephen & S Lee Eds, London, Smith Elder & Co 1908 p 219
823. Skiing. A Short History: Times (London), Apr 12, 1954 p 5
824. Skornickel GR Jr: A Very Remarkable Piece of Acting: William Gillette as Sherlock Holmes: Brackenridge, Penn, Privately Printed, 1981
825. Small GW, Borus JF: Outbreak of Illness in a School Chorus. Toxic Poisoning or Mass Hysteria: N Engl J Med 308:632–635, 1983
826. Smith EB, Beerman H: Sherlock Holmes and Dermatology: Int J Dermatol 16:433–438, 1977
827. Smith E, Hart FD: William Murrell, Physician and Practical Therapist: Br Med J 3:632–633, 1971
828. Smith S: Mostly Murder: Toronto, Clarke, Irwin & Co 1960
829. Smith SM, Brown HO, Toman EP, Goodman LS: The Lack of Cerebral Effects of *d*-tubocurarine: J Am Soc Anesthesiol 8:1–14, 1947
830. Smyth F: Cause of Death. The Story of Forensic Science: NY, Van Nostrand Reinhold Co 1980

831. Snow CP: Two Cultures and a Second Look: Cambridge, Cambridge U Press 1964
832. Snyder C: There's Money in Ears, But the Eye is a Gold Mine; Sir Arthur Conan Doyle's Brief Career in Ophthalmology: Arch Ophthalmol 85:359–365, 1971
833. Society. Entertainments, Balls etc.: Queen, Lady's Newspaper, Dec 31, 1898 p 1148
834. Sollmann T: A Manual of Pharmacology and Its Application to Therapeutics and Toxicology: 7th ed, Phila, WB Saunders Co 1948 p 353
835. Some Observations on Sherlock Holmes and Dr. Watson at Barts: St Bartholomew's Hosp J 55:270–275, 1951
836. South African Hospitals Commission: Evidence of Dr. Conan Doyle: Br Med J, Aug. 1900 p 383
837. [Sovine JW] Barton H: The Singular Bullet: Baker Street J 9:28–32, 1959
838. Starrett V: Answers. Oliver Wendell Holmes and Conan Doyle: Am Notes Queries 1:42–43, 1941
839. ______ The Private Life of Sherlock Holmes: Chicago, U Chicago 1960
840. ______ Introduction: *in* Sherlock Holmes: A Play Wherein is Set Forth The Strange Case of Miss Alice Faulkner, by William Gillette Based on Sir Arthur Conan Doyle's Incomparable Stories, Santa Barbara, Helen Hallbach Pub 1974 pp v-xiv
841. Stavert G: A Three-Paragraph Problem: Dr. Watson's Military Service: Sherlock Holmes J 13:99–103, 1980
842. ______ The Southsea Connection: Baker Street J 1982 pp 6–9
843. ______ Elementary, My Dear Doctor. Dr. Conan Doyle's First Few Weeks in Southsea: Southsea, unpublished presentation to London Sherlock Holmes Society 1981, 11 pages
844. ______ Letter to A.E. Rodin: July 22, 1982
845. ______ Letter to A.E. Rodin: Aug 26, 1982
846. Steegmann AT: Syndrome of the Anterior Spinal Artery: Neurology 2:15–35, 1952

847. Stein J Ed: The Random House Dictionary of the English Language: NY, Random House 1966 pp 836–837, a. p 176, b. p 926, c. p 555, d. p 960, e. p 179
848. Steiner PE: Disease in the Civil War. Natural Biological Warfare in 1861–1865: Springfield, Ill, Charles C Thomas Pub 1968 p 14
849. Stern MB: Arthur Conan Doyle. A Phrenological Case Study: AB Bookmans Weekly, May 3, 1982 pp 3465–3467
850. Stevenson RL: My Wife: XXVII *in* Songs of Travel, Vol 14, Edinburgh ed, Collected Works, London, Chatto & Windus 1895 p 335
851. ______ Strange Case of Dr. Jekyll and Mr. Hyde: London, Longmans Green 1886
852. Stewart TG: An Introduction to the Study of the Diseases of the Nervous System being Lectures Delivered in the University of Edinburgh during the Tricentenary Year: Edinburgh, Bell & Bradfute 1884
853. ______ Address to the Graduates in the University of Edinburgh 1st August 1879: Edinburgh, Oliver & Boyd 1879 pp 8–11
854. Still GF: The History of Paediatrics. The Progress of the Study of Diseases of Children up to the End of the XVIIIth Century: Oxford, Oxford U Press 1931 p 139
855. Stirling AW: Random Reminiscences of Last Century European Ophthalmologists: Arch Ophthalmol 26:727–741, 1941
856. Stoker B: Sir Arthur Conan Doyle Tells of His Career and Work, His Sentiments Towards America, and His Approaching Marriage: World (NY), July 28, 1907
857. Strohl EL: The Fascinating Lady Mary Wortley Montagu 1689–1762: Arch Surg 89:554–558, 1964
858. Strümpell A: Lehrbuch der Speciellen Pathologie und Therapie der Inneren Krankheiten: Leipzig, FCW Vogel 1884 pp 199–201
859. Stumpf SE: Momentum and Morality in Medicine: Ann Intern Med 67:10–14, 1967
860. Sutherland R: What Life was Really Like at 221b Baker St.: Medical Post, Sept 21, 1982 p 34

861. Symons J: The Tell-Tale Heart. The Life and Works of Edgar Allan Poe: NY, Harper & Row Pub 1978
862. ______ Portrait of an Artist. Conan Doyle: London, André Deutsch 1979 p 36, a. p 44, b. pp 69–74, c. pp 102–106, d. p 100
863. Tabes: Stedman's Medical Dictionary: 22nd ed, Baltimore, Williams & Wilkins Co 1972 p 1250
864. Tattersfield AE: Smoking in Patients with an Advanced Lung Disease: Br Med J 286:163–164, 1983
865. Taylor AS: A Manual of Medical Jurisprudence: 12th Am ed, C Bell Ed, Lea Brothers & Co 1897 pp 226–229, a. pp 469–473, b. pp 194–196, c. p 383, d. pp 281–306, e. p 369, f. pp 476–479
866. This Week: New Republic 63:219 July 16, 1930
867. Thompson CJS: Magic and Healing: London, Rider & Co 1947
868. Thomson B: The Story of Scotland Yard: NY, Literary Guild 1936 p 132, p 219–220
869. Thomson D: England in the Nineteenth Century 1815–1914: Harmondsworth, Middlesex, Penguin Books 1950 p 208
870. Thomson HD: Masters of Mystery. A Study of the Detective Story: London, Wm Collins & Co 1931 Chapter 2, a. pp 168–176
871. Throat Irritation and Cough: Hampshire Times, Dec 19, 1885 p 2
872. Tilton EM: Amiable Autocrat. A Biography of Dr. Oliver Wendell Holmes: NY, Henry Schuman 1947
873. Tracy J: The Encyclopaedia Sherlockiana, or a Universal Dictionary of the State of Knowledge of Sherlock Holmes and his Biographer John H. Watson, M.D.: Garden City, NY, Doubleday & Co 1977 pp 285,361–362, a. p 120, b. pp 128–129
874. Tracy J, Berkey J: Subcutaneously, My Dear Watson. Sherlock Holmes and the Cocaine Habit: Bloomington, Ind, James A Rock & Co 1978
875. Transactions of the Ophthalmological Society of the United Kingdom Session 1890–91 with List of Officers, Members,

Etc.: London, JA Churchill Vol XI p xvi, 1891; Vol XII, 1891–92; Vol XIII, 1892–92

876. Transcript: Arthur Conan Doyle: University of Edinburgh 1876–1881
877. Trautmann J, Pollard C: Literature and Medicine. Topics, Titles and Notes: Phila, Society for Health & Human Values 1975
878. Trevor P: A British Commando. An Interview with Conan Doyle: Strand Mag 21:633–640, 1901
879. Trudeau EL: An Autobiography: Garden City, NY, Doubleday, Doran & Co 1934
880. Truzzi M, Morris S: Sherlock Holmes as a Social Scientist: Psychology Today 5:62–66 Dec 1971

TS: Warren, Samuel (1807–1877), author: Vol 20 DNB . . . see reference 558

881. Tuck G: Sir A. Conan Doyle: Times (London), July 9, 1930 p 21
882. Tureen LL: Circulation of the Spinal Cord and the Effect of Vascular Occlusion: Assoc Res Nerv Ment Dis 18:394–437, 1938
883. Turner AL: History of the University of Edinburgh 1883–1933: London, Oliver & Boyd 1933 p 102
884. Turner W: An Introduction to Human Anatomy Including the Anatomy of the Tissues: Edinburgh, Adam & Charles Black 1877
885. Typhoid and the Army: Times (London), Nov 13, 1901 p 14
886. Upper Norwood Literary and Scientific Society: War and Its Effects, As Seen in Marine Organisms: Norwood News & Crystal Palace Chronicle, Oct 22, 1892 p 5
887. Vaisrub S: Holmes or Spade: JAMA 238:2721–2722, 1977
888. Vallery-Radot R: The Life of Pasteur: trans from French by RL Devonshire, NY, Sun Dial Press 1937
889. Van Liere EJ: Dr. Watson and Nervous Maladies: Baker Street J 28:100–108, 1947
890. ——— The Therapeutic Doctor Watson: W Va Med J 47:148–150, 1951

891. ______ Sherlock Holmes the Endocrinologist: Q Phi Beta Pi, Jan 1952 pp 335–337

892. ______ "Dr. Watson's Universal Specific": Baker Street J 2 n s: 215–220, 1952

893. ______ Sherlock Holmes and the Portugese Man-of-War: W Va Med J 48:1–8, 1952

894. ______ Brain Fever and Sherlock Holmes: W Va Med J 49:77–80, 1953

895. ______ Physiology at the University of Edinburgh and Sir Arthur Conan Doyle: W Va Med J 50:94–96, 1954

896. ______ The Surgical Doctor Watson: W Va Med J 53: 186–187, 1957

897. ______ Doctor Watson, General Practitioner: W Va Med J 55:364–367, 1959

898. ______ A Doctor Enjoys Sherlock Holmes: NY, Vantage Press 1959

899. ______ Dr. John H. Watson and the Subclavian Steal: Arch Intern Med 118:245–248, 1966

900. Vash G: The States of Exhaustion of Mr. Sherlock Holmes: JAMA 197: 664–665, 1966

901. Veith I: Hysteria. The History of a Disease: Chicago, U Chicago Press 1965 p 106

902. Virchow R: Die Cellularpathologie in ihrer Begründung auf Physiologische und Pathologische Gewebelehre: Berlin, A Hirschwald 1858

903. ______ The Effect of Koch's Remedy on the Internal Organs of Tuberculous Patients: Br Med J 1:127–129, 1891

904. Vivisection and M. Pasteur. Lively Meeting at Southsea: Hampshire Times, Apr 17, 1886 p 2

905. Wade A Ed: Martindale. The Extra Pharmacopoeia: 27th ed, London, Pharmaceutical Press 1977 p 1763, a. pp 693, 971

906. Wade HW: Postmortem Findings in Acute Jelly-Fish Poisoning with Sudden Death in Status Lymphaticus: Am J Trop Med Hyg 8:233–241, 1928

907. Walkowitz JR: Male Vice and Feminist Virtue: Feminism and the Politics of Prostitution in Nineteeth-Century Britain: Hist Workshop 13:79–93, 1982
908. Wall A: Guinea Pig or Man?: Daily Express (London), Oct 29, 1910 p 4
909. Walls HJ: The Forensic Science Service in Great Britain: A Short History: J Forensic Sci Soc 16:273–278, 1976
910. Walsh JJ: Cures. The Story of the Cures that Fail: NY, D Appleton & Co 1923, a. pp 127–128, b. pp 201–202, c. pp 165–170, d. p 276
911. The War. The Langman Field Hospital. Inspection by the Duke of Cambridge: Times (London), Feb 22, 1900 p 10
912. Ward AC: Sherlock Holmes versus John Thorndyke and Reginald Fortune: Windsor, England, Gaby Goldscheider, 1982
913. Warren Commission: The Assassination of President Kennedy: NY, McGraw-Hill Book Co 1964
914. Warren S: The Diary of a Late Physician Being a New Edition of Selected Passages: NY, Saalfield Pub Co 1905
915. Waterloo, Battle of: 15th ed, Vol X Micropaedia, Encyclopaedia Britannica, Chicago, U Chicago 1974 pp 570–571
916. Watson EHL: Conan Doyle as Poet: Bookman (London), 76:237–239, 1929
917. Watt I: Conrad in the Nineteenth Century: Berkeley, U California Press 1979 Chapt 4
918. Waugh CG, Greenberg, MH, Ed: The Best Science Fiction of Arthur Conan Doyle: Carbondale, South Ill U Press 1981
919. Wedderburn N: Depression of Immune Response to Moloney Leukaemia Virus by Malaria Infection: Nature 242:471–473, 1973
920. Weil-Nordon P: Some Aspects of Sir Arthur Conan Doyle's Works and Personality: *in* Sir Arthur Conan Doyle Centenary 1859–1959, London, John Murray 1959 pp 11–27, a. p 12

921. Weintraub S: London Yankees. Portraits of American Writers and Artists in England 1894–1914: NY, Harcourt Brace Jovanovich 1979, a. p 6
922. Weiner JS: The Piltdown Forgery: London, Oxford U Press 1955 p 105
923. Wheelwright EG: The Physic Garden: Medicinal Plants and Their History: Boston, Houghton, Mifflin Co 1935
924. Whittemore R: William Carlos Williams. Poet from Jersey: Boston, Houghton, Mifflin Co 1975
925. Widdup C: Inspired by Plymouth Doctor: Western Morning News (Plymouth), Dec 28, 1971
926. Wilcox A: Manual for the Microscopical Diagnosis of Malaria in Man: Washington, US Dept HEW 1960 pp 26–27
927. Willcox PHA: The Trial of Dr. W.R. Hadwen: J R Coll Physicians Lond 4:227–233, 1970
928. Williams G: Virus Hunters: NY, Alfred A Knoff 1971 pp 154–175
929. Williamson JN: "The Latest Treatise Upon Pathology": Baker Street J 6:208–214, 1956
930. Wilson JG: The Influence of Edinburgh on American Medicine in the 18th Century: Proc Inst Med Chicago 7:129–138, 1929
931. Wintle AS: Compulsory Vaccination: Evening Mail (Portsmouth), July 14, 1887 p 2
932. ______ Compulsory Vaccination: Evening Mail (Portsmouth), July 21, 1887 p 2
933. Wissemen JL Jr: Scrub Typhus: *in* Cecil Textbook of Medicine 15th ed. W McDermott, JB Wyngaarden Eds, Phila, WB Saunders Co 1979 pp 327–328
934. Witches and Witchcraft: Hampshire Post, Apr 4, 1890 p 8
935. Wolff J: That Was No Lady. A Reply to Mr. Stout in Which are Included Some Observations Upon the Nature of Dr. Watson's Wound: Am J Surg 58 n s 310–312 1942

936. Woolford JV: Conan Doyle: Br Heritage, Dec–Jan 1980–81 pp 44–45
937. World Health Statistics: Geneva, World Health Organization, Vol 35, No 1, 1982 pp 37–38
938. World Health Statistics Annual. Vital Statistics and Causes of Death: Geneva, World Health Organization 1981
939. Wormley TG: Is Gelsemic Acid Identical with Aesculin?: Am J Pharm 10:1–8, 1882
940. Wrenshall GA, Hetenyi G, Feasby WB: The Story of Insulin. Forty Years of Success Against Diabetes: Toronto, Max Reinhardt 1962
941. Wright AE: On the Results Obtained by Anti-typhoid Inoculation: Lancet 2:651–654, 1902
942. ——— The Inoculation of Troops Against Typhoid Fever and Septic Infection: Times (London), Sept 28, 1914
943. Wright AE, Douglas SR: An Experimental Investigation of the Role of the Blood Fluids in Connection with Phagocytosis: Proc R Soc Lond 72:357–370, 1903
944. Wright AE, Semple D: Vaccination Against Typhoid Fever: Br Med J 1:256–259, 1897
945. Wright-St Clair RE: Doctors Monro. A Medical Saga: London, Wellcome Historical Medical Library 1964
946. Wynder EL, Hoffmann D: Tobacco and Health. A Societal Challenge: N Engl J Med 300:894–903, 1979
947. Yellen S: Sir Arthur Conan Doyle: Sherlock Holmes in Spiritland: Int J Parapsychol 7:33–57, 1965

INDEX

INDEX

Books are indicated by italics. Except for listings under Doyle, Arthur Conan, short stories are indicated by quotation marks and fictional characters by parentheses. Items listed in the appendices, but not mentioned by name in the text, are not indexed.

INDEX

INDEX

INDEX

INDEX

INDEX

INDEX

-P-

-Q-

-R-

The End Of The Beginning